FEDERAL IMPARTIALITY

Disagreements on constitutional rights (such as racial and religious discrimination or abortion) are increasingly divisive. From the role of abortion in US presidential elections to debates about the competence creep of EU fundamental rights, the question arises: should the power to decide these matters rest with a central/federal union, or be left to individual states?

This book addresses this crucial *federal boundary question* from both theoretical and comparative perspectives. It explores how the proper allocation of decision-making power in federal systems can enhance impartiality and reduce polarisation.

The book both develops and critiques the influential constitutional theory of James Madison, architect of the US Constitution and modern federalism. By tracing Madison's intellectual debt to David Hume and to common law rules on bias, it identifies gaps in his account of impartiality. It also shows how a revised Madisonian framework remains relevant to contemporary struggles in both the US and the EU over managing discord through federal structures.

The book's comparative dimension explores three categories of rights, each reflecting particular forms of social disagreement: (i) minority rights, which often trigger group bias and spark division between majorities and minorities; (ii) ideologically divisive rights, such as abortion; and (iii) cases where group and ideological bias overlap, such as those pitting religious freedoms against ideologically contested measures, including bans on ritual slaughter or religious apparel in public employment.

By combining comparative and theoretical contributions, the book demonstrates both the perils and the promise of federalism in securing impartiality and navigating social faction.

Volume 34 in the series Hart Studies in Comparative Public Law

Hart Studies in Comparative Public Law

Recent titles in this series:

The Dynamics of Exclusionary Constitutionalism
Mazen Masri

Constitutional Courts, Gay Rights and Sexual Orientation Equality
Angioletta Sperti

Australian Constitutional Values
Edited by Rosalind Dixon

Human Rights in the UK and the Influence of Foreign Jurisprudence
Hélène Tyrrell

The Nordic Constitutions
Edited by Helle Krunke and Björg Thorarensen

Regulation in India
Design, Capacity, Performance
Edited by Devesh Kapur and Madhav Khosla

New Media and Freedom of Expression
Rethinking the Constitutional Foundations of the Public Sphere
András Koltay

Why Religious Freedom Matters for Democracy
Comparative Reflections from Britain and France
for a Democratic 'Vivre Ensemble'
Myriam Hunter-Henin

The Role of Monarchy in the Modern Democracy:
European Monarchies Compared
Edited by Robert Hazell and Bob Morris

Responsible Government and the Australian Constitution:
A Government for a Sovereign People
Benjamin B Saunders

Federalism and the Rights of Persons with Disabilities: The Implementation
of the CRPD in Federal Systems and its Implications
Edited by Delia Ferri, Francesco Palermo and Giuseppe Martinico

Constitutional Courts, Media and Public Opinion
Angioletta Sperti

Judicial Review and Electoral Law in a Global Perspective
Edited by Cristina Fasone, Edmondo Mostacci and Graziella Romeo

Judicial Bricolage: The Use of Foreign Precedents by Constitutional Judges in the 21st Century
Edited by Tania Groppi, Marie-Claire Ponthoreau and Irene Spigno

Automation in Governance: Theory, Practice and Problems
Edited by Yee-Fui Ng and Matthew Groves

Federal Impartiality

Navigating Divisive Rights in the EU and the US

Mohamed Moussa

•HART•
OXFORD • LONDON • NEW YORK • NEW DELHI • SYDNEY

HART PUBLISHING

Bloomsbury Publishing Plc

Kemp House, Chawley Park, Cumnor Hill, Oxford, OX2 9PH, UK

1385 Broadway, New York, NY 10018, USA

Bloomsbury Publishing Ireland Limited, 29 Earlsfort Terrace, Dublin 2, D02 AY28, Ireland

HART PUBLISHING, the Hart/Stag logo, BLOOMSBURY and the Diana logo are trademarks of Bloomsbury Publishing Plc

First published in Great Britain 2026

A catalogue record for this book is available from the British Library.

A catalogue record for this book is available from the Library of Congress.

Library of Congress Control Number: 2026933374

ISBN: HB: 978-1-50998-728-3
ePDF: 978-1-50998-726-9
ePub: 978-1-50998-727-6

Typeset by Compuscript Ltd, Shannon

For product safety related questions contact productsafety@bloomsbury.com

To find out more about our authors and books visit www.hartpublishing.co.uk. Here you will find extracts, author information, details of forthcoming events and the option to sign up for our newsletters.

ACKNOWLEDGEMENTS

My debt is great and owed to many. I am grateful to my daughter, Sophia, for inspiring me, and to my wife for her intellectual and emotional support throughout this process. I also thank my family for teaching me everything that truly matters.

I am deeply grateful to Professor Alison Young for her mentorship throughout my academic career and for her feedback on this book. I also wish to thank Professor Mark Tushnet for his excellent feedback and ongoing support. I am also grateful to Darren Harvey and Oana Stefan for their valuable feedback on chapter six, and to Bruce Ackerman for his insightful comments on earlier drafts of chapters two to four. I am grateful to my colleagues at the Cambridge Centre for European Legal Studies (CELS) and the Centre for Public Law (CPL) for their support and for hosting events that allowed me to reflect on many of the ideas explored in this book. I am particularly thankful to the Cambridge Centre for Research in the Arts, Social Sciences and Humanities (CRASSH) for awarding me a generous research grant. This gave me the time and space away from academic duties to develop key parts of the research and to engage with a broad range of interdisciplinary ideas. I would also like to express my gratitude to Nikhil Purohit for his meticulous assistance in editing this manuscript.

CONTENTS

TABLE OF CASES

The EU

The ECtHR

Germany

The United Kingdom

The United States

Other Authorities

TABLE OF LEGISLATION

The EU

The US

The UK

Introduction

I. The Boundary Question and the Challenge of Divisive Rights

In classical novels, we often encounter the phrase that someone is of 'a delicate constitution'.[1] The word 'constitution' itself originates from a metaphor of the human body, suggesting that a constitutional system functions as a corporate body, where individuals are akin to its cells.[2] This etymological analysis helps understand the dangers of modern-day polarisation. From Plato to contemporary scholarship, extreme factionalism and polarisation have been to a constitution what a mortal autoimmune disease is to the human body.[3] When the pathology of faction afflicts the constitutional body, its metaphorical cells – ie, the citizens – may become 'unable to accomplish anything in common', risking dysfunction or even disintegration of the body politic.[4]

In an era of culture wars, rights are often a particular source of social conflict. As Alexy noted, 'the constitutional rights catalogue regulates in a highly open manner what are in part deeply controversial questions about the basic normative structure of state and society'.[5] These conflicting views are evident in issues such as abortion, discrimination, bioethics, and others, which, although expressed in legal jargon and within judicial avenues, originate from competing moral and ideological views as well as inter-group competition.[6] For example, if one looks at the 2024 US presidential debate between Kamala Harris and Donald Trump, a considerable time was spent debating whether a right to abortion exists and whether the decision should be centralised at the federal level or kept to states. In the EU, some argue that EU human rights have become a 'source of Euroscepticism' and disagreement on the legitimacy of the European project itself.[7]

[1] C Dickens, *David Copperfield* (London, Penguin Classics, 2004) ch 1, para 5 ('He was double my mother's age when he married, and of but a delicate constitution.'); J Austen, *Love and Friendship and Other Youthful Writings* (C Alexander ed, London, Penguin Classics, 2015) Introduction, p xliii.

[2] Eg, Plato, *Republic* (Robin Waterfield tr, Oxford, Oxford University Press, 1993) 556d–e; Aristotle, *Politics* (Ernest Barker tr, RF Stalley ed, Oxford, Oxford University Press, 1995) bk 5, ch 1.

[3] Plato (n 2).

[4] ibid.

[5] R Alexy, *A Theory of Constitutional Rights* (Oxford, Oxford University Press, 2010) 2.

[6] A Clapham, 'Human Rights Policy for the European Community' (1990) 10 *Yearbook of European Law* 311 ('rights might operate as a double-edged sword. Not only are they a cohesive force but they may well be divisive'.).

[7] C Leconte, 'The EU Fundamental Rights Policy as a Source of Euroscepticism' (2014) 15 *Human Rights Review* 83.

It is perhaps no coincidence that the modern reincarnation of federalism emerged with the promise of providing a 'remedy' to the mortal 'disease' of factionalism[8] – what contemporary scholarship refers to as 'polarization'.[9] The American framer James Madison's most influential paper, *Federalist No. 10*, explicitly presents federalism as a mechanism that achieves two primary purposes: to 'remedy' factionalism and to better protect fundamental rights.[10] To him, federalism offers a unique advantage not available in unitary systems (eg, Norway) – the advantage of *impartiality*. As will be explored in chapter two, Madison's argument explains how federalism can neutralise and balance competing group biases, thereby encouraging conflicting groups not only to act *impartially* but also to converge on rights-friendly outcomes and 'gradually' mitigate the risks of factionalism over time.[11]

Despite the widespread influence of Madison's theory, the problem is that the experience of US federalism and the EU constitutional project seem to present *a mixed image* in terms of both polarisation and the protection of rights. This complexity often arises from a confusion about when to centralise rights (ie, make the Union lead) and when to decentralise them (make the states be in the driver's seat). Getting this balance wrong can often be catastrophic. In the US, federalism was, for a significant period, associated with the disregard for minority rights.[12] For example, federalism and decentralisation 'served as a code word' for 'racism' for quite some time.[13] It was only through centralisation following the New Deal, among other factors, that a 'golden' chapter in the history of civil rights for African Americans was written.[14] In contrast, a move towards centralisation of abortion rights triggered half a century of deeply polarising debate.[15]

Conversely, in the EU, a specific form of decentralisation, combined with procedural checks by the Court of Justice of the European Union ('CJEU') and the European Court of Human Rights ('ECtHR'), appears to have better diffused tension over abortion.[16] On the other hand, the EU's de facto decentralisation – compelled by unanimity voting on racial and religious minority rights – has resulted in lamentable conditions for minorities in many Member States, in stark

[8] J Madison, 'Federalist No. 10' in A Hamilton, J Madison and J Jay (eds), *The Federalist Papers* (I Shapiro ed, New Haven, Yale University Press, 2009) 48 (Federalist No. 10).

[9] MG Spencer, 'Hume and Madison on Faction' (2002) 59 *William and May Quarterly* 869, 885.

[10] Madison, Federalist No. 10 (n 8) 48.

[11] Madison, *Federalist No.* 51.

[12] A R Amar, *The Bill of Rights: Creation and Reconstruction* (New Haven, Yale University Press 1998) 7.

[13] Riker famously said, 'If in the United States one disapproves of racism, one should disapprove of federalism.': WH Riker, *Federalism: Origin, Operation, Significance* (Boston, Little, Brown and Company, 1964) 155.

[14] MJ Klarman, 'Rethinking the Civil Rights and Civil Liberties Revolutions' (1996) 82 *Virginia Law Review* 1.

[15] See, eg, F Fabbrini, 'The European Court of Human Rights, the EU Charter of Fundamental Rights, and the Right to Abortion: Roe V. Wade on the Other Side of the Atlantic' (2011) 18 *Columbia Journal of European Law* 1.

[16] See ch 5.

contrast to the EU's commendable role in centralising equal pay and addressing sex discrimination.[17]

A. The Book's Main Question

Given these puzzling patterns, the book grapples with the question of why 'federal laboratories' often deliver Madison's promised 'public cure' to polarisation, while in other instances, they produce 'deadly viruses'.[18] In other words, why does centralisation frequently serve as a beneficial safeguard for rights and societal harmony, while in other cases, it results in glaring constitutional violations and widespread polarisation? The proposed book explores the underlying structural factors that differentiate the effective role of federalism in resolving conflicts over rights from situations where federalism falls short.

In essence, it seeks to answer part of the '*boundary question*', namely, how the allocation of power between the central authority and the constituent states influences the substantive protection of rights and the social acceptance of these rights. An integrative union like the EU or the US brings together several constituent systems together with the union legal system, and the crucial question becomes how to draw the boundary between these different systems. Is abortion, for example, a state matter or a union matter? What about minority rights, etc? When should the union have a hands-on or hands-off approach, to which questions, and on what grounds? A key message the book seeks to convey is that the boundary question – determining when the union should accelerate, brake, or coordinate – is not merely procedural. It not only shapes the distribution of powers between the union and its member states but also has significant implications for the quality of rights protection and levels of polarisation.

To address these questions, the book conducts a comparative analysis of the paradigmatically rich experiences of the US and the EU in managing social discord over rights through multilevel constitutionalism. The comparison focuses on the allocation of power between the central authority and states in the context of fundamental rights. It narrows its scope to three main distinct categories of fundamental rights, each giving rise to specific forms of social disagreement. These are: (i) minority rights that often create divisions between majorities and minorities; (ii) morally divisive rights (such as abortion) that split majorities upon themselves; and (iii) rights that encompass elements of both types (eg, religious freedoms and church-state relation cases).

While comparative analysis could be an end in itself, the book offers further theoretical contributions. It re-evaluates Madison's foundational theory concerning the federal division of powers and fundamental rights. Although constitutional

[17] See ch 3.

[18] RA Schapiro, *Polyphonic Federalism: Toward the Protection of Fundamental Rights* (Chicago, University of Chicago Press, 2009) 42.

and political scholars have grappled with the issue of social conflict since time immemorial, Madison argued that this objective could only be realised by first achieving the 'requisite' impartiality, which, in his view, could only be attained through federalism.[19] According to Madison, to secure social agreement and effectively shield rights from local majoritarian biases, the power to define these rights must be centralised, at least at a minimal level, where the central authority establishes a threshold of protection that states cannot fall below. Madison's perspective, therefore, links impartiality with the centralisation of rights.

This Madisonian theory of federalism has significantly influenced case law and academic literature in both the US and the EU.[20] However, this influential viewpoint fails to account for the varied outcomes of federalism and the numerous instances where centralisation exacerbates rather than alleviates social conflict over rights. The book's comparative analysis not only revisits Madison's theory and its contemporary echoes in the EU and the US but also develops a comparatively grounded, accessible framework for allocating the federal boundary across different types of rights.

This way, the book provides a missing link in EU scholarship and the broader field of comparative federalism. In recent years, EU scholarship has produced a wealth of literature that compares the allocation of power within the EU and the US from a federal perspective. This includes, for example, Schütze's work 'From Dual to Cooperative Federalism' and Harvey's work on 'process federalism'.[21] Other comparative efforts have delved into the question of how federalism allocates power over rights, as seen in the works of Fabbrini and Pérez.[22] While these works offer valuable insights, they do not specifically address the puzzle of why federalism, in both the US and the EU, often presents a mixed image, exacerbating conflicts instead of resolving them and failing to enhance the protection of rights. The boundary question regarding rights remains unanswered, and the search for a criterion to balance unity with diversity and harmonisation with decentralisation persists.[23] As shall be explored throughout the book, confusion on how to draw the boundary remains commonplace in EU case law as well as the recently proposed Treaty amendments.[24]

[19] See, eg, J Madison, 'Vices of the Political System of the United States, April 1787' in RA Rutland and WME Rachal (eds), *The Papers of James Madison*, vol IX (Chicago, The University of Chicago Press, 1975) 345–358, point number 11.

[20] See, eg, *City of Richmond v JA Croson Co* 488 US 469 (1989) (Scalia J, concurring); for an overview of literature, see M Moussa, 'The Shackles of Veto: On the American Parallel of Article 19 TFEU and Its Tension with Procedural Justice' (2023) 25 *Cambridge Yearbook of European Legal Studies* 122.

[21] R Schütze, *From Dual to Cooperative Federalism: The Changing Structure of European Law* (Oxford, Oxford University Press. 2009).

[22] F Fabbrini, *Fundamental Rights in Europe* (Oxford, Oxford University Press, 2014) 33; AT Pérez, *Conflicts of Rights in the European Union: A Theory of Supranational Adjudication* (Oxford, Oxford University Press, 2009) 70.

[23] E Spaventa, 'Should We "Harmonize" Fundamental Rights in the EU? Some Reflections About Minimum Standards and Fundamental Rights Protection in the EU Composite Constitutional System' (2018) 55 *Common Market Law Review* 999.

[24] Qualified majority voting and unanimity. Note No 15 (CONF 3815/96), 18 April 1996, EC/IGC/CONF.3815/96.

The question continues to present even further in the 'more mature' US federal scholarship as well.[25] Dean Chemernisky raised the query of when 'is it worth experimenting [through decentralisation]' and 'when is experimentation to be rejected because of a need to impose a [central] mandate'?[26] Likewise, Schapiro emphasised the puzzle of not knowing 'how and when to promote plurality and redundancy without undermining uniformity and finality'.[27] Similarly, Rodriguez questioned 'at what point' decentralising rights and 'other forms of diversity degenerate from being democracy-reinforcing and constructive into producing rights violations or even create chaos'?[28]

Moreover, many strands of US literature and judicial opinions conflate the nature of impartiality and its connection with the boundary question, leading to diametrically opposed conclusions regarding the boundary question. This includes either expanding impartiality to argue for overcentralisation across various types of rights,[29] or arguing for complete decentralisation, as exemplified by Justice Kavanaugh in the recent abortion case, *Dobbs*.[30] Through a comparative assessment of the relationship between federal impartiality, divisive rights, and the boundary question, the book provides a much-needed guide on how to allocate powers over these rights in both the US and the EU. It also offers insights on how to maximise federalism's capacity to resolve conflicts involving rights falling within the so-called culture wars.

II. Why the EU and the US Federalism

Whenever a work proposes to compare the EU and the US, two compounded questions are frequently raised: first, what do we mean by a federation – which leads to the question of whether the EU can properly be called one – and second, whether the EU and the US are in fact comparable, and why such a comparison is warranted. The questions are addressed in turn.

Federalism is a broad church and can mean different things to different people. For the purposes of this book, the term denotes a particular structure referred to as 'coming together' – in Stepan's terms[31] – or 'integrative federalism' – in Lenaerts' terms[32] – that describes a constitutional model formed by already 'independent' states which 'voluntarily' share their powers without 'losing their individual

[25] C Barnard, 'Restricting Restrictions: Lessons for the EU from the US?' (2009) 68 *Cambridge Law Journal* 575.

[26] E Chemerinsky, *Constitutional Law*, 7th edn (Burlington, Aspen, 2023) 338.

[27] RA Schapiro, *Polyphonic Federalism* (Chicago, University of Chicago Press, 2009) 46.

[28] CM Rodríguez, 'Negotiating Conflict Through Federalism: Institutional and Popular Perspectives' (2013) 123 *Yale Law Journal* 2094.

[29] Eg, C Sunstein, *The Partial Constitution* (Cambridge, MA, Harvard University Press 1993).

[30] See chs 4 and 5.

[31] S Alfred, 'Federalism and Democracy: Beyond the US Model' (1999) 10 *Journal of Democracy* 19.

[32] K Lenaerts, 'Constitutionalism and the Many Faces of Federalism' (1990) *38 American Journal of Comparative Law* 205.

identities'.[33] This is unlike the 'devolutionary' or 'holding together' models, such as Belgium, for instance, which divide the power of a unitary state into smaller subunits. As Lenaerts, the president of the Court of Justice of the European Union, noted, the EU and the US are paradigmatic examples of an integrative federal model.[34]

Second, given the different historical and structural details of the EU and the US, it is important to provide a prefatory note regarding their comparability. Despite many divergences in details, the two systems share a 'normative' denominator[35] and a 'family' resemblance[36] that have long generated *functional comparisons* not only in literature[37] but also in judicial opinions, both in the Court of Justice of the European Union ('CJEU')[38] and the Supreme Court of the US ('SCOTUS').[39] This stems from the fact that the US federal structure, like the EU, came into being through a constitutional process of 'coming together'[40] or integration.[41] As many have remarked, in both experiences, pre-existing states voluntarily agreed to integrate into a continent-sized polity.[42]

To varying degrees, they both experienced debates regarding the divisibility of sovereignty and the contested extent of central authority, particularly concerning minority rights, among other things.[43] This commonality is what makes a comparison of the two systems 'obvious and fruitful'.[44] The two systems remain thematically 'the least different', if not 'the most similar', among other possible

[33] Alfred (n 31) 19; for a definition of a federation see SR Larsen, *The Constitutional Theory of the Federation and the European Union* (Oxford, Oxford University Press, 2021) 14–19.

[34] Lenaerts (n 32) 236; 'It is humbling for an American scholar of federalism to admit that the most interesting developments in federalism are happening in Europe, not the United States': EA Young, 'What Can Europe Tell Us About the Future of American Federalism' (2017) 49 *Arizona State Law Journal* 1109.

[35] Fabbrini (n 22) 33.

[36] On comparing constitutional 'families', see V Jackson, 'Comparative Constitutional Law: Methodologies' in M Rosenfeld and A Sajo (eds), *The Oxford Handbook of Comparative Constitutional Law* (Oxford, Oxford University Press, 2012) 67.

[37] See, eg, T Sandalow and E Stein (eds), *Courts and Free Markets: Perspectives from the United States and Europe* (Oxford, Oxford University Press, 1982); M Cappelletti, M Seccombe and J Weiler, *Integration Through Law: Europe and the American Federal Experience* (Berlin, de Gruyter, 1986); E Young, 'Protecting Member State Autonomy in the European Union: Some Cautionary Tales from American Federalism' (2002) 77 *New York University Law Review* 1612.

[38] See, eg, Case C-491/01 *British American Tobacco (Investments) and Imperial Tobacco* ECLI:EU:C:2002:476, Opinion of AG Geelhoed, para 108; Case C-34/09 *Ruiz Zambrano* ECLI:EU:C:2010:560, Opinion of AG Sharpston, paras 172–173.

[39] See, eg, *Printz v United States* 521 US 898, 976–977 (1997) (Breyer J, dissenting).

[40] Alfred (n 31).

[41] Writing extrajudicially, Lenaerts (n 32) 236.

[42] ibid.

[43] J Resnik, 'Federalism(s)' Forms and Norms: Contesting Rights, De-Essentializing Jurisdictional Divides, and Temporizing Accommodations' (2014) 55 *Federalism and Subsidiarity* 363.

[44] D Halberstam, 'Comparative Federalism and the Issue of Commandeering' in R Howse and K Nicolaidis (eds), *The Federal Vision: Legitimacy And Levels Of Governance In The United States And The European Union* (Oxford, Oxford University Press, 2001) 329.

comparator constitutional polities.[45] The relevant difference in structure and scope is highlighted in more detail in chapter one as well as throughout the book. Moreover, given the well-established scholarly practice of treating the EU and the US as the leading examples of integrative federalism, these two systems provide fertile ground for testing classical claims about how integrative federalism can mitigate factionalism and polarisation – especially in an era where both sides of the Atlantic are experiencing increasing polarisation and ongoing culture wars.

III. Justification and Methodology for Case Selection

The rationale for focusing on fundamental rights in exploring the relationship between federalism and social faction lies in the fact that the definition, scope, and limitations of rights invariably reflect the competing ideologies present within heterogeneous societies such as the US and the EU. Rights often mirror – and even intensify – the dynamics of factional struggle and contemporary culture wars. However, analysing rights in isolation is insufficient. Scholars have pointed out the often-overlooked 'connections between the two grand traditions of constitutional law: structure and rights'.[46] The foundational theories of federalism held that structure, rather than rights, is 'the key to promoting individual liberty'.[47] When the structure is flawed and consistently fails to prevent governmental violation, an ex-*ante* 'paper guarantee' alone cannot deter the government,[48] and its ex-post remedies often do little for victims.[49] Moreover, as chapters three and five will show, dissenters to certain rights claims frequently rely on structural or boundary-based arguments as their primary line of resistance. For these reasons, it is essential to examine the dialectical relationship between rights and structure to fully understand the socio-constitutional dynamics at play.

In terms of the methodology of selecting the comparative cases, the book follows what Jackson terms 'functional contextualism'.[50] Focusing on functions has a potent explanatory force in highlighting the varied ways rights operate within each jurisdiction.[51] The contextualist dimension ensures that the particularities of each system are not overlooked.[52] With this in mind, the selected cases are those that can effectively illustrate and contextualise the functional question of

[45] Fabbrini (n 22) 29.
[46] HK Gerken, 'Federalism All the Way Down' (2010) 124 *Harvard Law Review* 4, 74.
[47] ibid citing Amar (n 12).
[48] '[V]iolations of these parchment barriers have been committed by overbearing majorities in every State': From James Madison to Thomas Jefferson, October 1788, in *Selected Writings of James Madison* (Ralph Ketcham ed, Indianapolis, Hackett Publishing, 2006) 81, 159.
[49] Eg, M Tushnet, *Taking the Constitution Away from the Courts* (Princeton, Princeton University Press, 2000) 166.
[50] Jackson (n 36) 67.
[51] For definitions of various comparative methods, see Jackson (n 36) 67.
[52] See ch 1.

whether – and to what extent – jurisdictional authority over a given right is allocated to the centre or to the component states.[53] This analysis of the jurisdictional locus is then juxtaposed with a second layer of inquiry: to what extent does movement along the centralisation–decentralisation spectrum influence social acceptance of rights and levels of political polarisation?

To this end, the book compares three paradigmatic types of conflicts over rights which are functionally analogous across the US and the EU. These categories reflect not only recurring disputes over whether such rights should be centralised or not, but also their tendency to provoke significant social disagreement and sometimes polarisation.

The first category is minority rights. These conflicts bring to the forefront the division between majority and minority groups – tensions which, as will be shown, were a central justification for the federal model itself, premised on offering stronger protections for minorities. Today, such rights remain at the heart of constitutional tensions in both systems. For example, the recently enforced Danish 'Ghetto Law' classifies neighbourhoods based on the birthplace of citizens' parents. Under this law, individuals whose parents come from a 'non-western country' may face termination of public housing contracts.[54] For some, EU intervention against such measures is seen as federal overreach; for others, it is a necessary safeguard for minority rights. The racial tension in US constitutional law and history is well-known enough to warrant a summary here but shall be explored in chapter three.[55]

The second category concerns rights associated with so-called 'morality politics' – issues that provoke strong moral, partisan, or ideological commitments. These include matters such as abortion or bioethics, which often divide and split majorities unto themselves. By examining the relevant case law, we observe how these deeply contested societal questions, rooted in moral, religious, or ethical beliefs, are translated into language. This process of legal distillation allows for functional comparability across the two jurisdictions.

The third category involves cases that combine elements of the two previous types – those that simultaneously engage questions of minority protection and moral or ideological division. The book will take on the thorny question of the relationship between federalism, religion, and ideology. As a 'multifaceted'[56] or 'shape shifting'[57] phenomenon, religion can be 'both a matter of identity (akin

[53] M Moussa, 'Beyond Incomplete Dichotomies: A Structural Typology of Dual Rights in the EU and the US' (2023) 24 *German Law Journal* 261.

[54] Case C-417/23 *Slagelse Almennyttige Boligselskab – Afdeling Schackenborgvænge and Others v Ministry of Transport and Housing* (2025).

[55] See ch 3.

[56] T Khaitan and JC Norton, 'The Right to Freedom of Religion and the Right against Religious Discrimination: Theoretical Distinctions' (2019) 17 *International Journal of Constitutional Law* 1132, 1132–1134, 1144.

[57] R McCrea, 'Singing from the Same Hymn Sheet? What the Differences between the Strasbourg and Luxembourg Courts Tell Us About Religious Freedom, Non-Discrimination, and the Secular State' (2016) 5 *Oxford Journal of Law and Religion* 183.

to race) and a matter of belief (akin to political opinion)'.[58] Put differently, religion may function as a source of group conflict when it operates as a marker of group identity (chosen or otherwise), rooted in the ethnic and ostensibly immutable characteristics of its adherents.[59] By contrast, religion may also assume a broader ideological role, indirectly structuring cross-group cultural wars that fracture society without being confined to the claims of a particular religious group. To unpack this, the book covers a wide array of cases, ranging from religious exemptions to church–state arrangements. Taken together, these three categories serve as a litmus test for the interaction between power distribution, institutional orders and societal conflict.[60] Through their comparison, the book assesses federalism's purported ability to manage polarisation and to promote the substantive protection of rights.

IV. Structure of the Book

Overall, the book theoretically and comparatively assesses the role of federal impartiality as a guide for defining the boundary question regarding socially divisive rights in the US and the EU. This analysis is structured around three interconnected themes: the boundary question, impartiality, and divisive rights. Addressing each involves an interweaving of doctrinal, theoretical, and comparative analysis, respectively.

Theme I: Comparing federal constitutional doctrines:

Chapter one outlines the doctrinal and practical challenges associated with defining the federal boundary concerning fundamental rights. This is achieved by comparing the constitutional and judicial principles governing the allocation of powers within the US and the EU systems.

Theme II: Federal impartiality as a theory to guide the boundary question:

Chapter two embodies the book's theoretical linchpin. It engages with the foundational theory that underpins federalism's claim to better regulate divisive rights. This theory is embodied in Madison's *Federalist No. 10*, where he advocated for federal impartiality as a basis for his argument that all rights should be centralised and placed within the federal domain. This section of the book adopts a balanced approach to this influential theory. On the one hand, it partly defends its premises, and through comparative testing, it elucidates the conditions necessary to make centralisation more conducive to protecting certain divisive rights. On the other hand, the book cautions against the common error of universalising this theory across all types of rights. To illustrate why this is a mistake and how courts

[58] R McCrea, 'I Faith at Work: The CJEU's Headscarf Rulings' (*EU Law Analysis*, 14 March 2017) eulawanalysis.blogspot.com/2017/03/faith-at-work-cjeus-headscarf-rulings.html accessed 3 August 2025.
[59] Khaitan and Norton (n56).
[60] See, eg, N MacCormick, *Institutions of Law: An Essay in Legal Theory* (Oxford, Oxford University Press, 2007); S Voigt, *Institutional Economics: An Introduction* (Cambridge, Cambridge University Press, 2019).

and scholarship often uncritically fail in this regard, chapter four traces Madison's intellectual roots to David Hume as well as the common law doctrines on bias.[61]

Madison's federal impartiality theory is premised on the idea that by uniting different states, federalism increases the diversification of conflicting interests. The clash of these interests creates uncertainty, which encourages various groups to agree on more objective outcomes and thus act *more impartially*.[62] This perspective has been globally influential, suggesting that the central level is a better 'guardian' of rights, or, as Madison terms it, a 'universal negative' with the authority to veto state legislation on rights.[63] However, what is often overlooked is that Madison, in formulating this influential argument, drew upon Hume's work but omitted Hume's distinction between rights involving principle-based and interest-based factions. This omission has significant implications for Madison's theory, as it prevents the application of the centralisation argument to a range of rights. To clarify this point, chapter four aligns Hume's typology of factions with common law doctrines on bias, which distinguish between pecuniary and non-pecuniary forms.[64] These doctrines recognise that bias underpinning a conflict may stem not only from economic interest but also from strongly held ideological commitments – what Hume would call 'factions of principle'.[65]

Reading Madison's impartiality theory in conjunction with Hume's typology and common law doctrines on causes of bias, the book illustrates that federal impartiality is context sensitive and contingent on the issue at stake. In particular, for rights driven by agreement on strongly held moral convictions (such as abortion or assisted dying), Madison's condition of interest diversification is absent. As a result, the conception of federal impartiality becomes unattainable. Centralisation of rights under such circumstances can even lead to opposite outcomes to those intended. Chapter four elaborates a multifactorial criterion to distinguish different types of divisive rights in relation to the boundary question, which helps refine the Madisonian theory further.

Theme III: Comparing divisive rights and their interaction with the federal boundary:

The remainder of the book puts this theoretical framework to the test and explores its implications for the division of powers in federal systems through a comparative analysis of case law across chapters three, five, and six. Taken together, they identify when centralisation within a federal – structure fosters more impartial law-making and rights-friendly outcomes – and when it falls short. They also

[61] A Gibson, 'Madison's Republican Remedy: The Tenth Federalist and the Creation of an Impartial Republic' in JN Rakove and CA Sheehan (eds), *The Cambridge Companion to the Federalist* (Cambridge Companions to Philosophy, Cambridge, Cambridge University Press, 2020) 274.

[62] Madison, Federalist No. 10 (n 8).

[63] CF Hobson, 'The Negative on State Laws: James Madison, the Constitution, and the Crisis of Republican Government' (1979) 36 *William and Mary Quarterly* 215.

[64] M Moussa, 'Expanding the *Nemo Judex* Rule: Reflections on Non-Pecuniary Bias' [2025] *Judicial Review* 1; P Cane, *Administrative Law*, 5th edn (Oxford, Oxford University Press, 2011) 72.

[65] See ch 4.

shed light on how federalism can address the social contention surrounding rights and help cultivate an 'agreement to disagree' ethos.

Chapter three serves as an illustrative case of factions of group interest. It examines the judicial, legislative, and socio-political developments surrounding racial minority rights and equal pay in the US and the EU. This comparison highlights the effectiveness of the federal impartiality argument and how centralisation significantly enhanced the protection of these rights and fostered their greater social acceptance. Chapter five turns to abortion and serves as an example of a principle-based faction, characterised by a conflict between decisional autonomy and foetal personhood. While the US has shifted from centralising[66] to decentralising abortion rights,[67] the EU, conversely, has adopted a 'mediated plurality' approach. Namely, it leaves the matter to the discretion of states while maintaining the potential for central intervention.[68] The book illustrates why the EU's approach is more suitable for morally divisive matters. Beyond abortion, the book demonstrates how this argument holds true for several examples of divisive rights falling under the category of 'faction of moral principle'.

Chapter six addresses the more complex cases where interest-based (group bias) and principle-based (ideological) bias overlap, offering a nuanced framework for approaching compounded factional conflicts. These arise in cases involving religious freedom and ideologically contested issues such as bans on ritual slaughter or religious apparel in public employment, arrangements for religious funding, religious exemptions, or the placement of religious symbols in public spaces, among others.

In its entirety, the book provides a theoretically grounded, comparatively informed guide for drawing the federal boundary over various types of divisive rights in the US and the EU. This aids in optimising federalism's potential to safeguard rights and mitigate internal conflicts over increasingly contested rights in an era marked by culture wars. At the same time, it cautions that federalism is a double-edged sword, and getting the federal balance wrong can heighten the risks of polarisation or undermine rights. In making these claims, the book couples its doctrinal and comparative focus with insights from federal constitutional theory, history of ideas, social psychology, and constitutional economics.

[66] *Roe v Wade* 410 US 113 (1973).
[67] *Dobbs v Jackson Women's Health Org* 597 US 215 (2022).
[68] Case C–159/90 *SPUC v Grogan* ECLI:EU:C:1991:378, [1991] ECR I–4685.

1

Federal Doctrines and Rights in the EU and the US

I. Introduction

This chapter provides readers with a brief introduction to some basic federal doctrines used in both systems, which are essential for understanding the normative theory and the case law discussed in the remaining chapters. The second section offers an overview of the competing theories used to draw federal boundaries. The third section summarises the role of the Union's Charter, or the Bill of Rights, and to what extent these instruments apply to constituent states. The fourth section introduces the main constitutional doctrines designed to maintain the balance of powers between the Union and the states while showing the common contestation over how to apply these doctrines to the boundary question in both systems. It is important to stress that the doctrinal analysis provided here is intended to be concise, serving only to familiarise the reader with the key concepts used in the case law discussed in subsequent chapters. It is by no means an exhaustive doctrinal analysis, as a comprehensive discussion of the relevant jurisprudence of each system alone would require a series of books.

II. A Primer: Federal Theory and the Boundary Question?

For many visitors to the UK, it comes as a surprise that watching live TV without first obtaining a licence is a criminal offence.[1] For constitutional observers, however, the fact that the Parliament can criminalise or regulate any conduct is simply a manifestation of the absolute sovereignty model inherent in nation-states. Following Hobbes' *Leviathan*, citizens have relinquished the question of whether the sovereign has the power to regulate certain areas; the jurisdiction of Parliament is never questioned. This marks, at least theoretically, a crucial distinction between the absolute sovereignty model and federalism as a divided power model. It is the difference between *any* and *some*. While the absolute sovereignty model grants the power to regulate *anything*, federalism distributes regulatory

[1] Communications Act 2003, s 363.

authority between different levels of government, *some* areas here and *some* there. The federal Parliament must first establish its own competence before it can legislate on a given matter. This makes it essential to determine where each jurisdiction (federal or state) ends and the other begins – a fundamental inquiry known as the *boundary question*.

Federal scholarship has long grappled with this question, which remains equally puzzling in both the EU and the US. What makes the boundary question over divisive rights more difficult is that the three leading theories of federalism in the United States – dual, cooperative, and process federalism – which have migrated into EU scholarship, do not, in my view, provide a sufficient answer to the pressing questions around.[2]

The earliest theory is *dual federalism*, which imagines the relationship between the Union and the states as a 'layered cake' with each level of government exercising *exclusive powers* in its own distinct layer. The theory carries a strong normative commitment to preserving clear boundaries between state and federal authority. Yet this clarity is largely impractical. As many have observed, reality does not come conveniently 'packaged into boxes'.[3] Take, for example, discrimination against minorities in housing: is it a matter of social welfare (traditionally local), or an economic service subject to Union regulation?[4] The same dilemma applies to abortion – is it a morally local question, or a medical service with cross-border economic dimensions?

The limits of dual federalism led to the rise of *cooperative federalism*, often compared to a 'marble cake' where the union and state powers are intermingled.[5] This model acknowledges the practical reality of overlapping jurisdictions and rejects the notion of exclusive spheres of power. While descriptively more accurate, cooperative federalism, as Schapiro notes, still lacks a normative account of *how* to coordinate this overlap.[6] Even a marble cake requires *a recipe*: we need to know how much 'chocolate' (Union law) and how much 'vanilla' (state law) goes into the federal recipe. For contested issues like abortion or housing discrimination, the theory does not provide a normative path to balance promoting rights while controlling factionalism.

Dissatisfaction with cooperative federalism led to what is termed 'New federalism' or the partial return of the 'undead' dual federalism,[7] which swung 'the pendulum' towards the classical checks of pre-cooperative federalism.[8] Without

[2] For an account summary applying these theories to the EU, see R Schütze, *From Dual to Cooperative Federalism: The Changing Structure of European Law* (Oxford, Oxford University Press, 2009).

[3] RA Schapiro, *Polyphonic Federalism: Toward the Protection of Fundamental Rights* (Chicago, University of Chicago Press, 2009) 56.

[4] Case C-417/23 *Slagelse Almennyttige Boligselskab – Afdeling Schackenborgvænge and Others v Ministry of Transport and Housing* ECLI:EU:C:2025:98, Opinion of AG Ćapeta (Danish Ghetto Case).

[5] M Grodzins, *The American system: A new view of government in the United States* (Piscataway, Transaction Publishers, 1966) 60–153.

[6] Schapiro (n 3).

[7] EA Young, 'The Puzzling Persistence of Dual Federalism' (2014) 55 *Federalism and Subsidiarity* 34.

[8] RE Ryan, *Federalism and the Tug of War Within* (Oxford, Oxford University Press, 2011) 68.

fully denouncing the overlap and the marble cake-like interactions, the US Supreme Court seems to shift the default line from the 'uncritical overlap of cooperative federalism to a model emphasizing more protected zones of exclusive state and federal power'.[9] Unlike the other theories which have migrated from the US into EU scholarship, this one remains largely an American one. Others perceive this swing not as a standalone theory but rather as a partial revival of dual federalism.[10]

Another theory is *process federalism*. Its central idea is that state interests are protected through their role in composing the federal institutions and through their role in the decision-making process. On this view, the political process itself should be sufficient to protect local interests, and courts ought to defer to that process unless a procedural defect has occurred.[11] The difficulty, as Schapiro argues, is that process federalism is essentially a theory of judicial review, not 'a theory of federalism'.[12] It does not tell us whether matters such as abortion should be regulated through the state political process or the federal one. Moreover, those engaged in running the political safeguards of federalism still need substantive guidance on when to centralise or localise regulation.[13] This is particularly clear in the EU context, as highlighted in the 2024 Draghi Report on the Future of Europe, which notes the widespread confusion among policymakers over when and how to invoke subsidiarity to maintain the Union-state balance.[14]

In short, while each theory offers important insights, none provides a sufficient framework for addressing the boundary disputes over contentious rights questions. One of the book's central aims is to offer a more flexible and layered approach – one that allows for overlapping and graduated categorisations of when, and to what extent, the Union should be involved in regulating divisive rights.[15] Before turning to that analysis, the next section briefly contrasts some of the key jurisprudential and doctrinal tools developed within each system to navigate the complex relationship between constitutional structure and rights protection. The argument is rooted both in revisiting the foundational theory of federalism and in testing through comparative empirical analysis. For now, let's briefly contrast some of the jurisprudential and doctrinal tools each system has devised to navigate the relationship between structure and rights.

[9] ibid 101.

[10] Young (n 7).

[11] The theory is traced back to H Wechsler, 'The Political Safeguards of Federalism: The Role of the States in the Composition and Selection of the National Government' [1954] *Columbia Law Review* 543. For its application in the EU see X Groussot and D Harvey (eds), 'Process-Oriented Federalism in EU Law' (EULawLive Press, Dec 2024).

[12] Schapiro (n 3) 87.

[13] ibid.

[14] M Draghi, *The Future of European Competitiveness: A Competitiveness Strategy for Europe* (European Commission, 9 September 2024) 310.

[15] H Kleinlein, 'Federalisms, Rights, and Autonomies: The United States, Germany, and the EU' (2017) 15 *International Journal of Constitutional Law* 1169.

III. The Structural Scope of Federal Rights in the US and the EU

The interaction between structure and rights in a federation usually raises two questions. First, whether a federal bill of rights exists or only state-level constitutional rights are present. If a federal bill of rights exists, the next question is whether it applies to the states – ie, whether it is centralised (or *incorporated*, to use American terminology) – or whether states are insulated from the federal bill and apply their own version of constitutional rights in a decentralised manner. As we shall see, neither system initially had a bill of rights. However, a Bill of Rights was later adopted in the US, and a Charter of Fundamental Rights was belatedly introduced in the EU, both of which began to play a role in centralisation, albeit to varying degrees. The scope and function of federal rights in both systems share some similarities but differ in some important ways, as summarised below.

A. The Evolution and Scope of the American Federal Rights

In the US, state constitutions predated the federal Constitution and were the main source for protecting individual rights.[16] Even after the Bill of Rights was added in the form of the first ten amendments to the Constitution, it was 'universally understood' to apply only to the federal government.[17] For decades, the Supreme Court invalidated just one federal law based on the Bill – the infamous *Dred Scott* decision, which denied citizenship to enslaved people and classified them as property. The ruling contributed to tensions that led to the Civil War.[18]

Following the Union victory, the Reconstruction Amendments (Thirteenth, Fourteenth, and Fifteenth) redefined the US constitutional structure. The Thirteenth abolished slavery, the Fourteenth centralised *citizenship and due process* protections, and the Fifteenth secured voting rights regardless of race. The Fourteenth Amendment is the most relevant to the book's analysis. Its goal was to centralise the definition of citizenship and to put certain rights outside the prerogative of the states. To this end, the provision has three main clauses: (i) '*The Due Process Clause*' secured the basic natural rights to life, liberty, and property; (ii) '*The Privileges and Immunities Clause*' seemed to carry more promise as it secured Union Citizenship's broader category of rights; and (iii) '*The Equal Protection*

[16] See generally A Amar, *The Bill of Rights: Creation and Reconstruction* (New Haven, Yale University Press, 1998).

[17] *Barron v Mayor & City Council of Baltimore* 32 US 243 (1833); constitutional historians indicate the trivial role of the Bill in this era by reference to the fact that Tocqueville's detailed study of American democracy did not make any mention thereof: see RJ Reinstein, 'Completing the Constitution: The Declaration of Independence, Bill of Rights and Fourteenth Amendment' (1993) 66 *Temple Law Review* 117.

[18] *Dred Scott v Sandford* 60 US 393 (1857).

Clause' uncoupled liberty from equality, and accordingly, equal treatment became an independent right.[19]

However, two subsequent decisions negatively impacted the scope of the Fourteenth Amendment. Firstly, the ambitious 'privilege and immunity' clause had a '*false start*' in the *Slaughterhouse* cases.[20] The Supreme Court held that the clause did not extend the rights embodied in the Bill to states, and ever since, the clause has become '*a dead letter*'.[21] Secondly, the '*ironically named Civil Rights Cases of 1883*',[22] the Court had restricted the authority of Congress to horizontally apply equal rights against private individuals. Confining this curial clause to state action only meant that restaurants, hotels, and railway companies continued to deny their services to blacks.[23] For half a century, the post-Civil War 'Reconstruction Amendment' had become almost only centralisation on '*paper*'.[24]

Effective centralisation started in the early twentieth century when the Court launched a process of 'incorporation' relying on the 'Due Process Clause' of the Fourteenth Amendment.[25] Through this judicial innovation, the Court gradually extended to states *most* of the Bill's *enumerated rights* (rights listed in the first ten amendments) as well as other *unenumerated rights* (unwritten rights implicit in the penumbra of the Constitution).[26] Simply put, incorporation involves *a process of rights centralisation* by removing them from the realm of state plurality and bringing them under the authority of the federal constitution and the federal branches of government.

Equally important was the advent of cooperative federalism's expansion of the federal regulatory authority and its concomitant structural centralisation, which

[19] Reinstein (n 17) 117–125.

[20] *Slaughterhouse Cases* 83 US (16 Wall) 36 (1872); E Chemerinsky, *Constitutional Law* (Burlington, Aspen, 2019) 736.

[21] RH Fallon, *The Dynamic Constitution* (Cambridge, Cambridge University Press, 2012) 128; noting that the only case where the Court used the clause was in 1999 to invalidate a California law that limited welfare benefits for new residents in the state to the level of the state they moved from; *Saenz v Roe* 526 US 489 (1999).

[22] ibid.

[23] In other spheres, the Court endorsed a law authorising literacy test and poll tax as pre-requisite to vote which, in fact, excluded the black franchise. *Williams v Mississippi* 170 US 213 (1898).

[24] B Ackerman, *We the People, Volume 3: The Civil Rights Revolution* (Cambridge, MA, Harvard University Press, 2014) 30. '[The] dream of first-class citizenship had sunk to a cruel nadir': AH Kelly, WA Harbison and H Belz, *The American Constitution, Its Origins and Development*, 7th edn (New York, WW Norton & Co Inc, 1991) vol 2, 580.

[25] The process of reaching this conclusion involved judicial artisanship. The difficulty lies in the fact that, until today, the Court has neither overruled *Barron* (holding that the Bill does not apply to states) nor *Slaughterhouse* (rejecting that the Bill's privilege and immunities clause extended to states). Choosing not to overrule the precedents, the Court interpreted the word 'liberty' in the Due Process Clause to encompass those rights enumerated in the Bill which are deemed fundamental. DE Hall and JP Feldmeier, *Constitutional Law: Governmental Powers and Individual Freedoms* (London, Pearson, 2012) 320. The roadmap of applying different degrees of judicial scrutiny is encapsulated in footnote number four by Justice Stone in the *Carolene products case* 304 US 144 (1938).

[26] US Constitution, amend IX; See R Dworkin, 'Unenumerated Rights: Whether and How Roe Should Be Overruled' (1992) 59 *University of Chicago Law Review* 381.

led to what is called '*New Deal – Civil rights synthesis*'.[27] Decades of activism, along with the conducive global and domestic political ambience post-World War II, synthesised civil rights with the New Deal structure, putting the latter in the service of the former to revolutionise rights and equality in the US.[28] This was epitomised in the *Brown* decision[29] and subsequent Voting Rights and Civil Rights Acts, ending overt segregation in several spheres of life.[30]

This synthesis led to a profound impact on the American Constitution, both in terms of the substance and structure of rights. *Substantive rights-wise*, while the era was about African American 'liberation', it generated a major ripple effect on areas such as sex equality, criminal process and others.[31] *Structure-wise*, the civil rights era represented a 'defeat' in numerous areas to the notion of decentralisation and states' rights. The federal jurisdiction boundary moved to territories traditionally considered on the states' side. The atrocities committed by some states in resistance to black rights made decentralisation seem to be on 'the wrong side of history'.[32]

However, by the 1990s, the Court revived limits on federal power. In judgments often likened to the EU's *Tobacco Advertising Case*,[33] the US Supreme Court curbed Congress's authority under the Commerce Clause and Reconstruction Amendments,[34] signalling a shift towards 'new federalism' or a partial return to the 'undead' dual federalism.[35] The incorporation process and its centralisation of most rights remains the departure point, yet debates on abortion, religious freedom, and some aspects of culture wars continue to raise questions about the federal authority, as the case studies in subsequent chapters show.

B. The Evolution and Scope of the EU Fundamental Rights

Whereas in the US, political pressure compelled drafting a Bill shortly after ratification,[36] in the EU, the initial political circumstances pointed in the other

[27] A term coined in Ackerman (n 24) 109.
[28] ibid 109, 192–232.
[29] *Brown v Board of Education of Topeka* 347 US 483 (1954).
[30] LM Friedman, *A History of American Law*, 4th edn (Oxford, Oxford University Press, 2019) 687.
[31] ibid. Notably, it is only in 1971 that the Court started realising that the Fourteenth Amendment bans discrimination against women which ushered in a new jurisprudence on gender discrimination. *Reed v Reed* 404 US 57 (1971). Prior to this, the Court upheld denial of women's right to practice law in *Bradwell v Illinois* 83 US (16 Wall) 130 (1873), as well as female jury exclusion in *Hoyt v Florida* 368 US 57 (1961). An Equal Rights Amendment for women was introduced and almost gained ratification in the 1970s but fell short by three states.
[32] Schapiro (n 3) 46.
[33] E Young, 'Protecting Member State Autonomy in the European Union: Some Cautionary Tales from American Federalism' (2002) 77 *New York University Law Review* 1612, 1647.
[34] *United States v Lopez* 514 US 549 (1995); *United States v Morrison* 529 US 598 (2000).
[35] Young (n 7) 34.
[36] This does not mean that the founding document did not contain any rights, because akin to how Amar showed the US Constitution contained some rights before the Bill, the Treaty of Rome contained a market provision which was seen to protect some rights. Eg, EC Treaty (Treaty of Rome, as amended)

direction.[37] Not only was the Treaty of Rome born silent on fundamental rights, leaving the matter to the constitutions of Member States, but also during the period from 1957–1969, the Court of Justice of the EU ('CJEU') emphatically rejected arguments to rely on national fundamental rights to challenge the actions of Community institutions[38] or to read their treaties as entailing explicit or implicit protection of rights.[39] As the Court started to constitutionalise the treaty and break away from the 'international law plus' model,[40] fundamental rights started to play a role in Community law. This was instigated by the ruling in *Stauder* (1969) followed by the well-known *Solange* saga between the CJEU and the German Constitutional Court (FCC).[41]

Given the lack of a written source, the question is how did the CJEU extract the unwritten rights – to use the American jargon – from the European constitutional traditions? Parallels can be drawn with the task of the US Supreme Court in discovering whether an unenumerated right exists and then assessing whether it is sufficiently fundamental to warrant centralisation. As mentioned earlier, the US Supreme Court does not adhere to one approach which maximises its discretion.[42] Of 'particular significance' to the Court's task is the European Convention on Human Rights ('ECHR').[43] While the Court consistently referred to the ECHR as a 'special source of inspiration',[44] it has never considered it formally binding so as to retain freedom to diverge and move beyond it.[45] Using this methodology, following the decades after *Strauder*, the CJEU developed a rich fundamental rights jurisprudence in several areas.[46]

art 7 (non-discrimination based on nationality); and EC Treaty (Treaty of Rome, as amended) art 119 (equal pay for equal work among men and women); for the American perspective see Amar (n 16).

[37] See generally G de Búrca, 'The Evolution of EU Human Rights Law' in P Craig and G de Búrca (eds), *The Evolution of EU Law*, 2nd edn (Oxford, Oxford University Press, 2011).

[38] Case 1/ 58 *Stork v High Authority* ECLI:EU:C:1959:4, [1959] ECR 17, para 17.

[39] Cases 36, 37, 38, and 40/59 *Geitling v High Authority* ECLI:EU:C:1960:36, [1960] ECR 423; Case 40/64 *Sgarlata and others v Commission* ECLI:EU:C:1965:36, [1965] ECR 215, [1966] CMLR 314; it rejected even the possibility of relying on fundamental rights as a general principle that could aid the interpretation of the treaty. *cf* Case 35/67 *Van Eick v Commission* ECLI:EU:C:1968:39, [1968] ECR 329, 342.

[40] AS Sweet, *The Judicial Construction of Europe* (Cambridge, Cambridge Univeristy Press, 2005) 156; Case 26/62 *Van Gend en Loos* ECLI:EU:C:1963:1, [1963] ECR 13.

[41] BVerfGE 37, 271 (*Solange I (Re Internationale Handelsgesellschaft)*). For an English translation, see [1974] 2 CMLR 540; BVerfGE 73, 339 (*Solange II (Re Wünsche Handelsgesellschaft)*). For an English translation, see [1987] 3 CMLR 225.

[42] On the evolution of European general principles, see R Schütze, *European Constitutional Law*, 2nd edn (Cambridge, Cambridge University Press, 2016) 431–436.

[43] C-260/89 *ERT and others* ECLI:EU:C:1991:254, [1991] ECR I- 2925, 437–438, para 41; C-402/05 P and C-415/05 *Kadi and Al Barakaat International Foundation v Council and Commission* ECLI:EU:C:2008:461, [2008] ECR I-6351, para 283.

[44] P Craig and G De Búrca, *EU Law: Text, Cases, and Materials*, 7th edn (Oxford, Oxford University Press, 2020) 385; eg, Case 4/73 *Nold v Commission* ECLI:EU:C:1974:51, [1974] ECR 491; Case 36/75 *Rutili v Minister for the Interior* ECLI:EU:C:1975:137, [1975] ECR 1219.

[45] ibid.

[46] Eg, the right to lawyer-client confidentiality: Case 155/79 *AM & S Europe Ltd v Commission* ECLI:EU:C:1982:157, [1982] ECR 1575. On prohibition of retroactivity of penal norms, see Case 63/83 *Kirk* ECLI:EU:C:1984:255, [1984] ECR 2689.

In 1992, unwritten fundamental rights gained textual endorsement. The 1992 Maastricht Treaty on the European Union comprised the first recognition of fundamental rights as part of EU law.[47] In the Treaty of Amsterdam, the Copenhagen criteria for admission were granted treaty status.[48] The *acquis* aimed at ensuring respect for human rights as a condition of membership. Article 13 EC Treaty (now Article 19 TEU) was introduced, conferring power on the EU to adopt legislation to combat discrimination on a range of grounds within the existing Union competences. The Article, however, as its contemporary successor, was limited by the requirement of unanimity as explained in chapter three.[49]

It took 30 years from the Court's *Stauder* decision for the EU to have a 'written' Bill of Rights. To 'showcase' the achievement in the field, the European Council proposed the adoption of the EU Charter of Fundamental Rights ('CFR'). The Charter was drafted and solemnly 'proclaimed' in 2000, yet its legal status was unclear.[50] Following the failure to ratify the ill-fated Constitutional Treaty, the Charter was eventually given binding legal status by the Lisbon Treaty in 2009. According to Article 6(3) of the Charter, there are three sources of EU fundamental rights: the Charter as the written Bill, the unwritten source of general principles drawn from common constitutional tradition, and the European Convention on Human Rights ('ECHR') as an 'external bill of rights'.[51]

Having covered the question of whether an EU federal bill of rights exists in its written and unwritten formats, this takes us to the second question of whether it applies to Member States. It will be recalled that the American Bill originally did not apply to states until after the Reconstruction Amendments and the subsequent process of incorporation. In Europe, fundamental rights originally applied only to EU institutions, but then by the end of the 1980s, the CJEU extended the review to Member States.[52] However, EU rights are partially centralised or 'half-way' incorporated.[53] Even with the advent of the Charter, the same position applies. Article 51(1) of the Charter provides that the rights, freedoms, and principles protected by the Charter are addressed to the Member States 'only when they are *implementing* Union law'.[54]

[47] See generally de Búrca (n 37) 480.
[48] ibid.
[49] E Spaventa, 'Should We "Harmonize" Fundamental Rights in the EU? Some Reflections About Minimum Standards and Fundamental Rights Protection in the EU Composite Constitutional System' (2018) 55 *Common Market Law Review* 999, 1017.
[50] De Búrca (n 37) 480–481.
[51] R Schütze, 'Three "Bills of Rights" for the European Union' (2011) 30 *Yearbook of European Law* 131.
[52] Case 5/88 *Wachauf v Germany* ECLI:EU:C:1989:321, [1989] ECR 2609. For a comparison, see AT Pérez, 'The Federalizing Force of the EU Charter of Fundamental Rights' (2017) 15 *International Journal of Constitutional Law* 1080.
[53] ibid.
[54] Charter of Fundamental Rights of the European Union 2000, art 51(1) [emphasis added].

The term 'implementing' has been interpreted broadly; a leading case is *Fransson*, where Member States are deemed to be 'within the scope of EU law'.[55] The case involved the matter of imposing tax penalties in criminal proceedings – a matter that might initially seem outside the EU's reach – but the Court found EU law to apply. This was because part of the VAT revenue is allocated to the EU's own resources, and Article 325, TFEU, obliges Member States to 'counter illegal activities' affecting the Union's financial interests.[56] Consequently, contrary to the arguments of several Member States and even the Commission, the tax penalties in question were held to constitute implementation of the EU law. However, in the absence of this 'degree of connection' with the EU law, the Charter has, on other occasions, been found not to apply to Member States.[57]

In sum, the EU scholarship has categorised the case law on the meaning of 'implementing' into four main groups: (i) agency situations, where Member States are enforcing Union acts and measures;[58] (ii) situations where states derogate from the EU law (as in ERT);[59] (iii) cases where states act within the broader category of 'the scope of EU law' (as highlighted in *Fransson*); and (iv) certain 'non-classical' cases that might result in the deprivation of EU citizenship rights (such as *Zambrano*).[60] The case law on these categories is well established and need not be fully summarised here. The key takeaway is that the Charter is the 'shadow' of and travels in tandem with the EU treaties.[61] Unlike the US model of full incorporation, the EU Charter is not a 'free-standing' legal instrument;[62] rather, its application depends on the existence of a 'degree of connection' to the EU law.[63] This crucial contrast was captured by the Advocate General in her opinion in *Zambrano*:

> The 'incorporation' case-law, based since then on the 'due process' clause of the Fourteenth Amendment, does not *require an inter-state movement nor legislative acts from Congress* … The federalising effect of the American incorporation doctrine is well

[55] Case C–617/10 *Åklagaren v Åkerberg Fransson* EU:C:2013:105.

[56] E Spaventa, 'Fundamental Rights in the European Union' in C Barnard and S Peers (eds), *European Union Law*, 3rd edn (Oxford, Oxford University Press, 2020) 259.

[57] Case C-206/13 *Cruciano Siragusa v Regione Sicilia*, EU:C:2014:126, para 24; Case C-198/13 *Hernándezc and others* EU:C:2014:2055.

[58] See Craig and De Burca (n 44) 450; eg, Case C–55/19 *CCOO & Deutsche Bank* EU:C:2019:402. The logic of this situation is explained in Schütze (n 42) 458.

[59] *ERT and others* (n 43) para 41.

[60] The term is from M Dougan, 'Judicial Review of Member State Action under the General Principles and the Charter: Defining the Scope of Union Law' (2015) 52 *Common Market Law Review* 1201, 1226. Notably, the call upon the Court to use Union citizenship as a medium towards incorporating the Charter is challenged by the text of Art 25(2), TEU, which has built-in double 'safeguards' and the limitation of Art 6(1). See K Lenaerts and P Van Nuffel, *EU Constitutional Law* (T Corthaut ed, Oxford, Oxford University Press, 2022) 25.009.

[61] K Lenaerts and JA Gutiérrez-Fons, 'The Place of the Charter in the EU Constitutional Edifice' in S Peers and others (eds), *The EU Charter of Fundamental Rights: A Commentary* (Oxford, Hart Publishing, 2014) 1568.

[62] K Lenaerts, 'EU Federalism in 3-D' in E Cloots, G De Baere and S Sottiaux (eds), *Federalism in the European Union* (Oxford, Hart Publishing, 2012) 15.

[63] *Siragusa* (n 58) para 32.

> known. A change of that kind would alter, in legal and political terms, the very nature of fundamental rights under EU law. It therefore requires both an evolution in the case-law *and* an unequivocal political statement from the constituent powers of the EU (its Member States) [emphasis added][64]

To further deliver the point, we can apply this contrast to some of the case studies examined in this book. As explored in chapter five, for an issue such as abortion to trigger the application of the Charter, the Court must first determine whether it falls within the scope of the EU law as an inter-state or cross-border service.[65] Similarly, in cases of discrimination against racial minorities in housing,[66] the Court must identify a connecting factor to EU law; without such a link, neither the Charter nor the EU law would apply. Matters in the United States are somewhat more straightforward. Most of the Bill of Rights applies directly to the states: if a right exists, the courts will apply it at the state level.

That being said, US courts can still preserve state prerogatives from federal reach, as demonstrated in *Dobbs*, where the Supreme Court held that abortion is neither explicitly nor implicitly included in the Bill of Rights, and therefore, no federal right extends to the states.[67] However, in doing so, US courts must engage substantively with the question of whether a right exists, whereas EU courts may exclude matters from the scope of the Charter simply on the basis of the absence of cross-border implications or a connection to the EU law, even if there is an explicit Charter provision on the matter.

Despite this crucial divergence between the two systems, two important commonalities emerge. First, courts in both jurisdictions exercise considerable discretion: in the EU, to determine whether there is a sufficient connection to the EU law;[68] and in the US, to decide whether a right is implicitly contained within the penumbra of the Bill of Rights. Second, and closely related, the way in which both courts interpret these questions is underpinned by a conception of what type of federalism courts endorse. The way these matters are interpreted directly shapes the balance of state-union powers.[69] This dialectical relationship between interpretation and federalism will be examined in greater detail in the case law on abortion, minority rights, and religion, where courts' interpretive choices often reflect a normative vision of the role the central authority ought to play in regulating divisive rights.

[64] Case C-34/09 *Ruiz Zambrano* ECLI:EU:C:2010:560, Opinion of AG Sharpston, paras 172–173.

[65] Case C–159/90 *SPUC v Grogan* ECLI:EU:C:1991:378, [1991] ECR I–4685.

[66] Danish Ghetto Case (n 4).

[67] *Dobbs v Jackson Women's Health Org.* 597 US 215 (2022).

[68] Pérez (n 52) 1084 (the precise 'intensity of the necessary connection' seems to remain 'elusive').

[69] This point is made in various contexts. See, eg, C Barnard, 'Restricting Restrictions: Lessons for the EU from the Us?' (2009) 68 *The Cambridge Law Journal* 575, 575–576; H Eklund, 'The Margin of Discretion and the Boundary Question in EU Fundamental Rights Law' (2022) 59 *Common Market Law Review* 1407.

IV. A Few Comparative Remarks

Exigencies of space preclude contrasting all the institutional details of the two models; therefore, a few remarks will have to suffice. The convergence and divergence can be cursorily highlighted with regard to, among others, the following two aspects: (i) the constitutional principles on the allocation of powers and shields against excessive centralisation; and (ii) legislative powers on fundamental rights.

A. Doctrines Governing Allocation of Powers and Shields against Overcentralisation

In both systems, the power of the centre to act on rights is constrained by the principle of *conferral*[70] – in the EU jargon – and its American equivalent of *enumerated powers*.[71] In both, the Centre, unlike the constituent states, does not possess absolute residual powers but is confined to what is granted in their founding document. In theory, both systems require the Centre to first determine a legal base or a conferred power before being able to legislate. Recall the distinction between 'any' and 'some' powers discussed at the beginning of this chapter: here, the principles of conferral and enumerated powers are designed to ensure that the Union remains within its prescribed limits, confined to those 'some' areas of authority rather than assuming power over '*any* law-making'.[72]

Additionally, each system embraces doctrines which – albeit conceptually and genealogically different – serve somehow the similar role of being a 'shield' against overcentralisation.[73] In the US, the Tenth Amendment remains the main 'textual marker of federalism',[74] ensuring protection of some aspects of state autonomy by providing that all power not conferred upon Congress is reserved 'to the People or to the States'.[75] The meaning of this provision oscillated between two approaches. The first approach is that the Court viewed the Tenth Amendment as 'nothing more than a truism',[76] a simple 'reminder' that the federal government may only 'legislate' if it has a conferred 'authority under the constitution' and, thus, makes no distinctive role than the enumerated powers doctrine. The second

[70] Art 5 TFEU.

[71] Madison famously affirmed that '[t]he powers delegated by the proposed Constitution to the federal government are few and defined.': J Madison, 'Federalist No. 45' in A Hamilton, J Madison and J Jay (eds), *The Federalist Papers* (Ian Shapiro ed, New Haven, Yale University Press, 2009) 48.

[72] G Davies, 'Democracy and Legitimacy in the Shadow of Purposive Competence' (2015) 21 *European Law Journal* 2, 18 (emphasis added).

[73] M Klamert, M Kellerbauer and J Tomkin, *Commentary on the EU: Treaties and the Charter of Fundamental Rights* (Oxford, Oxford University Press, 2019) 70; TFEU Protocol (No 2) on the application of the principles of subsidiarity and proportionality [2016] OJ C202/206.

[74] Schapiro (n 3) 48.

[75] US Constitution, amend X (stressing that all power not enumerated, namely conferred upon Congress, is reserved to the People or to the States).

[76] *United States v Darby* 312 US 100 (1941), 123.

approach appears when the Court moves away from cooperative federalism, where it utilised the Tenth Amendment to create 'a zone' of exclusive state activity and to declare unconstitutional federal laws 'intruding' into this zone.[77] The controversy surrounding which interpretation of the Tenth Amendment should prevail persists judicially and academically.[78]

In the EU, there are twin principles which supplement the conferral principle and act as a shield of state regulatory powers: proportionality and subsidiarity. While conferral asks whether an EU power to act in a certain area *exists*, subsidiarity asks *whether the EU should* exercise it, and proportionality asks to *what extent* this power should be used. Subsidiarity is more complex in its enforcement than proportionality. The latter is mentioned in Article 5(4), TEU, mandating that '[the] content and form of Union action shall not exceed *what is necessary to achieve the objectives of the Treaties*'.[79] The Court allows the legislator a wide discretion and rarely strikes down a measure on the grounds of proportionality, but, unlike subsidiarity, invalidation does happen.[80] Judicial formulation of the proportionality test has developed across time, and its level of scrutiny depends on the nature of the measure. Yet, it generally revolves around whether the measure is *suitable* and *necessary* to achieve a *legitimate* aim, and/or whether it is *manifestly inappropriate* to the objective sought.[81]

Subsidiarity has 'no immediate [explicit] analogue in America'.[82] The principle prescribes that in areas not falling within the EU's exclusive competence (ie, those shared with Member States), matters should be dealt with at the level of government closest to those affected.[83] Article 5(3) notes that the Union may take action only 'if and in so far as the objectives of the proposed action cannot be sufficiently achieved by the Member States … but can rather, by reason of the scale or effects of the proposed action, be better achieved at Union level'[. The doctrine relies

[77] Chemernisky (n 20) 459–460; See *Nat'l Fed'n of Indep Bus v Sebelius* 567 US 519 (2012); *Murphy v National Collegiate Athletic* 584 US 200 (2018).

[78] F McDonald, RM Hardaway and A Hubjer, 'Tenth Amendment' in KL Hall, JW Ely Jr and JB Grossman (eds), *The Oxford Companion to the Supreme Court of the United States*, 2nd edn (Oxford, Oxford University Press, 2005).

[79] See, eg, Case T- 87/98, *International Potash* EU:T:2000:221.

[80] Case C-453/03 *ABNA and others* ECLI:EU:C:2005:741, [2005] ECR I-10423; Cases C-293/12 and C-594/12 *Digital Rights Ireland* EU:C:2014:238.

[81] Case C-491/01 *British American Tobacco* EU:C:2002:741, [2002] ECR I – 11453; Case C-426/93 *Germany v Council* ECLI:EU:C:1995:367, [1995] ECR I-3723, para 42; Case C-84/94, *United Kingdom v Council* ECLI:EU:C:1996:431, [1996] ECR I-5755, paras 57–58; Case C-331/88 *R v Minister of Agriculture, Fisheries and Food, ex parte Fedesa* ECLI:EU:C:1990:391, [1990] ECR I-4023. While seeking similar goals, the doctrinal details and the enforcement mechanisms of each doctrine vary considerably between the EU and the US, see D Chalmers, G Davies and G Monti, *European Union Law*, 5th edn (Cambridge, Cambridge University Press, 2024).

[82] EA Young, 'A Comparative Perspective' in R Schutze and T Tridimas (eds), *Oxford Principles of European Union Law* (Oxford, Oxford University Press, 2017) 159.

[83] Klamert, Kellerbauer and Tomkin (n 73). The doctrine has a long historical pedigree dating back to the Catholic Church and the Roman empire. See also D Halberstam, 'Federal Powers and the Principle of Subsidiarity' in VD Amar and MV Tushnet (eds), *Global Perspectives on Constitutional Law* (Oxford, Oxford University Press, 2009) 34.

on both *ex ante* political enforcement and *ex post* judicial scrutiny. The political enforcement is through engaging the national Parliament to scrutinise drafts of the EU legislative measures for compliance with subsidiarity through the 'Early Warning Mechanism'.[84]

With regard to the judicial enforcement of the principle, the CJEU seems to embrace a light version of 'process of federalism' which mainly relies on political safeguards in policing the jurisdiction boundaries.[85] Thus far, the CJEU has never relied on subsidiarity to invalidate a Union measure despite it being raised by the parties.[86] Yet, even for the political enforcement, the doctrine is contested as an effective tool of policing the boundaries and was labelled as a 'wrong idea in the wrong place in the wrong time'.[87] The recently published Draghi Report stressed the enigma of the 'limited' use of the subsidiarity mechanism by national Parliament and the general confusion of when 'more EU law' is needed and when not.[88]

To sum up, while seeking similar goals, the federal constitutional doctrines and their enforcement mechanisms vary considerably between the EU and the US.[89] Yet, a common thread runs through the debates on subsidiarity in the EU and the Tenth Amendment in the US: in both systems, there is widespread dissatisfaction with how these doctrines are applied to achieve an appropriate balance between Union and state powers, and ongoing disagreement over what that balance ought to be. This reflects the persistent contestation and complexity of the boundary question that is common to both systems. Relatedly, central powers have often been exercised broadly despite the existence of these doctrinal constraints. This can even be seen in powers related to fundamental rights discussed in the next section.

B. Legislative Powers on Fundamental Rights and their Limits

The US Reconstruction Amendments granted the federal legislature the power to 'enforce' their substantive provisions 'by appropriate legislation'.[90] By contrast, the

[84] TFEU Protocol (No 2) on the Application of the Principles of Subsidiarity and Proportionality [2016] OJ C202/206.

[85] *UK v Council* (n 81), paras 46 and 47; C-233/94 *Germany v Parliament* (Deposit guarantee directive) ECLI:EU:C:1997:231, [1997] ECR I-2405, paras 24–28; *British American Tobacco* (n 81) paras 177–185; Cases C-154/04 & C-155/04 *Alliance for Natural Health* ECLI:EU:C:2005:449, [2005] ECR I-6451, paras 99–108; Case C-114/01 *AvestaPolarit Chrome Oy* ECLI:EU:C:2003:448, [2003] ECR I - 8725, para 56; Case C-518/07 *Commission v Germany* ECLI:EU:C:2010:125, [2010] ECR I-1885; Case C-176/09 ECLI:EU:C:2011:290, *Luxembourg v Parliament* [2011] ECR I-3727.

[86] ibid.

[87] G Davies, 'Subsidiarity: The Wrong Idea, in the Wrong Place, at the Wrong Time' (2006) 43 *Common Market Law Review* 63.

[88] Draghi (n 14) 310.

[89] For a comparison, see GA Bermann, 'Taking Subsidiarity Seriously: Federalism in the European Community and the United States' (1994) 94 *Columbia Law Review* 331.

[90] US Constitution, amend XIV, s 5.

EU legislator lacks similar proactive 'pure' fundamental rights competence except for Article 19, TFEU, which empowers the Council within the limits of conferred competences to 'take appropriate action to combat discrimination' on particular grounds.[91] This power, however, is largely constrained by the need for a unanimous vote of members of the Council (the EU's equivalent of the Second Chambers). The implication of this veto power will be further discussed in chapter three. Related to non-discrimination legislation is Article 157 on equal pay between men and women, which deposits its original economic purpose to prevent 'social dumping'. It played a revolutionary role in equal treatment between men and women within EU Member States as shall be explored in the subsequent chapter.[92]

A comparative note on 'pure' human rights competence is that the US has no equivalent of the EU-like veto power in the Federal Senate. However, Section 5 of the Reconstruction Amendment has its own court-imposed constraints. First, because of the previously discussed '*ironically named Civil Rights Cases of 1883*'. This Congressional power cannot be used to legislate against private actors (ie, no horizontal effect in the EU jargon). Further, the US Supreme Court came to place a ceiling or judicial veto on the scope of this legislative power. In *City of Boerne (1997)*,[93] the Court held that the Congress cannot create new rights or grant more generous interpretations of existing rights (say to religious minorities) beyond what the Court decided. Congress just enforces what the Court reads into the Constitution.[94] As the Court put it, 'Congress does not enforce a constitutional right by changing what the right is; it has been given the power *to enforce, not the power to determine* what constitutes a constitutional violation.'[95] This type of judicial veto as well as the Member State veto has implications for the case study examples, which will be covered in chapters three (racial minorities) and six (religious minorities).

Beyond 'pure' fundamental rights competence, the two systems share some comparable market and implied powers, which are extensively used in rights-related legislation. In the US, the commerce clause has been the 'deep reservoir' of federal powers.[96] Despite the clause's original economic purpose to regulate interstate commerce, it has been frequently utilised in regulating fundamental rights and to achieve social ends which were originally within the state's police power. For instance, it was used to pass the Civil Rights Act, which extended

[91] E Muir, 'Fundamental Rights: An Unsettling EU Competence' (2014) 15 *Human Rights Review* 25.

[92] C Barnard, *EU Employment Law* (Oxford, Oxford University Press, 2012) 254.

[93] This departs from the more generous view in *Katzenbach v Morgan* 384 US 641 (1966). See discussion in Chemerinsky (n 20) 433.

[94] See summary in BL Adkins and others, *Federalism-Based Limitations on Congressional Power: An Overview* (Congressional Research Service, CRS Report R45323, 31 January 2023).

[95] *City of Boerne v Flores* 521 US 507 (1997) [emphasis added]. Subsequent cases, however, are not 'entirely consistent'. See Fallon (n 21) discussing the difference between reasoned Judgment Model versus Truth Model in judicial decision-making.

[96] OH Stephens Jr and JM Scheb, *American Constitutional Law: Civil Rights and Liberties* (Boston, Cengage, 2011) vol 2, 106.

race and gender discrimination to private actors.[97] It was even argued that '[T]he Commerce Clause, not the Fourteenth Amendment, was deemed the primary source of constitutional authority supporting the major civil rights statutes of the 1960s.'[98] However, with the advent of new federalism, the Court, starting with *Lopez* and then *Morrison* began – though inconsistently[99] – to reinvigorate some limits on the Congress' power to regulate non-economic activity, such as the previously mentioned case on violence against women.[100]

Somewhat similarly, Article 114, TFEU, and its predecessors provide the Union with the power to establish and ensure the functioning of the EU's internal market needed to complement the four market freedoms which enable goods, persons, services, and capital to move freely across Member States.[101] The CJEU's scrutiny is generally 'soft' in checking the boundary of the EU '*ratione materiae*' while 'harder' in reviewing its compatibility with fundamental rights.[102] It is true that in *Tobacco Advertising* the Court did strike down a measure adopted through Article 114.[103] In subsequent cases, however, the CJEU – unlike the US Supreme Court post *Lopez* – consistently returned to its soft approach,[104] which revived critiques that Article 114 is '(almost) boundless'[105] and that *Tobacco Advertising* was a 'false dawn'.[106]

According to the 'centre of gravity' test,[107] the CJEU identifies the legislation's principal – as opposed to the ancillary – objective. If the principal aim relates to the functioning of the common market, Article 114 can be used as the basis of Union action.[108] As de Witte succinctly remarked, it is perfectly constitutional to

[97] See ch 3.

[98] SR McAllister, 'Is There a Judicially Enforceable Limit to Congressional Power Under the Commerce Clause?' (1996) 44 *University of Kansas Law Review* 217, 224–225. Subsequently, for instance, it was the basis for federal statutes on Partial-Birth Abortion Ban Act of 2003, 18 USC, s 1531.55.

[99] In *Gonzales*, the Court upheld the Congress's use of the Commerce Clause to ban cultivation and possession of small amounts of marijuana for medical purposes.

[100] *United States v Morrison* 529 US 598 (2000); *NFIB v Sebelius* 567 US 519 (2012).

[101] For discussion of harmonisation and its levels (minimum, exhaustive, optional, and new approach harmonisation), see C Barnard, *The Substantive Law of the EU* (Oxford, Oxford University Press, 2019) ch 14.

[102] T Tridimas, 'Fundamental rights, general principles of EU law, and the Charter' (2014) 16 *Cambridge Yearbook of European Legal Studies* 361, referring to Case C-380/03 *Germany v European Parliament and Council of the European Union* ECLI:EU:C:2006:772, [2006] ECR I-11573 (Tobacco Advertising II); Case C-210/03 *R (on the application of Swedish Match AB) v Secretary of State for Health* ECLI:EU:C:2004:802, [2004] ECR I-11893.

[103] Case C-376/98 *Germany v European Parliament and Council of the European Union* ECLI:EU:C:2000:544, [2000] ECR I-8419 (Tobacco Advertising I).

[104] *Swedish Match* (n 102); *Tobacco Advertising II* (n 102); *Alliance for Natural Health* (n 85); Cases C-154/04 & C-155/04 *Alliance for Natural Health* ECLI:EU:C:2005:199, Opinion of AG Geelhoed; Case C-58/08 *Vodafone* ECLI:EU:C:2010:321, [2010] ECR I-4999.

[105] Schütze (n 42) 231.

[106] ibid quoting D Wyatt, 'Community Competence to Regulate the Internal Market' (Oxford Legal Studies Research Paper No. 9/2007).

[107] Centre of gravity was first articulated in Case C-300/89 *Commission v Council* ECLI:EU:C:1991:244, [1991] ECR I-2867 (Titanium Dioxide).

[108] The analysis is informed by the brilliant chapter of B de Witte, 'A Competence to Protect: The Pursuit of Non-Market Aims Through Internal Market Legislation' in P Syrpis (ed), *The Judiciary, the*

use Article 114 for fundamental rights legislation *as long as* the 'authors' of the measure make 'a plausible case' that it either helps remove disparities between national provisions which hinder the four market freedoms or removes disparities of competition.[109] Moreover, if the divergence on fundamental rights among national systems creates appreciable distortion to the market, Article 114 can be easily invoked to harmonise national rights in this regard.[110] In this way, the Union has long used the Article to achieve a number of social ends and enact fundamental rights-related legislation. Examples include labour rights,[111] right to receive and impart information, aspects of freedom of expression,[112] disability rights,[113] and others.[114]

Another relevant comparable competence is the so-called 'Flexibility Clause'[115] of Article 352, TFEU, which empowers the Union to adopt 'appropriate measures' that prove necessary to attain one of 'the objectives' set out in the Treaties, where the latter do not provide the 'necessary powers'.[116] The EU has long adhered to an expansive interpretation of the Article in numerous fields, including fundamental rights.[117] For instance, it was used to establish a European Monitoring Centre on Racism and Xenophobia. More recently, it was the legal basis for setting up the Fundamental Rights Agency.[118] This power is, however, limited by the need for a unanimity vote and the fact that it cannot be used to harmonise (unify state laws) in areas where the treaties ban such harmonisation. This residual power, as its phrasing shows, is conceptually similar, with some procedural differences, to the US *Necessary and Proper Clause* providing the Congress with the power to adopt measures that aid in attaining the ends contemplated by other constitutional

Legislature, and the EU Internal Market (Cambridge, Cambridge University Press, 2011) 25; M Dougan, 'Minimum Harmonization and the Internal Market' (2000) 37 *Common Market Law Review* 853; see the examples he discusses in notes 30–31.

[109] ibid; see also Case C-491/01 *British American Tobacco (Investments) and Imperial Tobacco* ECLI:EU:C:2002:476, Opinion of AG Geelhoed, paras 100–101.

[110] V Kosta, *Fundamental Rights in EU Internal Market Legislation* (London, Bloomsbury Publishing, 2015) 31.

[111] Directive 96/71/EC concerning the posting of workers in the framework of the provision of services. While the Directive does not seem to be framed in a rights language, the Commission's Explanatory Memorandum of its first proposal contained references to the Community Charter of Fundamental Social Rights of Workers; among others, see ibid.

[112] Article 11(2) of Directive 2010/13/EU on Audio-visual Media Services Directive states first, that the media shall enjoy freedom of expression; and, secondly, that Member States must ensure media pluralism.

[113] Directive (EU) 2019/882 (European Accessibility Act), after basing its adoption on the need to harmonise the market by 'preventing barriers … arising from divergent accessibility requirements' Art 103 reads 'this Directive seeks to ensure full respect for the rights of persons with disabilities …'.

[114] For an analysis of market powers used in areas of health and data protection, see Kosta (n 110).

[115] Klamert, Kellerbauer and Tomkin (n 73).

[116] TFEU EC Treaty, art 308]. Noting, however, that the recourse to this EU power is not limited to the field of a specific union policy, but rather to 'broad objectives of the treaties': ibid.

[117] J Weiler, 'The Transformation of Europe' (1991) 100 *Yale Law Journal* 2403, 2445–2446.

[118] Council Regulation (EC) No 168/2007 establishing a European Union Agency for Fundamental Rights.

provisions.[119] The American clause, too, was used to affirm the federal regulation of voting rights,[120] immigration,[121] and many others.[122]

Table 1.1 Key EU and US powers compared

Issue	**EU**	**US**
Key Central Powers used with rights	1) Market Power: Art 114, TFEU (Tobacco Advertising test) 2) Art 19, TFEU (limited by veto) 3) Art 157, TFEU (equal pay between men and women)	1) The Commerce Clause (varying jurisprudence, eg, *Filburn* (1942) to *Morrison* (2000)) 2) Section 5 of the 14th Amendment (limited to state action, not horizontal effect, & limited by SCOTUS interpretation as ceiling)
State power shields	The Conferral principle Subsidiarity & proportionality	The 'enumerated powers' principle The 10th Amendment

C. A Note on the Centralisation/Decentralisation Spectrum

Given the critiques associated with dual federalism and the prevailing reality of mostly overlapping competences in modern federalism, a brief clarification of the centralisation–decentralisation dichotomy is warranted. In previous work, I have identified at least ten categories illustrating the various ways in which Union and state law can intersect. Accepting the descriptive accuracy of the *marble cake* metaphor – where federal and state powers are intermingled – does not preclude scalar categorisation; even a marble cake requires a recipe that determines how much vanilla (state law) and how much chocolate (Union law) are intermixed.[123] While I do not intend to revisit all the various categories (federal cake recipes), two terms are particularly relevant for the present analysis: one leaning towards centralisation, and the other reflecting what I refer to as *mediated plurality*.

Centralisation comes in various forms, but its simplest variant is either a ceiling, where states cannot provide more protection, or a floor (maximum and minimum

[119] US Constitution, art I, s 8, cl 18.

[120] In the Voting Rights Act the Clause combined with s 5 of the Fourteenth Amendment were expressly invoked by Congress: Public Law 91-285, title III, s 301(a)(2)(b) (June 22, 1970). The use of the clause was affirmed by the Court's reasoning in *Katzenbach v Morgan* 384 US 650-651 (1966).

[121] RJ Reinstein, 'The Aggregate and Implied Powers of the United States' (2019) 69 *American University Law Review* 15; see, eg, *Arizona v United States* 567 US 387 (2012).

[122] It is used constantly in providing the constitutional authority for most federal criminal statutes and more recently to justify the indefinite detention of 'sexually dangerous' prisoners. *United States v Comstock* 560 US 126, 156 (2010).

[123] M Moussa, 'Beyond Incomplete Dichotomies: A Structural Typology of Dual Rights in the EU and the Us' (2023) 24 *German Law Journal* 364.

harmonisation in the EU jargon), where states are free to expand. For example, granting a federal parental leave of two weeks, but states are free to provide a more generous leave. Centralisation is not always legislature-led. There are various ways that the Union's courts can vary the level of centralisation in the way the review is conducted. The judicial oversight can be *hands-on* or off.[124] As is well known, the CJEU has an 'incomplete jurisdiction' to directly invalidate national law,[125] its role is to provide the legal interpretation on the compatibility of national law with EU Law while national courts remain responsible for applying rules to the facts.[126] However, the way the Court, for example, frames the referred question and provides its answer can vary across the spectrum, affording national courts a wide 'margin of discretion',[127] or 'highly prescriptive' approach[128] with no room for 'manoeuvre'.[129] Likewise, as Tridimas noted, the Court's proportionality analysis 'hides diverse standards of scrutiny' depending on the issue at hand.[130] Others have expressly stressed the federal 'dimension of proportionality'.[131]

Somewhat comparably, yet more explicitly, in the US, the standard of judicial review impacts how much regulatory discretion states enjoy. Unlike the EU's implicit scale of standards, the US Court 'expressly' refers[132] to a three-tiered scrutiny framework in equal protection and fundamental rights caselaw – ranging from rational basis review to strict scrutiny[133] – which has significant implications for state legislative autonomy and federalism more broadly. Under strict scrutiny, state measures are presumed unconstitutional unless they serve a 'compelling governmental interest' and are 'narrowly tailored' to that interest.[134] This test has often been described as 'strict in theory, but [usually] fatal in fact'.[135] By contrast, rational basis review is 'highly deferential' to states.[136] The challenged law enjoys a 'presumption of constitutionality' unless it is shown that it does not pursue a

[124] T Tridimas, 'Constitutional Review of Member State Action: The Virtues and Vices of an Incomplete Jurisdiction' (2011) 9 *International Journal of Constitutional Law* 737, 738, providing a typology of three broad categories of the Court's approach.

[125] ibid 738 ('ECJ rulings on interpretation thus become a proxy for constitutional review.').

[126] ibid.

[127] Eklund (n 69).

[128] F De Witte, 'Sex, Drugs & EU Law: The Recognition of Moral and Ethical Diversity in EU Law' (2013) 50 *Common Market Law Review* 1545.

[129] Takis (n 124) 738.

[130] T Tridimas, 'The Principle of Proportionality' in T Tridimas and R Shcutze (eds), *The Oxford Principles of the European Union* (Oxford, Oxford University Press, 2018) vol 1, 250–251; see analysis of proportionality in cases discussed in ch 6.

[131] A Steinbach, 'The Federalism Dimension of Proportionality' (2022) 28(1–3) *European Law Journal* 36.

[132] Tridimas (n 130) 250–251.

[133] For tiers of review outside equal protection, see: AZ Huq, 'Tiers of Scrutiny in Enumerated Powers Jurisprudence' (2013) 80 *The University of Chicago Law Review* 575.

[134] Mark T, *Weak Courts, Strong Rights, Judicial Review and Social Welfare Rights in Comparative Constitutional Law* (Princeton, Princeton University Press, 2009).

[135] G Gunther, 'Foreword: In Search of Evolving Doctrine on a Changing Court' (1972) 86 *Harvard Law Review* 1, 8.

[136] Chemernisky (n 20) 690.

'legitimate' goal (understood usually widely) or the means used to achieve it are not rationally related.[137] As will be seen in chapter six, shifting from one test to the other carries strong federal implications.

Turning to *mediated plurality*, this concept lies in the often-overlooked intermediate spot between centralisation and full decentralisation, referring to a *hands-off approach* by the Union that allows for regulatory diversity among Member States on the same issue. In its most differential form, the Union reminds the states of its competence to intervene but avoids ruling on merits on technicality. Abortion in the EU is a good example.[138] It cannot fit in the traditional binary of centralisation since the EU does not regulate it, nor have its courts pronounced a right to abortion. Yet, it cannot be said to be fully decentralised because the EU states' freedom to regulate the matter is not unqualified. The court in *Grogan* reminded Member States of the EU's authority over the matter as a service within the internal market but on a technicality did not pronounce on substance.[139]

A slightly more active, yet still deferential, version of this plurality sees the Court play a slightly larger role but remain 'respectful' of the normative choices of constituent states. This is what de Witte terms 'procedural proportionality'.[140] This light-touch 'variant' of proportionality does not seek to 'reorient' or second-guess the state's policy or moral preference.[141] Instead, while states retain primary regulatory authority, the Union reviews their implementation to ensure coherence and to prevent discriminatory or protectionist inconsistencies.[142] In effect, the Union Court accepts '*prima facie* the substance of the moral or ethical choice' made by constituent states and examines 'policy inconsistencies that betray underlying protectionist or discriminatory intentions'.[143] This approach characterises much of the EU's handling of nationally sensitive issues such as gambling or broader public morality questions.[144] This can find some echoes in parts of the US Supreme Court's rational basis jurisprudence, among other things.[145]

For the purposes of this book, the term *centralisation* refers to a minimum legislative floor or a 'hands-on' approach to judicial scrutiny. By contrast, *mediated*

[137] *O'Gorman & Young, Inc v Hartford Fire Insurance Co* 282 US 251, 257–258 (1931).
[138] See ch 5.
[139] *Grogan* (n 65).
[140] De Witte (n 128) 1546.
[141] ibid.
[142] ibid 1571.
[143] ibid.
[144] Case C-36/02 *Omega* ECLI:EU:C:2004:614, [2004] ECR I-9609; see generally De Witte (n 128).
[145] Think of the Supreme Court's 'four-years moratorium' on capital punishment from 1972 to 1976. After that, it affirmed that the death penalty is not 'categorically impressible' and, with some conditions, states are free to abolish it, as a few did, or retain it, as did the majority. Nevertheless, the Supreme Court occasionally intervenes and invalidates the punishment for certain types of crimes – rape – or for certain offenders – minors and the intellectually disabled. See MJ Perry, *Constitutional Rights, Moral Controversy, and the Supreme Court* (Cambridge, Cambridge University Press, 2008) 80; *cf* Case note, 'The Dormant Commerce Clause and Moral Complicity in a National Marketplace' (2024) 137 *Harvard Law Review* 980.

plurality denotes a more deferential, light-touch or 'hands-off' form of review.[146] The nuances of each model will be explored in subsequent chapters: chapter three considers cases where a centralised, interventionist approach is advisable; chapter five turns to instances where mediated plurality is preferable; and chapter six examines scenarios in which both approaches may be combined to some extent. However, to determine whether a hands-on or hands-off arrangement is appropriate, we first require a guiding normative framework – this is the task of the next chapter, which refines and develops the theory of federal impartiality.

V. Concluding Remarks

This chapter introduced the competing theories for drawing the boundary in federal systems – dual, cooperative, and process federalism – highlighting both their relevance and their limitations in addressing the issue of divisive rights. It also contrasted the position of federal rights in the US, where federal rights are fully incorporated and apply directly to the states, and in the EU, where rights are only partially centralised and apply to Member States solely when they are implementing the EU law. The chapter further examined the doctrinal tools designed to ensure that the Union acts only within its conferred – or *enumerated* – powers, to use the American terminology. These tools include safeguards against over-centralisation, such as the EU's principle of subsidiarity and the Tenth Amendment in the United States. Despite these mechanisms, both systems face criticism regarding the limited effectiveness of these safeguards in constraining Union power, and the absence of a practically workable, normatively grounded criterion for determining when centralisation is appropriate and when local diversity should be preserved. The next chapter argues that federal impartiality theory can, at least partly, fill this normative void.

[146] This also applies in matters where there is a union legislation, but a derogation allows a state to diverge on particular areas. As we saw from ERT derogation, this does not mean that states can do what they like, and the centre can still intervene; so again, overlap is unavoidable, but the degree of union involvement varies.

2

The Theoretical Foundation: The Federal Promise of Impartiality

'No man is allowed to be a judge in his own cause. With equal, nay with greater reason, a body of men, are unfit to be both judges and parties, at the same time; yet, what are many of the most important acts of legislation, but so many judicial determination.'

James Madison[1]

'For the end of civil Society, being to avoid, and remedy those inconveniences of the state of Nature, which necessarily follow from every Man's being Judge in his own Case.'

John Locke[2]

'O fairest of mankind except in the dispute of mine

You are the controversy, the opponent and the judge combined.'

Al-Mutanabbi's poem to the 10th century Aleppo Ruler[3]

I. Introduction

Federalism's eighteenth-century reincarnation is closely connected with its claim to provide a more 'impartial' arbiter of citizens' rights and their disagreements.[4] To fully appreciate this claim, this chapter explains the nature and limits of 'impartiality' and how it affects federalism and its boundary question. Heeding Machiavelli's advice to 'take the government back to its original principles',[5] the analysis will start from a foundational canon of constitutional law and theory which has been consistently used to justify the creation of government. Namely, that the government is needed to act as *an* umpire of conflicting rights and, thus, ensure respect for the maxim '*nemo judex in causa sua*' or 'no individual should judge their own

[1] J Madison, 'Federalist No. 10' in A Hamilton, J Madison and J Jay, *The Federalist Papers* (Shapiro ed, Yale University Press, 2009) 42 (Federalist No. 10) (emphasis added).

[2] J Locke, *Second Treatise of Government and A Letter Concerning Toleration* (M Goldie ed, Oxford, Oxford University Press, 2016) ch VII, 90 (emphasis added).

[3] Translation by the author, for a classical translation of Al-Muttanabi's work and a biography see AJ Arberry, *Poems of Al-Mutanabbi: A Selection* (Cambridge, Cambridge University Press, 1967) 70.

[4] Madison, Federalist No. 10 (n 1) 42.

[5] N Machiavelli, *Discourses on Livy* (HC Mansfield and NTarcov trs, Chicago, University of Chicago Press, 2009) bk 3, ch 1.

cause' [hereinafter the '*nemo judex* rule']. The *nemo judex* rule, as we shall see, was explicit and central to Madison's defence of federalism.

However, a tremendous amount of confusion stems from conflating the nature of impartiality and the *nemo judex* rule when applied to an individual judge or holder of public office compared to the group settings of labelling an institution collectively as biased or impartial. Therefore, this chapter elucidates the main attributes of the rule when applied to group and institutional settings. Particularly, it builds on and further updates Madison's application of the doctrine to legislative decision-making within the federal structure in his most celebrated paper, Federalist No. 10.

This chapter is divided into four sections. Following the introduction, section II traces the use of the *nemo judex* rule from Locke to Madison, who memorably relied on the rule to formulate an argument in favour of setting up a federal union. Section III unpacks the overlapping philosophical and institutional assumptions underlying Madison's impartiality argument, while updating it with some contemporary comparative insights. It shows how impartiality in institutional settings differs from impartiality when applied to individual decision-makers and what these differences entail for the federal allocation of powers. Section IV engages with a critical aspect by drawing attention to the problem of inertia in the Federalist No. 10 and how it may be harnessed.

In its entirety, the chapter offers a refined interpretation of Madison's theory concerning impartiality, factions, and the federal division of powers. Its primary objective is to establish the intellectual groundwork for the ensuing chapters, marked as four, five, and six, which are dedicated to empirical and comparative assessment of institutional impartiality's underlying *nemo judex* argument, including its uses and limits, as well as when it can be used as a guiding compass for the boundary question.

II. Impartiality as Institutional and Group-Based

In the aftermath of storming the US Capitol in January 2021, a debate ensued on the existence of a presidential power of self-pardon which could have been invoked by Trump to avoid impeachment or pre-empt future indictment. In questioning the legality of such a pardon, commentators cleared textual ambiguity by resorting, among other things, to the *nemo judex* rule.[6] Reliance on the maxim comes as no surprise, given that it is considered a cornerstone of natural justice to

[6] Eg, C Sunstein, 'Trump Can't Pardon Himself' (*Bloomberg Opinion*, 8 January 2021) www.bloomberg.com/opinion/articles/2021-01-08/trump-can-t-pardon-himself?srnd=premium&fbclid=IwAR1x4OKxFGt4DvrcURoHOK1GyQ-AxsHSYmM8or-E6DyZtMAUeTJeYWAS1 accessed 3 August 2025; while Trump did not pardon himself, Biden did pardon his son which also gives rise to *nemo judex* concerns.

most, if not all, legal traditions.[7] For instance, its use in the UK goes as far back as the leading seventeenth-century *Bonham* case by Sir Edward Coke.[8] In the EU, not only has the maxim been invoked before the CJEU,[9] but it also lays the foundation of the right to an impartial tribunal enshrined in the increasingly important Article 47 of the EU's Charter of Fundamental Rights.[10] In the US, the Supreme Court has invariably invoked the doctrine,[11] and it was described by Justice White as a 'first principle'.[12]

While the maxim is crucial for preventing a judge, a president, or a holder of public office from deciding a matter on which they have a personal interest, this book's focus diverges from this individualised, traditionally litigation-related context. Instead, the book places emphasis on the maxim's relevance when applied to the *macro* level of *group* decision-making processes of public institutions acting in their *collective* and *corporate* capacity.[13] The chapter will, in due course, thoroughly unpack the meaning of institutional impartiality, but to illustrate it, for now, consider a simple example. Unlike the traditional individual scenario of two parties and the judge being related or having an interest aligned with one of them, imagine 'white parliamentarians' making decisions regarding the rights of the 'black minority'; 'male legislators' determining whether 'females' ought to have equal wages; or an assembly of farmers deciding on the amount of farm subsidy.[14] It can be seen that here decision-makers are not directly involved in litigation or a personal dispute related to these matters; they cannot be seen in *strictu senso* as being parties and judges to their causes, and, thus, the traditional individual scope of the *nemo judex* rule as consistently applied in administrative law is not breached.[15]

However, the group or institutional scope of the *nemo judex* rule takes on a different dimension. Parliamentarians dealing with issues like equal pay or workplace discrimination, for instance, are affiliated with and may have 'natural affinity towards' groups that sometimes hold mutually incompatible interests on

[7] GF Wharton, *Legal Maxims, with Observations and Cases* (Chicago, Alpha, 1865) 101–102.

[8] *Dr Bonham's Case* (1610) 77 Eng Rep 638 (CP) 652; 8 Co Rep 107a, 118a (Coke, CJ) (holding that a college of physicians given statutory powers to punish unlicensed medical practice could not act as 'judges, ministers, and parties' at the same time); *Dimes v Grand Junction Canal* (1852) 3 HLC 759, 793.

[9] See, eg, Case C-824/18 *AB et al v Krajowa Rada Sądownictwa*, ECLI:EU:C:2020:1053, Opinion of AG Tanchev, para 134; Case C-199/11 *Europese Gemeenschap v Otis and others* ECLI:EU:C:2012:684, para 39.

[10] Eg, Case C-64/16 *Associaçao Sindical dos Juízes Portugueses* EU:C:2018:117; Case C-619/18 *Commission v Poland* EU:C:2019:531.

[11] Eg, *Gutierrez de Martinez v Lamagno* 515 US 417 (1995).

[12] *Arnett v Kennedy* 416 US 134, 197 (1974) (White J, concurring in part and dissenting in part).

[13] The distinctive aspect of the maxim's macro application is that it applies to collective decision making in juristic persons and involves a dispute between two corporate parties. The issue has metaphysical aspects, which I do not engage with here, see B Epstein, *The Ant Trap: Rebuilding the Foundations of the Social Sciences* (Oxford, Oxford University Press, 2015).

[14] J Waldron, 'Legislatures Judging in Their Own Cause' (2009) 3 *Legisprudence* 125.

[15] For an overview, see M Elliott and J Varuhas, *Administrative Law: Text and Materials* (Oxford, Oxford University Press, 2017) ch 9.

these matters.[16] This can involve issues such as 'male monopoly versus female economic advancement'[17] or competing groups' vying for 'material, sociocultural, and political advantage'.[18] After all, neuroscience shows that we have biological impulses to act not only selfishly but '*groupishly*', and our reasoning can be biased by our tendency to support our groups.[19] Given the scarce nature of resources, the majority group is 'less prosperous' the more weight is placed on the interests of minorities.[20] Does this create a situation where the legislative majority is, in effect, judging its own case? The individual-focused application of the *nemo judex* rule rarely addresses this institutional dimension.[21] Properly assessing it requires moving beyond the standard scope of the rule in administrative and civil procedure law and moving into the realm of macro constitutional theory.

This macro, or group, lens of the *nemo judex* rule has long played a central part in political philosophy and constitutional theory in both western[22] and eastern traditions.[23] Space does not allow comprehensive exploration of its universal history, but suffice it to mention that John Locke, among others,[24] saw the main justification for the state, as he repeatedly explained, as providing 'an indifferent

[16] 'Individuals … may have a natural affinity towards other individuals from similar backgrounds with similar life experience. If not consciously and overtly, then unconsciously and tacitly, individuals tend to favour such persons.': DA Wood, 'Judicial Fairness and System Bias' in S Parker and CJG Sampford (eds), *Legal Ethics and Legal Practice: Contemporary Issues* (Oxford, Oxford University Press, 1995) 4.

[17] A Sachs, 'The Myth of Judicial Neutrality: The Male Monopoly Cases' (1975) 23 *The Sociological Review* 104.

[18] T Khaitan and JC Norton, 'The Right to Freedom of Religion and the Right against Religious Discrimination: Theoretical Distinctions' (2019) 17 *International Journal of Constitutional Law* 1132, 1132–1134 (emphasis added).

[19] J Haidt, *The Righteous Mind: Why Good People Are Divided by Politics and Religion* (London, Vintage, 2012).

[20] Waldron (n 14); 'the tyranny of kings is replaced with the tyranny of parliaments': JHH Weiler, 'The Normative Dimension of the Three Waves of Judicial Review' [2020] *Quaderni costituzionali* 235.

[21] One of the few occasions is *Calder v Bull* (1798), which Waldron summarises: Waldron (n 14).

[22] '[S]eeing every man is presumed to do all things in order to his own benefit, no man is a fit arbitrator in his own cause': T Hobbes, *Leviathan* (R Tuck ed, Cambridge, Cambridge University Press, 1996) pt I, 104.

[23] For example, in Muslim intellectual tradition, the maxim can be traced to a *Hadith* prohibiting a person from being a witness in their own cause; see I Abd al-Barr, *Al-istizkar* (Al-Asriya, 2012) 6/105. The maxim was also implicit in jurists' and theologians' justification of rulership, which they saw as necessary means to settle disputes inevitably bound to rise among individuals. See, eg, I Khaldun, *The Muqaddimah: An Introduction to History* (Abridged edn, Princeton, Princeton University Press, 1967) 103–105; F al-Dīn al-Rāzī, *The Great Exegesis* (12th Century AD, reprint, Cairo, 1933) Surat 38: 26; Al-Ghazzālī, *Moderation in Belief* (Chicago, Chicago University Press, 2013) 231: 'if mankind, given their different classes, diverse desires and disparate opinions, are left to their own devices without decrees that they obey and that unify their factions they would end in ruin. It is an epidemic that has no remedy other than a strong [ruler].' Al-Taftazani, *Shareh al-'Aq'aed al-Nasfia* (Dar al-Taqwa, 2020) 423. Al-Sanhuri passingly notes that a ruler was tasked to '*résoudre les conflits et de trancher les différends*': Abde-Razzaq Al-Sanhūri, *Le Califat: Son Évolution vers une Société des Nations Orientale* (Librairie Orientaliste, 1926).

[24] The rule was used to justify the separation of power: 'If the adjudicator could make law, then those parties would be subject to 'arbitrary control', for the adjudicator might change the rules of the fight mid-way': see L Claus, 'Montesquieu's Mistakes and the True Meaning of Separation' (2005) 25 *Oxford Journal of Legal Studies* 419, 431.

judge' which had been lacking in the state of nature.[25] Locke started by warning of the implications of man's 'self-love' in acting as a judge in his own case in the state of nature:

> [I]t is unreasonable for Men to be *Judges in their own Cases*, that self-love will make Men *partial* to themselves and their Friends … God hath certainly appointed *Government to restrain the partiality* and violence *of Men*.[26]

Locke then contrasted the 'peace' that would follow from introducing the sovereign state as an impartial 'umpirage', which through the '*Legislative*' would end 'all Differences' and become a 'Bar to the state of War among [individuals]'.[27] Two important points to note on Locke here. Firstly, like earlier writers, he saw the legislative as exercising a *judicial task in a broader sense* by acting as an 'umpire' whose function is to 'dispense justice', attained through respect for the corporate application of the *nemo judex* rule.[28] Secondly, Locke posited that in such broader judicial or institutional settings, collective decisions should be made 'only by the will and determination of the majority'.[29]

This corporate understanding of the *nemo judex* rule has travelled to and developed a particular relationship with the founding of American federalism. Madison, who drew on Locke's work, extended the logic of the *nemo judex* rule a step further. His most celebrated paper – Federalist No. 10 – used the very same maxim to offer a brilliant argument against majority rule in unitary small states and to propose instead an integrative federalism or what he terms a 'compound republic' model. Whilst he explicitly concurs with Locke that legislative acts are often nothing but a '*judicial determination*', he diverges in seeing majority rule in small republics not arising from respect for the *nemo judex* rule but rather as *a flagrant violation* thereof. This was an argument that Madison consistently repeated in many contexts up to his late writings, 50 years after the ratification of the Constitution.[30]

Troubled by the 'disease' of internal factions and pondering on the 'vices' of the American states prior to the Union,[31] Madison lamented the absence in the then-existing structure of a '*disinterested and dispassionate umpire*' to resolve disputes

[25] Locke (n 2) ch XIX, 227.
[26] ibid ch II, 13 (emphasis added).
[27] ibid 227.
[28] MJC Vile, *Constitutionalism and the Separation of Powers* (Carmel, Liberty Fund, 2012) 27–28.
[29] Locke (n 2) ch XIX, 227; book II, 96.
[30] J Madison, *Selected Writings* (R Ketcham ed, Indianapolis, Hackett Publishing, 2006) 81; J Madison, 'Proposed Principles for the Federal Convention to George Washington, April 16, 1787' in RA Rutland and WME Rachal (eds), *The Papers of James Madison* (Chicago, University of Chicago Press, 1975) vol IX, 382–387; J Madison, 'State and Federal Power and the Public Good to Thomas Jefferson, October 24, 1787' in RA Rutland and WME Rachal (eds), *The Papers of James Madison* (Chicago, University of Chicago Press, 1975) vol X, 209–214.
[31] J Madison, 'Vices of the Political System of the United States, April 1787' in RA Rutland and WME Rachal (eds), *The Papers of James Madison* (The University of Chicago Press 1975) vol IX, 345–358, point number 11.

'between different passions and interests in the State'.[32] To demonstrate the point, in a letter to Jefferson, he questioned the very basis of majority rule in small republics – what could be equated with today's nation-states:

> If two individuals are under the biass of interest or enmity agst. A third, the rights of the latter could never be safely referred to the majority of the three. *Will two thousand individuals be less apt to oppress one thousand, or two hundred thousand, one hundred thousand?*[33]

The reflection will be further developed and find its most memorable expression in the Federalist No. 10. The relevant passage merits quotation in full:

> *No man is allowed to be a judge in his own cause*; because his interest would certainly bias his judgment, and, not improbably, corrupt his integrity. With equal, nay with greater reason, *a body of men, are unfit to be both judges and parties*, at the same time; yet, what are many of the *most important acts of legislation, but so many judicial determinations*, not indeed concerning the rights of single persons, but *concerning the rights of large bodies of citizens*; and what are the different classes of legislators, but advocates and parties to the causes which they determine? … *the most numerous party*, or, in other words, the most powerful faction must be expected to prevail.[34]

To illustrate this point, Madison used three examples from legislation on economic matters. A vivid one to discuss here is debtor-relief laws. Reacting to the depressed economic conditions following the Revolutionary War, state legislators – captured by majorities who were debtors – enacted a variety of debt-relief laws to the detriment of creditors. These included laws staying the collection of debts, allowing payment in instalments or in commodities.[35] Through these legislative acts, debtors directly controlled the outcome of pending cases between them and creditors, thus making themselves both a party and a judge of their own controversy. Madison depicted the debtor relief law proposal as a dispute premised on 'a question to which the creditors are parties on one side, and the debtors on the other'. The predicament here is that 'the parties are and must be themselves the judges', and the outcome is settled not on the basis of what is just or right but according to what 'the most numerous party, or, in other words, the most powerful faction' desired it to be.[36]

If we accept Madison's diagnosis, one must inquire: can the majoritarian nature of republican constitutionalism ever be reconciled with the dictates of impartiality and the *nemo judex* rule? How does popular control, which requires *a self-judging majority*, fit with the *prohibition of self-judging*? Madison/Publius found the answer

[32] Madison, 'Proposed Principles for the Federal Convention, April 16, 1787' in *Selected Writings* (n 30) 43.

[33] Madison, 'State and Federal Power and the Public Good to Thomas Jefferson, October 24, 1787' in *Selected Writings* (n 30) 81 (emphasis added).

[34] Madison, Federalist No. 10 (n 1) 22 (emphasis added).

[35] Eg, JW Ely Jr, 'The Contract Clause: Origins and Early Development' (2015) 4 *Brigham-Kanner Property Rights Conference Journal* 199.

[36] Madison, Federalist No. 10 (n 1) 22.

in a compound republic, or what is now termed 'integrative federalism'.[37] By integrating many states into a larger political orbit, 'the Society becomes broken into a greater variety of interests, of pursuits, of passions, which check each other'.[38] This 'enlargement of the sphere' qualitatively increases the diversity of interests, which then 'naturalize the evil of each other'[39] and modify '*the sovereignty* as that it may be *sufficiently neutral* between different parts of the Society'.[40]

The proposed institutional remedy, in general, and its relation to the *nemo judex* rule, is complex and presupposes many overlapping assumptions. It also, understandably, leaves out some of the insights which contemporary literature and comparative experiences have revealed. The following section unpacks Madison's argument, but before proceeding, four prefatory notes are due.

First, an obvious and common objection to Madison, which often puzzles readers, is the fact that parliaments and judges are distinct entities.[41] How, then, can we use the term 'judging' to describe the actions of a legislative majority in order to assess whether they are 'judging' their own cause? How can Madison explicitly describe legislation as a form of 'judicial determination'?[42] Readers might think that this equivocation collapses the two institutions of the legislature and judiciary and, thus, runs counter to the currently ubiquitous tripartite understanding of the separation of powers. This objection can be answered in two ways.

To begin with, there is a long legal history,[43] as well as etymological roots,[44] of the word 'Parliament' to indicate that the legislature acted as a 'superior court' and performed the function of providing the correct interpretation of law.[45] However, we need not explore this history here. A simpler approach, for our purposes, is to equate the word 'judge' here with 'decision-maker'. After all, Waldron notes, 'politics involves deciding controversies in society'.[46] In this sense, the rule would be

[37] On the distinction between integrative and devolutionary federalism, see ch 1.

[38] Madison, Federalist No. 10 (n 1) 43.

[39] DW Howe, 'The Political Psychology of the Federalist' (1987) 44 *The William and Mary Quarterly* 485.

[40] ibid [emphasis added].

[41] Waldron (n 14). There could be ontological reading of the word 'judging' here to indicate that federalism brings to existence of a new corporate body to decide as a judge or epistemological in terms of how the group decides when they get together. This book will explore the latter and keeping the ontological aspect to future work.

[42] Madison, Federalist No. 10 (n 1).

[43] Vile remarked that earlier theories of natural law perceived law as 'divinely-inspired' and 'unchanging', thus legislators were interpreting (ie, judging) what the law 'really was': Vile (n 28) 27–28; he also adds that in 1655, Sir Henry Vane still saw the legislative and executive powers as elements of the 'supreme judicature', citing '*A Healing Question*' (London, 1655) in W Scott (ed), *Somers Tracts*, vol VI, 310–12. The Old Testament saw the administration of the state as a function of justice; to rule meant to judge and the generic term of ruler was in olden times judge, W Julius, 'Tribal life of the Epic Period' in H Smith (ed), *The Historians' History of the World* (London, The Encyclopaedia Britannica Company, 1926) 289.

[44] Kelsen tells us that in French, the word '*parlement*' originally meant 'Court': H Kelsen, *Peace through Law* (Clark, Lawbook Exchange, 2000) 21.

[45] See generally CA Desan, 'The Constitutional Commitment to Legislative Adjudication in the Early American Tradition' (1997) 111 *Harvard Law Review* 1381.

[46] Waldron (n 14) 125.

interpreted as commanding that 'no person should be the decision-maker of their own controversy' without confining the word 'judge' to this narrower context of litigation and courtrooms.

Just as it is well-established, the *nemo judex* rule extends beyond the judiciary to apply to administrative and executive bodies,[47] who are prohibited from deciding matters in which they have personal interests; the rule can, at some level, also be extended to legislative bodies. UK courts, for instance, have rejected the 'fancied distinction' between judicial and executive decisions when applying common law rules of procedural fairness to non-judicial bodies.[48] Yet, in parliamentary systems, the executive is the majority in Parliament. If those same actors are subject to the *nemo judex* rule in their executive capacity, it would be difficult to claim that upon entering the legislature, they somehow become supra-human entities immune from bias. As the debtor-relief laws example illustrates, it is not inconceivable for legislators to act as parties to their own cause. Indeed, an entire field of law – *investor–state arbitration* – has emerged to address the biases of legislatures. Admittedly, there are institutional challenges that have traditionally made it difficult to apply the *nemo judex* rule to legislative bodies. However, as we shall see, Madisonian ideas provide, under certain conditions, a workable solution for checking legislative bias and for legislature 'to act more judiciously' without collapsing the distinction between judges and legislatures altogether.[49]

Turning to the second prefatory note, most of the Federalist Papers' analysis below would be Madison's, but when reference is made to ideas shared with Hamilton, I will use their collective pseudonym: 'Publius'. Relatedly, while the subsequent analysis will engage with supporting parts of other Federalist Papers, such as Federalist No. 51, the majority and the central claim originate from Federalist Paper No. 10, and, thus, for ease of reference, the book will refer to the argument as the 'Federalist impartiality argument'.

Thirdly, I use the term 'minority rights' in the contemporary sense for racially and religiously non-dominant groups, as well as women, as an underprivileged group.[50] This was not the meaning of minorities Publius had in mind,[51] yet it can

[47] Eg, *Ridge v Baldwin* [1964] AC 40 (Reid LJ).

[48] ibid, critiquing the 'fancied distinction between decisions which are 'administrative' and decisions which are 'judicial' or 'quasi-judicial''.

[49] JN Rakove, 'Politics Indoors and out-of-Doors: A Fault Line in Madison's Thinking' in JN Rakove and CA Sheehan (eds), *The Cambridge Companion to the Federalist* (Cambridge, Cambridge University Press, 2020) 381. Rakove notes that 'whether Madison was more intent on describing certain categories of *legislation* as being inherently (or even ontologically) judicial in their very nature, or whether he simply wanted *legislators* to act more judiciously (or even judicially) in their deliberations' (emphasis added).

[50] I adhere to the core, uncontested category of minorities, and do not engage with well-known debate over a universal definition that captures all minority groups; see H Hannum, 'The Concept and Definition of Minorities' in M Weller (ed), *Universal Minority Rights: A Commentary on the Jurisprudence of International Courts and Treaty Bodies* (Oxford, Oxford University Press, 2007) 49–74.

[51] Although the factor of 'dominance' can be inferred from Madison's statement on 'ambition to dominate', Dahl remarks that Madison meant to protect elite minorities 'of wealth, status, and power' from

be extended to contemporary minorities, and thus, in some respect, the analysis will have to extend and reinterpret the logic of their argument to the contemporary conditions in light of recent scholarship and comparative experience covered in the preceding chapters.

Fourthly, Madison used the terms 'neutrality' and 'impartiality' interchangeably, and maybe even used neutrality more frequently.[52] He is not alone in this. Except for a few unsuccessful attempts in philosophy to separate the two terms, almost all public law[53] and constitutional theory literature use the two terms interchangeably.[54] Related synonyms include the 'rule against bias' or the 'nemo judex rule'.[55] Following this tradition, the book uses the terms neutrality and impartiality interchangeably.[56] As will be explained in section III, and developed more fully in chapter four, Madison's notion of impartiality corresponds closely to the 'British legal tradition' concepts of judicial and administrative bias.[57]

Fifthly, one must explain the meaning of Publius' frequently used term 'faction'.[58] In Federalist No. 10, Madison lamented the widespread spirit of faction into which the American society and public good were divided. In fact, his invocation of neutrality was an attempt to resolve the centuries-old struggle to check the evils of faction as 'the scourge' of healthy constitutional government.[59] To appreciate the originality of Madison's use of neutrality to remedy the 'disease of faction', we need first to understand the latter term.[60]

Madison defined a faction as:

> a number of citizens, *whether amounting to a majority or minority of the whole*, who are united and actuated by some common impulse of passion, or of interest, adverse to the rights of other citizens, or to the permanent and aggregate interests of the community.[61]

their 'bitter enemies – the artisans and farmers of inferior wealth, status, and power, who … constituted 'popular majority', RA Dahl, *A Preface to Democratic Theory* (Chicago, University of Chicago Press, 2006) 30. For historical analysis, see MJ Klarman, *The Framers' Coup: The Making of the United States Constitution* (Oxford, Oxford University Press, 2016).

[52] Eg, Madison noted that sovereignty 'may be *sufficiently neutral* between different parts of the Society'; see Madison, 'State and Federal Power and the Public Good to Thomas Jefferson, October 24, 1787' (n 30) 209–214.

[53] The role of the state is to be a 'neutral and impartial organiser of the exercise of various religions, faiths and beliefs': *R (S) v Governors of Denbigh High School* [2006] UKHL 15, [2007] 1 AC 100; Case C-148/22 *Commune d'Ans* ECLI:EU:C:2023:378, Opinion of AG Connells, fn 40: 'I do not believe that a strict distinction should be drawn between the two concepts.'

[54] Eg, MH Kramer, 'Impartiality in a System of Governance' (2019) University of Cambridge Faculty of Law Research Paper No. 10/2019 2.

[55] See, eg, AA Olowofoyeku, 'The "Nemo Judex" Rule: The Case against Automatic Disqualification' [2000] *Public law* 456.

[56] Kramer (n 54) 18.

[57] A Gibson, 'Madison's Republican Remedy: The Tenth Federalist and the Creation of an Impartial Republic' in JN Rakove and CA Sheehan (eds), *The Cambridge Companion to the Federalist* (Cambridge, Cambridge University Press, 2020) 274.

[58] Madison, Federalist No. 10 (n 1) 41.

[59] ibid.

[60] PH Schuck, 'Against (and for) Madison: An Essay in Praise of Factions' (1996) 15 *Yale Law & Policy Review* 553, 553.

[61] Madison, Federalist No. 10 (n 1) 41 (emphasis added).

In other writings, Madison illustrated his definition by providing examples of the different groups which are natural to all constitutional systems. He noted that:

> civilized societies are divided into *different interests and factions*, as they happen to be creditors or debtors – Rich or poor – husbandmen, merchants or manufacturers – members of different religious sects – followers of different political leaders – inhabitants of different districts – owners of different kinds of property ....[62]

These groups and their underlying interests 'divide [citizens] into different classes, actuated by different sentiments and views.'[63] This description of factions as groups or corporate classes within the society aligns with his view of the state as a corporate judge deciding not the rights of single citizens but that of groups or, as he puts it, 'large bodies of citizens'.[64]

Notably, Madison's worry is not the mere existence of these diverse groups or factions, which he saw as an inescapable outcome of the difference 'embedded' in human nature and the 'complexity of modern societies'.[65] His concern was with two specific 'mischiefs' associated with factionalism. Notably, when he uses the term 'faction' in a negative context; it seems to carry a more limited meaning, referring not to all societal groups but those engaged in either of the two mischiefs.

The first mischief is closely connected to Publius' classical view of partiality and the 'public good', which will be discussed shortly. The second is related to violence, which will be evident with regard to abortion opposition groups in chapter five. With this in mind, Madison's vilification of factions refers, first, to cases where the determination of public law matters is surrendered to the partial determination of those groups who team up to shape the rights of other citizens in line with their 'narrow and selfish' or dogmatic motives, rather than with (as Madison put it) 'the permanent and aggregate interests of the community'.[66] Whenever there is 'an apparent interest or common passion unites a majority', Madison wondered, 'what is to restrain them from unjust violations of the rights and interest of the minority, or of individuals?'[67]

The second mischief is the tendency of excessive factionalism to *degenerate into violence*. This concern came not only through reflection on various historical examples referenced in the *Federalist Papers* but also from the American events that immediately preceded the Philadelphia Convention, where armed insurrection took place in Massachusetts in the well-known 'Shay's Rebellion'.[68] Farmers took up arms under the leadership of Revolutionary War veteran, Captain Shay, and engaged in large-scale military insurgencies which could have 'plunged

[62] Madison, 'Vices of the Political System of the United States' (n 31) 355 (emphasis added).

[63] Madison, Federalist No. 10 (n 1) 22 (emphasis added).

[64] ibid 22 (emphasis added).

[65] JN Rakove, *A Politician Thinking: The Creative Mind of James Madison* (Oklahoma, Oklahoma University Press 2017) vol 14, 9.

[66] Schuck (n 61) 562.

[67] Madison, 'Vices of the Political System of the United States' (n 31) point 11.

[68] 'The tempestuous situation, from which Massachusetts has scarcely emerged [ie, Shays's Rebellion] evinces that dangers of this kind are not merely speculative.': Hamilton, *Federalist No. 21* 95.

[the state] into *civil war*.'[69] Fearing that factional struggle may frequently lead to 'flying to arms and tearing a State to pieces',[70] Madison explicitly sets out Federalist No. 10's aim to 'break and control the violence of faction'.[71] Delineating Madison's shift from the general meaning of faction as *a societal group* to the other two particular negative uses to denote sources of bias or violence is important when quoting his passages.

Having clarified the meaning of the five terms, we now proceed to analyse the premises of the Federalist impartiality argument and what it entails.

III. The Premises of Federalist Impartiality Argument and their Relativity

Publius' proposed remedy rests on four complementary premises: one is rooted in mixed human nature and the discoverability of the 'public good'; second is the diversity of interest as a constitutional check; third is the outcome of the first two on the quality of decision-making through 'relative' increase in impartiality; and fourth is the interaction between the impartiality underlying the *nemo judex* rule relative to other values underpinning the Federalist structure which I call 'relativity in the second sense'.

A. Mixed Human Nature and the Public Good

To make a *macro* claim about legislative politics, Madison deep-dived into the *micro* domain of the human psyche. Much like classical philosophers, he viewed the polity as a collective individual.[72] Madison asked, 'What is government itself but the greatest of all reflections on human nature?'[73] This perspective runs across the Federalist,[74] and indicates that, to its authors, public decision-making is, to some extent, 'analogoues' to the human mind.[75] Therefore, 'we should not shut our eyes to the nature of man.'[76]

[69] Hamilton, *Federalist No. 6* 21.

[70] Madison, *Federalist No. 43* 213.

[71] Madison, Federalist No. 10 (n 1) 22. It is even common across the Federalist Papers to find the word violence or its synonyms to accompany any reference to faction. See, eg, Hamilton, *Federalist No. 29* 136.

[72] Eg, Aristotle, *Politics* (E Barker tr, Oxford, Oxford University Press, 1995) bk 39, 1281: 'when all meet together, the people may thus become something like a single person'.

[73] J Madison, 'Federalist No. 51' in A Hamilton, J Madison and J Jay, *The Federalist Papers* (I Shapiro ed, New Haven, Yale University Press, 2009) 252 (Federalist No. 51). Elazar notes that in contradistinction to nation-state, 'federalism can be seen as consistent with human psychology': DJ Elazar, *Exploring Federalism* (Alabama, University of Alabama Press, 1987) 30.

[74] See, eg, Madison, *Federalist No. 63* as analysed in Howe (n 39) 499–500.

[75] Howe (n 39).

[76] Notes on Suffrage Commenting on the Debates of 1787, 1821–1829; Speech, Virginia Convention of 1829, December 2,1829; Notes on Majority Governments, 1833 (Documentary History of the Constitution of the United States, Washington, DC, 1905).

The nature he refers to is of mixed character. Publius rejects both 'the supposition of universal venality … [and] universal rectitude'.[77] This mixed character bears resemblance to Plato's famous passage that saying a 'man is stronger than himself' seems 'ridiculous'.[78] For the same person must be both the stronger and the weaker at the same time. Plato noted that absurdity disappears once we realise that within the 'soul resides' a 'better' side and a 'worse' one.[79] When the 'smaller forces' of the better side overpower the numerous 'worse' ones, the person (and, by analogy, the polity) shows its better side.[80] In a similar fashion, Madison stresses that 'fallible' human faculties are pushing in the conflicting directions of interest, passions, pride, as well as reason.[81] He notes that 'the mild voice of reason, pleading the cause of an enlarged and permanent interest, is but too often drowned before public bodies as well as individuals, by the clamours of an *impatient* avidity for immediate and *immoderate gain*'.[82] Nevertheless, the better side of the very same human nature may, under the right conditions, favour 'the love of justice' and 'public good' over 'partial considerations'.[83]

This conceptualisation of better and worse sides of human nature indicates that, for Madison, justice and public good 'objectively exists'.[84] Through overcoming the worse side of our nature, the '*general good*' can be identified.[85] This raises two central questions: (i) what are these negative impulses that block the ability to discover this public good; and (ii) how can these impulses be controlled so that the polity may express its *better*, more just *self*?

To answer this, Madison drew upon the then-prevalent tripartite taxonomy of human motives: reason, passion, and interest.[86] While Madison does not explicitly define each term, it is clear that, for him, enlightened reason aligns with the public good, whereas it is primarily 'unreasonable' interest and impulses of 'passion' that distort judgment and blind individuals to the clear demands of justice. Few would deny, at least in the abstract, that the enforcement of contracts is both just and desirable. Yet, in the aftermath of the Revolutionary War, the

[77] Hamilton, *Federalist No. 76* 371.
[78] Plato, *Republic* (Robin Waterfield tr, Oxford, Oxford University Press, 1993).
[79] ibid.
[80] ibid.
[81] Madison, *Federalist No. 37* 169. For an analysis of humanity's mixed nature and the notion of fallibility with the capability to learn, see V Ostrom and B Allen, *The Political Theory of a Compound Republic: Designing the American Experiment* (New York, Lexington, 2008) 37–39. For a brilliant analysis of mixed human nature, see Al-Ghazali, *Iḥyāʾ ʿUlūm al-Dīn* (Al-Habib Omar, ed, Gawami' Al-kalam, 2014) vol 3; *Quran*, ch 91, v 7–9.
[82] Madison, *Federalist No. 42* 206.
[83] Madison, Federalist No. 10 (n 1) 46–47.
[84] Howe (n 39) 494 discussing Hamilton's note that 'It is a just observation, that the people commonly intend the Public Good': A Hamilton, 'Federalist No. 71' in A Hamilton, J Madison, and J Jay, *The Federalist Papers* (I Shapiro ed, New Haven, Yale University Press, 2009) 351. See also Rakove (n 65) 110; Dahl (n 51) 158–159.
[85] Madison, Federalist No. 51 (n 73) 255 (emphasis added); *Federalist No. 58* 288.
[86] J Elster, 'The Political Psychology of Publius: Reason, Passion, and Interest in the Federalist' in JN Rakove and CA Sheehan (eds), *The Cambridge Companion to the Federalist* (Cambridge, Cambridge University Press, 2020).

pursuit of 'immoderate gains' led debtor majorities to manipulate legal frameworks at the expense of creditors.[87] Similarly, although many agree in principle with prohibitions on arbitrary discrimination, ingrained biases often lead to the reinterpretation – or rationalisation – of such principles to justify the mistreatment of racial minorities.[88]

The question, then, is how the constitution can constrain these impulses standing in the way of attaining the public good.[89] Publius saw placing exclusive reliance on public virtue as impractical since 'enlightened statesmen will not always be at the helm',[90] and experience showed that 'passions … not the reason, of the public, would sit in judgment'.[91] In this 'reason-passion-interest schema',[92] Madison recognised that reason is 'normatively superior' but 'practically' feebler as a spur for action than self-interest.[93] Building on insights from his Princeton teacher, who saw that prudence (self-interest) could aid conscience in controlling passion,[94] Madison opted for enlisting 'self-interest' to the service of reason and public good. While he denounced pursuit of short-term 'gain'[95] and 'unreasonable indulgences',[96] he saw that pitting competing 'immoderate' impulses against one another cancels out each other and mutually naturalises their evil.[97]

This may appear paradoxical – self-interest as both the problem and the remedy. This apparent tension disappears when we realise that human inclination to self-interest has a mixed nature too, or a spectrum whose middle aligns with reason and the public good. Where excessive and immoderate pursuit of short-term interest is checked by similar forces, the majority will prudently lean to the better, reasonable side of its mixed human nature, which would come closer to the public interest. This seems analogous to Aristotle's *golden mean*, where self-interest cannot be eradicated, but reason aligns with the middle ground between excess (of self-interest) and deficiency (of complete disinterest).

As Ostrom remarked, for Publius the political process serves as a 'constraint'[98] on short-term calculus – which permits 'momentary passions and immediate interests' – 'allowing reason to work its way' to the long-term calculus of 'policy,

[87] Madison, *Federalist No. 42* (n 82) 204.

[88] This existence of public good will play a role in Madison's idea that the nefarious faction will crumble, see next section.

[89] '[T]he passions of men will not conform to the dictates of reason and justice': Hamilton, *Federalist No. 15* 66.

[90] Madison, Federalist No. 10 (n 1) 43.

[91] Madison, *Federalist No. 49* 248.

[92] Elster (n 86).

[93] A Vermeule, 'Veil of Ignorance Rules in Constitutional Law' (2001) 111 *Yale Law Journal* 399, 429.

[94] Howe (n 39) 485.

[95] Madison, *Federalist No. 42* (n 82) 206.

[96] Madison, *Federalist No. 58* (n 85) 288.

[97] V Ostrom and B Allen, *The Political Theory of a Compound Republic: Designing the American Experiment* (New York, Lexington Books, 2008) 36.

[98] ibid 9.

utility or justice'.[99] Both short-term and long-term inclinations emanate from human nature, and the role of political constraint is to encourage the good side to prosper. Time and again, Publius tells us that by eclipsing unbridled passion and unreasonable interest, it makes 'reason, justice and truth ... regain their authority over the public mind'.[100] While many of these 'psychological axioms'[101] were not novel to constitutional thinkers, ancient and modern, the innovation is to use these axioms in providing a practically workable constitutional check, as explained in the next premise.

B. Diversity of Interest as a Constitutional Check

Madison took great interest in analysing the gulf of religious tolerance enjoyed in eighteenth-century America compared to the '[t]orrents of blood' spilt in Europe.[102] Despite their common ancestral origin and heritage, he realised that America, unlike Europe, was religiously diverse, and its multiplicity of sects had restrained larger sects from dominating others. This way, America simply secured a level of tolerance that 'no appeal to revolutionary principles ... could have accomplished'.[103]

This was the *eureka moment* of modern federalism. From that realisation, Madison marched to the conclusion that will shape his work on the US Constitution. He noted that in the same way that 'multiplicity of sects' protects religious rights, the increased 'multiplicity of interest' in a large compound republic can provide a 'built-in check'[104] for civil rights against oppressive factions.[105] Unsurprisingly,

[99] Hamilton, Federalist No. 6 (n 69) 22; 'Since passions induce a high rate of time discounting, institutional designers can extend the subjective time horizon of the agents by creating a setting that is unfavourable to the emergence of passion.': Elster (n 86) 214.

[100] Madison, Federalist No. 63 (n 74) 307. Surely, the notion of 'public good' is more challenging for political theory than for constitutional law. The latter seeks a modest 'real world' practical understanding thereof rather than minute philosophical analysis. What Publius meant by the term has triggered controversy, see, eg, Dahl (n 51) 30; *cf* the critique of the inherent amorality of the American constitution in R Albert, 'America's Amoral Constitution' (2020) 70 *American University Law Review* 773.

[101] Dahl (n 51) 8; see generally Howe (n 39).

[102] J Madison, 'Memorial and Remonstrance against Religious Assessments, 20 June 1785' in RA Rutland and WME Rachal (eds), *The Papers of James Madison* (The University of Chicago Press 1975) vol VIII, 298–304.

[103] L Banning, *The Sacred Fire of Liberty: James Madison and the Founding of the Federal Republic* (Ithaca, Cornell University Press, 1998) 207; Rakove (n 65) 117.

[104] CR Sunstein, 'Interest Groups in American Public Law' (1985) 38 *Stanford Law Review* 29, 40.

[105] Earlier formulation of similar ideas can be found in Voltaire: 'If you have two religions in your countries, they will cut each other's throat; if you have thirty religions, they will dwell in peace. Look at the great Turk, he governs Guebres, Banians, Creek Christians, Nestorians, Romans.' Voltaire, *Selections from the Philosophical Dictionary* (Project Gutenberg, 2005) 303. This reasoning also seems to independently concur with a Quranic insight which implies that multiplicity imbedded in humanity protects diverse religious practices. The relevant verse reads '[a]nd were it not that God *checks the people, some by means of others*, there would have *been demolished monasteries, churches, synagogues, and mosques* in which the name of God is much [praised]' Saheeh International, *Quran* 22:40. For a recent

a few years later, in Federalist No. 51, Madison compared religious and political factions. In politics, as in religion, diversity of interest – understood to be *multiplicity of sects* – was the safest guarantee against the risk of one group 'capturing the reins of government and turning it to its own interests'.[106] The degree of security in both cases will depend mainly on the extent of diversity, which, in turn, is presumed to depend, in part, on the size of the polity.

The core of Madison's remedy for checking the biases and evils of factionalism is not to completely eradicate the causes of conflict by eliminating the natural differences and diversity among societal groups. Rather, he sought to harness diversity as a positive force. Impartiality is made possible *not despite diversity but because of it*. The gist of the idea is to 'counteract' faction with faction and each group's ambition to dominate with an equivalent ambition. Madison realised that as a pre-condition to 'carry into effect schemes of oppression', groups sharing 'malevolent' impulses must 'concert' their interests and 'act in unison'.[107] To prevent this concert, a compound republic, or what is now termed 'integrative federalism' provides a remedy.

By integrating different states under one multi-layered constitutional umbrella, the number of diverse interests and actors as well as factions, will significantly increase beyond the narrower scope of the state level. Thus, the 'opportunity' of coordinating interest and 'concert[ed]' action between nefarious factions becomes restrained, rendering them less 'politically [e]ffective'.[108] The component of the Madisonian insight can be broken down into the following syllogism composed of two premises (P_1, P_2) and a conclusion (C):

P_1: Integrative federalism diversifies interests, which makes '*concert*' more difficult.

P_2: **Non-neutral** collective decision-making requires '***concert***' among common interests.

C → Integrative federalism renders non-neutral decision-making more difficult. Q.E.D.

The first premise, that *interest diversification makes concert more difficult*, is the linchpin of Madison's impartiality argument. And, as case studies show later, the absence of this premise's components would have significant consequences with regard to particular types of rights discussed in chapters five and six. Then, one needs to first dwell further on two conditions which explain why concert between factions would become more difficult in an integrative federation, and why this would disadvantage pursuit of malevolent interests compared to reasonable ones.

formal fatwa (legal opinion) relying, among other grounds, on this very same verse in the context of religious tolerance see Dar Al-Iftaa, Fatwa 4121, 06/8/2017 www.dar-alifta.org/AR/ViewFatwa.aspx?sec=fatwa&ID=14039 accessed 3 August 2025.

[106] N Feldman, *Divided by God: America's Church-State Problem-and What We Should Do About It* (New York, Farrar, Straus and Giroux, 2006) 27.

[107] Madison, Federalist No. 10 (n 1) 45.

[108] Dahl (n 51) 30.

First, and chiefly, the increased diversification of interest and stakeholders must be examined alongside a key – yet often under-examined – term from the Federalist No. 51, 'coalition'.[109] To be effective on the federal level, a local majority cannot act alone but must form a coalition from a number of states. For illustration, one may take an example from ethnic minorities. Although Publius did not have our contemporary minorities in mind,[110] the logic of the Federalist No. 10 can be extended to and illustrated by an example of such minorities. Assume we have five equally populated states, each dominated by a racial majority but also having other dispersed racial minorities. The states then come together into an integrative federation. For simplicity, let us assume the racial ratios follow and correspond to represented interests at the legislature as indicated in the chart below:

Figure 2.1 Diversification in Integrative Federalism

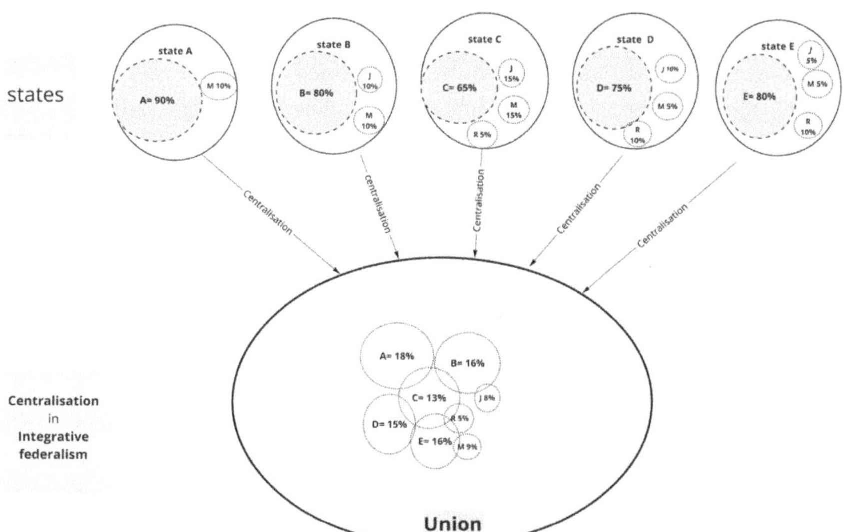

As seen from the chart, each local majority gets diluted at the union level (for example, group A goes from 90 to 18 per cent, and group B from 80 to 16 per cent). A mighty local majority cannot act effectively at the federal level without forming a coalition across states. However, the reason for the coalition's effectiveness is the very same reason for its vulnerability. In such inter-state settings, a coalition must inescapably involve a high assortment of interests and actors, which makes it more challenging to cater for the divergent interests, opinions, and changing circumstances of the constituent parts of such a coalition. Under certain conditions, cracks appear, and it becomes more difficult for a coalition either to 'act

[109] Madison remarked that 'a *coalition* of a majority could seldom take place on any other principles than those of justice': Madison, Federalist No. 51 (n 73) 255 (emphasis added).

[110] Dahl (n 51) 30; see also the interpretation caveats introduced in section I earlier.

in unison' or dominate the course of federal action.[111] As divergent actors across states or at the federal level (such as the central judiciary, the executive, or even activists) pursue different paths, challenges unravel for locally dominant groups. This, according to Publius, in turn, makes it difficult for these factions to maintain complete control over perpetuating their excessive privileges or immoderate interests.

Given that this applies to all groups or factions, they neutralise the evils of one another. As a consequence, either inaction follows, or pursuit of reasonable interest prevails over immoderate pursuits. Inertia will be examined later in this chapter. But the other possibility is premised on the view that the new conditions make it rational for factions to move to their second-best shot or common modicum rather than the unbridled pursuit of interest at the local level.[112] As Barry puts it, '[w]here the pursuit of maximum short-run gain makes everyone lose compared with some 'reasonable' gains; it actually becomes a matter of self-interest to aim at the 'reasonable solution' provided everyone else does likewise'.[113] This is aided by the following underexplored mechanism mentioned briefly in Federalist No. 51.

The second, albeit as a derivative, supplemental mechanism in the Federalist syllogism is *uncertainty as conducive to impartiality*. It is derivative because it depends on diversification of conflicting interests. And it is supplemental because often, as in the case with Thatcher and her anti-equal pay allies, as discussed later, interest diversification by itself achieves the required goal of checking the anti-right coalition. However, in cases where this is not enough, uncertainty could be of further incidental help. To clarify this point, I cast some light on the connection between uncertainty and impartiality in literature prior to explaining how it overlaps, with some necessary limitations, with the Madisonian claim to hinder concert among factions.

The constitutional economist and Nobel laureate James Buchanan and his co-authors posited that through thickening the 'veil of uncertainty', 'fairness may be induced',[114] and actors would 'adopt more impartial perspective' in constitutional choice.[115] Unlike Rawls' abstract veil, here uncertainty refers to actors who, while well-aware of their position in society, are unable to 'accurately anticipate the particular ways in which they will be affected by the prospective … rules'.[116] To the extent that certainty exists, actors 'led by self-interest calculus …. [to]

[111] Madison, Federalist No. 10 (n 1) 45.

[112] ibid. It is important to note that there are other members who may be prone to propose principles of justice regardless of their interest, but they are unlikely to command a majority except in ideal polities. As shall be discussed, when the conditions of the impartiality argument are met, these virtuous members have better ambiance to propose their views and garner acceptance.

[113] B Barry, *Political Argument: A Reissue* (Oakland, University of California Press, 1990) 255.

[114] V Vanberg and JM Buchanan, 'Interests and Theories in Constitutional Choice' (1989) 1 *Journal of Theoretical Politics* 54: 'individual is led by his self-interest calculus to concentrate on choice options that eliminate or minimize prospects for potentially disastrous results'.

[115] ibid 55.

[116] Contra Rawls' impractical veil where decision makers somehow should not know what position they will occupy in society: see J Rawls, *A Theory of Justice* (revised edn, Cambridge, MA, Harvard University Press, 1999) 118–123.

minimize prospects for potentially disastrous results' will opt for 'arrangements that might be called *fair* in the sense that patterns of outcomes generated under such arrangements will be broadly acceptable, regardless of where the participant might be located in such outcomes'.[117] Relatedly, Buchanan and Vanberg add that a concern for 'stability' may also induce impartiality.[118] Namely, a concern that the agreed arrangement would be unlikely to endure but rather would be subject to continuous renegotiation if 'designed to serve one's own particular interests'.[119]

In a more robust, legally grounded analysis, Vermeule examined the role of uncertainty in 'dampen[ing] self-interest' in constitutional and legislative domains.[120] He taxonomised a wide array of examples of norms purposefully using uncertainty to increase impartiality.[121] This includes, for instance, the Twenty-Seventh Amendment, which delays legislative pay raises to the next cycle so legislators cannot know certainly they will be the beneficiary of the raise.[122] Or the requirement of 'generality' and 'prospectivity' as a means to limit the legislator's ability to certainly identify who will bear the cost of a given bill. Others refer to the simple examples of conscription, lottery rules in some armies, or jury selection rules.[123] In all these rules, certainty is reduced as a device to reach 'decisions that mimic those an impartially motivated decision-maker would produce'.[124]

Albeit sharing similarity with Buchanan's veil of uncertainty, the role of uncertainty in the Federalist argument is more limited. Uncertainty here does not itself directly bring out impartiality but rather indirectly, gradually, and contingent on other factors. In Federalist No. 10, uncertainty plays a role in generating self-fulfilling doubt, which gradually helps undermine and destabilise oppressive factions and their ability to concert. While the weakening of oppressive coalitions could pave the way for relative impartiality, it does not necessarily follow but rather depends on the diversification of interest and the fulfilment of other conditions charted out in the remainder of the chapters.

With that in mind, how would uncertainty help Publius' cause? Madison noted that strong factions, 'prompted by the *uncertainty* of their *conditions*', will be

[117] G Brennan and JM Buchanan, *The Reason of Rules: Constitutional Political Economy* (Liberty Fund, 2008) 30.
[118] ibid.
[119] ibid.
[120] While Buchanan distinguished between constitutional design and post-constitutional choice (namely legislation), Vermeule erases the distinction and offers a wide array of examples from the American legal system and beyond: Vermeule (n 93) 400.
[121] The 'point of a veil rule is to prevent self-interested decision-making': ibid 403.
[122] ibid: while introducing the Amendment Madison remarked 'in which case it cannot be for the particular benefit of those who are concerned in determining the value of the service'. J Gales (ed), *1 Annals of Congress* (Gales & Seaton, 1789) 457–458.
[123] S Voigt, 'Veilonomics: On the Use and Utility of Veils in Constitutional Political Economy' in LM Imbeau and S Jacob (eds), *Behind a Veil of Ignorance? Power and Uncertainty in Constitutional Design* (Cham, Springer, 2015) 9.
[124] Vermeule (n 93) 403.

'gradually induced' to wish for just governance.[125] The 'conditions' that Madison refers to as brought by a federation, which are unavailable under unitary small states, are that local powerful factions face more divergent interests, leading to pressure to act from multiple stakeholders. Simultaneously, opposing factions of equal strength advocate for different directions, further complicating the decision-making landscape. These dynamics create a heightened degree of uncertainty regarding predicting and controlling the outcome. Additionally, there is a further element of uncertainty with regard to the resilience, cohesion, and trust among the members of each faction or coalition.

The latter form of uncertainty is fed by two fears. First, there is the concern of defection of its constituent members under effective bargaining from other constitutional actors. For example, conservative southern senators were converted into voting for the Civil Rights Act under shrewd pressure by President Johnson,[126] in addition to the pressure from religious organisations.[127] To a lesser extent, the European Commission, through infringement procedures and bargaining, managed to get Member States to amend unequal pay laws.[128] Second, there is the uncertainty resulting from growing 'distrust' among members of a coalition pursuing an oppressive goal. As Madison remarked, 'where there is *consciousness of unjust or dishonorable purposes*, communication is always checked by *distrust*, in proportion to the number whose concurrence is necessary'.[129]

Implicit in this line of thinking is that a more principled, 'pro-right coalition' with its inclination to just outcomes is comparatively more stable and, to some extent, less likely to lose its basic constituent core of members with the *shifting sands* of diversified interests. Madison seemed to have alluded to this bifurcation:

> a coalition, which notwithstanding the rivalship and local prejudices which might prevent it on ordinary occasions, *would not fail to take place, when not merely prompted by common interest, but justified by equity and the principles of the constitution*'.[130]

For instance, past experience reveals that a defection of a black rights activist senator to the other side is less likely than that of a southern anti-civil right senator, and, thus, an inter-state coalition of the former is relatively more stable and, thus,

[125] Madison, *Federalist No. 51* (n 73) 255.

[126] Eg, C Risen, *The Bill of the Century: The Epic Battle for the Civil Rights Act* (London, Bloomsbury, 2014) 255, referring to the Arizona Senator who was swayed by a 'white House promise' to open a facility in his constituency to mint silver dollars.

[127] ibid 269, referring to the unlikely vote of senators such as Jack Miler of Iowa; on the role of religious groups, see CW Whalen and B Whalen, *The Longest Debate: A Legislative History of the 1964 Civil Rights Act* (Santa Ana, Seven Locks Press, 1989) 233.

[128] For an insightful summary of the infringement procedures and their impact, see J Pillinger, *Feminising the Market: Women's Pay and Employment in the European Community* (Cham, Springer, 2016) appx 4, 186–187.

[129] Madison, Federalist No. 10 (n 1) 46 (emphasis added).

[130] Madison, *Federalist No. 58* (n 85) 283 (emphasis added).

other things being equal, more likely to prevail over an inter-state collation of the latter.[131]

Behavioural evidence suggests that in multi-party negotiations, a coalition seeking to maximise the interest of its members through starkly unequitable shares of others 'took longer time to form' and 'was harder to maintain'.[132] Relatedly, two Nobel economic laureates have demonstrated that the 'opprobrium attached to unfairness imposes constraints' on the pursuit of self-interest.[133] This may indicate that anti-right coalitions which *consciously* seek 'unjust' purposes are labouring against psychological forces which may affirm Madison's remark on the distrust eroding the core of these coalitions.[134] However, one must be cautious of attributing the thinnest meaning of 'right' or 'fairness' to a case where unfairness is 'conscious' and generally perceived as so. To wit, it may not apply to other kinds of overlapping and morally divisive rights where multiple interpretations are possible yet irreconcilable, and each party genuinely sees it as just. We shall revisit this issue later in chapters four and five.

With this in mind, the proposed structure makes it so that, as Madison stressed, 'a coalition of a majority of the whole society … seldom take place on any other principles than *those of justice and the general good*'.[135] Once the conditions of diversification of interest and inability to concert are met, strong factions would experience a degree of 'uncertainty of their condition'.[136] The faction which is dominant at the state level and freely engaging in self-dealing may not maintain its ability to do so on the federal level. To the extent that inability to concert and uncertainty exist, and once resistance and domination attempts fail, factions would be 'induced' to move to their second-best shot, which, in many cases, would be closer to 'those of justice and the general good'.[137] Uncertain debtors may prefer contract enforcement over taking the risk of the federal majority swelling the interest. It seems to be what has happened with debt relief laws. As Halberstam notes, the introduction of the Bankruptcy Clause and the Contracts Clause in the

[131] See ch 4.

[132] I Van Beest, E Van Dijk and H Wilke, 'The Interplay of Self-Interest and Equity in Coalition Formation' (2004) 34 *European Journal of Social Psychology* 547; I Van Beest and others, 'Do-No-Harm in Coalition Formation: Why Losses Inhibit Exclusion and Promote Fairness Cognitions' (2005) 41 *Journal of Experimental Social Psychology* 609. For summary of literature, see D Druckman and LM Wagner, 'Justice and Negotiation' (2016) 67 *Annual Review of Psychology* 387.

[133] D Kahneman, *Thinking, Fast and Slow* (Basingstoke, Macmillan, 2011) 259; D Kahneman, JL Knetsch, and R Thaler, 'Fairness as a Constraint on Profit Seeking: Entitlements in the Market' (1986) 76 *The American Economic Review* 728.

[134] Elster used the Ultimatum game theory to expound Montaigne's insight that when uncertainty and 'doubt' arise as to 'which is the shortest road, we should keep going straight ahead.': J Elster, 'Mimicking Impartiality' in K Dowding, RE Goodin and C Pateman (eds), *Justice and Democracy* (Cambridge, Cambridge University Press, 2004); M de Montaigne, *The Complete Essays* (London, Penguin, 1996).

[135] Madison, *Federalist No. 51* (n 73) 255 (emphasis added). While federalism makes uniting difficult for good and wicked factions, to Madison, the commonly shared conceptions of good act as lubricant to facilitate agreement of the better group will make coalition based on good causes more likely than malicious ones.

[136] ibid.

[137] ibid.

US Constitution 'protected creditors' against the biases of 'local levellers' by 'lodging' the decision over debt relief 'squarely with the central government'.[138]

The takeaway of the discussion is to show how interest diversification, principally, and uncertainty, subsidiarily, make concerted action among malevolent coalitions more difficult, which helps destabilise them. As previously mentioned, hindering the ability of malevolent factions to form stable coalitions is the core of the Federalist's goal to make non-neutral decisions more difficult. Since 'diversity is a group-level characteristic', the next step is to examine the relationship between group attributes and 'institutional outcomes', and to explore how these factors influence partiality, particularly what it means to make bias more difficult to sustain at the group level.[139]

C. Relative Increase of Impartiality: How to Define it?

If the Federalist syllogism establishes that integrative federalism's diversification of interest makes partial decision-making more difficult, then it follows, *a senso contrario*, that such a structure makes *impartial* decision-making *easier*.[140] Indeed, the Federalist Papers, as well as Madison's other writings, are replete with stressing the objective of attaining 'the requisite impartiality'[141] and modifying sovereignty to become 'more impartial' (albeit not absolutely impartial) to different parts of society.[142]

It must be stressed then that when the conditions are right, federalism provides only a relative increase of impartiality or, to be accurate, a *decrease* in the effect of bias. Impartiality as a rule against bias is a negative quality. It indicates either the absence of bias or *controlling/decreasing its effect*. In the traditional individual context, where two parties are in conflict, it is relatively easy to find a neutral third party. This is not the case in constitutional politics. There is no absolute collective 'third-party enforcer' unless you invite a foreign parliament to vote on your own domestic issues, which is patently illogical.[143] What is possible, however, is to mitigate the violation of the *nemo judex* rule by controlling the impact of bias rather than eliminating its causes.

Differently put, institutional impartiality is 'a scalar rather than an all-or-nothing property'.[144] A legislature formed exclusively of white members debating

[138] D Halberstam, 'Federalism: Theory, Policy, Law' in M Rosenfeld and A Sajó (eds), *The Oxford Handbook of Comparative Constitutional Law* (Oxford, Oxford University Press, 2012) 592.

[139] AP Harrison, 'Can Racial Diversity among Judges Affect Sentencing Outcomes?' (2024) 118 *American Political Science Review* 940.

[140] As shall be discussed later, there is another *contrario* possibility, which is to make no decision at all.

[141] Eg, Madison, *Federalist No. 54* 269; Hamilton to refers to partiality in *Federalist No. 59* 295.

[142] Madison, 'State and Federal Power and the Public Good to Thomas Jefferson, October 24, 1787' (n 30). The connection he sees between impartiality and justice is apparent in this letter as well as the vices of confederation that legislature's violation of *nemo judex* leads to 'Injustice of the laws of States.'

[143] T Ginsburg and Z Elkins, *Public Choice and Constitutional Design* (Chicago, University of Chicago Press, 2009) 9–11.

[144] Kramer (n 54) 1.

affirmative action would be more biased compared to one that included a combination of other races. A legislature fully dominated by debtors would be more partial in deciding debt-relief laws than a parliament representing other interests.[145] If we hark back to the chart (Figure 2.1), for 'simple arithmetical reasons', the dangers of unrestrained majority are higher in states; the smaller and less complex the polity, the easier for the wrong kinds of unrestrained majorities to form.[146] Conversely, when a locally dominant majority is not federally so, minorities are relatively more protected by a more diversified majority which, subject to some conditions, are relatively less partial decision-makers.[147] The relativity aligns with Madison's realisation that bias cannot be eradicated, but we can 'control its effects'.[148]

To appreciate this relative increase in impartiality, it is necessary to define impartiality in the context of collective decision-making. In the Madisonian sense, impartiality is a less abstract and more functionally oriented concept than the broader accounts typically found in political philosophy.[149] As intellectual historians have noted, Madison's understanding departs from the conception of bias within the individual mind, which bears a striking resemblance – as chapter four will demonstrate – to the typologies developed in the 'British legal tradition' on judicial bias.[150] This narrower, functional conception of impartiality, coupled with the limited ambitions of constitutional law, as Vermeule observes,[151] spares us from navigating the sprawling terrain of philosophical disagreement over the meaning and feasibility of the ideal impartiality.[152] Stated differently, since 'the ambitions of constitutional law are far more modest', it does not seek to offer a 'uniquely best definition of impartiality', but rather aims to avoid 'decisions that all competing definitions of impartiality condemn'.[153]

With this in mind, partiality in individual decision-making is often defined, as the decision maker's 'close-mindedness' to different views.[154]

[145] Waldron provides an example in the context of credit regulation: Waldron (n 14) 125.

[146] Rakove (n 5) 118.

[147] The use of the term 'likely' because there is still a possibility that all factions forming the diverse majority might still concur to hate and oppress one minor group.

[148] Madison, Federalist No. 10 (n 1).

[149] See generally 'Impartiality', (*Stanford Encyclopedia of Philosophy*) plato.stanford.edu/entries/impartiality/ accessed 3 August 2025; AP Griffiths and others, 'Neutrality and Impartiality: The University and Political Commitment' (1976) 26 *Philosophical Quarterly* 197.

[150] 'Madison thus extended the central normative axiom of impartiality in the British legal tradition to the actions of groups of citizens and legislators.': Gibson (n 57) 274.

[151] Vermeule (n 93) 403.

[152] Ironically, however, many political philosophers writing in the US have largely overlooked Madison's own account, despite their framer's enduring practical influence. Eg, there is not a single reference of the Federalist No.10 argument in Rawls (n 116); and J Rawls, *Political Liberalism* (New York, Columbia University Press, 1993).

[153] Vermeule (n 93) 403.

[154] Kramer (n 54) 1; for a discussion of open-mindedness and impartiality as truth aptitude, see M Kramer, *Objectivity and the Rule of Law* (Cambridge, Cambridge University Press, 2007) 58–70. See discussion in CG Geyh, 'The Dimensions of Judicial Impartiality' (2014) 65 *Florida Law Review* 493; for the examination of the conditions of 'replicability' and 'inter-personally valid' criteria, see JCW Touchie, 'On the Possibility of Impartiality in Decision-Making' (2001) 1 *Macquarie Law Journal* 21.

This close-mindedness or antecedent unmoved view can be traced etymologically from the word 'pre-judice', namely as 'pre' (to mean before) and 'judice' (to mean judgement), signifying judgement formed in advance. Others define bias as a decision-maker's 'undue' imposition of his/her own interests or views *to the detriment and to the disregard* of other parties. In collective institutional settings, the dominant group or faction often plays the role of decision faculty, controlling the institutional mind. In this light, a relative increase in impartiality is the extent to which dominant groups are *compelled or enticed to consider and give weight* to the interests and views of other stakeholders in arriving at a decision. Or as SCOTUS defines it, as 'open-mindedness' whereby the decision maker considers 'views that oppose his preconceptions and remain *open to persuasion*'.[155] *Likewise, UK courts* define close mildness as not being 'susceptible to any reasonable persuasion'.[156]

Likewise, being institutionally biased indicates the degree to which the decision maker is rendered 'immune to contrary views', their position is unmovable and in practice not 'persuadable.'[157] Seen this way, the check underlying the Federalist argument is to relatively *minimise* the closed-mindedness or tendency of strong factions to consider different views and to allow the possibility of shifting their 'predisposition' from pursuing excessive interest to more moderate ones. As later chapters will show, this dynamic can be observed in how the same issues receive different majoritarian responses at the state level compared to the federal level, once federal checks are in place.

Analogies between individual and institutional impartiality can further illuminate this point. Publius' insight on attaining impartiality through introducing opposite interests resembles, to some extent, one of Kramer's notions of impartiality. Kramer notes that the strongest form of impartiality is the absence of any known personal stake in one's decision (something he perceives as 'not altogether possible' in the law-making process).[158]

Another less-ideal form of impartiality is 'an ability to let one's decision unaffected by one's awareness of that one has a stake therein'. To deactivate or reduce the impact of this awareness on the decision calculus, Kramer suggests introducing another personal stake to balance the already existing one. To slightly tweak his example, a parent is not neutral when deciding a dispute between their child and their neighbour's child as to who should be allowed to play first on a certain swing. However, if the parent is deciding the same issue between a twin of their own children, 'the personal stake of each of those relatives is offset by that of the other, the parent's impartiality is unimpaired'.[159]

[155] *Republican Party of Minnesota v White* 536 US 765, 778 (2002).

[156] *R v Inner West London Coroner, ex parte Dallaglio* [1994] 4 All ER 139.

[157] To reformulate H Woolf and others (eds), *De Smith's Principles of Judicial Review*, 2nd edn (London, Thomson Reuters, 2020) 536–537.

[158] Kramer (n 54) 2.

[159] ibid.

Kramer's example is, to some extent, comparable with the Federalist ambition to control the effects of bias rather than to eliminate it entirely – though it is important to distinguish between individual and institutional impartiality. At the individual level, impartiality, understood as a *rule against bias*, demands the absence – or at least the complete suspension – of bias in the mind of the decision-maker. In contrast, the institutional setting, where society effectively decides upon itself, cannot realistically aspire to such an idealised form. Instead, it aims for a less ideal conception of impartiality: the reduction of bias's impact on the decisional process, rather than its total eradication.

Another example is how Publius made census the benchmark of calculating both the state allocation of seats in the federal legislature and their contribution to taxes. This way, states should 'feel as little bias as possible to reduce or sweel or to reduce the amount of their numbers'. If census were the rule for representation alone, states would be tempted to inflate their inhabitants, whereas if the rule were used to decide their share of taxation alone, 'a contrary temptation would prevail'. Thus, using 'common measure' for both enlists opposite interests to 'reduce bias' and produce 'the requisite impartiality'.[160] Since this increase of institutional impartiality depends on countering biases with opposite forces, the effectiveness of this technique depends on the balance and the strength of the corresponding opposite forces.

At the risk of oversimplification, the Madisonian formula of controlling bias through federal structure can be expressed as:

Federal integration + centralisation = multiplies but dilutes bias.

This dilution of the effect of bias, to Madison, ensures a measure of protection of fundamental rights and guards against social factionalism. As this book will explore, certain conditions must be met for the formula to function effectively, and in some types of bias, it may not apply at all.

A possible objection is that bias (and, by corollary, its reduction) is a 'black box' which is hidden and, thus, difficult to prove.[161] However, this increase in institutional impartiality can be traced by contrasting the majority's attitude and their willingness to change their approach when acting locally compared to federally. Memorable comparative examples exist. It was only after the centralisation of minority rights in the twentieth century US, coupled with other factors, that the rights of minorities experienced a gradual improvement. Similarly, it was only after the CJEU managed to constitutionalise sex equality that equal pay was asserted in the face of state resistance. Beyond ethnic minorities, the Bankruptcy Clause and the Contracts Clause in the US Constitution did a similar job in controlling local biases, as discussed earlier.[162] In short, in all these examples, prejudicial state majorities, once integrated into the federal

[160] Madison, *Federalist No. 54* (n 141) 268–269.
[161] D Fox, 'Neuro-Voir Dire and the Architecture of Bias' (2013) 65 *Hastings Law Journal* 999.
[162] Halberstam (n 138) 592.

structure, under some conditions, get diluted, and minorities become *relatively* more secure.

It is worth stressing that that reasoning of the Federalist argument only applies to 'integrative federalism', not to the more worldly prevailing type of smaller 'devolutionary federalism' as in Belgium, Austria, or the UAE, where diversity of interest is less and relatively insufficient to meet the second premise of the Tenth Federalist (inability to concert and interest diversification).[163] Moreover, it does not apply where the central government lacks both de jure and de facto competence to intervene on the issue of minorities, as was the case with pre-New Deal America. Without an ability to decide, a collective judge, like an individual one, is just a bystander. The Federalist's rationale also collapses under some voting arrangements, as we shall examine later with the EU minorities in chapter three. For now, we turn to examine the second type of relativity stemming from impartiality's relation to federalism's objectives and other values.

D. Relativity in the Second Sense: Balancing and Displacing Impartiality

In individual traditional disputes, having an impartial judge is a necessary but insufficient condition. Rather, many other conditions must be secured, such as competent knowledge, accessibility, and redundancy through having recourse to appeal, and many others. If this is the case for individual impartiality, then the relative collective type of group impartiality is, likewise, desirable but not alone sufficient. Harkening back to the common law jurisprudence on impartiality, it is well-known that impartiality can be either 'displaced' for necessity[164] or overridden for competing public value.[165] The same applies to group impartiality.

For instance, while the Federalist argument implies that enlarging the polity increases impartiality, the practical implication of the 'size principle' ensures, among other things, that enlargement be kept 'within a practicable sphere', not a Kantian-style world government.[166] This is to ensure effective government and social solidarity among citizenry.[167] Other objectives such as 'efficiency' or 'energetic governance' often supersede impartiality.[168] This could be exemplified by the cases where effectiveness consideration led to empowering specialised

[163] On the inevitable role of having autonomous state powers, see ch 4.

[164] P Craig, *Administrative Law*, 9th edn (London, Sweet and Maxwell 2021) 431.

[165] DJ Galligan, *Due Process and Fair Procedures : A Study of Administrative Procedures* (Oxford, Oxford University Press, 1996) 123–127; E Chemerinsky, 'The Values of Federalism Dunwoody Distinguished Lecture in Law' (1995) 47 *Florida Law Review* 499. Here, 'values' are used in the federal theory sense – as public goals – rather than in the sense associated with Art 2, TEU, which will be briefly addressed in the final chapter.

[166] I Kant, *Perpetual Peace: A Philosophical Essay* (Phoemixx Classics Ebooks, 2021).

[167] Madison, *Federalist No. 51* (n 73) 255.

[168] Hamilton, *Federalist No. 23* 110.

administrative agencies with a combination of judicial and legislative functions, rendering these agencies, in some respects, 'judges of their own authority'.[169]

This brings us to the 'second sense' of impartiality's relativity.[170] Madison was emphatic that in constitutional settings we are constantly confronting 'imperfect options',[171] where a choice must be made of the 'GREATER, not the PERFECT good'.[172] Impartiality, albeit valuable, is one element in this choice calculus which 'constantly trades off against and competes with other values'.[173] It can be superseded or traded off in two broad situations, to borrow Hamiltonian language: when 'necessity urges' or when the 'greater good invites':[174]

Figure 2.2 Impartiality and the Calculus of Federal Values

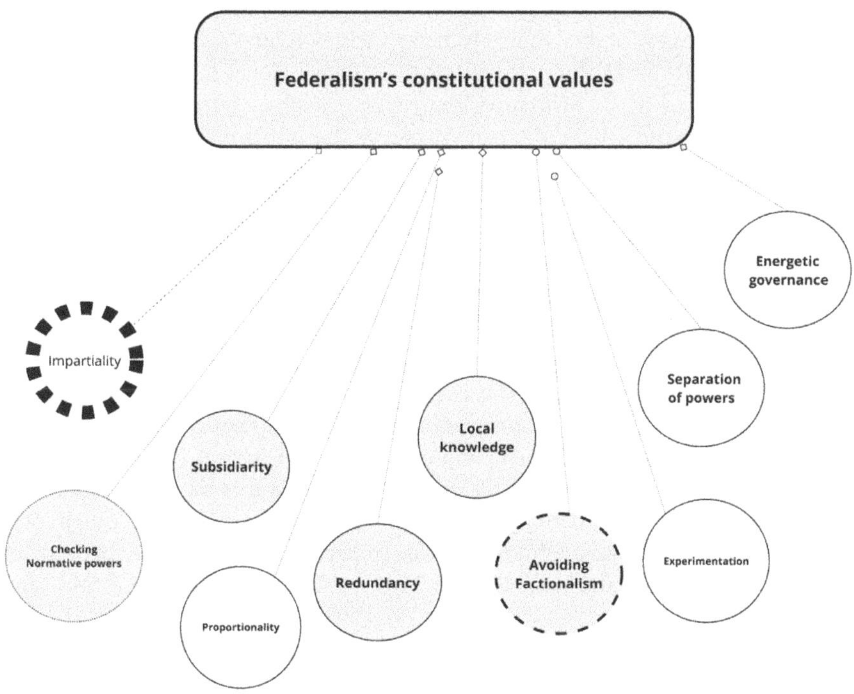

The first scenario – necessity – refers to cases where the violation is inevitable because of the impossibility of securing any impartial entity, or when the alternative decision-making arrangement is equally 'partial'.[175] The second, *greater good*,

[169] I Shapiro and CW McCarthy, 'Are Federal Agencies the Sole Judges of Their Own Authority?' (*Regulation*, Summer 2011) 4 (libertarian critique).
[170] Ostrom calls this the Federalist 'relative advantage principle': Ostrom and Allen (n 98) 35.
[171] ibid 35.
[172] Madison, *Federalist No. 41* para 3. Madison's emphasis.
[173] A Vermeule, 'Contra Nemo Iudex in Sua Causa: The Limits of Impartiality' (2012) 122 *Yale Law Journal* 384, 389.
[174] Hamilton, *Federalist No. 59* (n 141) 291.
[175] Vermeule (n 173) 415.

refers to instances where impartiality is theoretically achievable but the cost of securing it would be disproportionate to the public values sacrificed. These scenarios correspond to Robert Alexy's distinction between *factual impossibility* and *legal impossibility* in the optimisation of constitutional principles.[176] Factual impossibility arises when no impartial adjudicator can be secured. Legal impossibility arises when securing impartiality would require unjustifiable encroachment on other entrenched values, rendering such optimisation constitutionally untenable.[177]

The first scenario – necessity due to the factual impossibility – is already a well-known defence to exclude the *nemo judex* rule.[178] *If everyone would be disqualified, none is.*[179] This will be the case for some rights explained in chapter five where impartiality will become impossible in this sense. But to take an institutional example of necessity/factual impossibility is the doctrine of *Kompetenz Kompetenz* or the related supremacy of the Union's judiciary, which is long settled in America but hotly debated in the EU.[180] Empowering the Central Court to decide on its own jurisdiction and assert its own supremacy vis-a-vis state courts could be seen as incompatible with the *nemo judex* rule. However, the violation is inevitable because, as things stand, it is either the state courts or the centre that can have the final say. Entrusting the latter may be preferred by reference to 'the greater good' stemming from other values such as ensuring 'equality of states' recently reaffirmed by CJEU's president.[181] Similarly, consider Publius' reasoning for entrusting Congress with the power to regulate its own elections; given that 'discretionary power over election ought to exist somewhere',[182] the requirement of ensuring a 'firm union' and '[self] preservation' of the federal government should prevail.[183]

The second type – trade-off for greater good – arises when pursuing impartiality is *factually possible* but *legally unaffordable*. This can be illustrated by an example from the UK's Westminster, which composed of representatives from four polities: England, Scotland, Northern Ireland, and Wales. England is the only nation with no devolved Parliament and, except for a few years, members from the other countries voted on English affairs.[184] While a more impartial group might be theoretically possible by contending that non-English MPs would be more removed and, thus,

[176] Alexy defines optimisation of principles by the 'fact they can be satisfied to varying degrees, and the appropriate degree of satisfaction depends on what is factually … and legally possible'. Legal possibility is determined by 'opposing principles and rules': R Alexy, *A Theory of Constitutional Rights* (Oxford, Oxford University Press, 2010) 47–48. The distinction between legal and factual realities has long pedigree in Islamic legal theory: see, eg, Al-Tilmsany, *Muftah al- Wuṣū*, (Dar-al Rashad, 2019).

[177] Alexy (n 176).

[178] See, eg, *Phillips v Eyre* (1870) LR 6 QB; T McKevitt, 'The Rule of Necessity: Is Judicial Non-Disqualification Really Necessary' (1995) 24 *Hofstra Law Review* 817.

[179] Eg, *United States v Hatter* 532 US 557 (2001).

[180] See ch 2, s 3.

[181] 'Press release following the judgment of the German Constitutional Court of 5 May 2020' (Court of Justice of the European Union, Press Release No. 58/20, 8 May 2020) curia.europa.eu/jcms/upload/docs/application/pdf/2020-05/cp200058en.pdf accessed 3 August 2025.

[182] Hamilton, *Federalist No. 59* (n 141) 292 stressing that 'every government ought to contain in itself the means of its own preservation'.

[183] ibid.

[184] This was during the introduction of English Votes for English Matters (EVEL) in 2015, which in July 2021, was removed.

impartial to English affairs, then they alone should vote on English matters to the exclusion of English MPs.[185] This obviously would be – to use an English thinker's terms – 'nonsense on stilts'[186] as it disproportionately destroys values of accountability, local knowledge and others. Other examples abound, where the US Constitution, for instance, empowers the Congress to decide on its own interest despite the availability of the judiciary as a more impartial umpire. This is usually justified on the grounds of political accountability or institutional autonomy.[187]

To reiterate, when violation of the collective *nemo judex* rule is inevitable and necessary or when impartiality is legally unaffordable, one has to look for a 'calculus' or trade-off that attains more 'optimisation' of federalism's matrix of values while paying due regard to the de facto structural dynamics and the available safeguards to remedy impartiality absence. This can include values/goals such as local knowledge, avoiding polarisation, *energetic governance*, normative pluralism or what Cover calls 'jurisdictional redundancy'.[188] Chapter three shows that for racial minority rights and sex equal pay, there are no competing values that hinder the availability of federal impartiality. In contrast to other types of rights whose 'centre of gravity'[189] rests more heavily on morally divisive convictions, like those discussed in chapters five and six, violation of the *nemo judex* rule is inevitable. This is because all potential decision-makers are equally biased, which would behove more careful balancing to attain the most optimal balancing of other federalism values.

To recap, this section has covered the main attributes of the *nemo judex* rule in macro constitutional politics as: (i) institutional and group-based, not merely individual; and (ii) relative in two senses. It has also unpacked, while incorporating contemporary insights, the two main premises of the Federalist argument, namely: (i) interest diversification; and (ii) the ensuing uncertainty, which together increase impartiality at the federal level. The next section moves to examine a fundamental point left out by Publius, which may restrain integrative federalism's capacity to produce an impartial decision-making process.

IV. The Problem of Inertia in Madison's Argument

While expounding the Federalist argument through the syllogism showing that integrative federalism makes *non-neutral* decision-making more *difficult*, we marshalled a *senso contrario* interpretation that a compound republic makes *neutral*

[185] Assuming that the legislated matters do not affect the budget or issues that would affect the non-English polities.

[186] J Bentham, 'Rights, Representation, and Reform: Nonsense upon Stilts and Other Writings on the French Revolution' in P Schofield and others (eds), *The Collected Works of Jeremy Bentham* (Oxford, Oxford University Press, 2002) 317–401.

[187] Eg, *Bradlaugh v Gosset* (1884) 12 QBD 271; Vermeule (n 93) 287–288.

[188] RM Cover, 'The Uses of Jurisdictional Redundancy: Interest, Ideology, and Innovation' (1980) 22 *William & Mary Law Review* 639.

[189] The term comes from Case C-300/ECLI:EU:C:1991:244, [1991] ECR I-2867.

decision-making easier. However, this is not the only possible *contrario* interpretation. There is another equally valid one, which is that it *may make no decision at all possible*.[190] That is 'inertia' or perpetuating 'the status quo'. Neutralising factions can yield inaction.[191] This logical insight has been affirmed empirically by federalism scholars such as Stepan and others who showed that federalism creates a potential for 'structurally induced bias' in favour of the 'status quo'.[192]

Beyond institutional hurdles,[193] the problem with the status quo, as Sunstein remarked, is that it often gives a deceptive impression of 'neutrality'.[194] On some occasions, lingering injustices will be cloaked in the habitual state of things and might elude the attention of the 'indifferent', 'sang-froid' decision-making entity, which would favour inertia over disturbing the seemingly neutral status quo.[195] However, as pre-civil rights America and other examples have made clear, the status quo is often neither 'neutral nor just'.[196]

Behavioural research, too, has demonstrated that status-quo bias does not only restrain individuals but also organisations, be it a private firm[197] or a public institution.[198] This pattern is also clear from reflecting on the history of the US or the contemporary conditions of the EU minorities. Blame is usually levelled against component states for their *harmful action* against minorities,[199] as France with Roma minorities, for instance, while the centre is blamed for its *inaction*.[200]

Overcoming this inertia requires what we might call 'inertia-disrupting forces'. This includes popular activism, or what is known as federalism's 'popular safeguards',[201] and/or friction emanating from resisting states, which forces the central government to intervene.[202] Occasionally, the pressure to act could

[190] I thank my colleague Hasan Spiker for drawing my attention to this.

[191] AC Stepan, *Arguing Comparative Politics* (Oxford, Oxford University Press, 2001) 337–339; Halberstam (n 138) 598.

[192] ibid.

[193] For a summary on the institutional elements in Congress which perpetuate the status quo, see: Stepan (n 191).

[194] CR Sunstein, *The Partial Constitution* (Cambridge, MA, Harvard University Press, 1993) 1.

[195] Locke describes the sovereign as an 'indifferent Judge': Locke (n 2) ch IX, 124.

[196] Sunstein (n 194) 1.

[197] R Hastie and RM Dawes, *Rational Choice in an Uncertain World: The Psychology of Judgment and Decision Making* (Thousand Oaks, Sage, 2009) 102.

[198] Eg, W Samuelson and R Zeckhauser, 'Status Quo Bias in Decision Making' (1988) 1 *Journal of Risk and Uncertainty* 7, 45–46.

[199] For a contrast of the treatment of civil rights cases in state courts compared to federal court, see MJ Klarman, *Brown V. Board of Education and the Civil Rights Movement: The Supreme Court and the Struggle for Racial Equality* (Oxford, Oxford University Press, 2007) 459.

[200] See ch 3 for discussion of France and other states' harmful action towards Roma minorities and for condemnation of EU's inaction.

[201] Popular safeguards refer to people's direct and indirect control not only of governmental performance, but also of the meaning of constitutional norms. See CJEU's historic decision: '[T]he vigilance of individuals concerned to protect their rights amounts to an effective supervision in addition to the supervision entrusted': Case 26/62 *Van Gend en Loos* ECLI:EU:C:1963:1, [1963] ECR 1; see M Tushnet, 'Social Movements and the Constitution' in M Tushnet and others (eds), *The Oxford Handbook of the US Constitution* (Oxford, Oxford University Press, 2015) 244–255.

[202] HK Gerken and A Holtzblatt, 'The Political Safeguards of Horizontal Federalism' (2014) 113 *Michigan Law Review* 57.

emanate from 'external events'[203] such as the Cold War's impact on the Civil Rights Revolution, or the Haider Affair's impact on the EU legislation on racial discrimination.[204] One can clearly trace the dynamics of these forces in minority rights in the US, and in the EU equal pay with some variation. While the following chapter provides a detailed exploration of the two examples, a concise summary is presented here only on the point of inertia and its disruption.

In pre-civil rights America, despite the existence, after the New Deal, of a *relatively* more impartial federal decision-maker that met the Federalist No. 10 requirements, the rights of African Americans stagnated for decades in a 'cruel nadir'.[205] To overcome the status quo, many elements had to come into play. First, popular safeguards were expressed through the National Association for the Advancement of Coloured People's ('NAACP') unabated 'constitutional war' on racism. It selected test cases, patiently assembled small yet incremental legal victories,[206] and along with other forces, coordinated social mobilisation that attracted the intervention of the Supreme Court and later Congress.[207]

Second, 'external factors' were pivotal too. Popular activism coincided with conducive socio-political factors globally and domestically. During and after WWII, it was difficult to reconcile the condemnation of the Nazis and then communist ideology with the reality of racial injustice in the US.[208] This gave blacks an 'irrefutable moral claim'.[209] Domestically, the New Deal's industrialisation led to substantial demographic changes, coupled with the Great Migration of five million African Americans to the North, which produced a 'potent Northern black political presence'.[210]

Even state frictions and resistance have, according to Klarman and others, played a role too.[211] Massive southern resistance laid 'bare the violence at the core of white supremacy' which, due to the media broadcast of violent confrontations, showed supremacists 'at their worst' and African Americans at 'their best'.[212] Popular opinion grew more and more supportive of empowering minorities, which incentivised Congress's legislative intervention. To put it succinctly, it was

[203] The term 'external events' is defined as events well-beyond the control of constitutional actors that significantly influence constitutional rules or even the structure. See Z Elkins, T Ginsburg and J Melton, *The Endurance of National Constitutions* (Cambridge, Cambridge University Press, 2009).

[204] G de Búrca, 'The Evolution of EU Human Rights Law' in P Craig and G de Búrca (eds), *The Evolution of EU Law* (Oxford, Oxford University Press, 2011).

[205] AH Kelly, WA Harbison and H Belz, *The American Constitution, Its Origins and Development*, 7th edn (New York, WW Norton & Co, 1991) vol 2, 580.

[206] For a detailed historical account, see R Kluger, *Simple justice: The history of Brown v. Board of Education and Black America's struggle for equality* (London, Vintage, 2011).

[207] LM Friedman, *A History of American Law*, 4th edn (Oxford, Oxford University Press, 2019).

[208] Kelly, Harbinson and Belz (n 205) 582; MJ Klarman, 'Rethinking the Civil Rights and Civil Liberties Revolutions' (1996) 82 *Virginia Law Review* 1.

[209] Kelly, Harbinson and Belz (n 205).

[210] Klarman (n 209) 33.

[211] Klarman (n 199) ch 8.

[212] ibid 421 and 442.

popular safeguards, such as the NAACP, and external factors, such as the Cold War, as well as state friction that together contributed, among other factors, to forcing the central government out of its status-quo comfort zone.

If one turns to the EU equal pay story, similar common elements exist with some necessary variations. Political events and activism called into question the absent social role for the European Community, which led to the adoption of the Social Action Program (1973). Additionally, the CJEU, unlike its American counterpart, had an institutional incentive to act and overcome inertia to help the Court expand its power and rescue the 'European project' from its political stagnation in the 1970s. Still, 'women's organisations'[213] and euro-law associations[214] contributed to prompting, shaping, and enforcing the EU rules in this regard.[215] Euro-law associations 'fashioned test cases', and their professors and affiliated judges indirectly advised the CJEU and national judges on 'doctrinal issues'.[216] Indeed, numerous research traced the backscenes of landmark cases from that era and documented this influence.[217] More importantly, these networks of 'vigilant',[218] popular/social actors were pivotal to 'post-ruling mobilisation' which helped induce Member States to exercise their role in the EU legislature, as will be explored in greater detail later.[219]

The takeaway is that in integrative federalism, the risk of inertia is latent in the Madisonian theory and should not be taken lightly but may be 'harnessed'.[220] If overcome, then the impartiality argument indicates that the two conditions of interest diversification and uncertainty should, at least in theory, pave the way for more impartial law-making processes when rights are centralised at the federal level. This way, the simplified Madisonian formula can be updated to:

Federal integration + centralisation + overcoming inertia = multiplies but dilutes bias.

[213] Sweet briefly refers to 'the relationship between the development of sex equality law after *Defrenne* II and the construction of networks of lobby groups, union officials, law professors, and litigators': AS Sweet, *The Judicial Construction of Europe* (Oxford, Oxford University Press, 2005) 191; S Mazey and J Richardson, 'Institutionalizing Promiscuity: Commission-Interest Group Relations in the European Union' in AS Sweet, W Sandholtz and N Fligstein (eds), *The Institutionalization of Europe* (Oxford, Oxford University Press, 2001) 71.

[214] See generally A Vauchez, *Brokering Europe: Euro-Lawyers and the Making of a Transnational Polity* (Cambridge, Cambridge University Press, 2015).

[215] Alter refers to the presence of societal actors who share the CJEU's substantive objectives as among the largest factors shaping the Court's role: K Alter, *The European Court's Political Power: Selected Essays* (Oxford, Oxford University Press, 2010) 4. See also G de Búrca, 'EU Race Discrimination Law: A Hybrid Model?' in G de Búrca de and J Scott (eds), *Law and New Governance in the EU and the US* (Oxford, Hart Publishing, 2006) 97.

[216] For a detailed study of the role of these associations in the CJEU's landmark cases, see Alter (n 216) ch 8.

[217] ibid; A van der Vleuten, *The Price of Gender Equality:Member States and Governance in the European Union* (Abingdon, Routledge, 2016).

[218] On collective vigilance in the EU, see M Dawson and E Muir, 'Collective Vigilance in Protection Fundamental Rights in the EU: Lesson from the Roma' (2011) 48 *Common Market Law Review* 766.

[219] Alter (n 216) 18.

[220] Paraphrasing RH Thaler and CR Sunstein, *Nudge: Improving Decisions About Health, Wealth, and Happiness* (London, Penguin, 2009) 7.

Testing this theoretical claim is undertaken in the next chapters, which further elucidate, revise, and introduce some caveats to the Federalist's impartiality argument.

V. Concluding Remarks

To unpack the interconnection between impartiality and federalism, this chapter focused on understanding the notion of institutional impartiality itself. It traced how Madison reformulated the classical use of the *nemo judex* rule to propose a new theory of integrative federalism. This type of federalism, he argues, is liable to produce a more impartial law-making process than unitary smaller states. Put differently, Madison's theory is analogous to the common law rule of '*automatic disqualification*' of judges for bias, which he extended to disqualify sub-state legislatures, pending review by the Union legislature.[221] However, it was clarified that federal must be distinguished from individual impartiality. The former is relative, not absolute, and more amenable to being traded off due to the imperfect nature of constitutional choices. The chapter analysed the premises of Madison's *nemo judex* argument, which posits that enlarging the federal orbit enlists two factors for attaining institutional impartiality, namely, the diversification of conflicting interests and its concomitant uncertainty. However, the last section illustrated the challenge latent in the Federalist impartiality argument. Implicit in the Madisonian syllogism is a risk of inertia which must be overcome to harness the potential of increased impartiality.

Two questions follow from this theoretical analysis. Firstly, one may ask whether the federal impartiality argument holds in practice as it does in theory. This has significant implications for the boundary question: if the argument proves valid in practice, then allocating certain rights to the federal 'central floor' will yield a more neutral approach to these rights. Secondly, if both the impartiality argument and the central floor categorisation are indeed effective, one must then consider whether this framework can be applied universally to all types of rights, or whether certain nuances necessitate treating different categories of rights differently. The upcoming chapter addresses these first questions through comparative examples drawn from both the EU and the US.

[221] M Moussa, 'Expanding the *Nemo Judex* Rule: Reflections on Non-Pecuniary Bias' [2025] *Judicial Review* 1, para 31.

3

The Possible Impartiality: Minority Rights as a Faction of Interest

I. Introduction

Drawing on chapter two's analysis of the federal impartiality theory, this chapter seeks to answer the ensuing question of whether practice matches federalism's theoretical promise. To what extent, and under what conditions, does centralisation of rights produce a more impartial decision-making process? If centralisation is indeed effective, should the federal boundary be drawn by placing these rights at the central floor or ceiling level?

The chapter approaches these questions as follows: after the introduction, section II explains how Madison's impartiality argument, after harnessing inertia, indeed works in the two successful examples of EU equal pay and the American civil rights era. Not only did centralisation produce more impartial, better protection of rights, but it also helped change social attitudes whereby the public were 'gradually induced' to embrace these rights.[1] Section III, however, highlights how institutional and jurisprudential flaws can undermine the potential of federalism's impartiality. One example focuses on the EU's reliance on state veto power under Article 19, TFEU, which limits the EU's ability to protect racial and ethnic minorities.

It should be noted that this chapter's analysis predominantly uses minority rights as an illustrative case of societal conflict of interest (or faction of interest in Madison's and Hume's terms). By this, I refer to racial, ethnic, and religious minorities, as well as women, as power minorities.[2] The rationale behind considering the dispute surrounding the scope of minority rights as a faction or interest-based conflict is rooted in the fact that membership in a 'cognate group' not only

[1] J Madison, 'Federalist No. 51' in A Hamilton, J Madison and J Jay, *The Federalist Papers* (I Shapiro ed, New Haven, Yale University Press 2009) 255 (Federalist No. 51).

[2] H Hannum, 'The Concept and Definition of Minorities' in M Weller (ed), *Universal Minority Rights: A Commentary on the Jurisprudence of International Courts and Treaty Bodies* (Oxford, Oxford University Press, 2007). These groups, whose status as minorities or underprivileged communities is not contested, offer a clear foundation on which to build the analysis. Matters become more complicated, however, when individuals claim membership in a group that others do not recognise as such – particularly on moral grounds. In such cases, the issue becomes both a group conflict and a value conflict. For further discussion, see ch 6 on mixed factions and the exploration of the limits of value diversity in any constitutional system.

affects economic collective and self-interest, but also because in societies '*power and advantage – material, sociocultural, political* – are distributed in ways that are sensitive to certain personal characteristics'. Members of these groups compete with other dominant groups to reduce gaps in group advantages which could be 'political, material or socio-cultural' in nature.[3]

II. Does Practice Uphold Theory: How Self-Interested Factions are '*Gradually Induced*' to Protect the Rights of Others?

Recall that Madison remarked that the two elements – diversity of interest and inability to concert – will not alter the mixed nature of humanity or turn them into disinterested 'angels'.[4] Yet, he insisted that once introduced, the majority would 'seldom take place on any other principles than *those of justice and the general good*'.[5] Two sentences are worth remembering: Madison asserts that strong factions are 'prompted by the uncertainty of their conditions' to be '*gradually induced*' to embrace just governance.[6] This suggests that centralisation does not merely yield more impartial outcomes but may also serve to foster broader social acceptance over time. The question is if and how this gradual inducement happens.

I will briefly highlight the gradual shift in local factions' attitude through a cursory reference to examples from the EU and the US experiences. Perhaps, to grasp the dynamics, one may need to separate what happens at the decision-maker (representative) level and the popular local reaction. Surely, the two levels have a dialectical and simultaneous influence, but separation here is only for the sake of explanation. Prior to exploring the two comparative examples, a brief overview might help guide the details of the case studies.

At the federal level, once the conditions of a more impartial decision-maker are met and factors/safeguards combine to create sufficient momentum to leave inertia, competing interests start to collide, and inter-state coalitions are sought. In fact, initially, unlike what Madison predicts, a coalition is often successfully formed across several states and united with the goal to block minority rights (anti-right coalition). Further, they mount resistance to either perpetuate the status quo, bend the purported action their way, or water down the proposed legislative measures. Such a coalition often succeeds in imposing the status quo for some time. However, if the inertia-disrupting pressure persists, the Federalist impartiality argument comes into play, and the anti-rights coalition would start to teeter.

[3] T Khaitan and JC Norton, 'The Right to Freedom of Religion and the Right against Religious Discrimination: Theoretical Distinctions' (2019) 17 *International Journal of Constitutional Law* 1132, 1132–1134 (emphasis added).

[4] Madison, Federalist No. 51 (n 1) 251 (emphasis added).

[5] ibid 255 (emphasis added).

[6] ibid.

Once members of such a coalition realise their inability to cater to the evolving interests in their component constituents, and/or uncertainty creeps into their coalition, or when their resistance and domination attempts start to become increasingly difficult, the fate of the coalition takes one of two possible paths. Either they are slowly 'induced' to move to their second-best shot or common modicum across factions, which in many cases would be more equitable than the excessive pursuit of interests at the local level. This was the case with EU equal pay. Alternatively, when the pressure of other actors and inertia-disrupting factors come into play with the associated uncertainty (as discussed earlier), the ranks of the coalition witness 'growing apostasy'. This slowly erodes the anti-right coalition's core, paving the way for a pro-right intervention.[7] This was the case of the American southern coalition.

But how can private actors at the state level, who oppose minority rights, be 'gradually induced' to accept the new rights? They are not likely to give up without a fight; as comparative constitutional history reveals, resistance is likely, if not bound, to occur.[8] Racism and sexism are complex phenomena rooted in skewed views of the inferiority of certain races/sexes and long-harboured prejudices but also involving some tangible individual and group interests.[9] The redistributive policies of desegregation, equal pay, and affirmative action may very well affect members of the local majority. The group and self-interest involved are susceptible to tangible incentives,[10] and once central intervention becomes evidently assertive, the new calculus of interests often makes compliance with federally legislated equality not the worst option. Over time, compliance in turn contributes to softening some of these prejudices.[11]

However, to keep expectations realistic, a few caveats are explained after contrasting the two cases to remark that the Federalist No. 10 is neither linear nor mechanical. The improvement is only relative. Namely, softening prejudices does not mean elimination; thus, often racism turns into a softer form, yet lingers. Second, the systems usually apply to average opponents of race/sex equality rather than those with radical tendencies. This adds to the relative impartiality explained earlier and perhaps aligns with Madison's insistence on reducing rather than eliminating factionalism. Third, the social attitude shift does not happen overnight but often takes decades, as a brief examination of the two examples below illustrate.

[7] R Mann, *When Freedom Would Triumph: The Civil Rights Struggle in Congress, 1954–1968* (Baton Rouge, LSU Press, 2007) 238, 164–165. Mann refers to erstwhile proponents of civil rights unexpectedly switching sides; this includes Russell's three fellow Georgians; Dean Rusk, Atlanta Mayor and Ivan Allen.

[8] MJ Klarman, *Brown V. Board of Education and the Civil Rights Movement* (Oxford, Oxford University Press, 2007) ch 8.

[9] Mann (n 7) 164–165, 238; see also discussion in ch 5, s III.

[10] L Bobo and JR Kluegel, 'Opposition to Race-Targeting: Self-Interest, Stratification Ideology, or Racial Attitudes?' (1993) 58 *American Sociological Review* 443; DO Sears and CL Funk, 'The Role of Self-Interest in Social and Political Attitudes' (1991) 24 *Advances in Experimental Social Psychology* 1.

[11] ibid; see also text to notes 31–32.

A. The EU Equal Pay

France, seeking to preserve its economic interests, successfully 'insisted' on the inclusion of Article 119 (now Article 157, TFEU) to ensure equal pay between men and women in the Treaty of Rome, 1957.[12] The rationale was not to protect a right to equality. Rather, it stemmed from purely economic considerations to prevent 'social dumping'.[13] With free movement of goods, Member States whose legislation allows unequal pay would have an advantage over France by paying women less and, thus, producing at lower costs. Even with this narrow scope, the provision was 'poorly implemented' and lay *inert* in the community for almost two decades.[14] As discussed earlier, political events and activism as federalism's popular safeguard called into question the economic focus of the European project and its meagre social role, which led to the adoption of the Social Action Programme (1973).[15] The CJEU in *Defrenne II* (1976) recognised that equal pay does not only serve an economic purpose but also has social objectives; thus, paving the way for equality as an EU fundamental right. The Court declared the Article to be effective and, thus, empowering women to invoke it directly before domestic courts to challenge discriminatory national laws.[16]

'Coinciding'[17] with these judicial decisions, Equality Directives were proposed by the Commission, backed by the European Parliament.[18] However, some Member States, primarily the UK and Denmark, mounted resistance and used the Council (roughly the EU's federal chamber) to water down the proposals in order to approximate them to their national laws.[19] Worse still, most states did not even implement the directives. In its 1979 report, the Commission found that only two states had fully implemented the Equal Pay Directive.[20] This led the Commission to bring infringement procedures against seven Member States, including France itself, which initially proposed Article 119, and the UK as a main opponent.[21] Gradually, however, opposing states realised their lack

[12] Ca Barnard, *EU Employment Law*, 4th edn (Oxford, Oxford University Press, 2012) 254.
[13] ibid.
[14] J Pillinger, *Feminising the Market: Women's Pay and Employment in the European Community* (Cham, Springer, 2016) 84.
[15] E Ellis and P Watson, *EU Anti-Discrimination Law* (Oxford, Oxford University Press, 2012) 25; Barnard suggested that the promotion of equality by the ECJ has served to legitimise the Union and to strengthen political integration: C Barnard, 'The Principle of Equality in The Community Context: *P, Grant, Kalanke and Marschall*: Four Uneasy Bedfellows?' (1998) 57 *Cambridge Law Journal* 352.
[16] Case 43/75 *Defrenne v Sabena II* ECLI:EU:C:1976:56, [1976] ECR 455.
[17] M Bell, *Racism and Equality in the Euopean Union* (Oxford, Oxford University Press, 2008) 45.
[18] 'The first direct elections to the European Parliament in 1979 saw the highest proportion of women represented in the European Parliament': Pillinger (n 14) 69.
[19] AS Sweet, *The Judicial Construction of* Europe (Oxford, Oxford University Press, 2004)185; The UK, in particular, was determined to fit the directive into the UK Equal Pay Act 1970: Pillinger (n 14) 85.
[20] Pillinger ibid.
[21] Eg, Case 61/81 *Commission v UK* ECLI:EU:C:1982:258, [1982] ECR 2601; Pillinger (n 14) appx 4, 186–187.

of complete ability to control the outcome[22] and in the area of sex equality, the young European Community soon 'eclipse[d] the [ancient] British' and other European parliaments.[23]

Nothing better depicts the restraint in states' capacity to block change than their struggle to prevent extending equality to social security. Ironically, it was the Iron Lady's majoritarian government that spearheaded veto attempts to stall and block the legislation. As predicted in the Federalist argument, Thatcher and her allies, however, lost their ability to 'dominate' the outcome for a number of reasons. First, the CJEU constitutionalised sex equality by anchoring its reading of it into a treaty rather than a legislative provision.[24] Thus, it insulated its judgments from the possibility of reversal by the Council, making the only way to change its rulings through the treaty amendment. This way, an area falling under unanimous voting became subject to the CJEU's pen strokes. Moreover, inertia stood on the side of equality since coordinating a treaty amendment or court-packing is no easy task for European states with divergent agendas.[25]

Second, recognising the direct effect of Article 157, TFEU, allowed female workers to file cases across Europe for private gains as well as to challenge discriminatory national laws.[26] The involvement of national courts increased the political cost further for reluctant national governments. Third, and crucially important, was the role of activism and popular safeguards in securing 'post-judgement mobilisation' that raised the political cost of non-compliance for national governments.[27] The *Drake* case provides a suitable example. The case involved discrimination by granting allowances only for men who leave the workforce to care for disabled persons. Upon winning in the CJEU,[28] equality groups launched a media campaign and lobbied both houses of the UK Parliament.[29]

[22] A quote that best captures how things went out of the UK government's control is that made by the UK permanent representative to the Council of Ministers who noted that 'I don't think we would have agreed to this measure if we had known about the implications that it would have to the government now over the Equal Pay Act': quoted in Pillinger (n 14) 89.

[23] Sweet (n 19) 181.

[24] Eg, in 1987, the UK and France promised to veto the proposal to extend equality to occupational pensions. The ECJ, however, pre-empted their effort by its decision in Case C-262/88 *Barber* ECLI:EU:C:1990:209. Similarly, the draft legislation dealing, among other things, with maternity leave was stalled for years in the 1980s due to the veto of the UK. Once again, the Court pre-empted the legislature with its rulings in Case C-177/88 *Dekker* ECLI:EU:C:1990:383; and Case C-179/88 *Hertz* ECLI:EU:C:1990:384. See also the UK's arguments against constitutionalising equality of occupational pensions: Case 170/84, *Bilka Kaufhaus v Weber* ECLI:EU:C:1986:204 [1986] ECR 1607, para 13. For commentary, see Sweet (n 19) ch 4; Pillinger (n 14) 89 (remarking that the UK was the crucial veto point within the Council of Ministers on social provisions).

[25] K Alter, *The European Court's Political Power: Selected Essays* (Oxford, Oxford University Press, 2009) 111; C Harlow and R Rawlings, *Pressure through Law* (Abingdon, Routledge, 2013) 282.

[26] Sweet (n 19) 148; for a comparative account on how Member States were pressured into compliance, see A van der Vleuten, *The Price of Gender Equality:Member States and Governance in the European Union* (Abingdon, Routledge, 2016) chs 3 and 4.

[27] Alter (n 25) 111.

[28] Case 150/85 *Drake v Chief Adjudication Officer* ECLI:EU:C:1986:257, [1986] ECR 1995.

[29] Alter (n 25) 111; Harlow and Rawlings (n 25) 282.

The campaign made 'it politically too embarrassing for the supposedly family-oriented Conservative government' to deprive vulnerable and disabled caretakers of benefits. Consequently, the UK government extended benefits to women who leave the workforce to care for a disabled family member.[30]

As per private actors at the Member State level, employers preferred to pay damages for potential plaintiffs rather than restructuring their business on the basis of equal pay. However, the calculus changed as well as employers' preferences after *Marshall II*.[31] There, the CJEU held that victims of discrimination could rely on Article 6, Equal Treatment Directive, to override national laws placing a ceiling on compensation. A study found that in the two years following the implementation of *Marshall II*, the average award in sex discrimination cases rose more than fourfold from £2,940 to £12,172.[32] This contributed to making employers more willing to adjust to the EU policies.[33]

A counterfactual thought experiment of the *Marshall saga* helps illustrate why centralisation can be crucial for underprivileged groups. The defendant's and the UK's primary argument in that case focused on the *boundary question*, contending that the dispute concerned a matter of domestic law and, thus, fell outside the scope of EU law.[34] The Court rejected this reading of the relevant directive, instead offering an interpretation that brought the case within the ambit of EU law. But had the Court accepted the UK's argument and dismissed the claim as a domestic matter, Mrs Marshall would have been left without an effective remedy. Given the UK's doctrine of unfettered parliamentary sovereignty, the Act was otherwise unchallengeable, and legal reform would have depended entirely on the political will of the majority – potentially leaving generations subject to the existing legal framework. EU intervention in *Marshall* cases served to correct some of the market-driven inequalities as well.

Overall, and gradually, despite Member States' earlier reluctance to enforce equality, their economic interest shifted to ensure that others would adhere to equal pay to prevent comparative market advantage of cheaper production costs.[35] Clear evidence of the gradual inducement is that a few years later in subsequent

[30] ibid.

[31] Case C–271/91 *Marshall v Southampton and South-West Hants Area Health Authority (No 2)* ECLI:EU:C:1993:335, [1993] ECR I-4367.

[32] Alter (n 25) 169–170; The statutory maximum for race claims was removed by the Race Relations (Remedies) Act 1994.

[33] Alter (n 25) 169–170.

[34] Case 152/84 *Marshall v Southampton and South West Hampshire Area Health Authority (Teaching) (No. 1)* ECLI:EU:C:1986:84, para 29: 'The respondent considers that the provision of a State pension constitutes an aspect of social security and therefore falls within the scope not of Directive No 76/207 but of Directive No 79/7, which reserves to the Member States the right to impose different ages for the purpose of determining entitlement to State pensions.'

[35] The Equal pay article was adopted based on a French proposal tied to this economic purpose, yet it failed to push for harmonisation in the face of strong German opposition: see C Barnard, 'The Economic Objectives of Article 119' in T Hervey and D O'Keeffe (eds), *Sex Equality Law in the European Union* (Chichester, Wiley, 1996).

treaty revisions, Member States, despite having the chance to reverse the change, *unanimously opted for codifying the Court's jurisprudence* on equality, further stressing the role of Article 157, TFEU. They also adjusted their national laws to 'catch-up' with the Union's 'evolving jurisprudence'.[36] Many scholars concur that the Treaty of Rome opened avenues for sex equality that were not then possible through national systems.[37] By pitting the conflicting economic interests of Member States against each other, the treaty played a role in breaking the domestic majoritarian control over equal pay issues. This eventually led to a gradual shift in attitudes and perspectives.

B. The American Civil Rights

If one turns to the other side of the Atlantic, the well-known battle of American Civil Rights also aligns with the logic of the Federalist impartiality argument. First, the New-Deal structure, along with incorporation, equipped the federal umpire with the de facto jurisdiction to intervene. Then, black legal activism coupled with conducive external factors pushed the indifferent federal umpire from its inertia, which was best epitomised judicially by the *Brown* decision.[38] The legislator, however, took more time to be pushed out of inaction.[39] As the Congress contemplated engagement, white Southerners formed a strong coalition, mainly from Democrat and far-right Republican senates under the leadership of the 'racist', yet astute, former majority whip 'Richard Russell'.[40]

Lacking the power to veto, the coalition relied on 'filibuster', which is a parliamentary device utilised to block a vote on a Bill by a 'prolonged debate' derived from the Dutch word '*vrijbuiter*' meaning 'freebooter' 'plunderer' or 'pirate'.[41] The filibuster could be ended only when at least two-thirds of the senators agree to end discussion and bring the Bill to a vote, a step called 'cloture'. Given the difficulty of securing a two-thirds vote, for years the southern coalition used the device to defeat civil rights legislation and subsequently to leverage its terms to dilute the 'tepid' civil rights legislation in 1957.[42]

[36] Sweet (n 19) 194; Vleuten (n 26) chs 3 and 4.

[37] '[B]y accident rather than by design the signatories of the Treaty of Rome had the laid the foundation for development of EC policy for women': Pillinger (n 14) 81; France's 'foot-in-the-door' negotiating stance when the original TEC was being drafted, therefore, paid off in a way which could hardly have been anticipated in 1957: Ellis and Watson (n 15) 26.

[38] *Brown v Board of Education* 347 US 483 (1954).

[39] On why the Congress lagged far behind, see M Klarman, *From Jim Crow to Civil Rights: The Supreme Court And the Struggle for Racial Equality* (Oxford, Oxford University Press, 2006) 451.

[40] Russell told Business Week: 'I'm not an anthropologist, but I've studied history. And there is no case in history of a mongrel race preserving a civilization, much less creating one.': Quoted in Mann (n 7) 181.

[41] ibid 34.

[42] Klarman (n 39) 325.

However, seven years later, a sequence of events and the joint impact of diverse factors had significantly eroded the southern coalition.[43] This includes a multiplicity of actors with different incentives and skills, such as President Johnson's shrewd bargaining, Dirksen, the leader of the Republicans' flexibility, Martin Luther King's activism, religious groups' lobbying, and brewing unrest, as well as conducive socio-political factors domestically and globally and their impact on public opinion.[44] Russell and his southern allies were disturbed by '*the growing apostacy in their own ranks*' and bitterly complained that their alliance no longer 'fought civil rights in *concert*'.[45] Eventually, after the longest filibuster in American history (three months), the Senate passed the Civil Rights Act, 1964, 'the most sweeping civil rights measure in the past century'.[46]

The Act, among other things, banned segregation in hotels, motels, and restaurants.[47] It also prohibited discrimination in private employment. It addressed discriminatory practices on the basis of race, colour, religion, or national origin as well as sex.[48] A year later, there was momentum to adopt the 1965 Voting Rights Act, eliminating state measures that disenfranchised African Americans.[49] As the Supreme Court upheld the Act and further 'completed the destruction' of the poll tax by its decision in *Harper*, hundreds and thousands of new voters were registered by 1966.[50] Shortly afterwards, the Civil Rights Act 1968, commonly known as the Fair Housing Act, was approved. The Act banned discrimination in the sale of houses, which maintained a de facto segregation of neighbourhoods.

The acts, mainly the first two, introduced what Sunstein terms a 'dramatic shift' from exclusive reliance on 'compensatory' adjudication to administration,[51] through relying on 'a new set' of agencies to enforce racial justice.[52] This included the Equal Employment Opportunity Commission ('EEOC'), the Department

[43] See generally CW Whalen and B Whalen, *The Longest Debate: A Legislative History of the 1964 Civil Rights Act* (Santa Ana, Seven Locks Press, 1989); DB Rodriguez and BR Weingast, 'The Positive Political Theory of Legislative History: New Perspectives on the 1964 Civil Rights Act and Its Interpretation' (2003) 151 *University of Pennsylvania Law Review* 1417; Mann (n 7).

[44] Eg, polls revealed that the percentage of those who deemed civil rights to be the nation's most urgent issue rose from 4% before Birmingham to 52% afterward: Klarman (n 39) 436.

[45] Mann (n 7) 164–65, 238 (emphasis added) referring to erstwhile proponents of civil rights unexpectedly shifting camps.

[46] ibid citing Congressional *Quarterly Weekly Report* (14 February 1964) 2/14/64, 293.

[47] *Katzenbach v McClung* 379 US 294 (1964). On the same day, the Court upheld the Civil Rights Act as it applied to hotels, in *Heart of Atlanta Motel, Inc. v United States* 379 US 241 (1964).

[48] On the historical debate on how sex was included in the Act, see S Mayeri, 'Intersectionality and Title VII: A Brief (Pre-)History' (2015) 95 *Boston University Law Review* 713.

[49] Upon challenge, the Court upheld the Act based on Congress' section five power to enforce the 'Reconstruction Amendment' in *Katzenbach v Morgan* 384 US 641 (1966). Regretfully, half a century later, the Supreme court undermined a significant part of the Act in *Shelby County, Ala. v Holder* 570 US 529 (2013).

[50] *Harper v Virginia Bd of Elections* 383 US 663 (1966).

[51] CR Sunstein, *The Partial Constitution* (Cambridge, MA, Harvard University Press, 1993) 322.

[52] B Ackerman, *We the People, Volume 3: The Civil Rights Revolution* (Cambridge, MA, Harvard University Press, 2014) 154.

of Housing and Urban Development ('HUD'), and the Department of Health, Education, and Welfare ('HEW'), which all 'crafted' creative 'administrative setups' to achieve equality across different spheres of life.[53] The new governance model has significantly aided and complemented private and judicial enforcement in revolutionising racial equality, and since then, 'overt discrimination went underground'.[54]

The point is that a combination of factors and divergent interests leading up to the enactment of the said acts would not have been possible had minority-related matters been left to the regulation of southern states, where the pursuit of local majorities' 'immoderate' interests loomed large. This led decentralisation and state autonomy in America to be tainted, in the minds of many, by a 'charge of racism'. Civil rights have come to 'represent a defeat' to state autonomy, and numerous scholars at the time saw the decline of state authority as 'a cause for celebration'.[55]

If we look at the popular level, as is well-known, opponents of desegregation mounted 'massive resistance' in the decade following *Brown*. However, as the federal intervention became assertive, attitudes started to change for the main bulk of white opponents, excluding radicals.[56] Regarding school desegregation, Klarman noted that preference shifted to the second-best. Unlike extreme racists, moderate whites, whose top preference was to reject desegregation, still would prefer integration to school closures. The federal intervention meant that resistance would lead to school closure, and thus, their preference shifted to embracing desegregation. More importantly, the 1964 Civil Rights Act mandated school desegregation as a condition of receiving federal funds, or else they risk costly litigation. Given that the South was the poorer region, this carrot/stick incentive carried through 'HEW' policy guidelines,[57] coupled with 'judicial prodding', proved remarkably effective.[58] Many defiant southern schools started to de-segregate at a higher pace.

Similar changes occurred in businesses as well as on social fronts. Among the incentive measures used for businesses was the 'contract compliance' policy, which required 'contractors of the federal government to increase the representation of [women, racial and religious] minorities' in their workforces as a condition

[53] ibid 154–55 and 169: see discussion on the shift to 'government by numbers' and 'statistic of hope'; for an informative overview of the Acts and the role of administrative enforcement, see CJ Back, *The Civil Rights Act of 1964: An Overview* (Congressional Research Service, 2020) 80, 33 ff.

[54] LM Friedman, *A History of American Law*, 4th edn (Oxford, Oxford Universirty Press, 2019) 685.

[55] RA Schapiro, *Polyphonic Federalism: Toward the Protection of Fundamental Rights* (Chicago, University of Chicago Press, 2009) 47.

[56] Klarman noted that resistance only ended after Eisenhower had showed willingness to use federal troops. Although the deployment of these forces 'bolstered massive resistance in the short term'. Klarman (n 39) 187.

[57] HEW Guidelines are established by the Office of Education, Department of Health, Education and Welfare (HEW), for use in qualifying school districts for the receipt of the federal funds.

[58] Schapiro (n 55) 45.

for the 'award and the continuation of the contract'.[59] A survey of 53 cities found 'widespread compliance' with the Civil Rights Act and business leaders advertising the urgency of compliance with law.[60]

On a broader social front, while incentives opened an avenue for compliance, the resulting interracial contact is empirically associated with an increase in tolerant attitudes.[61] This has come to be known as 'inter-group contact theory'.[62] The 'contact theory' even made it to the Supreme Court, which, until recently, relied on this theory and its evidence for encouraging diversity in higher education.[63] Court aside, broader social research noted that already by the 1980s, 'the American public now nearly unanimously endorses the idea that blacks should have opportunity equal to whites for jobs and schooling'.[64] Even in the army context, surveys found that whites who served in integrated 'combat units underwent profound changes' in their racial attitudes.[65] The point is that overall federal intervention and incentives facilitated interracial contact, which in turn increased tolerance and softened, albeit not eliminated, racism at the popular level. This may not have been possible had minority rights been left within states' prerogative without federal intervention.[66]

The workability of the Madisonian argument is not limited to the experience of African American minorities but extends to a broader range of cases which has been judicially acknowledged[67] and academically examined.[68] While space precludes a detailed examination of these examples, a brief reference to judicial recognition will suffice. In *City of Richmond*, Justice Scalia invoked Madison's argument, offering an extensive survey of what he described as the 'prophesy' concerning the 'dangers of [factional]oppression' at the state level.[69] He observed that '[a]n acute awareness of the heightened danger of oppression from political factions in small, rather than large, political units dates to the very beginning of

[59] S Fredman, *Discrimination Law* (Oxford, Oxford University Press, 2011) 334.

[60] Mann (n 7) 218.

[61] CT Clotfelter, *After Brown: The Rise and Retreat of School Desegregation* (Princeton, Princeton University Press, 2006) 190–200; Bobo and Kluegel (n 10) 460.

[62] CG Ellison and DA Powers, 'The Contact Hypothesis and Racial Attitudes Among Black Americans' (1994) 75 *Social Science Quarterly* 385 (defining the contact hypothesis as the belief that 'particularly close and sustained contact, with members of different cultural groups promotes positive, tolerant attitudes').

[63] *Grutter v Bollinger* 539 US 306 (2003), paras 326–327; *cf* MA Graber, 'Harvard's Diversity Chicken Comes Home to Roost' (*Verfassungsblog*, 9 July 2023) verfassungsblog.de/harvards-diversity-chicken-comes-home-to-roost/ accessed 3 August 2025.

[64] Clotfelter (n 61) 190-200.

[65] Klarman (n 8) 47.

[66] For an analysis of the decision, see M Adams, 'Shifting Sands: The Jurisprudence of Integration Past, Present, and Future' (2004) 47 *Howard Law Journal* 795, 823–825.

[67] *City of Richmond v JA Croson Co* 488 US 469 (1989) (Scalia J, concurring).

[68] D Halberstam, 'Federalism: Theory, Policy, Law' in M Rosenfeld and A Sajó (eds), *The Oxford Handbook of Comparative Constitutional Law* (Oxford, Oxford University Press, 2012) 592; see also M Moussa, 'The Shackles of Veto: The American Parallel of Art 19 Tfeu and Its Tension with Procedural Justice' (2023) 25 *Cambridge Yearbook of European Legal Studies* 122.

[69] *City of Richmond v JA Croson Co* 488 US 469 (1989) (Scalia J, concurring).

our national history.'[70] The examples he surveyed included state-level discrimination against 'Chinese'[71] and 'Hispanic' minorities, among others.[72]

C. Clarifications, Qualifications, and Rebuttals

Having briefly sketched the two experiences, a clarification is due on why rights should be placed on the central floor and not at ceiling level. This is followed by a few caveats on the scope of the impartiality argument, as well as engagement with some of the critical literature of the *nemo judex* argument.

i. Why Federal Floor, not Ceiling?

The implication of the Federalist impartiality argument is that minority rights should be positioned within the central floor level, rather than the ceiling. However, it is important not to mistakenly interpret this implication as advocating for maximum centralisation; that would lead to replacing constituent states with a unitary 'superstate', relegating states to mere enforcers of central laws.[73] Such an interpretation would be erroneous, both conceptually and empirically.

First, to conceptually distinguish federalism from mere administrative decentralisation, states must retain a consistent legislative role. Central ceilings – where states are barred from going further – should be reserved for cases where unity or uniformity is at serious risk. More importantly, the impartiality argument itself may support this point. The legislative contribution of states plays a significant role in overcoming inertia, which was latent in the Madisonian syllogism. We saw that state resistance or friction between states has sometimes contributed to jolting the federal umpire out of inertia.[74] Many contended that the existence of states with diffused powers, while facilitating 'prolonged resistance', eventually led to a more durable result.[75] They served to 'impede and ultimately promote' the outcome once black Americans started to incrementally assume a role in state and local institutions.[76]

The states' crucial role has philosophical roots, too. The complexity of federal-state dynamics is what makes it well-suited to the mixed human nature highlighted

[70] ibid.

[71] *Yick Wo v Hopkins* 118 US 356 (1886).

[72] *Hernandez v Texas* 347 US 475 (1954).

[73] N MacCormick, *Questioning Sovereignty: Law, State, and Nation in the European Commonwealth* (Oxford, Oxford University Press, 1999) 191; similarly, see DL Shapiro, *Federalism: A Dialogue* (Evanston, Northwestern University Press, 1995) 71–106; Schapiro (n 55). In the EU, see K Lenaerts, 'Some Thoughts on the State of the European Union as a Rights-Based Legal Order' [2014] *Revue de droit de l'Union européenne* 71.

[74] See earlier discussion on inertia.

[75] DJ Elazar, *American Federalism: A View from the States* (New York, Longman, 1984) 11–14.

[76] Shapiro (n 73) 105.

in the Federalist argument. Contrary to the view of a 'unity' of 'the constitutional soul' preached by nation-states' intellectual forefathers,[77] Elazar notes that '[f]ederalism can be seen as consistent with … the human personality [which] is forged out of the interaction of several components that may pull in contradictory directions. Patterns of personal behaviour are forged out of the resolution of these contradictions.'[78] Indeed, 'monopoly on coercion [is] truly broken', says Rapaczynski, 'only in a system in which some forms of governmental authority exist independently from one another, and not as emanation from a single source of legitimate power'.[79]

Secondly, once central intervention sets the tone and removes the harms of partiality, it provides a corrective force to reorient the federal feature of *jurisdictional competition*.[80] Analogously, this is why we speak of a *minimum wage* (a floor), not *uniform wages* (a ceiling). States normally attempt to attract capital and workers through offering more attractive environments. We saw how states used to compete to lower women's pay to keep lower production costs. Once the EU placed minimum rules of engagement, the tone shifted to ensuring equal protection, which was followed by other states.[81] Some states continue to go above the federal floor and offer more protective work-related rights to women. The rich literature on competitive federalism shows that for this dynamic to function equitably, states must retain legislative autonomy – hence, the case for a federal floor rather than a ceiling.

Thirdly, while many states are more prone to majority-friendly laws, occasionally a few states may have, for cultural, social, historical, or economic reasons, minority protective norms which may inform the federal floor or help spark change. We have seen that France, out of economic motivation, unknowingly infused the seed of equal pay in the EU. New Jersey, in 1947, had already passed a constitutional amendment banning school segregation seven years before *Brown*.[82] It is for the combination of these reasons that minority rights should be kept in *the centralised floor* category, where the federal standards serve as a *safety net*, leaving states free to diverge above.[83]

[77] J Tully, *Strange Multiplicity: Constitutionalism in an Age of Diversity* (Cambridge, Cambridge University Press, 1995).

[78] DJ Elazar, *Exploring Federalism* (Tuscaloosa, University of Alabama Press, 1987) 30.

[79] A Rapaczynski, 'From Sovereignty to Process: The Jurisprudence of Federalism after Garcia' [1985] *Supreme Court Review* 341, 390; for the argument that states may still check the federal government even 'where they lack autonomy', see J Bulman-Pozen and HK Gerken, 'Uncooperative Federalism' (2008) 118 *Yale Law Journal* 1256, 1263.

[80] R Vaubel, 'Enforcing Competition among Governments' [1999] *Constitutional Political Economy* 10, 327.

[81] Literature also shows that states play a crucial role in checking the abuse of the federal executive and/or the risk of lobby groups capturing the reigns of the federal government. Rapaczynsk (n 79) 380–389; J Bulman-Pozen, 'Federalism as a Safeguard of the Separation of Powers' (2012) 112 *Columbia Law Review* 459.

[82] Klarman (n 39) 105–106 listing examples of few states initiating desegregation before *Brown*.

[83] Beyond minority rights, states often offer a better locus for rights, pluralism, and redundancy that is suited to ideological conflict, which will be examined in the next chapter.

ii. Qualifications

While the previous section established the workability of the impartiality argument through comparative examples, three caveats must be addressed:

Firstly, the increase in impartiality is not necessarily continuous/linear. To echo Ackerman's remark, the constitutional structure is 'not an Enlightenment machine that can operate flawlessly'.[84] Inertia is one of two possible logical outcomes of the impartiality argument. Safeguards, popular vigilance, and external factors help ensure the constitutional outcome will not fall somewhere between Madison's 'wicked factions and a blessed coalition'.[85] The Madisonian argument seeks to reduce, rather than eliminate, causes of bias. Inertia can always reassert itself, as it did gradually in the United States.[86] It is true that while the Civil Rights era revolutionised race in America, racism remains 'a powerful force', and in many spheres racial disparities are evident.[87] Similarly, in Europe, the pay gap as 'a moving target'[88] persists despite improvement.[89]

Secondly, a brief note is warranted on the impact of the rise of the two-party system on Madison's argument.[90] The literature on this is vast, but a few remarks must suffice. Scholarship is divided: some argue that the emergence of strong parties renders Madison's theory 'obsolete',[91] while others maintain the Madisonian analysis 'never lost its thrust'.[92] In my view, a strong party system can place some pressure on the requirement of fluid diversification of interests that underpins the federal impartiality argument – particularly where parties are strong enough to discipline legislators who deviate from the party line. Yet, this does not necessarily

[84] Ackerman (n 52) 61.

[85] M White, *Philosophy, the Federalist, and the Constitution* (Oxford, Oxford University Press, 1989) 165–166.

[86] Clotfelter (n 61) 183, explaining how federal forces and NAACP 'gradually lost their resolve' to press the case for desegregation. Similarly, see analysis of 'betrayal' of the Supreme Court to the civil rights era by the *Shelby County* decision in Ackerman (n 52) 330–437; PI Rose, *The Unsteady March: The Rise and Decline of Racial Equality in America* (Chicago, University of Chicago Press, 2001) 5 (describing the march as 'two steps forward one back').

[87] Friedman (n 54) 685–687.

[88] J O'Reilly and others, 'Equal Pay as a Moving Target: International Perspectives on Forty-Years of Addressing the Gender Pay Gap' (2015) 39 *Cambridge Journal of Economics* 299.

[89] Women are paid 16.3% lower than their male counterparts; see 'Gender Pay Gap Statistics' (*EUROSTAT*, March 2022) ec.europa.eu/eurostat/statistics-explained/index.php/Gender_pay_gap_statistics accessed 3 August 2025.

[90] See generally R Hofstadter, *The Idea of a Party System: The Rise of Legitimate Opposition in the United States, 1780–1840* (Oakland, University of California Press, 1969); for analysis of the late Madison writing on parties, see JN Rakove, *A Politician Thinking: The Creative Mind of James Madison* (Oklahoma, University of Oklahoma Press, 2017) vol 14, 187–191.

[91] Most notably, Calhoun's critique of the 'errors' of the 'plan of the convention' analysed in J Read, *Majority Rule versus Consensus* (Lawrence, Kansas University Press, 2009) 49; see generally R Muirhead and NL Rosenblum, 'The Uneasy Place of Parties in the Constitutional Order' in M Tushnet, MA Graber and S Levinson (eds), *The Oxford Handbook of the United States Constitution* (Oxford, Oxford University Press, 2016) 225.

[92] Reformulating H Wechsler, 'The Political Safeguards of Federalism: The Role of the States in the Composition and Selection of the National Government' (1954) 54 *Columbia Law Review* 543, 545; see CR Sunstein, 'Interest Groups in American Public Law' (1985) 38 *Stanford Law Review* 29.

vitiate the logic of Madison's argument. As many have shown, parties in the United States are not monolithic factions, and they are 'markedly decentralized'.[93] They contain, in effect, 'parties within parties' – or *factions within factions*.[94] As previously noted, major civil rights votes cut across both Republican and Democratic lines, a pattern that recurs in many contemporary controversies. More importantly, for present purposes, this challenge does not carry over to the EU, where the party system remains 'half-baked'.[95]

Thirdly, returning to the analogy between human nature and decision-making, flawed outcomes can stem from more than just bias – and even bias arises from multiple sources that the Federalist argument does not fully address. Following Galligan's taxonomy, bias can be traced to three main causes: (i) 'personal' bias, the classical application of *nemo judex* in administrative law; (ii) 'group' bias, rooted in natural affinity toward one's group or shared experiences – addressed in the previous chapter through the lens of institutional *nemo judex*; and (iii) 'cognitive' bias,[96] encompassing unexamined assumptions, reasoning errors, and influence from dominant but inaccurate 'information cascades'[97] or social misconceptions.

The federal impartiality argument is limited only to the excessive pursuit of personal or group interest, not other distortions in judgment, especially cognitive biases. Madison recognised the importance of enhancing deliberation to mitigate similar errors in reasoning through improved representation, but he was disappointed with the outcomes during his time, referring to the elected representatives as a 'very scanty proportion who will share in the drudgery of business'.[98] More broadly, contemporary scholarship cautions against relying on legal structure alone to combat discrimination, given the enduring role of extra-legal forces.[99] A fortiori, the limits of procedural or structural theories – such as the Federalist's vision of impartiality – must be acknowledged, however vital their role.[100]

[93] L Kramer, 'Understanding Federalism Symposium: Federalism's Future' (1994) 47 *Vanderbilt Law Review* 1485 1524–1528.

[94] See D DiSalvo, *Engines of Change: Party Factions in American Politics, 1868-2010* (Oxford, Oxford University Press, 2012); D DiSalvo, 'Party Factions and American Politics' (*National Affairs*, Summer 2025) www.nationalaffairs.com/publications/detail/party-factions-and-american-politics accessed 3 August 2025.

[95] RD Kelemen, 'The European Union's Authoritarian Equilibrium' (2020) 27 *Journal of European Public Policy* 481, 489.

[96] DJ Galligan, *Due Process and Fair Procedures: A Study of Administrative Procedures* (Oxford, Clarendon Press, 1996) 438–440.

[97] CR Sunstein and EA Posner, 'The Law of Other States' (2006) 59 *Stanford Law Review* 162.

[98] Upon scanning the list of his colleagues of elected members in the House, Madison wrote 'a very scanty proportion who will share in the drudgery of business'. Madison to Edmund Randolph, March 1, 1789, PJM, 11: 453; see also Rakove (n 90) 155. While impartiality may not directly tackle cognitive bias, the diversity fostered by integrative federalism can help disrupt entrenched assumptions and error cascades – provided the context avoids polarisation and decision-makers remain open to self-correction, something explored more in ch 5.

[99] 'Ellis and Watson (n 15) 8; Klarman (n 39) 476 'white supremacy ultimately depended more on extra-legal forces than on law'.

[100] Madison did seem to acknowledge that constitutional design alone is 'insufficient to control the caprice and wickedness of man': Madison, *Federalist No. 57* 281. Likewise, Hamilton noted, 'it would

iii. Rebuttals of Some Nemo Judex *Scepticism*

Some constitutional law literature, such as Vermeule's 'Contra Nemo Iudex', doubts partly the importance of the *nemo judex* rule in public law, while others in political science circles, such as Dahl, denounce the Madisonian argument *in toto*. Both are discussed in turn.

Vermeule offers a ranging analysis of the *nemo judex* rule in American public law fused with some comparative insights. On the one hand, the argument of this book partly concurs with Vermeule's on the point of optimisation of values when impartiality is unattainable or costly in order to account for the greater good, which he illustrates through brilliant examples.[101] On the other hand, I disagree with Vermeule on a few issues raised in his article, which lead him to label the *nemo judex* rule a 'banal counsel',[102] and its use as intellectual 'burping'.[103]

First, implicit in Vermeule's analysis is a conflation of the nature of *nemo judex* as both an instrumental and institutional rule with norms that are categorical and individual. This is epitomised by his comparison between the *nemo judex* rule and the rule against 'intentional murder' to demonstrate that the former, unlike the latter, is not a robust rule.[104] However, this comparison is inaccurate because banning murder is substantive or categorical, but *nemo judex* is mainly procedural. Unlike substantive rules, procedural rules are usually means to other goals.[105] For instance, the requirement of impartiality is a means to attain sound decision-making, and similarly, the requirement of confrontation is more conducive to the attainment of truth, at least according to mainstream interpretation.

To illustrate the difference, contrasting the sanction of violating procedural laws compared to substantive laws can be helpful. Many procedural laws explicitly require a certain harm to be proven for nullity or allow rectification if the purpose of the rule was attained despite violation, as can be seen from the famous UK's 'no difference principle', among other comparative examples.[106] Therefore, it is understandable to see a more flexible teleological approach to violations of procedural rules compared to substantive norms. A flaw in service would be rectified if the defendant somehow knew about the case and appeared before the court. Whereas a victim dodging a bullet would not rectify the violation or the charge of attempted murder.

Relatedly, in constitutional politics, the *nemo judex* rule applies collectively and in corporate capacities, as Vermeule himself made clear by rejecting narrower,

be idle' to blame the constitution for not attaining 'impossibilities' Hamilton, *Federalist No 16* 112. An interesting avenue for future exploration is whether the impartial collective judge is more effective when complemented by a comprehensive theory of group rights.

[101] A Vermeule, 'Veil of Ignorance Rules in Constitutional Law' [2001] *Yale Law Journal* 399, 415.

[102] ibid 389.

[103] ibid 384.

[104] ibid 384.

[105] Contrast the non-instrumental view, see, eg, TRS Allan, 'Procedural Fairness and the Duty of Respect' (1998) 18 *Oxford Journal of Legal Studies* 497.

[106] Eg, The UK Senior Courts Act 1981, s 31(2B); French Procedural Code, arts 114–115.

exclusively individual formulations of the maxim.[107] However, he then used the example of the rule of killing on an individual level to compare it to that of *nemo judex*. The comparison does not hold if one takes the rule against killing to the institutional or corporate level, as in cases of dissolving a corporation or dismantling a union, as in the USSR, or what political scientists term 'kill[ing] an organisation'.[108]

On a more exegetical note, Vermeule argues that Madison used the *nemo judex* rule in a metaphorical sense, which meant 'multiplying rather than attempting to reduce' violation of the rule.[109] This interpretation conflates the distinction between *impulse* and *action*. Federal integration indeed multiplies the *impulses* of bias – by incorporating more groups with their particular interests and predispositions – but it does not necessarily multiply *actions* based on those impulses. On the contrary, centralisation often reduces the number of legislative outcomes. One federal legislative act replaces what could have been many disparate – and potentially biased – state laws. If Vermeule's reading were correct, and centralisation multiplied violations of the *nemo judex* principle, one must wonder why the Contract Clause lodges debt relief with the federal government, where only one piece of legislation will be issued compared to multiple state laws. Multiplication would be more abundant by empowering states to legislate. Why would it increase when the decision is made at the federal level but not in the several states where the same legislation will undergo a pre-decision process 13 times?

Additionally, Vermeule's famous use of the fallacy of composition argument can be redeployed against his sceptical view of Madison's impartiality argument.[110] The fallacy refers to wrongly inferring that a certain property is true of the whole from the fact that it is true of some part of the whole. To take an example, knowing that the components of water (hydrogen and oxygen) are dry does not entail that water, too, is dry. The fact that constituent members of an institution are motivated by selfish or non-neutral motives does not entail that the institutional decision is also non-neutral. Recall Madison's analogy between the institutional mind, akin to the human mind, as well as Kramer's parent example, deciding between two children who have two opposite stakes, helps induce impartiality. Likewise, having two opposite stakes (represented by different members) may induce impartiality in the institutional mind, akin to Kramer's example for the human mind, subject to the caveats explained earlier.

Further, in contending that Madison's argument lacks an enforcement mechanism, Vermeule overlooks the role of uncertainty as a useful 'mechanism' as well as the role of the 'public good' as a common modicum for divergent forces, at least

[107] Vermeule (n 101) 392–394.

[108] M Eilstrup-Sangiovanni, 'What Kills International Organisations? When and Why International Organisations Terminate' (2020) 27 *European Journal of International Relations* 281.

[109] ibid.

[110] A Vermeule, 'The Judiciary Is a They, Not an It: Interpretive Theory and the Fallacy of Division New Perspectives on Statutory Interpretation' (2004) 14 *Journal of Contemporary Legal Issues* 549.

within the limited conditions discussed in the previous chapter.[111] This oversight seems puzzling, given Vermeule's subsequent leading scholarly work on the two notions of 'uncertainty'[112] and the 'common good', albeit in different contexts.[113] That being said, Vermeule does offer a thorough critique of Madison's work on the horizontal inter-branch separation of powers, which is beyond the scope of this book.[114]

Another genre of critique invoked against the Federalist No. 10 comes from Dahl, among others, noting that 'smaller countries are no more vulnerable to the evils of faction than the larger ones'.[115] He further supported his critique by referring to Scandinavian countries and the Netherlands as examples of small states with less factious ambience compared to large ones.[116] Such critiques, as Ostrom notes, miss the fact that integrative federalism is not merely about enlarging the size of the polity, but rather its complex and 'overlapping' structure, which distinguishes an integrative federation from other large unitary or decentralised states.[117] By focusing on the size of the republic alone, Dahl's argument and its ilk overlook federalism's dynamics of 'overlapping units of power', which have been discussed earlier with regard to the central floor and jurisdictional competition point.[118]

More importantly, such critiques rest on an overestimation of the value and reality of nation-states' promised 'homogeneity'.[119] Dahl notes, for instance, that '[Madison] overlooked the costs of heterogeneity and the advantages of homogeneity.'[120] However, this homogeneity, as many have noted, has always been an unfulfilled ideal which has even increasingly come under more strain in our multicultural world.[121] Seen from the prism of minority vs majority conflicts, if it

[111] A Vermeule, *The System of the Constitution* (Oxford, Oxford University Press, 2011) 42.

[112] A Vermeule, 'Veil of Ignorance Rules in Constitutional Law' (2001) 111 *Yale Law Journal* 399.

[113] A Vermeule, *Common Good Constitutionalism* (Cambridge, Polity Press, 2022).

[114] Contrast this with the other view that separation of powers was just an ancillary mechanism after the Federalist No. 10 as well as 'dependence on the people' which may be linked to the previous discussion on inertia: DJ Levinson and RH Pildes, 'Separation of Parties, Not Powers' (2005) 119 *Harvard Law Review* 2312, 2319.

[115] RA Dahl, *A Preface to Democratic Theory* (Chicago, University of Chicago Press, 2006) 168, quoting A Alesina and others, *The Size of Nations* (Cambridge, MA, MIT Press, 2003) 15: 'Our main argument [is] that democratization, trade liberalization, and reduction of warfare are associated with the formation of small countries, whereas historically the collapse of free trade, dictatorships, and wars arc associated with large countries.'

[116] ibid.

[117] V Ostrom and B Allen, *The Political Theory of a Compound Republic: Designing the American Experiment*, 2nd edn (New York, Lexington Books, 2008) 83–85: 'some have read Madison's observation as applying only to the extent of the republic'.

[118] Such critiques confuse integrative federalism which could improve minority rights and devolutionary federalism whose role is more questionable. 'Transnational federalism is the mirror image of federalism within a country.' Dahl (n 116) 98.

[119] Dahl (n 6) 168. Contra Dahl, it should be noted that federalism is premised on intertwining unity and diversity. Thus, diversity is a positive force if it is kept within the implication of size principle and its requirement of effectiveness and agreement on minimum tenets of solidarity required for the body politics to function.

[120] ibid 168.

[121] See generally Tully (n 77).

is true that a few small states maintain a protective level of minorities, the fact is that many do not.[122]

This is not confined to southern American states in the 1960s or the Global South, but to many western democracies, which Dahl celebrates as factionless homogenous societies. This chapter, for instance, has shown that equal pay was not protected in many European countries (including the Netherlands and Denmark) until the European Community's intervention. Ethnic and religious minorities remain a challenge across many states in Europe, including those Dahl idealised, as seen in the recent Danish Ghetto Law, which will be discussed shortly.[123] The contribution of properly functioning integrative federalism is to bring more states to protect their minorities, as happened in the EU and the US. Where a component state already upholds a minority-friendly legal and institutional framework, it functions like the healthy part of a constitutional body – one that does not require the Madisonian remedy for this specific area. It may, however, need it for other benefits associated with federalism.

Either way, speaking of the challenge of European racial minorities, the next section explores why the struggle of minorities in many EU states was not resolved through the Federalist argument, despite the existence of an EU central competence over minorities. This will also help revisit another critique of Dahl's of the Federalist argument, which he mistakenly saw as providing 'a convenient rationalization' for the state vetoes and unanimous voting.[124]

III. Why Impartiality does not Fully Work for Protecting EU Minorities?

To 'combat discrimination based on sex, racial or ethnic origin', among other grounds, Article 19, TFEU, requires unanimity of Member States in Council (which is the EU equivalent to a federal chamber).[125] Although the EU was armed with this centralising competence a quarter century ago, the legislative pool for this article remains relatively dry. This competence has been exercised only twice and was mainly due to an 'unusual twist of political fate'[126] or an external factor, as others term it.[127] In February 2000, Jörg Haider's radical right-wing party was

[122] Eg, 'Nation-states are, by disposition, integrationist, or assimilationist. They are the role models in world politics': S Choudhry, *Constitutional Design for Divided Societies: Integration or Accommodation?* (Oxford, Oxford University Press, 2008) 87.

[123] More recently, see Case C-417/23 *Slagelse Almennyttige Boligselskab – Afdeling Schackenborgvænge and Others v Ministry of Transport and Housing* (2025) (Danish Ghetto Case).

[124] Dahl (n 115) 168.

[125] Treaty on the Functioning of the European Union, art 19.

[126] M Bell, 'The Principle of Equal Treatment: Widening and Deepening' in P Craig and G de Búrca (eds), *The Evolution of EU Law*, 2nd edn (Oxford, Oxford University Press, 2011) 618.

[127] See ch 3's discussion on inertia; see also the term defined in Z Elkins, TGinsburg and James M, *The Endurance of National Constitutions* (Cambridge, Cambridge University Press, 2009).

elected to the Austrian government, which evoked a call for a reaction from the EU and prompted 'the fast-tracking' of the Commission's proposal for a directive on discrimination on grounds of racial or ethnic origin.[128] In June 2000, Member States adopted the Racial Equality Directive ('RED').[129] Shortly afterwards, the Union 'moved swiftly to complement'[130] this with the Framework for Employment Equality Directive ('FED'), which extended the prohibition of discrimination with regard to employment and to the grounds of 'religion or belief, disability, age, and sexual orientation'.[131]

Yet, more than two decades afterwards, and despite some 'symbolic'[132] improvement,[133] the EU is described as 'minority agnostic' with a 'skin deep' commitment[134] and unable to 'rectify historical inequalities'.[135] For example, the Commission's legislative proposal to extend protection against discrimination on grounds covered by FED beyond work has failed to pass since 2008. If the American Civil Rights Act 1964's three-month filibuster earned the title of 'longest debate in history', how may the Commission's proposal be described, having been in negotiation for more than 13 years?[136]

As EU law stands, it seems 'lawful' to deny services to someone manifesting a religious symbol, be it a Sikh turban, a Jewish yarmulke, or a Muslim headscarf.[137] Moreover, the EU's six million Roma minorities are still facing 'de facto' segregation in education, housing, and other spheres of life.[138] They underwent a fait accompli of inhuman expulsion by French authorities in 2010.[139] Statistics still

[128] Bell (n 126) 618.

[129] Council Directive (EC) 2000/43 implementing the principle of equal treatment between persons irrespective of racial or ethnic origin [2000] OJ L180/22. On how the Directive was adopted despite unanimity; it was argued that the new Austrian government 'would not dare oppose the Race Directive out of fear that this would legitimize the reproach of the government by the other fourteen member states … [as] a racist party' and if other Member States sought to oppose the proposal, 'they would be blamed and shamed for not putting their political power where their mouth is'. TE Givens and RE Case, *Legislating Equality: The Politics of Antidiscrimination Policy in Europe* (Oxford, Oxford University Press, 2014) 85.

[130] Bell (n 126) 618.

[131] Council Directive (EC) 2000/78 establishing a general framework for equal treatment in employment and occupation OJ L303/16.

[132] M Goodwin, 'Romani Marginalisation after the Race Equality Directive' in U Belavusau and K Henrard (eds), *EU Anti-Discrimination Law Beyond Gender* (Oxford, Hart Publishing, 2019) 179.

[133] M Möschel, 'Eighteen Years of Race Equality Directive: A Mitigated Balance' in U Belavusau and K Henrard (eds), *EU Anti-Discrimination Law Beyond Gender* (Oxford, Hart Publishing, 2019).

[134] Goodwin (n 132) 179.

[135] ibid 175.

[136] Whalen and Whalen (n 43).

[137] However, if these symbols were classified as an issue of race or ethnicity, the EU law would provide protection: A Śledzińska-Simon, 'Unveiling the Culture of Justification in the European Union: Religious Clothing and the Proportionality Review' in U Belavusau and K Henrard (eds), *EU Anti-Discrimination Law Beyond Gender* (Oxford, Hart Publishing, 2019) 207.

[138] Originally from India, the Roma migrated to Europe between 500 and 1000 AD, 'reaching Europe around the thirteenth century'. A Eliason, 'With No Deliberate Speed: The Segregation of Roma Children in Europe' (2017) 27 *Duke Journal of Comparative & International Law* 191, 194.

[139] M Dawson and E Muir, 'Collective Vigilance in Protection Fundamental Rights in the EU: Lesson from the Roma' (2011) 48 *Common Market Law Review* 761.

reveal a high level of anti-Roma sentiments across Europe,[140] and 'unscrupulous politicians' often successfully use Roma as 'a scapegoat' to 'refocus discontent'.[141] Despite some recent judicial pronouncements,[142] very few cases tackle the widespread anti-Roma, anti-Black racism, or anti-Semitism and Islamophobia.[143] As many have noted, the minority policies of several EU states, frequently phrased in the language of integration, serve de facto as a majoritarian tool to control 'groups of non-Western descent'.[144] Vauchez has illustrated the 'exclusionary' consequences resulting from the invocation of neutrality to conceal hostility towards religious minorities, particularly a 'strong dimension of Islamophobia'.[145]

Even the broader scope of RED compared to FED is still insufficient.[146] Although the RED extends beyond work-related discrimination, de Búrca remarked that the Directive is a 'more genuine framework in nature, in so far as it contains a general prescription … to which States must commit themselves, but without prescribing in detail how this is to be achieved'.[147] The Directive almost exclusively relies on 'passive' protection through 'complaints-based' enforcement, which is particularly insufficient to rectify historical inequalities of racism.[148] Article 19, TFEU, restrains 'proactive' legislator intervention,[149] incentive measures, and redistributive measures which are needed to rectify historical wrongs.[150]

[140] A 2014 Pew Research study found that majorities across almost all Member States hold deeply unfavourable views of the Roma (Italy: 85%; France: 66%; Greece: 53%; UK: 50%). 'A Fragile Rebound for EU Image on Eve of European Parliament Elections' (Pew Research Centre 2014) 30–33 www.pewglobal.org/2014/05/12/chapter-4-views-of-roma-muslims-jews/cited in European Commission Report accessed 3 August 2025.

[141] Goodwin (n 132) 172, referring to politicians from France and Hungary.

[142] Specifically, Case C-417/23 *Slagelse Almennyttige Boligselskab – Afdeling Schackenborgvænge and Others v Ministry of Transport and Housing* ECLI:EU:C:2025:98, Opinion of AG Ćapeta; Case C-83/14 *CHEZ Razpredelenie Bulgaria* EU:C:2015:480; Case C-54/07 *Feryn NV* EU:C:2008:397, [2008] ECR I-05187.

[143] Möschel (n 133) 155.

[144] T Loenen, 'The Headscarf Debate: Approaching the Intersection of Sex, Religion, and Race Under the European Convention on Human Rights and EC Equality Law' in D Schiek and V Chege (eds), *European Union Non-Discrimination Law: Comparative Perspectives On Multidimensional Equality Law* (Abingdon, Routledge, 2009) 314.

[145] S Hennette-Vauchez, 'Religious Neutrality, Laïcité and Colorblindness: A Comparative Analysis' (2020) 42 *Cardozo Law Review* 539.

[146] Council Directive (EC) 2000/43 implementing the principle of equal treatment between persons irrespective of racial or ethnic origin OJ L180/22, art 3.

[147] While RED applies to 'social protection, including social security and 'healthcare', no attempt is made by that instrument to define the consequent detailed rules. It is unclear what the impact of this provision will be': Ellis and Watson (n 15) 438.

[148] M Bell, 'Advancing EU Anti-Discrimination Law: The European Commission's 2008 Proposal for a New Directive' (2009) 3 *Equal Rights Review* 18.

[149] On the distinction between passive and proactive protection, see E Muir, 'Fundamental Rights: An Unsettling EU Competence' (2014) 15 *Human Rights Review* 25.

[150] Eliason notes that 'the Central European countries, which resemble the Alabama's and Mississippi's of the 1950s and 60s in their discrimination against Roma, have little incentive to enforce anti-discrimination policies': Eliason (n 138) 238. For a critique on the EU's focus on individual rights at the expense of redistributive justice, see A Somek, 'The Preoccupation with Rights and the Embrace of Inclusion: A Critique' in Dimitry Kochenov and others (eds), *Europe's Justice Deficit?* (Oxford, Hart Publishing, 2015) 297.

RED continues to leave positive action to Member States' discretion, and so far, there has been no single case before the CJEU tackling positive action on race. According to the Commission's own reckoning, the Directive 'is not enough to resolve the deep-rooted social exclusion … *Legislation needs to be combined with policy and financial measures.*'[151]

Many scholars concur in pointing to the requirement of unanimity as a major reason behind the stark disparity between the regulation of sex equality compared to ethnic and religious equality.[152] Unlike Article 157, TFEU, on sex equality, Article 19, TFEU, requires the Council – the upper legislative chamber – to 'act unanimously' after 'obtaining the consent of the European Parliament' in order to take appropriate action to combat discrimination.[153] What is overlooked in the existing critique of Article 19, TFEU, is that unanimity simply frustrates the logic of the Federalist impartiality argument.

It will be recalled that the main premise of the argument is to break the 'ability to concert' among local majority factions. However, here a consensus is not needed because unanimity allows any local majority single-handedly to block any purported measure at the EU level.

Figure 3.1 Centralisation with Unanimous Voting

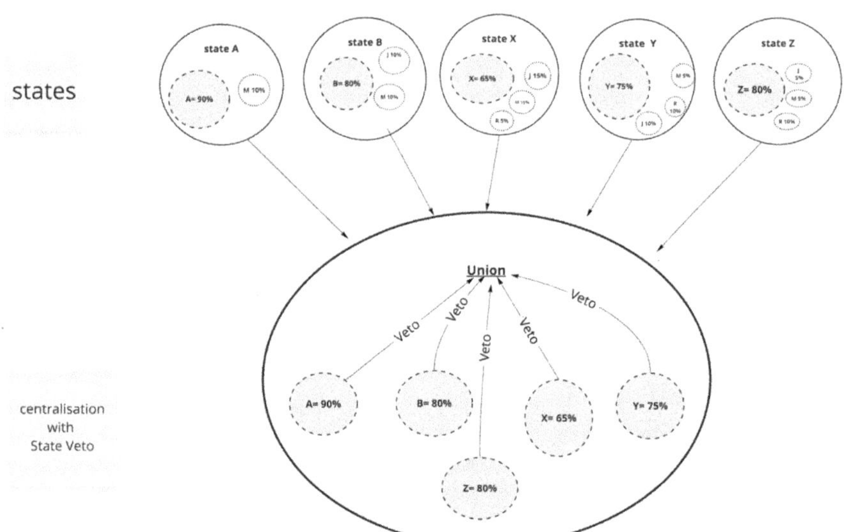

[151] European Commission, *Joint Report on the application of Council Directive 2000/43/EC and of Council Directive 2000/78/EC*, COM(2014) 2 final, 13 (emphasis added).

[152] E Spaventa, 'Should We "Harmonize" Fundamental Rights in the EU? Some Reflections About Minimum Standards and Fundamental Rights Protection in the EU Composite Constitutional System' (2018) 55 *Common Market Law Review* 999; B De Witte, 'Epilogue: The Limits of a Transformative Change in European Equality Law' in U Belavusau and K Henrard (eds), *EU Anti-Discrimination Law Beyond Gender* (Oxford, Hart Publishing, 2019) 364.

[153] Treaty on the Functioning of the European Union, art 19.

As is well-known, the Council members are ministers appointed by their states and are not elected as in the US Senate. Thus, whenever unanimity is required, one state's local majority has the power to *be the judge of its own cause* and veto a proposal notwithstanding the position of the elected European Parliament. With unanimity, contrary to Madison's reliance on diversity as a check, the increase of state diversity increases veto players, and, thus, the risk of inaction increases. Thus, in the EU, the unanimity hurdle has become more difficult since the 2004 enlargement and the growth of EU states, given that the higher the number of veto players, the less likely that a measure may pass. Differently put, unanimity is almost tantamount to decentralisation. When acting unanimously, the Council 'simply is the Member State governments'.[154]

An illustrative example of the dangers posed by veto can be found in the recent *Danish Ghetto Law*.[155] In pursuit of its 'No Ghetto 2030' strategy, Denmark enacted legislation mandating the relocation of individuals residing in designated social housing areas.[156] These areas were identified based on a range of socio-economic indicators, key among which was the proportion of residents with a 'non-western' background – a category that includes Danish citizens whose parents originate from outside the West. Suppose the EU Council sought to adopt legislation prohibiting such coercive and discriminatory practices, aimed at reducing the forced dispersal of minority communities. In such a scenario, the same Danish majority responsible for enacting the domestic law would be in a position to veto the EU initiative, effectively acting *as judge in its own cause*.

A full discussion of EU minorities or whether judicial review can overcome veto is beyond the scope of this chapter, since I extensively analyse it elsewhere and the issue of religious minorities is covered in chapter six.[157] The purpose of this cursory scan of EU racial minorities' struggle is twofold. First, to show the impact of unanimity on projecting majoritarian biases into practical legal outcomes. Second, to trace the genealogical connection of unanimity with some debates that Madison had to undergo 50 years after the constitutional convention in defence of the Federalist No. 10 argument. This will help refine the understanding of the impartiality argument and its incompatibility with state veto. The practical and conceptual points are briefly considered in turn.

Practically, unanimity reverses the logic of the Federalist No. 10 in two ways. First, it makes diversity of actors *a constitutional curse rather than a blessing* because it increases the likelihood of a veto, which hinders favourable intervention. This impact can be illustrated by comparison with other areas or institutions where

[154] RD Kelemen, 'Built to Last? The Durability of EU Federalism' in S Meunier and KR McNamara (eds), *Making History: European Integration and Institutional Change at Fifty* (Oxford, Oxford University Press, 2007) 56.

[155] LL Zurita, '"The Road to Hell Is Paved With Good Intentions" – Denmark's "Ghetto Laws" before the Court of Justice' (*European Law Blog*, 10 March 2025) www.europeanlawblog.eu/pub/y6mv9pbx/release/1 accessed 3 August 2025.

[156] *Danish Ghetto Case*, Opinion of AG Ćapeta (n 142) para 25.

[157] Moussa (n 68).

unanimity is not required. Most obviously, sex equality, generally unhindered by unanimity, remains the EU's most protected and 'judicialised' ground where nine directives have been successfully enacted and transposed.[158] But even within the field of racial and religious minorities, a more subtle comparison is the attitude of EU institutions with more federal/supranational composition, namely ones that better reflect the Federalist argument's requirements. The EU Commission and Parliament have been very active on this front, but all their attempts were crushed b y the EU Council's unanimity requirement.[159] A second negative impact of unanimity stems from its adverse effect on vanguard states' efforts in protecting their own minorities. This is because any single local majority could easily block the change across the whole EU on the one hand, while on the other, the free movement rules would make extending minority-tailored measures to all EU citizens costly for the vanguard state.[160]

On a different conceptual and comparative level, examining the unanimity practice in the EU helps clarify some unfounded critique levelled against Madison's Federalist No. 10. Dahl surprisingly construes the Federalist Papers as 'a convenient rationalization' for the state vetoes theory offered by John C Calhoun.[161] Since the Madison-Calhoun debate is extensively discussed elsewhere,[162] I will only highlight that Calhoun's proposed unanimity and veto embody, contrary to Dahl's assertion, an antithesis to the diversification logic underpinning the Federalist argument. This concise discussion aims to enhance our comprehension of the impartiality argument and the challenges posed by state veto, and set the foundation for the upcoming chapter, which will transition from state veto to federal veto.

Calhoun, the twice US vice-president and antebellum evil 'genius',[163] sought to prevent the potential abolition of slavery.[164] He developed a constitutional theory which turned 'the Madisonian legacy on its head' through substituting compound majority with state veto.[165] Calhoun's reliance on territorial veto, or what he terms

[158] For a list of the directives see U Belavusau and K Henrard, 'A Bird's Eye View on EU Anti-Discrimination Law: The Impact of the 2000 Equality Directives' (2019) 20 *German Law Journal* 614, fn 34.

[159] Moussa (n 68); See also European Parliament Legislative Resolution of 2 April 2009 on the Proposal COM(2008)0426, Amendment 37 of the EP, 2009, art 1, amendments 10 and 23. For an analysis, see R Xenidis, 'Multiple Discrimination in EU Anti-Discrimination Law: Towards Redressing Complex Inequality?' in U Belavusau and K Henrard (eds), *EU Anti-Discrimination Law Beyond Gender* (Oxford, Hart Publishing, 2019) 52–53.

[160] D Kochenov, 'European Union's Troublesome Minority Protection: A Bird's-Eye View' in J Boulden and W Kymlicka (eds), *International Approaches ot Governing Ethnic Diversity* (Oxford, Oxford University Press, 2015) 86.

[161] Dahl (n 115) 30 seems to have missed this point on veto which is manifested by his use of the example of Calhoun's theory of concurrent majorities, whereby states had the right to 'veto' or 'nullify' federal laws under some conditions. It appears that Dahl did not realise that Calhoun's ideas and veto rationale embody an antithesis to the diversification logic underpinning the Tenth Federalist.

[162] See generally Read (n 91) 121; Moussa (n 68).

[163] G Kateb, 'The Majority Principle: Calhoun and His Antecedents' (1969) 84 *Political Science Quarterly* 583.

[164] Read (n 91) 121.

[165] ibid 118–159.

'concurrent majority', rests on many premises that follow from his conceptualisation of sovereignty. He insisted that a veto was a right derived from the 'original sovereign character' of the people of the states since he saw the US Constitution as '*a union of political bodies*, as distinct from a Union of the people *individually*'.[166] Further, to show that unanimity is far from a constitutional anomaly, he drew an analogy between a state's legislative veto and the separation of powers' reciprocal checks whereby certain branches of government veto each other.[167]

One problem with Calhoun's argument is that he overlooked the role of foundational principles, including that of the *nemo judex* rule in constitutional theory and the Federalist Papers.[168] The incompatibility of Calhoun's theory with the latter came from no less authority than Madison himself, as the last surviving Founding Father.[169] Exigencies of space preclude full discussion of Madison's reply (which is well-discussed elsewhere);[170] I only highlight one point stressed by Madison on the analogy between state veto and executive veto in the separation of powers, and its concomitant impact on perpetuating inertia and, at times, injustice.

Madison dismissed any 'valid analogy' between 'reciprocal checks' among the three branches of government and 'a single state's' capacity to veto.[171] 'Disputes between independent parts of the same [government]' lead to a deadlock.[172] This is fundamentally different from 'disputes between a state Govt. and the Govt. of the [United] States'. Here, 'each party possessing … an organized Govt. … and having each a physical force to support its pretensions'.[173] In other words, while a reciprocal check seeks to prevent legislation in *toto*, state veto restrains only the central government while allowing a free hand to the state legislature to adopt laws as they please to the detriment of minorities. State veto, then, inverts the logic of the *nemo judex* rule by expanding, rather than restraining, state

[166] JC Calhoun, 'Speech Introducing Resolutions Declaratory of the Nature and Power of the Federal Government, January 22, 1833' in RL Meriwether and others (eds), *The Papers of John C. Calhoun* (Columbia, University of South Carolina Press 1980) vol XII, 18, 21.

[167] [W]ithout this there can be no constitution. …, it called by what check, or balance of power which, in fact, forms the constitution.' JC Calhoun, *A Disquisition on Government* (RK Cralle ed, A S Johnston 1851) 28.

[168] HV Jaffa, 'Calhoun versus Madison: The Transformation of the Thought of the Founding' (Bicentennial Celebration, Library of Congress Speech, 16 March 2021) www.loc.gov/item/2021688076/ accessed 3 August 2025.

[169] In his last work, Madison alluded to the dangers of Calhoun: 'Let the open enemy to it be regarded as a … Serpent creeping with his deadly wiles into Paradise': J Madison, 'Advice to My Country, 1834'; and to George Tucker, June 27, 1836 (Note in Madison's hand, Madison Papers, Library of Congress; Letters of Madison, IV, 435–36).

[170] Eg, Read (n 91) 42–45.

[171] Madison To Edward Everett, August 28, 1830 (Hunt, Writings of Madison, IX, 383–403).

[172] If states were to act opportunistically in cases of a federal deadlock, this would prompt federal institutions to sort out their deadlock and pre-empt state law. Conversely, state veto will ensure that this federal reconciliation would not happen, and state majorities would pursue their interests unbridled. See generally HK Gerken and A Holtzblatt, 'The Political Safeguards of Horizontal Federalism' (2014) 113 *Michigan Law Review* 57.

[173] 'Madison To Edward Everett' (n 171). For a commentary, see: Read (n 91) 42–45.

majorities' capacity to judge their own causes. The Civil War effectively resolved the Calhoun-Madison debate and assigned the idea of state veto to the American dustbin, although it was unconsciously resurrected in the EU through Article 19, TFEU.

To conclude this section, the objective was to demonstrate why unanimity voting over rights or state veto is inimical to the *nemo judex* rule practically and conceptually. Practically, a brief analysis of Article 119, TFEU's unanimity requirement, showed how it allows each state majority to judge its own interest and block change across Europe to the detriment of minorities. Conceptually, the analysis helped reveal Madison's rejection of unanimity as an interpretation of his theory, contrary to some mistaken critiques to the contrary.[174] Up to this point, this chapter has tested the effectiveness of the Federalist argument in various contexts and defended the argument against unfounded critiques with regard to state veto. The book now proceeds to raise its own critique of some unexamined gaps in Madison's argument, which relate to his views not only on state veto but also on federal veto, as well as his typology of faction.

IV. Concluding Remarks

This chapter embarked on a comparative and empirical journey to test and further revise the Federalist impartiality argument. According to the argument, minority rights are better situated at the central floor level, namely when the centre sets the minimum standard for rights protection, leaving states with the choice to go only above the floor. When the two conditions of 'diversification' and 'inability to concert' are met, and inertia-disrupting factors persist, centralising minority rights offers a *relatively more impartial decision-making process* and 'gradual' social inducement to accept the outcome of the process. Section I's comparison of the US civil rights and the EU equal pay demonstrated the effectiveness of the impartiality argument and how centralisation did lead to significant betterment of rights protection as well as broader social acceptance of these rights. The chapter also explored the negative practical and conceptual implications of unanimity or state veto, which simply frustrate the logic of the Federalist impartiality argument. As the examination of EU ethnic minorities under Article 119, TFEU, made clear, unanimity obviates uncertainty and the need to 'concert' altogether. It, thus, renders one state's majority capable of judging its own cause and blocking reform across the EU.

[174] Dahl (n 115) 30 seems to have missed this point on veto which is manifested by his use of the example of Calhoun's theory of concurrent majorities, whereby states had the right to 'veto' or 'nullify' federal laws under some conditions. It appears that Dahl did not realise the Calhoun's ideas and veto rationale embody an antithesis to the diversification logic underpinning the Tenth Federalist.

4

Non-Pecuniary Bias and the Omission of Factions of Principle

I. Introduction

The previous two chapters have illustrated and defended Madison's Federal impartiality argument against criticism. This chapter offers a critique from within the theory itself. Particularly, it shows that in formulating his definition of the causes of faction, Madison drew on Hume's faction trichotomy of factions of interest, passion, and principle, but reduced this to only two types, leaving out factions of principle. The chapter shows that his reduction has significant implications for impartiality and the boundary question. For factions of principle, Madison's condition of interest diversification is absent, rendering his conception of constitutional impartiality unattainable.

This chapter builds on the long-established categories in the common law rules on bias, which distinguish between pecuniary and non-pecuniary bias in public (though typically individual) decision-making.[1] It explores how this distinction can be extended to group decision-making and its implications for federal systems. The chapter begins by revisiting Hume and Madison's typology of the causes of faction and their corresponding sources of bias in decision-making, highlighting both the areas of overlap and omission. It then explains the implications of Madison's oversight for federal boundaries, particularly in relation to rights that arise in the context of culture wars and morality politics, such as abortion and assisted dying. The third section connects the Hume/Madison typology to the well-established common law categories of pecuniary and non-pecuniary bias. Finally, the fourth section offers a framework for distinguishing between these two types of faction and bias when they arise in group/federal decision-making, as opposed to individual settings.

II. Factions between Hume and Madison

As is well-known, Madison twice proposed a federal veto, or what he termed a 'universal negative', which the federal government would utilise to oversee state

[1] See, eg, H Woolf and others (eds), *De Smith's Principles of Judicial Review*, 2nd edn (London, Thomson Reuters, 2020) 532–540 (*De Smith's*).

laws and ensure protection of all rights.[2] The rejected proposal explicitly rested on the *nemo judex* rule and the assumptions of increased impartiality at the federal compared to the state level.[3] Even after rejection, Madison did not give up on the impartiality argument. He disappointingly wrote to Jefferson, lamenting the outcome while stressing the need for this 'universal negative' to consistently secure neutrality across the whole union.[4]

However, what Madison overlooked here is that the logic underlying the Federalist impartiality argument does not apply uniformly to all types of rights. In some cases, both centralisation and decentralisation would constitute an outright violation of the *nemo judex* rule and its underlying impartiality. That is a case of 'factual impossibility' where securing a relatively more impartial umpire is simply not possible. Perhaps, to properly grasp the distinction between different forms of divisive rights, we have to briefly cast light on the well-discussed genealogical connection between Madison's thoughts on faction and those of David Hume.

Literature on intellectual history suggests that Madison was arguably influenced by and borrowed from Hume's analysis.[5] In his essay, 'Of Parties in General', Hume subdivided what he termed 'real factions' into a trichotomy of *interest, principle*, or *affection*.[6] Affection's subdivision is irrelevant to our analysis and contemporary conditions, as it refers to emotional attachment 'felt for families in competition for a throne'.[7] The two other types are quite important. He distinguished between factions created through a 'clash of interests' and those from 'disagreement about matters of principles'.[8] While 'interest' is self-evident, he clarified that factious 'principles' could be derived from religious as well as philosophical views.[9] To further delineate the distinction between

[2] CF Hobson, 'The Negative on State Laws: James Madison, the Constitution, and the Crisis of Republican Government' (1979) 36 *William and Mary Quarterly* 215.

[3] J Madison, 'State and Federal Power and the Public Good to Thomas Jefferson, October 24, 1787' in RA Rutland and WME Rachal (eds), *The Papers of James Madison* (Chicago, The University of Chicago Press, 1975) vol X, 209–214.

[4] ibid.

[5] D Adair, 'That Politics May Be Reduced to a Science: David Hume, James Madison, and the Tenth Federalist' (1957) 20 *Huntington Library Quarterly* 343, 357. Despite strong similarity in terminology and phrasing, the extent of Hume's influence on Madison is subject to debate, see MG Spencer, 'Hume and Madison on Faction' in MG Spencer (ed), *David Hume and Eighteenth-Century America* (New York, Boydell & Brewer, 2005).

[6] D Hume, *Essays, Moral, Political, and Literary* (New York, Liberty Fund, 1985) 59.

[7] JA Harris, *Hume: An Intellectual Biography* (Cambridge, Cambridge University Press, 2015) 169–170; Hume (n 6) 63.

[8] ES Morgan, 'Safety in Numbers: Madison, Hume, and the Tenth Federalist' (1986) 49 *Huntington Library Quarterly* 95, 99 (contra Adair, he stressed the difference between Madison, who sought diversity, and Hume, who sought uniformity, where the former sought to control faction, Hume sought its elimination).

[9] 'Sects of philosophy, in the ancient world, were more zealous than parties of religion; but in modern times, parties of religions are more furious.' Hume (n 6) 63.

interest and principle, Hume dedicated 'well over' four pages to discussing relevant historical and then-contemporary incidents.[10]

But Madison, unlike Hume, was facing a 'real' pressing political predicament,[11] and lacked the luxury to engage in 'minute' theoretical analysis.[12] Understandably then, rather than developing Hume's typology further, he 'consolidated' it into a 'single' sentence'[13] in Federalist No. 10:

> A zeal for *different opinions* concerning religion, concerning Government and many other points …; an *attachment* to different leaders ambitiously contending for pre-eminence and power; or to persons of other descriptions whose fortunes have been *interesting* to the human passions, have in turn *divided mankind* … rendered them much more disposed to vex and oppress each other than to cooperate for their common good.[14]

More puzzlingly, in defining 'faction', Madison reduced this 'tripartite distinction' into two. A faction, Madison says, is a number of citizens who are 'united and actuated by some common impulse of passion, or of interest'. However, as White remarked, Madison does not include 'a number of citizens who are united and actuated by some common impulse of opinion [or principle]'.[15] Either way, as his proposal for universal negative makes clear, for Madison, factions, regardless of their causes, are best remedied by the federalising structure of Federalist No. 10.[16]

The question is whether Madison's consolidation of principle and interest and the overemphasis he places on the latter prevented him from developing a needed distinction, whose absence leaves a gap in the Federalist No. 10.[17] Formulated differently, should factious issues influenced more *by interest* be structurally dealt with in the same fashion *as* polarising ideological issues premised more *on principles*? By the latter, to reformulate Ackerman, I mean a *highly divisive* public policy issue where conflicting positions *are based less on interest* and *more on moral conviction* rooted in religious, laic, ideological or philosophical views.[18] Of course, the very same issue, as Hume remarked and as shall be explained in the next section, could be one of interest for the faction leader who

[10] ibid.
[11] Morgan (n 8) 99.
[12] Adair (n 5) 357.
[13] ibid.
[14] Madison, 'Federalist No. 10' in A Hamilton, J Madison and J Jay, *The Federalist Papers* (I Shapiro ed, New Haven, Yale University Press, 2009) 42 (Federalist No. 10).
[15] M White, *Philosophy, The Federalist, and the Constitution* (Oxford, Oxford University Press, 1989) 72–74 (discussing possible interpretations of this omission).
[16] Hobson (n 2) 215–233.
[17] On Madison's overemphasis on interest, see BA Ackerman, *We the People, Volume 1: Foundations* (Cambridge, MA, Harvard University Press, 1993) vol 1, 187–188.
[18] Akerman terms these factions 'ideological' to adapt them to 'today's usage': ibid.

benefits from mobilising the masses, but for the divided public, the issue is a matter of convictions and principles.[19]

The challenge is that when such issues enter the public domain and attract fierce popular disagreement, the condition of increasing 'diversification of interest' is unattainable. This is because a large federated heterogeneous society is 'rent into' two or three stable factions.[20] The 'immovable' issue of abortion in America gives a vivid illustration.[21] For half a century, Americans have been divided by it. Black, White, Asian, Protestant, Catholic, Jewish, Calvinist, Quaker, atheist, male or female eventually fall into two or three positions underpinned by either preference of the principle of decisional autonomy (thus, favouring liberalisation of abortion), or valuing prenatal life (thus, favouring prohibition), or some derivative subgroup of the two.[22] Whereas, the Federalist No. 10's logic is to increase the '*causes of faction*' to redeploy factions against themselves.[23] Here, the overarching principles serving as the '*causes of faction*' locally are identical to those existing upon federalisation. Thus, the polarising issue – to echo Adam Smith – collapses the 'whole of a large society' into 'two or three great' sides.[24]

Figure 4.1 Principled Faction and the Impossible Impartiality

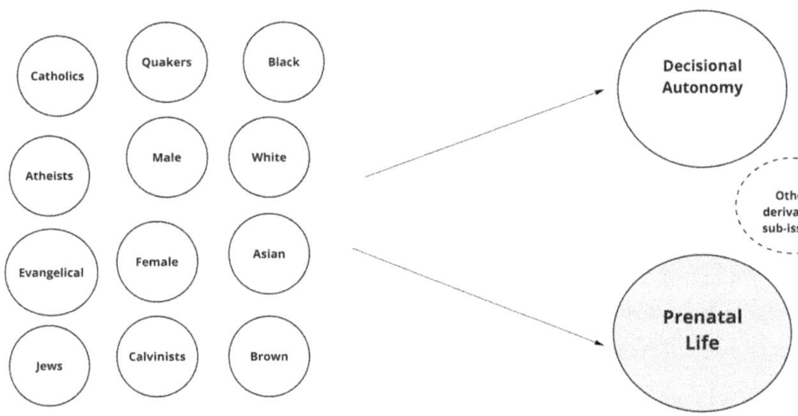

[19] Hume (n 6) 62; the definition will be further illustrated with examples in ch 5.

[20] Hume remarked, 'when the whole state is rent into two equal factions': ibid 58.

[21] Tribe calls it an 'immovable object' and 'unending debate': L H Tribe, *Abortion: The Clash of Absolutes* (New York, WW Norton & Company, 1992) 6.

[22] 'Public Opinion on Abortion' (Pew Research Center, 2025) www.pewforum.org/fact-sheet/public-opinion-on-abortion accessed 3 August 2025.

[23] 'Causes of faction' is a Madisonian term from Madison, 'Federalist No. 10' (n 14) 41.

[24] A Smith, *The Wealth of Nations* (AS Skinner ed, London, Penguin, 1999) bk 5, ch 1, pt iii; similarly, see Hume (n 6) 58.

Figure 4.2 Polarisation and Consolidation

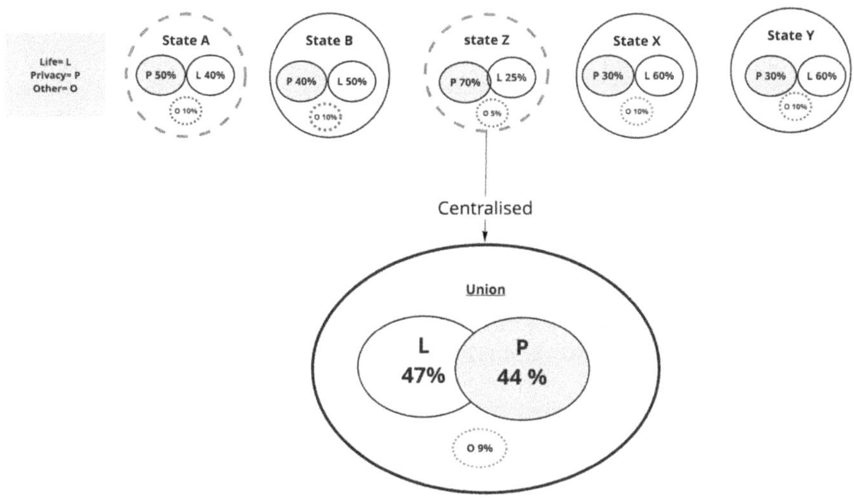

What happens here is a 'polar consolidation' of factions rather than 'diversification' thereof. These divisive rights lump otherwise heterogeneous groups into two or three 'great'[25] and 'stable' factions.[26] To visualise this point, let us harken back to our chart and imagine the very same five countries are divided by the issue of abortion. For the sake of simplicity, let us assume they fall into two main camps: those who are supporters of prenatal life, thus favouring abortion prohibition (P), and those supporting *choice autonomy* and, thus, for legalising abortion (L), in addition to a third position (O) of those who are disinterested or have a derivative position of one of the two main camps. The five countries form an integrative union which deems it appropriate to decide the matter.

While Madison sought to enlarge the political orbit to *increase* and *diversify* interested factions, here the polarising issue does the opposite. It *consolidates* and *collapses* different groups into fewer ones. More importantly, there is no real difference between the unitary state and the federal level. Here, the increase in the size and complexity of the polity does not bring a 'qualitative' increase in the principles underpinning the *causes of factions*. This is in contrast to minority rights, where enlarging the polity, as in the EU or the US, brings several new minorities and majorities, as well as a host of more divergent interests. And as we saw in earlier discussions and examples from the EU and the US, the federal majority usually does not mirror the local ones, and the dynamics of decision-making are significantly different. In instances of consolidation, not only are local and federal divisions similar, but also consolidated factions are quite stable, and, as discussed in the next chapter, the concert cannot be easily broken.

[25] Smith (n 24).
[26] Hume (n 6) 58.

What is noteworthy here is that the ideological dispute over abortion provides an example not only of a faction of principle, but it also exemplifies what was discussed earlier as impartiality's 'factual impossibility'. Dynamics at the federal level are no different from those of the state because there is *no impartial decision-maker on the horizon* or, as the famous book is entitled, 'no neutral ground' on which to stand.[27] Both state and federal majorities are equally partial in seeking to impose their own view on the other faction and their close-mindedness in accepting the other view. Whereas decentralising the issue means that each local majority judges its case and imposes its view, centralisation creates an all-or-nothing battle for the 'ultimate prize' of using legal authority to impose one faction's view across the whole union.[28] If we have six jurisdictions in our chart where each L/P faction imposes its view on three of them, centralisation allows one to get six jurisdictions while the other gets zero.[29] It becomes a battle of *coerce or be coerced*,[30] and each faction gears-up to 'prevail'.[31] It will be recalled that section I established that in situations of 'impossibility' of impartiality, one ought to look for other federal values and see which arrangement 'optimises' the greater number of values or alleviates the violation of the *nemo judex* rule.

While further discussion on abortion and the judicial misuse of the impartiality argument is offered in the next chapter, a few counterarguments must be addressed here. First, it could be argued that either sort of faction will boil down to a limited number of legislative choices, for instance, to pit those in favour of discriminating *vs* not discriminating against minorities; or to legalise abortion *vs* criminalise it, and, thus, diversification may not be a distinctive factor between the two types of factions. However, this would conflate 'causes' with 'outcome' and miss the advised Madisonian choice of the expression 'causes of faction'.[32] The minority aspects are underpinned by the diverging, shifting interests which, as shown, naturally increase as the polity orbit is enlarged. By contrast, principle-based factions are *caused* and *underpinned* by a limited set of values which do not increase no matter how much one augments the polity. In societies large and small, the abortion debate usually revolves around a limited set of competing values which do not vary, no matter how the polity augments.

Second, it could be contended that whilst Madison did not include principle in his definition, he analysed and was concerned with religious minorities

[27] K O'Connor, *No Neutral Ground?: Abortion Politics in an Age of Absolutes* (Abingdon, Routledge, 2020) 426: 'There may be circumstances in which no such position of neutrality exists.'

[28] AE Doan, *Opposition and Intimidation: The Abortion Wars and Strategies of Political Harassment* (Ann Arbor, University of Michigan Press, 2007) 9.

[29] A similar example is offered by RM Hills Jr, 'Federalism as Westphalian Liberalism' (2006) 75 *Fordham Law Review* 771.

[30] Absent an amicable compromise, coercion here could be seen collectively or individually. Collective coercion is simple; each faction wants to impose its view on the legal answer. Individually, pro-lifers may see abortion as alleged coercion or inflicting pain to the foetus, while pro-choicers would see it as coercion and bodily harm to the woman.

[31] Madison, 'Federalist No. 10' (n 14) 47.

[32] ibid 41.

and the role of religion.[33] However, it is important to stress that a discussion of religion is not necessarily a discussion of factions of principle. A 'multifaceted' phenomenon of religion could be a cause of group interest-based faction akin to race when used as a '*marker of group identity (chosen or otherwise)*'[34] and/or in others it can fuel ideological conflicts in culture war matters.[35] For example, non-practising individuals of Jewish or Muslim descent may face career disadvantages despite lacking religious conviction, making this an interest-based issue.

In contrast, other facets of religion, especially under the influence of state regulatory expansion, and what Habermas calls the 'translation proviso', enter ideological debates – such as abortion or assisted dying – by recasting religious arguments into broadly shared societal values. This process consolidates diverse groups into opposing factions structured around conflicting values.[36] Given the different historical context Madison was working in,[37] it seems he was possibly more pre-occupied with protecting the interests of religious groups in the first sense, which he saw, as Ackerman noted, as a 'durable' conflict compared to the ideological principle-based faction which was dropped out of his definition.[38] Chapter six will detail the various facets of religion as well as other examples of overlapping factions. Madison's original draft of the First Amendment may suggest, albeit in an under-theorised way, a distinction between aspects of religion that appeal to factions of principle (establishment) and those that give rise to factions of group interest. This distinction will be explored briefly in chapter six.

The last counterargument to tackle here is Justice Kavanaugh's neutrality assertion, which he used in *Dobbs* to justify the decentralisation of abortion.[39] Potentially misreading the Madisonian expression of being 'scrupulously impartial',[40] Justice Kavanaugh repeatedly stressed that by restraining the federal judiciary and leaving the matter completely to states, the Supreme Court becomes 'scrupulously neutral'.[41] This is a faux neutrality argument for the following reasons. First, neither Justice Kavanaugh nor other judges claim that states are neutral on abortion. In fact, he rightfully charted out states' rivalling

[33] J Madison, 'Federalist No. 52' in A Hamilton, J Madison and J Jay, *The Federalist Papers* (I Shapiro ed, New Haven, Yale University Press, 2009) 252.
[34] Khaitan and Norton (n 3) 129; T Khaitan, 'Directive Principles and the Expressive Accommodation of Ideological Dissenters' (2018) 16 *International Journal of Constitutional Law* 394.
[35] R McCrea, 'Faith at Work: The CJEU's Headscarf Rulings' (*EU Law Analysis*, 14 March 2017) eulawanalysis.blogspot.com/2017/03/faith-at-work-cjeus-headscarf-rulings.html accessed 3 August 2025.
[36] J Habermas and C Taylor, 'A Dialogue' in J Butler and others (eds), *The Power of Religion in the Public Sphere* (New York, Columbia University Press, 2011) 60.
[37] I mean the 'night watchman state' prevalent at his time.
[38] Ackerman (n 17) vol 1, 187–188; J Madison, 'Vices of the Political System of the United States' *Selected Writings of James Madison* (R Ketcham, ed, Indianapolis, Hackett Publishing, 2006).
[39] *Dobbs v Jackson Women's Health Org* 597 US 215 (2022) [3] (Kavanaugh J, concurring).
[40] Madison spoke of being 'scrupulously impartial' in *Federalist No. 57* which may have inspired Justice Kavanaugh's argument.
[41] *Dobbs v Jackson Women's Health Org* 597 US 215 (2022) [3] (Kavanaugh J, concurring).

factions between pro-life and pro-choice 'advocates'.[42] This poses the question then: if the federal umpire knows that state majorities are not neutral, then how does leaving the authority to non-neutral decision-makers turn the process or the outcome into a neutral one? Rather, the accurate description is that we are faced with a position of *impossible neutrality* because, as discussed earlier, in any situation, either the state or the federal majority will be acting as an ultimate umpire, superimposing its unchecked moral view.

Secondly, opting to defer to states is nothing but siding with one group at the expense of another on the jurisdictional question of whether regulation (be it pro-life or pro-choice) should be done federally or in a decentralised fashion. Deciding to decentralise is indeed 'taking sides' on that question and should not be conflated with abstaining from answering it or being neutral thereon. Thirdly, the judgement was not value-neutral on the competing views. Justice Kavanaugh dedicated a few lines to expressly side with the majority's disputed historical argument regarding the longstanding states' tradition of prohibiting abortion, which he sees as 'dispositive'.[43] More importantly, he did not object to the majority opinion's remark that the non-consensual issue of 'respect for and preservation of prenatal life *at all stages of development*' will be regarded as a legitimate state interest. Thus, it is difficult to reconcile this recognition with the opinion's professed neutrality on the competing values in question.

Fourthly, one may refer to the dissent's partially valid objection where they inquired, 'would [Justice Kavanaugh] say that the Court is being "scrupulously neutral" … if the Court allowed some States to use unanimous juries and others not? If the Court told the States: Decide for yourselves whether to put restrictions on church attendance?'.[44] Whilst raising accurate objections, the dissenters themselves have fallen prey to a similar mistake by laying the unfounded claim that their view represents neutrality, as 'it protects the [abortion] right against all comers'.[45] Yet, as the previous charts and discussion have illustrated, we are faced with a scenario of *impossible neutrality* since violation of the *nemo judex* rule is unavoidable, and neither side can claim impartiality. *Dobbs*' opinions and the judicial restraint argument are revisited later in chapter five, but what is needed first is to make sure that the distinction between the two types of factions is clear, which the next section undertakes.

To avoid falling into similarly misplaced assertions of neutrality in the context of factions of principle, the following two sections aim to further delineate the interest/principle distinction in two steps. First, the analysis traces its roots to the well-established categories of bias in common law rules on natural justice and judicial review. Second, it examines how these common law categories might be adapted when applied to group-level or federal decision-making, as opposed to their traditional application to individual decision-makers.

[42] ibid.
[43] ibid [2], fn 1 (Kavanaugh J, Concurring).
[44] ibid [20]–[21] (Breyer, Sotomayor, and Kagan, JJ, dissenting).
[45] ibid.

III. The Interest/Principle Distinction and Pecuniary/ Non-pecuniary Bias in the Common Law

The interest/principle distinction is as ancient as constitutional thought, among other fields.[46] Nonetheless, further clarity is desirable. Returning to the analogy between individual and collective decision-making, Madison's analysis effectively 'extended' the well-established common law analysis of causes of bias which can impugn decision-making.[47] A brief overview of the refined case law on the different causes of bias is, thus, instructive. Defined as 'a predisposition or prejudice against one party's case or evidence on an issue for reasons unconnected with the merits',[48] bias can emanate from various sources.

Three 'grounds' of bias are relevant.[49] First, traditional pecuniary (economic) interest arises where the judge/decision maker stands to make 'a financial gain' from the decision, such as having a share in the disputed property or corporate. The second type, 'personal bias', emerges from a 'special human association'[50] with one of the parties (eg, being a friend, a relative, or a neighbour).[51] Thirdly – and most importantly for this chapter – bias extends to non-pecuniary and 'strongly' held ideological philosophical conviction (eg. a judge who has extensively and vocally defended pro-life views adjudicating abortion-related cases in a Supreme Court context).[52]

The latter form is often called 'non-pecuniary bias' or, as the UK Supreme Court called it in the well-known *Pinochet No. 2* case, 'promotion of a cause' or cause-driven bias.[53] The case involved the extradition of the former Chilean Dictator. One of the Law Lords in the majority was the head of a charity affiliated with Amnesty International, which had intervened to defend the cause of extradition. Although he received no pecuniary remuneration for this charity role, the Court reversed the decision, reasoning as follows:

> In civil litigation the matters in issue will normally have an economic impact; therefore a judge is automatically disqualified if he stands to make a *financial gain as a consequence*

[46] Cicero discussed the relationship between the *Honestum* (the morally good, the honourable) and the *Utile* (the profitable, the beneficial, the advantageous): Cicero, *De officiis Book III* (Walter Miller tr, Cambridge, MA, Harvard University Press, 1913); T Besley, *Principled Agents?: The Political Economy of Good Government* (Oxford, Oxford University Press, 2007); M Sandel, *What Money Can't Buy: The Moral Limits of Markets* (London, Penguin, 2013).

[47] A Gibson, 'Madison's Republican Remedy: The Tenth Federalist and the Creation of an Impartial Republic' in JN Rakove and CA Sheehan (eds), *The Cambridge Companion to the Federalist* (Cambridge Companions to Philosophy, Cambridge, Cambridge University Press, 2020) 274.

[48] *R v Inner West London Coroner ex parte Dallaglio* [1994] 4 All ER 139, 151.

[49] Lord Widgery CJ in *Reg v Altrincham Justices, Ex parte N Pennington* [1975] QB 549, 552.

[50] DJ Galligan, *Due Process and Fair Procedures: A Study of Administrative Procedures* (Oxford, Oxford University Press, 1996) 446.

[51] ibid 446; see, eg, *Metropolitan Properties (FGC) Ltd v Lannon* [1969] 1 QB 577.

[52] M Moussa, 'Expanding the Nemo Judex Rule: Reflections on Non-Pecuniary Bias' [2025] *Judicial Review* 1; P Cane, *Administrative Law*, 5th edn (Oxford, Oxford University Press, 2011) 72.

[53] *R v Bow Street Metropolitan Stipendiary Magistrate, ex parte Pinochet Ugarte (No 2)* [2000] 1 AC 119.

> *of his own decision* of the case. But if, as in the present case, the matter at issue does not relate to money or economic advantage but is concerned *with the promotion of the cause*, the rationale disqualifying a judge applies just as much if the judge's decision will lead to the promotion of a cause in which the judge is involved together with one of the parties.[54]

Caselaw indicates that non-pecuniary bias is more subtle and subject to different legal tests, but it is often no less significant.[55] For instance, in *Hoekstra*, a judge published a newspaper article on the accession to the European Convention of Human Rights, describing it as offering 'a field day for crackpots' and being 'a pain in the neck for judges and a goldmine for lawyers'.[56] The appellate division held that the judge's commentaries established a reasonable apprehension that he might not approach cases involving human rights claims with the requisite impartiality.[57]

Further examples from jury selection are instructive. As is well-known, the jury selection process in the US starts with a room full of prospective jurors, and through a process of elimination known as 'voir dire', the jury panel is filtered and formed.[58] A traditional question to prospective jurors captures the principle-based or moral beliefs as a cause of bias. Prospective jurors are often asked, '[d]o any of you have any moral or philosophical beliefs that would prevent you from rendering a fair and impartial verdict?'[59]

This sort of moral non-pecuniary bias was also examined in capital punishment cases. The US Supreme Court found that it is constitutionally valid to exclude persons who are unwilling under any circumstances to impose capital punishment. The Court majority found this exclusion not to violate the defendant's rights to a jury or due process, since jurors holding these unmoved convictions may be seen by the state as unable to '*impartially* apply the law'.[60] Here, the impartiality referred to in the Supreme Court's ruling arises from rigid attachment to moral conviction, which is different from biases against groups such as defendants of different race or religion. Group interest, tribal instincts, or traditional forms of pecuniary interest do not play a role in these types of biases.

By contrast, tribal/group instincts affecting juries or judges can be analogised to the personal bias called 'special human association', or what Gilligan calls 'systemic bias'.[61] Neuroscientists inform us that while we possess biological impulses toward acting *selfish*, we also have impulses to be '*groupish*', which induce us to 'deploy'

[54] ibid [135] (emphasis added).

[55] *Pinochet* aside, the automatic disqualification in the UK only applies to the first two, but not non-pecuniary bias. The Court seems to require a 'higher threshold': see Moussa (n 52).

[56] *Hoekstra v HM Advocate [No 2]* (2000) JC 391 [19]–[20] (Hoekstra).

[57] ibid.

[58] JS Emery, LL Edwards and JS Edwards, *Civil Procedure and Litigation* (London, West Legal Studies, 2000) 562.

[59] ibid.

[60] *Lockhart v McCree* 476 US 62, 177–178 (1986).

[61] Galligan (n 50) 438.

our reason to 'support' our own group and tribe.[62] That groupish tendency colours our judgment with bias. A 'rare' example comes from cases where defendants sought to disqualify Jewish jurors in an antisemitic libel trial.[63] A more pervasive example is the extensive literature examining all-white juries or parliamentarians deciding the rights of minority African Americans.[64]

Be that as it may, the treatment of these different types of biases under common law and comparatively is fully explored elsewhere.[65] The purpose of this brief discussion is to demonstrate that moral non-pecuniary bias is a well-established category in case law, one that must be distinguished – as case law itself does – from pecuniary and association-based grounds of bias. The second purpose is to identify the corresponding bias that aligns with group settings and the terminology of factionalism used by both Madison and Hume. By reading both the case law on bias and the Hume/Madison typology, the following parallels emerge (summarised in the table below):

1) **Pecuniary bias** corresponds to what may be called in Madisonian theory the *faction of self-interest* when aggregated across a larger group of people (eg, debtor relief laws vs the interests of creditors).
2) **Human association bias** (relation to one of the parties) corresponds to tribal instincts, majority bias, and groupishness, which align with *factions of group interest* (eg, cases on racial/religious minority rights).
3) **Cause-driven bias** (promotion of moral cause) corresponds to *factions of principle* in Hume's terms (eg, abortion, assisted dying, and morality politics).[66]

Table 4.1 Typology of bias and faction

Bias ground in the common law	Hume/Madison Equivalent	Example
Pecuniary	Faction of interest (aggregated)	Debtor relief law
Association	Faction of [group] interest (being groupish)	Minority rights
Cause-driven	Faction of principle	Ideological conflicts over abortion/assisted dying, etc.

[62] J Haidt, *The Righteous Mind: Why Good People Are Divided by Politics and Religion* (New York, Vintage, 2013) (in moral and political matters, we are often groupish rather than selfish. We deploy our reasoning skills to support our team).

[63] '[A] defendant charged with criminal libel that included blatantly anti-Semitic messages' where the defence counsel sought to strike potential jury members who were Jewish on the theory that their affiliation alone would affect their impartiality; *Potter v State*, 216 S.W. 886, 888 (Tex. Ct. Crim. App. 1919). *cf Coleman v United States* 379 A.2d 951, 953–954 (DC 1977) (unsuccessful request to remove Catholic jurors where defendants were charged with, among other things, armed robbery of two Catholic priests inside a Catholic church), summarised in BI Bittker, SC Idleman and FS Ravitch, *Religion and the State in American Law* (Cambridge, Cambridge University Press, 2015) 678.

[64] K Abramowitz and AB Douglass, 'Racial Bias in Jury Selection Hurts Mock Jurors, not just Defendants: Testing one Potential Intervention' (2023) 47 *Law and Human Behaviour* 153.

[65] Cane (n 52) 72.

[66] The grounds of bias can overlap as covered in ch 6.

IV. Delineating the Distinction in Group/Federal Settings

Having surveyed the distinction between different types of biases at the level of the individual judge or decision-maker, it must be noted that extending this distinction to group-based or federal-level decision-making introduces an additional layer of complexity. At the group representative level, we encounter what Hume called 'faction leaders' – ie,what we now term politicians – and the represented public. Are both groups influenced by bias due to moral convictions, or are there distinct forces at play for each group?

Hume anticipated this distinction. To him, 'Faction of principle' implicates interest only for faction leaders but not the people. Opportunistic politicians, for example, benefited from mobilising the masses; profit-seeking abortion providers, too, have economic interests in the matter. But on 'the part of the people',[67] the general masses, it is a matter of principle, and they continue to judge abortion based on their 'belief system'.[68] This chapter adopts the perspective of the public as the primary lens through which to classify factions, given that it is the public's moral/ideological or tribal alignment that underpins widespread social disagreement and fuels growing polarisation. Focusing on public perception is also consistent with well-established judicial approaches to impartiality. For instance, in common law jurisdictions, courts assess bias from the standpoint of a reasonable lay observer; similarly, the CJEU employs a 'social perception' test to evaluate whether the appearance of impartiality has been maintained.[69]

To put the distinction succinctly: while factions of interest may involve both interests and principles, factions of principle are distinctive in that they are not grounded in self- or group interest. In factions of principle, moral convictions and value attachments dominate, and one's position is not necessarily tied to group identity. Consider the example of segregation. Though some may frame segregation in terms of distorted principles (eg, white supremacy), these are deeply interwoven with concrete economic and group interests: cheaper labour, group privileges, and economic advantage. Surely, minority rights advocates drawn from the dominant racial group, by contrast, transcend their tribal instincts and, thus, form a healthy component of the constitutional body – one that does not trigger the need for Madison's 'remedy'. For the broader public, however, interest-based incentives often remain operative. In such contexts, federal diversification can be effective in shifting attitudes by altering the payoff structure – for example, by reallocating costs or benefits in ways that promote inclusion. These interest-based dynamics are far weaker, or entirely absent, in pure factions of principle, such as debates surrounding assisted dying or abortion.

Stated differently, in factional disputes driven by group interest – such as equal pay or segregation – positions typically align with group membership, at least for

[67] Hume (n 6) 62.
[68] ibid. On the role of belief systems, see Doan (n 28) 10.
[69] *Commission v Poland* (Independence of the Supreme Court), C-619/18, EU:C:2019:531, para 74.

one side of the competing parties: Black individuals do not advocate for segregated restaurants, and working women do not oppose equal pay. By contrast, factions of principle involve competing values shaped by moral disagreements that cut across group boundaries and reflect deeper conflicts of normative commitments. For example, many women actively participate in anti-abortion campaigns. There are some cases of overlap between the two types, but let's articulate the distinction first, and the overlap is fully analysed in chapter six.

In many cases, the distinction is fairly intuitive. However, in a few cases it is not. In one case, particularly, I reckon the distinction might be slightly more difficult and may trick others into challenging the argument offered in this chapter. By this, I mean the case where disagreement exists as to whether the principle in question constitutes indirect discrimination against a particular group. More specifically, I anticipate some scholars who advocate that abortion should be protected not as a privacy right but rather as an indirect discrimination[70] may argue the following: given that the logic of the Federalist argument dictates that factions of interest apply to minorities, including women, and abortion is allegedly indirect discrimination against women, ergo, abortion should be centralised.

At the outset, it should be remarked that both the ECtHR[71] and the US Supreme Court consistently ignore calls to classify abortion as indirect discrimination and unequivocally treat it as a privacy issue.[72] Irrespective of the authoritative judicial answer, which might change, it is important to establish clear, unchanging criteria according to which similar confusions may be avoided. For that, I suggest the following four-pronged test.

A. Does Federalisation Qualitatively Increase the 'Causes' of Local Faction?

This criterion echoes the logic of the revised Federalist argument, which, by increasing the 'causes of faction', redeploys the danger of faction against itself.[73] For racial equality, at the smaller state level, there is usually one racially dominant group versus the minority. However, once racial equality is centralised, you take other races and different economic interests of different industries with different economic interests towards minorities. Recall that equal pay in the UK was animated by a neo-liberal agenda. Centralising equal pay pitted the interests of the UK factions against the more egalitarian French industry, which had a conflicting

[70] Eg, C MacKinnon, 'Reflections on Sex Equality Under Law' (1991) 100 *Yale Law Journal* 1281, 1319; CR Sunstein, *The Partial Constitution* (Cambridge, MA, Harvard University Press, 1993) 282–284.

[71] The ECtHR approaches abortion mainly on art 8 [private family life] but never on the basis of art 14 [equality]. See 'Guide on Article 8 of the European Convention on Human Rights: Right to respect for private and family life, home and correspondence' (European Court of Human Rights, December 2020) ks.echr.coe.int/documents/d/echr-ks/guide_art_8_eng accessed 3 August 2025.

[72] For an analysis, see E Chemernisky, *Constitutional Law*, 7th edn (Burlington, Aspen, 2020) 890.

[73] Madison, Federalist No. 10 (n 14) 41.

interest in ensuring that other Member States would not produce at a cheaper cost.[74] Conversely, for abortion, the conflicting principles (prenatal life and privacy) are identical to those existing upon federalisation. Thus, federalisation does not increase the principles underlying the factions involved.

Recalling the distinction made between 'causes' of faction and the outcome,[75] the outcome of equal/unequal pay is underpinned by the divergent range of interests, which increase as more stakeholders are involved through federalisation. In abortion, however, the overarching conflicting values serving as the 'causes of faction' locally are identical to those existing upon federalisation. It remains structured around a fixed clash of the same values, unaffected by the addition of new actors. Hence, Madison's simplified formula: '*Integration + centralisation = more causes of bias yet with diluted effect*' does not work here. The abortion debate usually revolves around a set of competing values which do not vary in polities, large or small.

In moral conflicts such as abortion, society's various groups tend to divide internally along the same lines – supporting either prenatal life or decisional autonomy – regardless of the size or diversity of the polity. Upon centralisation, these fixed values serve as a 'bridge', collapsing otherwise heterogeneous groups and facilitating a polarised 'alliance'.[76] In such cases, 'diversity ceases' to serve as a constitutional check.[77] Unlike the ephemeral, transitory nature of interest-based alliances, a value-based alliance may exhibit more resilience and longer 'staying power'.[78] Thus, federalisation does not bring about a qualitative change in the principles underlying the factions involved. Instead, centralisation merely raises the stakes by encouraging consolidation into opposing blocs – driven by a logic of 'coerce or be coerced' – which may, if anything, intensify polarisation, as illustrated in the figure below.

Figure 4.3 Principle vs Interest Centralisation

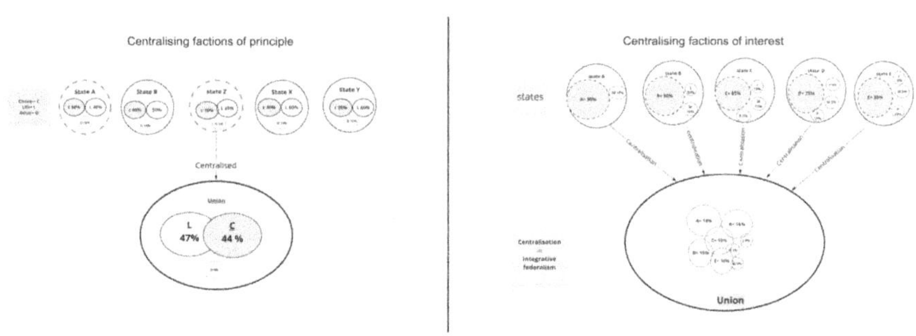

[74] See ch 4, s III.C.

[75] Madison, Federalist No. 10 (n 14) 41.

[76] ibid.

[77] N Feldman, *Divided by God: America's Church-State Problem -- and What We Should Do About It* (New York, Farrar, Straus and Giroux, 2006) 71 (noting that 'religious diversity might cease to protect non-establishment when different religious denominations could form alliances').

[78] Ackerman (n 17) vol 1, 187–188.

B. Demographic Makeup of Dissenters to the Divisive Right

The second prong is to look at the composition of the faction adverse to the right in question (be it abortion or racial equality), then explore whether the faction contains a sizeable number of the class of citizens who are presumed to be beneficiaries of the very same right. If the answer is yes, then it is a faction of principle; if not, then it is one of interest.[79] For example, it is extremely rare to consistently find a sizeable portion of the African American population arguing for discrimination against them or a working female objecting to equal pay. On the other hand, many leading anti-abortion activists are indeed women. Women from the working class, middle class, and intellectual elite oppose abortion.[80] Suffice to say that Europe's most restrictive judgment was penned by the Polish female judge.[81] In other words, here a dissenter's position does not necessarily tally with or follow from their group membership, nor does it trigger your tribal instincts. Moral conflicts of this kind fragment society along *lines of conscience rather than identity.*

A relevant example of such a cross-group 'single issue politics'[82] unfolded as I was writing the book. In late 2024, the UK Parliament debated the *Terminally Ill Bill*, which sought to legalise assisted suicide. In response, a diverse group of professors and practitioners from across the UK – representing a wide range of demographic backgrounds – jointly authored a letter opposing the Bill.[83] Some groups of terminally ill people publicly opposed the Bill,[84] and the Disabled People Organisation submitted a UN complaint against the Bill.[85]

[79] I refer here to those who reach such judgments for independent reasons – individuals who are less likely to be dismissed as having been manipulated into their views or as merely blinded by forces of habit.

[80] See generally M McKeegan, *Abortion Politics: Mutiny in the Ranks of the Right* (New York, Maxwell Macmillan, 1992).

[81] See ch 5. It could be argued that women opposed the Equal Rights Amendment despite it being a matter of interest. However, statistics showed that women who did so were acting on the interest of either the protection of their husbands from contact with female colleagues or the working class fearing increased competition. In Madisonian terms, they were part of the 'housewives' faction whose interests are adversely affected. See V Burris, 'Who Opposed the Era? An Analysis of the Social Bases of Anti-Feminism' (1983) 64 *Social Science Quarterly* 305.

[82] See definition: Wyn Grant, Oxford Reference available at www-oxfordreference-com.ezp.lib.cam.ac.uk/display/10.1093/oi/authority.20110803100508126; see also KA Kerr, 'Organizing for Reform: The Anti-Saloon League and Innovation in Politics' (1980) 32 *American Quarterly* 37, 37.

[83] M Elliott and others, 'The Perils of Assisted Dying' (*The Guardian*, 27 October 2024) www.theguardian.com/news/2024/oct/27/austerity-hurts-more-than-a-smack#:~:text=The%20perils%20of,law%2C%20Leiden%20University accessed 3 August 2025. For an analysis of the debate and summary of different views, see M Elliott, 'Assisted dying, Private Members' Bills and government neutrality' (*Public Law for Everyone*, 18 November 2024) publiclawforeveryone.com/2024/11/18/assisted-dying-private-members-bills-and-government-neutrality/ accessed 3 August 2025.

[84] S Kataria and A Payne, 'We disagree on assisted dying bill – MND patients' (*BBC*, 24 April 2025) www.bbc.co.uk/news/articles/cj0zn5j6g42o accessed 3 August 2025.

[85] 'DDPOs Plan UN Complaint Against Assisted Dying Bill' (*Disability Rights UK*) www.disabilityrightsuk.org/news/ddpos-plan-un-complaint-against-assisted-dying-bill#:~:text=Today%2C%20Deaf%20and%20Disabled%20people%27s,of%20Disabled%20People%20(UNCRPD) accessed 3 August 2025.

C. The Role of Financial Incentives in Changing Attitudes

A third distinguishing feature concerns the responsiveness of public attitudes to economic incentives. In interest-based factional disputes, financial inducements often shift behaviour. As discussed in the previous chapter, federal conditional spending significantly accelerated desegregation in schools, as well as hospitals and medical care centres.[86] The 'contract compliance' policy required 'contractors of the federal government to increase the representation of [women, racial and religious] minorities' in their workforces as a condition for the 'award and the continuation of the contract'.[87] The underlying logic, as cited by Justice White, was: 'stop the discrimination, get the money; continue the discrimination, do not get the money'.[88] This logic largely worked. Likewise, in Europe, a change of payoff altered employers' attitude to equal pay. Employers preferred paying damages for potential plaintiffs rather than restructuring their business on an equal pay basis. However, employers' attitude changed following the *Marshall II* ruling, which led to a fourfold increase in damages.[89] In contrast, principle-based factions are largely immune to financial incentives. It is unlikely that a financial bonus, for example, would substantially sway pro-life physicians. Beyond the economic interest of abortion providers, monetary incentives have little, if any, effect on the conviction of pro-life or pro-choice advocates.[90]

As the Social Psychology Encyclopaedia observes, moral convictions do not align with the economic 'rationality' of making choices that 'maximises' beneficial consequences.[91] Differently put, factions of interest involve competition over the finite resources of power, wealth or social advantage. As Madison notes, '[e]very shilling with which they over-burden the inferior number, is a shilling saved to their own pockets'.[92] By contrast, factions of principle do not always involve the finite resources issue. As Tushnet remarks, 'one group's resolution of the issues that divide it from the others' has no effect on the resolution of the same issues by another group',[93] or, as Hume puts it, 'two men travelling on the highway, the one east, the other west, can easily pass each other, if the way be broad enough: But two

[86] JO Shimabukuro, *Abortion: Judicial History and Legislative Response* (Congresional Research Service, 2019) 24.

[87] S Fredman, *Discrimination Law* (Oxford, Oxford University Press, 2011) 334.

[88] *Guardians Assn v Civil Service Comm'n, NYC* 463 US 582 (1983) [599] (White, J) (statement of Rep Lindsayon Title VI) (citing 110 Cong Rec 1542 (1964)); see discussion of funding termination technique in OM Fiss, 'The Fate of an Idea Whose Time Has Come: Antidiscrimination Law in the Second Decade after Brown V. Board of Education' (1974) 41 *Chicago Law Review* 742, 752–762.

[89] Case C–271/91 *Marshall v Southampton and South-West Hants Area Health Authority (No 2)* ECLI:EU:C:1993:335, [1993] ECR I-4367.

[90] FB Roy and DV Kathleen, *Encyclopedia of Social Psychology* (Thousand Oaks, SAGE Publications, 2007) 592; similarly, see CR Sunstein, 'Moral Heuristics' (2005) 28 *Behavioral and Brain Sciences* 531.

[91] Roy and Kathleen (n 90).

[92] Madison, Federalist No. 10 (n 14) 42.

[93] M Tushnet, 'Federalism and Liberalism' (1996) 4 *Cardozo Journal of International & Comparative Law* 329, 342.

men, reasoning upon opposite principles … cannot so easily pass.'[94] Perhaps, the tribal instinct activated with regard to group interest matters can be explained by the scarcity of resources and the fact that the 'less prosperous' the majority group is, the more weight is placed on the interests of minorities.[95]

Neuroscience research shows that the part of moral reasoning triggers a distinctly different part of our minds, which does not require the mathematical thinking part which you engage when thinking of matters that require calculation and economic rationality.[96] Similarly, political science literature characterises these divisive issues as those in which 'at least one advocacy coalition … portray[s] the issue as one of morality or sin and use[s] moral arguments in its policy advocacy'. It is argued that the adoption of 'morality policy does not involve high costs, nor does it produce high economic gains'.[97]

D. Lack of a Common Normative Baseline

One supplementary factor is that in factions of interest, competing parties do implicitly agree on the foundational value or the meta-norm governing the issue. The applicable norm is common to both parties, but their dispute is on interpreting and applying it to the disputed matter.[98] Recall the 'equal but separate' slogan in the segregation debates; the equality norm is common to the parties, but the debate was whether segregation violates equality or not. Segregationists interpreted it as 'separate but [still] equal'. Likewise, the European opponents of 'equal pay' tried to interpret the work nature as different or redefine 'pay' to deny any violation of equality. Simply put, what we have here is more of an interpretive dispute on the understanding of the norm or value in question, and judgment is affected by the group biases of the parties.[99]

By contrast, factions of principle involve a much deeper contestation over *which* moral value or belief should serve as the governing norm in the first place.[100] The disagreement is not about how to apply a common value but whether the other side's value is *relevant at* all to the particular dispute. Parties

[94] Hume (n 6) 62.

[95] see J Waldron, 'Legislatures Judging in Their Own Cause' (2009) 3 *Legisprudence* 125.

[96] Haidt (n 62) 63.

[97] P Kurzer, *Markets and Moral Regulation: Cultural Change in the European Union* (Cambridge, Cambridge University Press, 2001) 6.

[98] Factions of principle does not seem to fit in Madison's tripartite typology of human nature (reason, passion, and interest). Instead, they seem to belong to the classical definition of belief as something that can deceptively resemble reason, but it differs in that it lacks proof. Perhaps, this may stem from the fact that many of these issues revolve around epistemically challenging questions such as when life begins (abortion) or concerning death (assisted dying), among the other examples discussed in next chapter.

[99] This interpretive dispute is why a judge-like approach is needed.

[100] One can stretch the word 'common to Member States' in Art 2 of TEU to require that both parties concur on the value involved for centralisation; if the departure points are different values and irreconcilable then we have a faction of principle.

speak different beliefs and assess the matter according to a different (often irreconcilable) moral yardstick. In abortion debates, for example, one camp frames the issue around their belief in the sanctity of prenatal life, while the other appeals to autonomy and personal choice. Similarly, in assisted dying, one side invokes the inviolability of life, while the other emphasises dignity and the right to die.[101] Typically, at least one side rejects the relevance of the other's value, recognising that conceding its applicability would undermine its own normative position.[102] Pro-choice advocates, for instance, do not accept the foetus's right to life as a valid or relevant premise, and the literature frequently refers to abortion debates as a 'clash of absolutes'.[103]

This mutually exclusive value conflict contrasts sharply with issues such as 'separate but equal', where both sides acknowledge a shared normative baseline – equality – but disagree on how that value should be applied. In these interest-based conflicts, the dispute revolves around the interpretation of a common standard rather than its relevance. Parties agree that the rule of non-discrimination is the core governing framework. Any overlap with other interests (such as property rights claims underpinning a claim to the legitimacy of segregation in private restorations) may require balancing or place an incidental burden on the owner/s' right but does not generate mutually exclusive dynamics. As the US Supreme Court held in *Heart of Atlanta*, desegregation as 'reasonable regulation' did not 'deprive' the owner of his economic freedom and property rights.[104] Recognising property rights did not foreclose the case. By contrast, in abortion or assisted dying, accepting one side's framing as true and relevant (eg, prenatal life) necessarily negates the normative foundation of the other (eg, autonomy).

These dynamics are explicitly acknowledged in the US and German constitutional rulings. Justice Blackmun in *Roe* famously stated that if foetal personhood were established, 'the foetus's right to life would then be guaranteed' and any abortion right would 'collapse'.[105] Similarly, the German Federal Constitutional

[101] See, eg, R Shah, 'Assisted Suicide on the NHS would breach the ECHR' (*UK Human Rights Blog*, 1 November 2024) ukhumanrightsblog.com/2024/11/01/guest-post-assisted-suicide-on-the-nhs-would-breach-the-echr/ accessed 3 August 2025; *cf* A Deb and L Graham, 'No, legislating to allow euthanasia would not breach the European Convention on Human Rights' (UK Human Rights Blog, 7 November 2024) ukhumanrightsblog.com/2024/11/07/no-legislating-to-allow-euthanasia-would-not-breach-the-european-convention-on-human-rights/ accessed 3 August 2025.

[102] Contestation of the opposing side's core principles does not preclude non-radical members of both camps from sharing common goals. For instance, they may agree on the desirability of reducing the overall incidence of abortion, or they may be able to develop compromises based on a mutual willingness to 'agree to disagree'. Such outcomes become more feasible when antagonism is de-escalated – an idea explored in greater detail in ch 5.

[103] Tribe (n 21); EA Cook, *Between Two Absolutes: Public Opinion and the Politics of Abortion* (Abingdon, Routledge, 2019).

[104] *Heart of Atlanta Motel Inc v United States* 379 US 241, 261 (1964): 'The Fifth Amendment does not forbid reasonable regulation … Nor does the Act deprive appellant of its property.'

[105] *Roe v Wade* 410 US 113 (1973) 156–157.

Court held that '*a compromise* which guarantees the protection of the life of the one to be born and permits the pregnant woman the freedom of abortion *is not possible* since the interruption of pregnancy always means the destruction of unborn life'.[106]

This genuine moral clash has implications for the subsidiary mechanisms of uncertainty underpinning Madison's argument. He noted that diversification of interest allows only a coalition based on 'justice and common good' to be stable because the other coalitions will be suspicious of one another, and this uncertainty helps destabilise a malicious coalition.[107] In moral value-based conflicts, each faction genuinely believes itself to be morally correct and sees no reason to distrust its coalition partners. The result is stable, polarised alliances that are resistant to internal fragmentation, unlike the dynamics illustrated earlier with coalitions based on group interests.

E. Applying the Test

Bringing together the aforementioned factors clearly shows that disagreement on abortion is fundamentally a faction of moral principle in the context of the jurisdictional question and the *nemo judex* rule.[108] As discussed above: (i) centralising abortion in the larger territorial federation does not alter the causes of faction; (ii) neither are dissenters to the right in question mainly men, nor is a person's stance based on their social group membership; (iii) the attachment to the issue is unaffected by economic incentives; and (iv) parties to the debate do not share a common departure point as to the definition of life, nor whether life or choice should take precedence.

Before concluding, several caveats must be noted. First, while the four criteria outlined here – qualitative expansion of cause of bias, demographic asymmetry, and resistance to economic inducement – are cumulative and central to the analysis, the fourth factor, concerning normative standpoint, operates more as a supplementary consideration. Given the inherent ambiguity in defining morality or values, critics might seek to narrow the level of abstraction and reframe certain disputes as involving moral value disagreement. To avoid unnecessary detours, the fourth factor is treated as an auxiliary element, recognising that the first three are generally sufficient to distinguish between the two types of factions. Second, the two categories of factions discussed here serve as ideals; in practice, sometimes, they may – and often do – overlap. Chapter six will explore additional example cases where multiple factional dynamics intertwine.

[106] Quoted in M Nijsten, *Abortion and Constitutional Law: A Comparative European-American Study* (European University Institute, 1990) 100–102.
[107] Madison, *Federalist No. 51*, 255 (emphasis added).
[108] This is, however, independent from the substantive approach, and does not hinder the court from seeing it as a matter of indirect discrimination in the future.

V. Concluding Remarks

While this book thus far has defended Madison's impartiality theory, this chapter raises its own critique from within the logic of the theory itself. It highlights Madison's oversight of the distinction between factions of group interest and factions of principle – which were analogised to the common law distinction between pecuniary and non-pecuniary 'cause-driven' bias. In cases animated by factions of moral principle, the structural conditions necessary for Madison's impartiality logic to operate do not hold; in such contexts, centralisation does not necessarily yield more impartial decision-making. Given the significance of this distinction, the chapter has proposed a multi-factorial test to aid in differentiating between the two types of factions for the purposes of federal power allocation.

Yet, establishing that the impossibility of checking bias in cases of principle-based factions does not, by itself, resolve the boundary question. That is: the centre may not be neutral, but this does not automatically confer neutrality on the states. Where then should regulatory authority over such issues reside? In addressing this further boundary dilemma, a comparison between abortion regulation in the US and the EU offers valuable insights. The two systems have pursued diametrically opposed approaches, providing contrasting models that help refine our understanding of the implications of impartiality's absence and its bearing on the boundary question. Chapter six will add a layer of complexity by exploring issues where two factions merge. Taken together, the analysis in the chapters to follow will ultimately demonstrate how the drawing of federal jurisdictional boundaries shapes the management of disagreement across various factionalised disputes.

5

The Impossible Impartiality: Abortion as a Faction of Principle

> [T]here was *no neutral ground* on which HEW [Department of Health, Education, and Welfare], and its Secretary could comfortably stand, for any decision – to fund all, or none, or some abortions – would disappoint and enrage millions of Americans who were convinced that theirs was the only humane position.
>
> – J. A. Califano, former Secretary of the HEW[1]

> When those trained in the respective disciplines of medicine, philosophy, and theology are unable to arrive at any consensus, the judiciary, at this point in the development of man's knowledge, is not in a position to speculate as to the answer.
>
> – *Roe v Wade*[2]

I. Introduction

Before launching into the comparison of abortion across the Atlantic, it is worth recalling the distinction between non-consensual issues and fiercely polarising ones. Human nature makes disagreement, in most issues, inevitable.[3] Rights are no exception.[4] This is particularly the case when rights fall within the so-called 'morality politics',[5] 'culture wars',[6] or, to reformulate Hume, 'principle-based' disagreements such as abortion, bioethics, or euthanasia. However, being divisive or non-consensual does not entail being polarising. Like the poles of magnets, polarisation represents 'extreme endpoints'.[7] Polarisation is often defined as 'a process

[1] K O'Connor, *No Neutral Ground?: Abortion Politics in an Age of Absolutes* (Abingdon, Routledge, 2020) 1.

[2] *Roe v Wade*, 410 U.S. 113 (1973) para 160.

[3] The faculty of reason, being 'fallible' and prone to corruption by 'self-love' can give rise to factions of a theological or ideological nature. Madison, 'Federalist No. 10' 46–7; DW Howe, 'The Political Psychology of the Federalist' [1987] *William and Mary Quarterly* 485, 506.

[4] R Alexy, *A Theory of Constitutional Rights* (Oxford, Oxford Univeristy Press, 2010) 2.

[5] P Kurzer, *Markets and Moral Regulation: Cultural Change in the European Union* (Cambridge, Cambridge University Press, 2001) 6.

[6] Sociologist James Hunter brought the term 'culture war' to public attention in his best-selling book *Culture Wars: The Struggle to Define America* (New York, Basic Books, 1991).

[7] RF Baumeister and KD Vohs (eds), *Encyclopedia of Social Psychology* (Thousand Oaks, SAGE, 2007) 674.

where extreme views on some matter of public policy are more common'.[8] When polarisation occurs, each rival view judges the world in an all-or-none fashion, delegitimising the other 'as not simply false, but wildly, madly false – nonsense, totally unintelligible and literally unbelievable'.[9] Worse still, polarisation is a step closer to radicalisation, and 'lends itself' more easily to violence, particularly in areas of morality politics.[10]

Disagreement, then, as sown in human nature, cannot be removed by constitutional apparatus. Polarisation, on the other hand, could be avoided or lessened, or failing that, the constitutional structure may help temporise or prevent its escalation. Therefore, the goal of this chapter is not to see which side of the Atlantic eradicated disagreement on abortion but rather to examine which one managed to avoid, decrease, or temporise polarisation thereon and whether there is a normative lesson to be abstracted from the comparison on the role of *nemo judex* and federal division of power in influencing the outcome. In other words, the comparison is not about liberalising but depolarising the abortion debate; the two, depolarisation and liberalisation, do not always travel in tandem.

In comparing the case law and its impact on social reactions, this chapter will concentrate on three symptoms of polarisation that federalism should ideally prevent or mitigate: (i) increasing 'distance' between options favoured by rival factions – where, for example, one side may push for extremely harsh penalties on abortion while the other seeks to permit late-term abortions unconditionally, rather than striving for compromise; (ii) the protracted duration of the controversy, with neither side willing to reach a procedural settlement to 'agree to disagree', and each attempting to impose its moral stance on the other, or to reverse the status quo; and (iii) episodic occurrence of physical violence. This chapter will demonstrate how differing approaches to the federal boundary question have influenced the persistence of these three symptoms in the American abortion debate over the past five decades, while in Europe, with a few exceptions, these symptoms have largely remained absent.

The chapter begins by examining the United States before transitioning to the European Union in the third section. Each section starts by analysing the central jurisprudence governing the allocation of power over abortion regulation. This is followed by an exploration of how this central jurisprudence has influenced legal changes at the state level and its impact on social polarisation. Section IV highlights the stark differences in polarisation between the two regions, interpreted through the lens of chapter four's discussion of the omitted 'faction of principle' and the federalist impartiality argument. This analysis provides normative

[8] N McCarty, *Polarization: What Everyone Needs to Know* (Oxford, Oxford University Press, 2019) 9.

[9] R Wertheimer, 'Understanding the Abortion Argument' (1971) 1 *Philosophy & Public Affairs* 67; quoted in O'Connor (n 1) 79.

[10] AE Doan, *Opposition and Intimidation: The Abortion Wars and Strategies of Political Harassment* (Ann Arbor, University of Michigan Press, 2007): noting that once a group experiences failure and frustration because its efforts to influence the relevant actors have not materialised into favourable policy outcomes or societal behavioural changes, it may view violence as the only strategy available.

insights into the structural question of centralisation versus other forms of decentralisation of divisive moral principles. Section V looks ahead, assessing the implications of the argument for the future of abortion regulation on both sides of the Atlantic. Section VI broadens the lens, showing that abortion is far from exceptional by surveying other morally divisive issues that have become more polarised under centralisation and less so when over-centralisation was avoided. Finally, section VII concludes by reinforcing the chapter's central finding: that centralising a single view on morally contested issues is not neutral and often comes at a significant polarising cost.

II. America's Long-lasting Controversy

A. Case Law on who Judges Abortion, and how?

Whereas criminalising abortion in Europe goes back to Justinian codification in 534,[11] it was only in the nineteenth century when the American state legislatures started doing so.[12] Legislation was done by the state, not the federal government, because abortion was part of police powers over health and morals, which have traditionally been the province of states. By the 1960s, a combination of social and demographic forces produced a 'strong current of opinion' aiming to reform the severity of existing anti-abortion statutes.[13] Starting with Colorado in 1967, 19 states had relaxed their abortion ban by 1973, including four which had completely repealed criminal abortion laws.[14]

The adoption of these reforms does not imply that they were consensual. The morality of abortion and its concomitant epistemic ambiguity on the definition of life is, normally, a topic of debate.[15] However, the issue was neither 'fiercely divisive'[16] nor violent as it is today. Abortion took a much more polarising turn in the decade between the Supreme Court's intervention starting in *Roe* in 1973, and the ensuing political mobilisation and subsequent federal involvement from the 1980s onwards. Since then, the American 'tale' of abortion has been one 'of hopeless

[11] S Turenne, *Le Juge Face à La Désobéissance Civile En Droits Américain et Français Comparés* (Librairie Générale de Jurisprudence, 2007) 223.

[12] For a detailed account, see LH Tribe, *Abortion: The Clash of Absolutes* (New York, WW Norton, 1992) 28–38.

[13] MV Tushnet, *Abortion* (Facts On File Inc 1996) 1.

[14] Tribe (n 12) 46–48: the four started with Hawaii, then New York and Alaska, before Washington follows suit by a popular referendum.

[15] The contentious nature of regulating abortion in the 1960s on both sides is evidenced, for example, by the fact that the National organisation for women added abortion to its Bill of Rights, while two years later NARAL (the National Association for the Repeal of Abortion Laws) was formed. On the other hand, proto pro-life movement, predominantly Catholic, mobilised against the referendum in 1972 to legalise abortion in Michigan. For instance, see Tribe (n 12) 50; Doan (n 10) 9.

[16] RH Fallon Jr, 'If Roe were Overruled: Abortion and the Constitution in A Post-Roe World' (2007) 51 *Saint Louis University Law Journal* 611.

polarisation, personal hatreds, and political dysfunction'.[17] In what follows, I provide an overview of the origin and trajectory of this tale.

Unlike the EU Charter of Fundamental Rights and the ECHR, the American Constitution does not contain an explicit right to privacy. Still, Justice Douglas, writing for the majority in *Griswold* (1965), found a fundamental right to privacy implicit in the 'penumbras' of several provisions of the Bill of Rights.[18] In this case, the Supreme Court invalidated a statute criminalising the sale of or providing information on contraceptives, reasoning that the use of contraception falls within the right to privacy, which 'is protected from governmental intrusion'.[19] Less than a decade later, the Court expanded this right to privacy to include abortion.

In *Roe v Wade* (1973) and its companion case, *Doe* v *Bolton*, the Supreme Court held that the Constitution protects the right of a woman to choose abortion prior to viability.[20] *Roe* presented a challenge to a Texas law that prohibited all abortions except to save the mother's life. Whereas *Doe* involved a challenge to a Georgia law that banned abortions except when a doctor determines that the pregnancy would threaten the mother's life, there are serious foetal defects, or the pregnancy resulted from rape. Justice Blackmun, writing for himself and six others, read that the Fourteenth Amendment includes a right to personal privacy which embraces a woman's decision whether to carry a pregnancy to term.[21]

The Court adopted a periodic model by dividing pregnancy into three trimesters. During the first trimester, the government could not ban abortions and may only regulate abortions as other medical procedures, such as by requiring that they be performed by a licensed physician.[22] In the second trimester, the government also could not outlaw abortions, but the government 'may, if it chooses, regulate the abortion procedure in ways that are reasonably related to maternal health'.[23] For the third, which is subsequent to viability, the government may prohibit abortions, except if necessary to preserve the life or health of the mother.[24]

The judgment came as a strong federal intervention in what was previously seen as a traditional state arena and had the effect of invalidating forty-six state laws.[25] However, it was by no means the last federal intervention. Since then, the Court, Congress, and presidents have heavily intervened in regulating abortion. *Roe* and subsequent mobilisation instigated a 'flood of litigation' regarding different abortion aspects. This included mandatory waiting periods,[26] spousal

[17] M Ziegler, *Abortion and the Law in America: Roe V. Wade to the Present* (Cambridge, Cambridge University Press, 2020) 212.

[18] *Griswold v Connecticut* 381 US 479 (1965) 483, 485.

[19] ibid at 483.

[20] *Roe* (n 2).

[21] ibid.

[22] E Chemerinsky, *Constitutional Law* (Burlington, Aspen, 2019) 1200–1202.

[23] *Roe* (n 2) para 153.

[24] *Doe v Bolton* 410 US 179 (1973).

[25] MJ Klarman, 'Rethinking the Civil Rights and Civil Liberties Revolutions' (1996) 82 *Virginia Law Review* 10.

[26] *Planned Parenthood of Cent Mo v Danforth* 428 US 52 (1976); *City of Akron v Akron Ctr for Reprod Health, Inc* 462 US 416 (1983).

and parental consent,[27] locus of abortions,[28] viability, foetal testing, disposal of foetal remains,[29] and government funding of abortion.[30] One case in particular resembles the CJEU's case on providing advertisements for abortion services.[31] In *Bigelow v Virginia*, involving a Virginia statute, which, much like the Irish ban challenged before the CJEU in *Grogan*,[32] prohibited the advertising of abortion providers in other US states.[33] Unlike the CJEU's refusal to rule substantively on the issue, the American Supreme Court invalidated the Virginia statute.

More importantly, the Court had a chance to revisit *Roe* in another round of leading subsequent rulings. These rulings, however, were rendered in the *penumbras* of political mobilisation. From *Roe* to the year leading up to the 1980 presidential election, the issue of abortion triggered and *polarised consolidation*, especially on the side of the anti-abortion faction. Prior to *Roe*, opposition to abortion was 'predominantly Catholic'.[34] Federalising abortion and its ensuing mobilisation facilitated the consolidation of other actors, such as Evangelicals and Mormons, who, with Catholics, 'geared up' their 'machinery' to unite and mobilise sympathisers behind 'the anti-abortion flag'.[35] They found a political alliance with the Republican Party and its presidents, who explicitly called for reversing *Roe*. To this end, between 1980 and 1992, Republican Presidents Reagan and Bush appointed 'five new Justices to the Supreme Court (and Democrats none)'.[36] The judicial majority seemed 'poised' to overrule *Roe*.[37]

To the astonishment of many, the Court did not repeal *Roe*'s central holding. Yet, through *Casey* (1992), a bitter 5-4 decision, the Court narrowed down the scope of *Roe* and modified its trimester framework. The case involved the constitutionality of a Pennsylvania statute that imposed a 24-hour waiting period before an abortion could be performed; required a woman seeking an abortion to receive certain information designed to persuade her to choose childbirth over abortion; required a minor to obtain parental consent; and required a woman to provide spousal notice. The Court reaffirmed what it termed *Roe*'s core of assuring 'the

[27] *Planned Parenthood of Cent Mo* (n 26); *Bellotti v Baird*, 443 US 622 (1979); *Planned Parenthood Assn v Ashcroft* 462 US 476 (1983).

[28] *City of Akron* (n 26); *Simopoulos v Va* 462 US 506 (1983).

[29] *Planned Parenthood of Cent Mo* (n 26); *Colautti v Franklin* 439 US 379 (1979).

[30] Eg, *Harris v McRae* 448 US 297 (1980).

[31] *Bigelow v Va* 421 US 809 (1975).

[32] Case C–159/90 *SPUC v Grogan* ECLI:EU:C:1991:378, [1991] ECR I–4685.

[33] ibid.

[34] R Post and R Siegel, 'Roe Rage: Democratic Constitutionalism and Backlash' (2007) 42 *Harvard Civil Rights-Civil Liberties Law Review* 373.

[35] M McKeegan, *Abortion Politics: Mutiny in the Ranks of the Right* (Basingstoke, Macmillan, 1992) 18 ('Significantly, it was the women's movement that first galvanized born-again Christians to political action in the 1970s. After decades of political somnolence, conservative Protestants organized across the nation to defeat the ERA. Only after the amendment fizzled late in the decade did abortion become the religious right's top priority').

[36] RH Fallon Jr, *The Dynamic Constitution: An Introduction to American Constitutional Law and Practice*, 2nd edn (Cambridge, Cambridge University Press, 2013) 211.

[37] H Gillian, MA Graber and KE Whittington, *American Constitutionalism, Volume II: Rights and Liberties*, 2nd edn (Oxford, Oxford University Press, 2013) 608.

woman's right to terminate her pregnancy before viability'.[38] But in *Casey*, the Court replaced *Roe*'s trimester framework with the 'undue burden' standard. Under this standard, the government may regulate for the purpose of protecting potential life throughout the term of a pregnancy, as long as the law does not impose an 'undue burden' on the pregnant woman's decision whether to obtain or access abortion before viability.[39] Using this new framework, the Court upheld all of Pennsylvania's requirements, except spousal notification.[40]

Three decades after *Casey*, *Roe* indeed fell. In *Dobbs* (2022), the newly Trump-appointed justices helped form a majority to overrule *Roe* as well as *Casey*. Committed to what Sunstein terms 'due process traditionalism',[41] Justice Alito, writing for five others, held the Constitution not to confer a right to abortion. It was reasoned that such a right is neither 'deeply rooted in this Nation's history and tradition' nor 'implicit in the concept of ordered liberty'. The majority opinion mainly relied on a historical argument that until late in the twentieth century, 'there was no support in American law for a constitutional right to obtain an abortion'.[42] In every state, 'abortion had long been a crime'.[43] The common law made abortion 'criminal in at least some stages of pregnancy'. At the time the Fourteenth Amendment was ratified, 'three-quarters of the States had made abortion a crime at any stage of pregnancy, and the remaining states would soon follow'.[44] Absent a fundamental right at play, the Court utilised the lighter standard of rational basis review to uphold the Mississippi law banning abortion after 15 weeks of pregnancy.

The implications of *Dobbs* on the state and federal levels are still unfolding. What is crucial, however, is to understand how the United States arrived at this juncture. Contrasting the past half-century of developments with those in Europe may provide insights into the implications for the future. To this end, the next section summarises the enduring polarisation and conflict over abortion at the popular, state, and federal levels.

B. Consolidating Polarisation in the US

It will be recalled that the linchpin of Federalist No. 10 was 'interest diversification makes concert among factions more difficult'. The effect of the centralising

[38] *Planned Parenthood of South-eastern Pa v Casey* 505 US 833 (1992).

[39] For a comparative analysis, see: RB Siegel, 'The Constitutionalization of Abortion' in RJ Cook, JN Erdman and BM Dickens (eds), *Abortion Law in Transnational Perspectiv* (Philadelphia, University of Pennsylvania Press, 2014).

[40] ibid.

[41] CR Sunstein, 'Dobbs and the Travails of Due Process Traditionalism' (Harvard Public Law Working Paper No. 22-14, 29 June 2022) papers.ssrn.com/sol3/papers.cfm?abstract_id=4145922 accessed 3 August 2025.

[42] *Dobbs v Jackson Women's Health Organisation* 597 US 215 (2022) [6].

[43] ibid.

[44] ibid [16].

principle-based faction is not *diversification* but rather *consolidated polarisation*. Where the whole union, in Hume's words, is 'rend into two or three factions'.[45] Contrary to the goal of Federalist No. 10, centralising divisive principles helps *facilitate* rather than *break* 'concert', and *allows rather than prevents* them to 'act in unison'.[46] This is picturesque of the US abortion conflict as briefly discussed below.

Figure 5.1 Diversification vs Consolidation

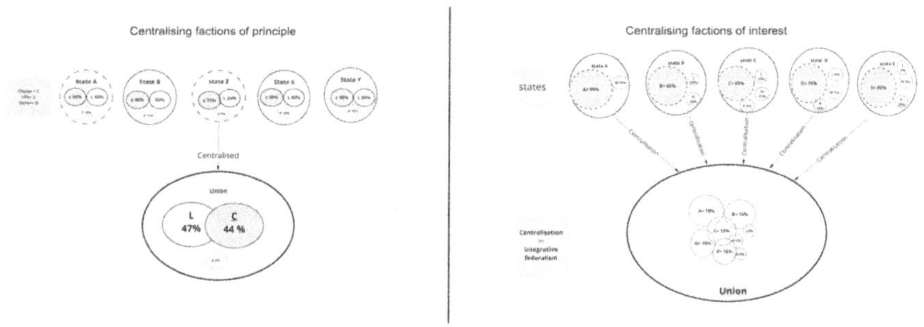

In the US, opposition and anti-abortion sentiment existed before the federal intervention that started with *Roe*. However, active opposition was predominantly Catholic, whereas Protestant clergy and Jewish rabbis were supportive of some 'abortion reform'.[47] Following federalisation, the US's heterogeneous groups *collapsed* into fewer ones marked largely by the divide between pro-life and pro-choice factions. Abortion became at the heart of culture wars pitting humanist secularists against cultural and religious traditionalists.[48] After federalisation, scholars pondered on a 'strange phenomenon',[49] a 'seismic shift'.[50] 'Suddenly', there were 'Catholics, Protestant Fundamentalists Mormons working together in various organizations … groups that would ordinarily ignore, … one another, were working side by side'.[51] Post and Seigel refer to a telling instance of consolidation. 'Paul Weyrich (a Catholic) and Howard Phillips (a Jew) met with Jerry Falwell [Southern Baptist] and other architects of the [religious] Right' to propose organising Protestant Evangelicals into an organisation entitled 'Moral Majority',[52] which was extremely active in mobilising anti-abortion sentiments during the Regan era.

[45] D Hume, *Essays, Moral, Political, and Literary* (Carmel, Liberty Fund, 1985) 62.
[46] Madison, 'Federalist No. 10' (n 3) 44.
[47] In 1967, 21 religious leaders announced on the front page of the *New York Times* that they would direct women in need of abortion services to doctors who were legitimate and safe: Tribe (n 12) 92.
[48] Doan (n 10) 162–163.
[49] DA Blanchard, *The Anti-Abortion Movement and the Rise of the Religious Right: From Polite to Fiery Protest*, 77 (New York, Twayne Publishers, 1994).
[50] As Feldman noted, 'a broader Catholic-evangelical alliance on social issues suddenly seemed possible for the first time'. N Feldman, *Divided by God: America's Church-State Problem -- and What We Should Do About It* (New York, Farrar, Straus and Giroux, 2006) 214.
[51] Blanchard (n 49) 77.
[52] Post and Siegel (n 34) 420–421.

Distinctive of consolidated principle-based factions is their durability and long 'staying power'.[53] The protracted nature of the controversy reflects the strength of polarisation. While activist organisations may change formation or be substituted, and their strength may wax and wane, the unifying power of the pro-life or pro-choice banner has persisted over the past 50 years.[54] Unlike the shifting winds of interest-based factions, where coalitions would teeter as their payoff changes, after half a century, neither faction lost its ground nor seems to be even 'mildly persuaded' by the views of the other.[55] Contrary to the examples of minority rights, federalisation did not break 'the concert' among factions, nor did the faction opposed to abortion rights slowly crumble like Thatcher's or Russel's southern Coalition, which, respectively, opposed rights to equal pay and racial equality.

The longevity of the conflict is evident from the fact that after more than 50 years of the decision in *Roe*, the issue is still controversial and was a key item in the 2024 presidential debate, where debate on abortion featured prominently. Candidates traded accusations on abortion. Harris supporters were pushing for the statute to protect abortion nationwide, and some of Trump's supporters sought a nationwide ban. Nine states put the issue on the ballots alongside the presidential election. The conflict is also expanding into a 'new battleground' over whether abortion pills used for early-term abortions can be mailed across states or should be federally banned.

Another indicator of strong polarisation over abortion is that it has occasionally degenerated into violence and even terrorism. Violence varied across a spectrum ranging from mild harassment to murder and bombing. Less violent, yet harmful, forms included picketing clinics or the homes of clinic staff members, vandalism, and threatening subcontractors dealing with abortion clinics.[56] A 'more ominous'[57] aspect was when hundreds of abortion clinics were bombed, and many more vandalised. Abortion doctors and staff were murdered,[58] whilst others received gunshot wounds.[59]

This lingering grassroots 'culture war' interacted dialectically, and often instrumentally, with politicians at the state and federal level.[60] Perhaps the most enduring impact of the latter is the transformation of the Supreme Court's composition.[61]

[53] B Ackerman, *We the People, Volume 1: Foundations* (Cambridge, MA, Harvard University Press, 1993) vol 1, 187–188.

[54] For an overview of these organisations, see P Saurette and K Gordon, *The Changing Voice of the Anti-Abortion Movement* (Toronto, University of Toronto Press, 2018).

[55] Tribe (n 12) 6.

[56] See generally Doan (n 10).

[57] Tribe (n 12) 171–172.

[58] O'Connor (n 1) 159–165; for a brief updated survey see Liam Stack, 'A Brief History of Deadly Attacks on Abortion Providers' *New York Times* (29 November 2015) www.nytimes.com/interactive/2015/11/29/us/30abortion-clinic-violence.html accessed 3 August 2025.

[59] Ziegler (n 17) 222; DA Blanchard and TJ Prewitt, *Religious Violence and Abortion: The Gideon Project* (Gainesville, University Press of Florida, 1993) 212.

[60] Doan (n 10) 10.

[61] MV Tushnet, *Taking the Constitution Away from the Courts* (Princeton, Princeton University Press, 2000) 138–139 ('Taking the Constitution Away').

Pro-life presidents Reagan, Bush, and most recently Trump have had the lion's share in judicial appointments, which aimed, among other things, at reversing *Roe*. These appointments, as Tushnet remarked, transformed Court membership, and, thus, 'the pro-choice victories themselves eroded with that transformation'.[62]

At the state level, before *Dobbs*, states were divided between embracing *Roe* and vehemently opposing it. On the one hand, as Friesen noted, 'few' states have 'expressly or by implication' accepted and moved beyond *Roe*.[63] On the other hand, in many states, *Roe* was followed by an unceasing onslaught of legislation aiming at eroding the federally established rights. This took the form of either enacting restrictive laws that could not possibly be constitutional under *Roe*, or states have opted to erect roadblocks to abortion by restricting its availability under differing circumstances or by imposing requirements that raise its cost, which has had the effect of a decline of local abortion providers and taking a toll on travel distance and cost.[64]

The occasional eruption of violence and the longevity of failure to reach a settlement tick two boxes of the symptoms of polarisation. Surveying the extremity of some state laws ticks the third. Some American state laws, unlike their European counterparts and empowered with some local popular support, tend toward extremes. In Alabama, abortion is illegal unless a physician determines it is necessary to prevent 'serious risk' 'to the physical health of the mother or major bodily function'.[65] The commission of this overarching category of 'illegal abortion' is classified as a felony in the law. While the law exempts the pregnant mother from punishment, for providers of abortion, it is punishable by up to 99 years of imprisonment.[66] Likewise, Texas's 'overlapping bans and penalties the harshest of which authorizes a term of life imprisonment for abortion offenders'.[67]

Moreover, states started to follow Texas's lead using a private bounty model to pit citizens against one another. In May 2021, Texas enacted SB8, which, reminiscent of the Roman *actio popularis*,[68] allows anyone to sue those involved in providing abortion care or practical support to patients in Texas, and win judgments of $10,000 or more.[69] When the Texas law reached the Supreme Court, the majority opinion left the door wide open for an infinite number of private

[62] ibid.

[63] For a survey, see J Friesen, *State Constitutional Law: Litigating Individual Rights, Claims, and Defenses*, 4th edn (London, LexisNexis 2006) 2, 55–58; PB Linton, *Abortion under State Constitutions: A State-by-State Analysis*, 3rd edn (Durham, Carolina Academic Press, 2020) 497–502.

[64] Doan (n 10) 153–154; see also Ziegler (n 17) 187–188.

[65] J Mascolo, ESQ, 'Alabama Abortion Laws' (*Findlaw*, 2024) www.findlaw.com/state/alabama-law/alabama-abortion-laws.html accessed 3 August 2025.

[66] Linton (n 63) 31–33. Though there have been proposals to punish pregnant women in state legislatures.

[67] RB Siegel and M Ziegler, 'Abortion's New Criminalization – A History-And-Tradition Right to Healthcare Access After *Dobbs*' (2025) 111 *Virginia Law Review* 413.

[68] Translated as 'action at Law of the People', which refers to action brought by a third party in the interest of the public/state as a whole. For its application in international law see, eg, separate opinion of Judge Bula-Bula in Arrest Warrant of 11 April 2000 (Congo v. Belg.), 2002 I.C.J. Rep. 3, 130 n. 96.

[69] Texas Senate Bill 8, Bill Text: TX SB8 (2021–2022).

individuals to utilise Texas state courts to launch an onslaught of litigation against abortion providers, which, among other things, will substantially hike up their running costs.[70] The examples of Texas and Alabama, along with similar 'copycat' laws,[71] represent one end of the spectrum, contrasting sharply with the laws in eight states plus Washington, DC, where no limits are currently set on abortion, even for late-term procedures. This widening gap between opposing positions is notably different from the way abortion regulation is approached in Europe.

Overall, and to recap, the abortion debate in the US has been defined by 'hopeless polarization',[72] 'ugliness',[73] 'violence', and 'fierce division'.[74] This half-century-old polarisation contrasts sharply with the tale of abortion on the other side of the Atlantic. The next part takes up this comparison, followed by an analysis of the reasons behind this stark difference.

III. Abortion in Borderless Europe

At the time *Roe* was decided, none of the European Community signatories allowed abortion except for the UK, which joined the community in the same year, 1973. Throughout the 1970s, the map of Member States' abortion regulation was predominantly restrictive. Only France in 1975 and Italy in 1978 liberalised their abortion regulation, while other members stood firmly against it. This is best exemplified by Ireland, which adopted a specific constitutional amendment enshrining the rights of the unborn; the Belgian King, who preferred to be declared unfit to rule than to sign a Bill legalising abortion, or the German Constitutional Court, which decided in 1975 that the Parliament is constitutionally bound to protect the life of the unborn. However, over the past decades, only two EU states have kept their ban, while the map of abortion in Europe has changed considerably. The remaining 27 Member States ('MS') shifted to legalise abortion, but, more importantly, they have done so, mostly, in a depolarised fashion where social norms have reflected gradual constitutional change.

The section begins with a summary of the EU case law addressing the jurisdictional purview over abortion, followed by a view from the states. Space allows only a broad overview of changing abortion regulation across MS. However, I dwell relatively more on Ireland, Germany, and Poland. This is because Ireland not only represents a major shift in its position on abortion, but also, its abortion laws have

[70] In January 2022, the Court majority turned down a request to send Texas abortion litigation back to the federal district court: *Re Whole Woman's Health, Et al. on Petition For Writ Of Mandamus* US No 21–962 (2022).

[71] A Durkee, 'Idaho Enacts Law Copying Texas Abortion Ban-And These States Might Be Next' (*Forbes*, 23 March 2022) www.forbes.com/sites/alisondurkee/2022/03/23/idaho-enacts-law-copying-texas-abortion-ban---and-these-states-might-be-next/?sh=2086faa25c05 [https://perma.cc/6DUH-5RBS] accessed 3 August 2025.

[72] Ziegler (n 17) 212.

[73] ibid 209.

[74] Fallon Jr (n 16).

the most significant interaction with the CJEU and ECtHR. Thus, understanding the Irish abortion journey is pivotal to understanding the EU-MS dynamics of the matter. Germany, too, changed its position and, most importantly, provided a model which has spread across many MS. Poland, on the other hand, is the outlier case where recent mobilisation has occurred.

A. European Case Law on who Judges Abortion

i. *The CJEU Jurisprudence*

The issue of abortion is not an active area of the CJEU jurisprudence, and the EU demands neither conformity nor harmonisation thereon. Thus, the CJEU prefers to leave abortion to MS's regulatory choice; yet, it keeps the potentiality to intervene not only on grounds of abortion as a fundamental right but also to ensure adherence to market freedoms. The first and only case where the CJEU was asked to examine MS abortion laws was *Grogan*.[75] The Society for the Protection of the Unborn Child ('SPUC'), relying on the Irish constitutional ban on abortion, sought an injunction to prevent student groups from distributing information on abortion services available in the UK. The Irish High Court referred to the CJEU the following questions: (a) whether abortion was a 'service' within the meaning of the Community's free movement rules; and (b) whether student groups have a right under Community law to distribute information concerning abortion services available in other Member States.[76]

The CJEU defined abortion 'solely in terms of the possible commerce and profit resulting from it'.[77] The Court dismissed claims on abortion as non-justiciable on the premise that the link between the Irish student unions and the UK was 'too tenuous' to trigger the application of Community Law.[78] Thus, in this case, European law could not prevent the Irish judiciary from issuing an injunction restraining students from distributing abortion information.[79] Whilst the Court impliedly opted to continue to leave the morally divisive issue to states, at the same time, it sent a 'credible threat' of potential intervention of the CJEU. By classifying abortion as a 'service', it meant that abortion fell within the purview of the EU's regulation of market freedoms across states, and the CJEU is, therefore, competent to intervene,[80] if need be, although it never has over the three decades following this ruling.

[75] *SPUC* (n 32).
[76] S Mullally, 'Debating Reproductive Rights in Ireland' (2005) 27 *Human Rights Quarterly* 78, 90–91.
[77] F Fabbrini, 'The European Court of Human Rights, the EU Charter of Fundamental Rights, and the Right to Abortion: Roe V. Wade on the Other Side of the Atlantic' (2011) 18 *Columbia Journal of European Law* 1, 17–18 ('Roe on the Other Side'); Mullally (n 76) 90–91.
[78] *Grogan* (n 32) para 24.
[79] Mullally (n 76) 90–91.
[80] *Grogan* (n 32) para 24.

Having opted to steer away from explicitly siding with pro-choice litigants, the Court also prevented the pro-life group's efforts to get the Union involved. This aligns with the hands-off approach of mediated plurality as defined in chapter one. In 2018, pro-life activists sought to challenge not national laws, but rather the Commission's alleged inaction on restricting abortion. The challenge was submitted by the European Citizens Initiative with the title '*Uno di noi*' (One of Us). As the name suggests, the initiative aimed mainly at the protection of the dignity and right to life from the moment of conception.[81] The Commission, however, adopted the contested Communication whereby it decided not to take any action on this initiative. The applicants argued that the Commission's discretionary power and 'right to stay passive' should be interpreted narrowly. The General Court disagreed, reasoning that the Commission enjoys a 'legislative initiative quasi-monopoly'[82] and broad discretionary powers to 'promote the general interest of the Union'.[83]

In a slightly relevant case, the Court did, however, take a wide definition of human embryo, but this was confined to the context of patenting biotechnological inventions. The Court found that the destruction of an embryo for the purpose of treating Parkinson's disease was unpatentable. In *Brüstle*, the Court held 'that any human ovum must, as soon as fertilized, be regarded as a "human embryo" within the meaning and for the purposes of application of Article 6(2)(c) of Directive on the legal protection of biotechnological inventions'.[84] The CJEU, however, attempted to distance itself in such a way as to limit the definition of an embryo to the scope of the said Directive without attempting to resolve the abortion debate.[85]

ii. *The Jurisprudence of the European Convention on Human Rights (ECHR)*

The ECHR is an international human rights treaty adopted in 1950 and has its own international court, the ECtHR. As an international agreement, it only binds its members under classic international law.[86] Therefore, states remain free as to 'which domestic legal status' to bestow upon this international convention.[87] However, the EU adds another layer to the threat of constitutionalisation and centralisation without directly centralising it.[88] Article 52(3) of the EU Charter is read by the CJEU to regard the ECtHR's jurisprudence as a 'special source of

[81] Case T-561/14 *European Citizens' Initiative One of Us and Others v European Commission* ECLI:EU:T:2018:210; see discussion in I Tucak and A Blagojević, 'Abortion in Europe' (2020) 4 *EU and Comparative Law Issues and Challenges Series* 1135, 1158–1161.

[82] *European Citizens' Initiative One of Us* (n 81) para 115.

[83] ibid 169.

[84] Case C-34/10 *Brüstle* v *Greenpeace* EU:C:2011:669, para 35.

[85] ibid; see also Tucak and Blagojević (n 81) 1158–1161.

[86] R Schütze, *European Constitutional Law*, 2nd edn (Oxford, Oxford University Press, 2016) 467.

[87] ibid.

[88] A von Bogdandy and J Bast, *Principles of European Constitutional Law* (Oxford, Hart Publishing, 2009) 486 (remarking that ECHR has a 'catalyst effect, but not legally binding').

inspiration'.[89] This way, the CJEU duly considers the ECtHR jurisprudence and often incorporates it directly into the EU legal order, making it constitutionally binding upon EU states.[90]

At the time the ECHR was adopted, abortion was a crime in all signatory parties, and the drafters did not protect a right thereto.[91] However, the Convention contained multiple provisions, such as the right to life, the right to private and family life, and freedom of information, which have gradually become relevant to case law on abortion.[92] Until 1990, the ECtHR did not decide on abortion. The first case to reach the Court originated from Ireland.[93] Overall, the Court has steered a cautious path, balancing the dictates of deferring to the moral choices of MS with placing some 'pressure' to ensure that the framework chosen by the MS is coherent, accessible, clear, and proportionate to the aim pursued by the given states.

On the one hand, the Court held that Article 8 on the right to private family life cannot be interpreted to confer a right to abortion and, thus, leaves the issue to the discretionary power of MS (their 'margin of appreciation' in ECtHR jargon). In *Vo*, the Grand Chamber justified invoking the margin of appreciation on two grounds. First, the issue of protecting the unborn child has not been resolved within the majority of MS. Second, Europe lacks a 'consensus on the scientific and legal definition of the beginning of life'.[94] Likewise, in *A, B, C* v *Ireland*, the Court spoke of 'the impossibility of finding a uniform European conception of morals including on the question of when life begins'.[95] It added that constitutional courts are not 'the appropriate *fora* for the primary determination as to whether a woman qualifies for an abortion which is lawfully available in a State' because 'it would be wrong to turn the High Court into a "licensing authority" for abortions'.[96]

On the other hand, once a state opts for a certain regulatory choice (be it more oriented towards prenatal life or decisional autonomy), the Court's jurisprudence ensures that a state's pursuit of the professed legal and policy aim is coherent, proportionate, and clear to the pregnant women.[97] Thus, '[o]nce the legislature decides to allow abortion [even only in therapeutic exceptions], it must not structure its legal framework in a way which would limit real possibilities to obtain it'.[98] When the

[89] Schütze (n 86) 467.

[90] See generally Síofra O'Leary, 'A Tale of Two Cities: Fundamental Rights Protection in Strasbourg and Luxembourg' (2018) 20 *Cambridge Yearbook of European Legal Studies* 3.

[91] Fabbrini (n 77) 19.

[92] ibid.

[93] See the Irish SPUC controversy in section II.A above.

[94] *Vo v France* App no 53924/00 (ECtHR, 9 July 2004). The ECtHR found that 'it is neither desirable, nor even possible' to provide an abstract answer to the question of whether the unborn is a person within the meaning of Art 2 of the ECHR.

[95] *A, B, and C v Ireland* App no 25579/05 (ECtHR, 16 December 2010).

[96] ibid para 258.

[97] For a summary on the Court's approach, see WA Schabas, *The European Convention on Human Rights: A Commentary* (Oxford, Oxford University Press, 2015) 81, 373; F Fabbrini, 'The Last Holdout: Ireland, the Right to Abortion and the European Federal Human Rights System' (2018) SSRN papers.ssrn.com/sol3/papers.cfm?abstract_id=3249400 accessed 3 August 2025 ('The Last Holdout').

[98] *Tysiąc v Poland* App no 5410/03 (ECtHR, 20 March 2007).

national law suffers '*manque de cohérence*', or fails to 'ensure clarity of the pregnant woman's legal position',[99] the Court found a violation of the Convention. While falling short of recognising a right to abortion, the ECtHR recognised the role of the state in ensuring that its policy choice does not impede the right to information.[100] And that severely ill-enforced state policies which result in 'either actual bodily injury or intense physical and mental suffering' can be seen as *cruel and inhumane or degrading treatment*, contrary to Article 3 of the ECHR.[101]

To recap, there seems to be a 'shared understanding', or perhaps a constitutional 'convention', as Dicey defines it, that informs the approach of the CJEU, the Commission, and the ECtHR.[102] By virtue of such a convention, abortion and other morally divisive matters are left to MS, but once they take a position, the EU maintains possible intervention to monitor its arbitrariness, coherence, and that it does not discriminate in its application. The convention is embraced by the EU Commission in its 2008 equality directive proposal, which, 'in line with subsidiarity principle' and the 'value of diversity', leaves untouched 'national laws on … *reproductive rights*'.[103]

B. EU States' Regulation: Social Dialogue and Legal Changes

i. Ireland

Ireland has been a stronghold of Catholicism. In the aftermath of the civil war and partition, the newly independent state saw the majority's Roman Catholic religion as an identity marker to distinguish 'Irish laws' from the 'polluting' forces of English law.[104] After the enactment of the English Act legalising abortion in 1967, and fearing liberalising tendencies of joining the European Market in 1973, Ireland was determined to proclaim itself as an 'abortion free zone'.[105]

One milestone in the Irish abortion journey is the Eighth Constitutional Amendment. To pre-empt the risk of legalising abortion in Ireland via 'judicial fiat',[106] the Pro-Life Amendment Campaign ('PLAC') proposed an amendment

[99] ibid; *RR v Poland* App no 27617/04 (ECtHR, 26 May 2011).
[100] ibid.
[101] ibid paras 149–162.
[102] Dicey defines conventions as 'understanding, habits or practices that 'regulate the conduct of the several members of the sovereign power': AV Dicey, *Introduction to the Study of the Law of the Constitution* (Basingstoke, Macmillan, 1959) 24:8.
[103] Proposal for a Council Directive on implementing the principle of equal treatment between persons irrespective of religion or belief, disability, age or sexual orientation COM/2008/0426 final, art 3(2) eur-lex.europa.eu/legal-content/en/ALL/?uri=CELEX%3A52008PC0426 accessed 3 August 2025 (The Equality Proposal).
[104] ibid 84.
[105] Kurzer (n 5) 168.
[106] Fabbrinni (n 97) 13 (noting that in 1974, 'the Irish Supreme Court had recognized a fundamental right to privacy … As a result, there was widespread preoccupation that the Irish Supreme Court would follow the path of the U.S. Supreme Court.').

enshrining the right to life of the unborn. Given the prevalent Catholic culture, the amendment was overwhelmingly approved by two-thirds of voters in 1983.[107] Yet, as Ireland is a member of a multilevel constitutional space, the amendment produced a 'cluster'[108] of litigation, not only domestically but also before the CJEU and the ECtHR. Although Ireland added Protocol 17 to the Maastricht Treaty to ensure that the Irish constitutional prohibition on abortion was insulated from any change that might be required as a result of European Union membership, the Protocol was of little effect.

Being part of a borderless Europe meant that some women could afford to circumvent the Irish ban and seek legal abortion in another MS, which unsettled the local norms' 'understated assumptions'.[109] This abortion tourism engendered judicial battles before the CJEU, the Irish Supreme Court, and a few times before the ECtHR. I explain each below, along with intervening referenda, solidifying the partial judicial victories. In *Grogan*, as previously mentioned, whilst the Court opted to continue to leave this morally divisive issue to states, it sent a 'credible threat' of potential intervention of the CJEU into Irish regulation of abortion as a service and, thus, within the potential reach of the market freedoms.[110]

Shortly afterwards, and again because of travel, the Eighth Amendment was tested judicially, but this time before the Irish courts. The seminal X case involved a 14-year-old girl who was pregnant as a result of rape and showed suicidal tendencies. Her parents arranged travel to England and informed the police of the incident, but the police reported the parents (not the rapist). The Attorney General secured an injunction restraining X from leaving Ireland for nine months, which was upheld by the High Court. As the case sparked massive controversy and global attention, the government paid all the fees for the appeal before the Supreme Court. The Court reversed the High Court's ruling, concluding that abortion is lawful when there was 'real and substantial risk' to the mother's life and recognising threatened suicide as one.[111]

After the CJEU and the Irish Supreme Court, the SPUC controversy and its concomitant right to travel and information reached the ECtHR. *In Open Door Counselling & Dublin Well Woman Centers*,[112] two centres were forced to close their nondirective pregnancy counselling services based on injunctions initiated by SPUC.[113] Both centres claimed that this restriction on the provision of information violated their right to privacy and to freedom of expression under the ECHR. In a judgment 'attempting to prevent encroachment upon contracting states' margin of appreciation', the Court concluded that the Irish prohibition on

[107] Irish Constitution 1937 (as amended by the Eighth Am 1983), art 40.3.3.
[108] Fabbrinni (n 97) 14.
[109] Kurzer (n 5) 180.
[110] *Grogan* (n 32). See also *Society for the Protection of Unborn Children v Coogan* [1989] IR 734.
[111] *The Attorney General v X* [1992] 1 IR 1 ('the X case').
[112] *Open Door Counselling & Dublin Well Woman v Ireland* App nos 14234/88, 14235/88, (1993) 15 EHRR 244.
[113] *Attorney General v Open Door Counselling & Dublin Well-Woman Centre* [1988] IR 593.

abortion information fell within the scope of permissible restrictions on the right to freedom of expression.[114]

The ECtHR found that the Irish prohibition pursued a legitimate public aim, ie, 'the protection of public morals'.[115] However, the ECtHR concluded that Ireland had not met the requirement of proportionality.[116] The absolute nature of the injunction against the applicants was found excessive, and for that, Ireland had violated Article 10 of the European Convention, protecting the right to freedom of expression. Having found a violation of Article 10, the ECtHR deemed it unnecessary to consider the scope of the right to privacy.[117]

The ECtHR followed a relatively similar approach in the case of *A, B & C*. Once again, the Court balanced deference to the margin of appreciation of MS whilst ensuring clarity and proportionality within national regulation. The case involved three women who travelled to the UK to obtain abortions and claimed that Ireland breached its ECHR obligation for not providing access to abortion. The Court, on the one hand, ruled that there was no right to abortion within the Convention and rejected the claim of the first two applicants who sought abortion on socio-economic grounds. On the other hand, the Court found Ireland in breach of Article 8 on private family life regarding the third applicant. For her, pregnancy threatened the recurrence of a rare cancer from which she had recently recovered and, thus, she should theoretically be entitled to abortion under Irish law. The Court reasoned, 'the uncertainty generated by the lack of legislative implementation of Article 40.3.3 [the Irish constitutional right to protect the life of mothers]', and more particularly by the lack of effective and accessible procedures under that provision, had resulted 'in a striking discordance between the theoretical right to a lawful abortion in Ireland on grounds of a relevant risk to a woman's life and the reality of its practical implementation'.[118]

These episodes of multilevel judicial dialogues triggered socio-political deliberation domestically, which led to subsequent rounds of constitutional referenda.[119] To maintain the country's moral purity and pro-life ethos, conservatives in 1992 and afterwards arranged for a constitutional referendum to reverse the Supreme Court's decision in X. However, the amendment was rejected. Instead, voters approved two other amendments solidifying the right to travel and information providing, thereby providing lawful inroads to circumvent the Irish ban on abortion.[120]

[114] Mullally (n 76) 94.

[115] *Open Door* (n 112) para 62.

[116] ibid 80.

[117] ibid.

[118] *A, B & C* (n 95) para 264.

[119] Fabbrinni (n 97) 7; L Field, 'The Abortion Referendum of 2018 and a Timeline of Abortion Politics in Ireland to Date' (2018) 33 *Irish Political Studies* 623.

[120] Thirteenth Amendment of the Constitution Act, No 13 (23 December 1992) (providing that Art 40(3)(3) be amended so as not to limit freedom of travel); Fourteenth Amendment of the Constitution Act, No 14 (23 December 1992) (providing that Art 40(3)(3) be amended so as not to limit freedom of information regarding abortion services).

The EU free movement secured an arguably very influential, yet subtle, factor in the Irish abortion shift.[121] In the *A, B & C* hearings, the Irish government acknowledged that in 2007 at least 4,686 women travelled to have an abortion,[122] and more recent statistics showed 'an average of nine women a day'.[123] The continuous influx 'accentuate[d] the tensions and contradictions in the national system of morality standards'.[124] As large numbers of Irish women availed themselves of the travel solution, the public questioned the logic of protecting life if abortion is obtainable abroad. It further 'exposed' the inequalities of a ban that could be easily circumvented only by those who could afford to do so.[125] This has resulted in the most sustained and open conversation on the island of Ireland regarding the meaning of abortion travel and women's reproductive health and rights.[126]

Media coverage of tragic cases,[127] along with social media documentation of the struggles of women travelling to seek abortion and the continued circulation of people, helped increase social and political deliberation.[128] In responding to public pressure, the issue of abortion formed a significant part of the 2016 general election. What was pivotal to the fate of the ultimate constitutional amendment was an Irish innovation in the realm of popular safeguards and deliberative constitutionalism. In July 2016, the Irish Parliament (Oireachtas) passed a resolution to convene the *Citizens' Assembly*.[129]

The Citizens' Assembly consisted of 100 members: the Chairperson, former judge of the Irish Supreme Court, Justice Mary Laffoy, and 99 citizens randomly selected by a polling company to provide a representative sample of the age, education level, wealth, and gender makeup of the Irish population.[130] The Assembly convened at the weekends and heard 'over eighty hours' worth of material from medical, legal, and ethical experts. The members were also provided with written submissions from members of the public, pre-recorded interviews with women affected by the Eighth Amendment, and presentations from multiple advocacy groups on the two sides of the debate.[131] The assembly produced a set of recommendations to the Oireachtas with the proposal of repealing the Eighth Amendment.

[121] See generally Fabbrinni (n 97); Kurzer (n 5).
[122] *A, B & C* (n 95) para 183.
[123] Fabbrinni (n 97) 25, citing A Kirk, 'Nine a Day: The Women who Have to Travel for Abortion as Ireland Prepares for Referendum' *The Telegraph* (24 May 2018) www.telegraph.co.uk/news/2018/05/24/nine-day-women-have-travel-abortions-ireland-prepares-referendum/ accessed 3 August 2025.
[124] Kurzer (n 5) 178.
[125] ibid.
[126] L Earner-Byrne and D Urquhart, *The Irish Abortion Journey, 1920–2018* (Cham, Springer, 2019); Fabbrinni (n 97) 7.
[127] E Carolan, 'Constitutional Change Outside the Courts: Citizen Deliberation and Constitutional Narrative (S) in Ireland's Abortion Referendum' (2020) 48 *Federal Law Review* 497, 507–508.
[128] Byrne and Urquhart (n 126) 135; noting that in 2008, the Safe and Legal in Ireland campaign developed three short videos in a series entitled 'Stop the Silence, End the Stigma' which was ranked the second most watched posting on YouTube in Ireland.
[129] Field (n 119) 615.
[130] ibid 614–615.
[131] ibid.

In 2018, Ireland has 'emphatically' approved the proposed constitutional amendment and thus repealed the Eighth Amendment.[132] Interestingly, a 'substantial anti-abortion consensus existed in Ireland' in the 1980s, as reflected by the overwhelming adoption of the Eighth Amendment by two-thirds of voters' approval.[133] However, in the span of time and through various factors, the Eighth Amendment was not only repealed, but also was repealed by around two-thirds of voters too. Shortly afterwards, the Parliament passed the Health (Regulation of Termination of Pregnancy) Act, which allows voluntary termination of pregnancy subject to the submission of a medical certificate that it has not exceeded 12 weeks and a waiting period of three days from the submission of the certificate.[134]

Without forcing a uniform answer from the EU, tension on a divisive issue has been defused gradually. The EU still played an indirectly important role. The free movement and the continued circulation of women accentuate the contradiction and 'understated assumption' of national standards and prompt their reconsideration.[135] This is an example of cross-fertilisation, which will be contrasted with the American experience. For now, the chapter briefly charts the abortion dynamics in other EU states.

ii. The Influential German Model and Other More Expansive Changes: A Broad Overview

In a 'diachronically opposed' opinion to *Roe*,[136] the German Constitutional Court ('FCC'), in 1975, invalidated the West German law that decriminalised abortion during the first 12 weeks after receiving abortion-dissuasive counselling. The Court concluded that the state's duty to protect prenatal life was derived from the Basic Law's protection of life and dignity: 'Where human life exists, human dignity is present to it.' The FCC warned the Parliament not to 'acquiesce' or jump on the bandwagon of popular beliefs and their 'passionate discussion of the abortion polemic'.[137]

The Court had another chance to decide upon abortion after the reunification of Germany. The Parliament adopted a law to reconcile the East German law (where abortion on request was legal until the 12th week after mandatory counselling) and that of West Germany (where abortion was criminal except in limited exceptions). Yet, once again, the FCC declared the 1992 Act unconstitutional,

[132] ibid.

[133] Kurzer (n 5) 152.

[134] Health (Regulation of Termination of Pregnancy) Act 2018, art 12.

[135] Kurzer (n 5) 180.

[136] GL Neuman, 'Casey in the Mirror: Abortion, Abuse and the Right to Protection in the United States and Germany' (1995) 43 *American Journal of Comparative Law* 273, 274.

[137] RB Siegel, 'The Constitutionalization of Abortion' in RJ Cook, JN Erdman and BM Dickens (eds), *Abortion Law in Transnational Perspective: Cases and Controversies* (Philadelphia, University of Pennsylvania Press, 2014) 23; BVerfGE 39,1, 643 (1975) (citing German Federal Parliament, Seventh Election Period, 96th Sess, Steno-graphic Reports, 6492) (FCC Abortion I case).

arguing that the state had a duty to protect human life. However, the FCC changed its approach and 'transformed understanding of the constitutional duty' to protect the unborn. In exemplary 'judicial activism',[138] the Court suggested dissuasive counselling instead of the threat of criminal prosecution.[139]

According to the Court, it is counselling rather than punishment that exacts what the pregnant woman owes 'without degrading her to a mere object of protection' and 'respects her as an autonomous person by trying to win her over as an ally in the protection of the unborn'.[140] Put differently, '[c]ounselling coupled with depenalization of abortion' would be more effective than the threat of punishment in meeting the state's duty to protect life; and at the same time, depenalisation is '*also* consistent with women's autonomy'.[141]

This led the legislature to adopt the hybrid framework, which allows abortion in early pregnancy (12 weeks) after dissuasive counselling. According to this law, abortion remains unlawful, but may not be punished, 'if it is performed at the request of the woman, by a medical practitioner, before the end of the twelfth week of pregnancy, after a mandatory counselling session and a three-day waiting period'.[142] This is in addition to the other grounds of indication of risk to the mother's health or if it is a result of rape.[143]

The significance of the German framework of coupling counselling with depenalisation is that it offers an example of horizontal influence across sister states in polycentric constitutionalism. The model has migrated and influenced many Member States, where courts either quoted it directly or followed its logic. As Reva Sigel, among others, noted, the German framework 'spread' across many parts of the region and 'looms large in European abortion constitutionalism'.[144]

For instance, the Hungarian Court rejected the time-limit model and held that the legislature could instead strike a balance through directed counselling measures or third-party verification.[145] The Court then discussed dissuasive counselling as a means 'of protecting unborn life that was *also* respectful of women's rights'.[146] The 2017 Croatian Constitutional Court decision upheld the existing abortion periodic legislation, which allows abortion unconditionally in the first 10

[138] Neuman (n 136) 314.

[139] BVerfGE 88, 203 (1993) [36]–[37] www.bverfg.de/entscheidungen/fs19930528_2bvf000290en.html accessed 3 August 2025 (Abortion II case, official court translation).

[140] ibid [214].

[141] ibid.

[142] Fabbrini (n 77) 12.

[143] ibid. Germany used to have a controversial article banning practitioners from advertising that they conduct abortion. However, the ban was removed in 2019, see A Ulbricht, *Who can talk about abortion? Information, offence, freedom of speech, and the advertising ban in Germany.* Politics 1 (2021).

[144] R Rubio-Marín, 'Abortion in Portugal New Trends in European Constitutionalism' in RJ Cook, JN Erdman and BM Dickens (eds), *Abortion Law in Transnational Perspective: Cases and Controversies* (Philadelphia, University of Pennsylvania Press, 2014) 23.

[145] Alkotmanybirosag (Constitutional Court), Decision 48/1998 (XI.23), Official Gazette (MagyarKozlony) MK 1998/105 (Hungary), s III, pt (3)(d), 26, official court translation available at public.mkab.hu/dev/dontesek.nsf/0/dae998e2349be7d2c1257ada005258a0/$FILE/en_0048_1998.pdf.

[146] ibid, s IV, pt (2)(a), 34, as discussed in Siegel (n 137) 27.

weeks. Yet, the Court has discussed at length, among other comparative examples, the German 1993 judgments and the legislative amendments based thereon and called upon the legislature to adopt a new Act with conditional abortion on a range of measures, among which is dissuasive counselling.[147]

The EU's diverse legal landscape is not, however, confined to the German model, and other MS have moved well beyond it. Spain is one example which modified its abortion regulation in 2010. Abortion was a crime until 1985, when a timid law was adopted to establish three exceptions for impunity of abortion, namely therapeutic (health), ethical, or criminological (eg, rape) and foetal anomalies.[148] The health exception included 'mental and anxiety arising from undesired pregnancy'.[149] Subsequently, in 2010, the Parliament passed a new law with the explicit purpose of reflecting 'the legislative trend prevailing among [European] state'.[150] The law noted in its preamble that one of its underlying principles was 'the protection of a space of autonomy for women'.[151] The law legalised abortion on request for the first 14 weeks after a three-day waiting period and attending a meeting where data about centres offering counselling is provided, but, unlike the German model, counselling is not required.[152] The law also allows for abortion between 14 and 22 weeks, but subject to medical indications of serious risk to the health of the pregnant woman or 'serious foetal anomalies'.[153]

In Portugal, although the Constitutional Court, in 1985, 'employed the reasoning of the 1993 German decision' to dispense with 'the need for expressly dissuasive counselling', it has moved beyond the German reasoning in its subsequent decisions.[154] The Court has twice approved the constitutionality of national referenda on adopting a time-limit model of abortion.[155] After the 1998 referendum narrowly rejected the periodic model, the 2007 referendum approved it with 59.25 per cent.[156] The Parliament then moved to enact a right to 'abortion by option of the woman, within the first ten weeks of pregnancy', subject to mandatory counselling and a three-day mandatory waiting period. Unlike the German model, the counselling here is explicitly nondirective and was upheld by the Portuguese Constitutional Court in its 2010 decision as compatible with the state's duty to protect life. In another decision, the Court spoke of the importance of nonpunitive measures aside from counselling, which can 'reduce unintended pregnancy, such as sexual education and family planning, and measures to encourage women to

[147] ibid.

[148] MT Requejo, 'The New Regulation of Abortion in Spain' (2011) 18 *European Journal of Health Law* 397.

[149] ibid. Siegel highlighted the parallels in the Spanish Court's reasoning in 1985 with the West German judgment of 1975: see Siegel (n 137) 31.

[150] Organic Law 2-2010 on Sexual and Reproductive Health and Voluntary Termination of Pregrnancy (Spain), pmbl II, translated in Fabbrini (n 77) 15.

[151] Requejo (n 148) 402.

[152] The Spanish Law, art 17; ibid 406.

[153] ibid.

[154] Rubio-Marín (n 144) 41.

[155] ibid.

[156] ibid 42–46.

opt for motherhood, such as employment-related protections and social support for student-parents'.[157]

Belgium, too, has recently adopted more expansive amendments. For almost two centuries, Belgium used to criminalise abortion as a crime against the family and public morals.[158] In 1990, the Parliament legalised abortion; however, the King indicated his inability to sign the Bill because it violates his conscience as a Catholic. Instead, he asked to be temporarily declared unfit to rule, and the Bill was eventually signed by the Council of Ministers. The 1990 law allowed abortion in the first 12 weeks where there is a 'situation of distress', a condition which was lifted by the 2018 Act.[159] By virtue of this law, voluntary abortion was removed from the criminal code and became unconditionally available upon request until the first 12 weeks.[160]

In Slovakia, abortion was decriminalised during its Communist era. After the Soviet's fall, the Assembly of the Czech and Slovak Federal Republic in 1986 successfully proposed a provision enshrining the right to life.[161] This was seen as an antidote to 'Communist and materialist ideologies' which had contaminated 'social morals and undermined respect for life'.[162] Prior to the country's accession to the EU, 31 members of the Slovak Parliament relied on the mechanism of abstract judicial review to challenge the constitutionality of decriminalisation in light of the new constitutional provision. Reasoning by comparison to other European states and beyond, the Constitutional Court in 2007 held that allowing abortion on request up to 12 weeks was constitutional. In fact, it was the only Court to 'validate abortion on request by reference to state obligations both to protect unborn human life and to respect the right of women to reproductive [autonomy]'.[163]

Cyprus remains one of the most religious countries in the EU, where religious identity serves as an important marker and the Orthodox Church influences politics and society.[164] Abortion was a crime in Cyprus before the country enacted a vaguely restrictive provision that decriminalised abortion on limited indications as risk to life, mental damage, and socio-economic grounds. In 2018, the country shifted to the periodic legislative model by decriminalising abortion in the first 12

[157] Differently put, if the state creates the social conditions to allow women to become mothers, 'they will': ibid 46.

[158] F De Meyer, 'Abortion Law Reform in Europe: The 2018 Belgian and Irish Acts on Termination of Pregnancy' (2020) 20 *Medical Law International* 3.

[159] Belgian Act on the Voluntary Termination of Pregnancy 2018.

[160] De Meyer (n 158) 5.

[161] After a heated debate, the Federal Assembly adopted a compromise provision, which read: 'Everyone has the right to life. Human life is worthy of protection even prior to birth'; see analysis in A Lamačková, 'Women's Rights in the Abortion Decision of the Slovak Constitutional Court' in RJ Cook, JN Erdman and BM Dickens (eds), *Abortion Law in Transnational Perspective: Cases and Controversies* (Philadelphia, University of Pennsylvania Press, 2014) 60.

[162] ibid 60.

[163] ibid 56.

[164] On the church's influence in Cypriot politics, see AK Aimilianidēs, *Religion and Law in Cyprus*, 3rd edn (Alphen aan den Rijn, Wolters Kluwer, 2019) 136–146.

weeks unconditionally, except for being conducted in an organised clinic by a medical gynaecologist.[165] The Orthodox Church expressed disagreement with the new amendment but has done so 'rather mildly'.[166] Beyond these convergent and divergent forms of legalising abortion in 25 MS, two kept their almost absolute ban, as summarised next.

iii. The Two States with an Abortion Ban

a. Poland

Poland may be considered the EU's outlier, where the country has experienced a measure of polarisation over abortion, albeit not as strong as in America. To properly examine the Polish situation, it might be helpful to have a cursory scan of its modern constitutional history, which shaped its contemporary abortion regulation. Following the collapse of Communism in the 1990s, and the corresponding increase of the already strong influence of the Polish Catholic Church,[167] political stakeholders agreed to the so-called 'abortion compromise'.[168]

The compromise found its way into the 1993 law whereby mothers, unlike medical professionals, will not face criminal sanctions, but abortion is unavailable on demand and allowed only in three cases: (i) a threat to the life or health of the pregnant woman; (ii) up to viability, if there is a high probability of severe and irreversible foetal defect or incurable illness endangering the life of the foetus; and (iii) up to the 12th week of pregnancy, where the pregnancy is the result of an unlawful act.[169] A short-lived law was passed in 1996 allowing abortion in the first trimester 'on grounds of material or personal hardship'.[170] However, the 1993 law was shortly restored after the Polish Constitutional Tribunal found the new law incompatible with the Constitution by interpreting the right to life provision to require protecting the unborn.[171]

From 1993 until late 2020, the abortion compromise remained intact, but two events of constitutional importance occurred meanwhile. First, in 2004, Poland joined the EU, subject to its transitional period ending in 2011 and subsequently followed the UK in the questionable opt-out from the Fundamental Rights Charter.[172] Second, in 2015, the country started its unfolding constitutional

[165] Article 169 as amended by law 21(1)/2018, discussed in Aimilianidēs (n 164) 181.

[166] ibid.

[167] 'Unlike other communistic countries in Europe, the Church in Poland retained a significant level of autonomy … and contributed to the public's high dissatisfaction of Soviets.' A Czerwinski, 'Sex, Politics, and Religion: The Clash between Poland and the European Union over Abortion' (2003) 32 *Denver Journal of International Law & Policy* 36.

[168] M Granat and K Granat, *The Constitution of Poland: A Contextual Analysis* (London, Bloomsbury, 2019) 202.

[169] ibid.

[170] Fabbrini (n 77) 13.

[171] K 26/96 (28 May 1997) Trybunal Konstytucyjny [Constitutional Court] (Poland).

[172] Czerwinski (n 167) 659.

crisis. The Law and Justice (PiS) party won the presidency and an absolute parliamentary majority, allowing them to govern single-handedly. A primary target of this populist government was the judiciary generally, and the Constitutional Court particularly. After openly clashing with the then-pre-captured Court, and illegally refusing to publish its politically inconvenient judgment,[173] the party has drawn a road map to convert the judiciary into 'the Government's enabler'.[174] The Parliament passed a number of laws which allowed the government to 'fire all judges of the Supreme Court and to replace the leadership of the lower courts, as well as to take over the system of judicial appointments from that moment forward'.[175]

One year after their ascension to power, the PiS proposed restrictions on abortion whereby foetal anomaly cannot be a ground for abortion, and neither is rape. However, the proposal stirred the Black Protest – a series of nationwide, large-scale protests organised between September 2016 and 2018, which ultimately led to the proposal's defeat. In 2020, however, the captured Constitutional Court stepped in to attain what PiS politicians could not.[176] Chaired by Mrs Julia Przyłębska, the Court invalidated the provision of the 1993 law which allowed abortion for foetal defects. The Court reasoned that the provision is incompatible with Article 38 of the Constitution enshrining the right to life, and Article 30 on human dignity.[177]

The judgment triggered massive protests to the extent that the Polish president undertook to interpret the judgment narrowly in the government's legislative proposal and allow abortion for certain anomalies.[178] Recent polls show that the majority of citizens reject the Court's ruling[179] and that since the Black Protest, there has been an increase in those favouring legalising abortion in the first trimester, though even with the new regime, they fell short of a majority to pass a new law.[180]

[173] P Laurent and KL Scheppele, 'Illiberalism Within: Rule of Law Backsliding in the EU' (2017) 19 *Cambridge Yearbook of European Legal Studies* 3, 15, 27; P Mikuli, *Poland's Constitutional Breakdown* (Oxford, Oxford University Press, 2020) 75–77.

[174] Mikuli (n 173) 79.

[175] F Zoll and L Wortham, *'Disciplining Judges', Weaponizing Judicial Discipline: Poland* (Michigan, EE Publishing, 2021).

[176] A Gliszczyńska-Grabias and W Sadurski, 'The Judgment That Wasn't (but Which Nearly Brought Poland to a Standstill): "Judgment" of the Polish Constitutional Tribunal of 22 October 2020, K1/20' (2021) 17 *European Constitutional Law Review* 130, 131.

[177] ibid 131.

[178] D Tilles, 'President proposes new "compromise" abortion law to resolve crisis in Poland' (*NFP*, 30 Oct 2020) notesfrompoland.com/2020/10/30/president-proposes-new-compromise-law-to-resolve-polands-abortion-crisis/ accessed 3 August 2025.

[179] See A Sas, 'Opinion on the Constitutional Court decision on abortion in Poland in 2020' (*Statista*, 31 January 2024) www.statista.com/statistics/1182787/poland-opinion-on-the-constitutional-court-decision-on-abortion/ accessed 3 August 2025; see also D Tilles, 'Majority of Poles support abortion protests and popularity of ruling party has dropped, polls show' (*NFP*, 1 November 2020) notesfrompoland.com/2020/11/01/majority-of-poles-support-abortion-protests-and-popularity-of-ruling-party-has-dropped-polls-show/ accessed 3 August 2025.

[180] W Sadlon, 'Polarization but Not Pillarization Catholicism and Cultural Change in Post-Transformation Poland' (2021) 12 *Religions* 10.

In December 2023, the ECtHR questioned the legitimacy of the election procedure of the Polish Constitutional Court, which decided the controversial 2020 Polish abortion judgment. The ECtHR held that 'the irregularities in the election procedure of the judges compromised the legitimacy of the Constitutional Court's bench, render on procedural grounds its ruling on banning abortion 'short of what the rule of law required'.[181] Although the ECtHR refrained from addressing the substantive issue of whether abortion should be permitted in cases of foetal defects, its judgment adds further pressure on the Polish Court and its contested abortion ruling. How the incumbent party may attempt to address these judicial irregularities and their implications for abortion policy remains to be seen.

Two things are to be noted. Poland is one of the relatively recent members of the EU. It joined the Schengen in 2007. The transition period and its concomitant restrictions on freedom of movement ended in 2011.[182] It is well-known and demonstrated in the case of Ireland that social change occurs in a time-honoured fashion. Secondly, despite the foregoing, as well as the constitutional breakdown, one can see that the level of Polish polarisation does not match up to America. Namely, extreme proposals such as those passed in the US to ban abortion in case of rape failed to gain sufficient approval among conservative politicians, nor do we see in Poland such laws enacted for excessively severe punishment of 99 years for abortion as in Alabama, for instance. Not only do mothers under Polish law not face criminal sanction, but also in December 2021, even the conservative Polish Parliament rejected a Bill that would introduce a harsher penalty for abortion.[183]

b. Malta

Malta is a southern European country with a small, homogeneous population of under 500,000, where Catholicism exercises an influential power and is even enshrined in the constitution.[184] Only in 2011 did the country have its first schism with Catholic doctrine by legalising divorce after a bitterly fought referendum.[185]

[181] *ML v Poland* App no 40119/21 (ECtHR 14 December 2023) para 174. See commentary in S Kasotny, 'How to Maneuver Around Acknowledging the Right to Access Abortion: Some Thoughts on the ECtHR's judgment in M.L. v Poland' (*EJIL: Talk!*, 11 January 2024) www.ejiltalk.org/how-to-maneuver-around-acknowledging-the-right-to-access-abortion-some-thoughts-on-the-ecthrs-judgment-in-m-l-v-poland/ accessed 3 August 2025.

[182] 'The transition aimed at introducing free movement gradually over a seven-year period.' See 'Frequently asked questions: The end of transitional arrangements for the free movement of workers on 30 April 2011' (*The European Commission*, MEMO/11/259, 28 April 2011) ec.europa.eu/commission/presscorner/detail/en/MEMO_11_259 accessed 3 August 2025.

[183] See 'Poland: Attempt to equate abortion with killing must be rejected' (*Amnesty International*, 30 November 2021) www.amnesty.org/en/latest/news/2021/11/poland-attempt-to-equate-abortion-with-killing-must-be-rejected/ accessed 3 August 2025.

[184] Constitution of Malta, art 2, provides that the 'Roman Catholic Apostolic' is the state religion.

[185] 'Malta Is The Last EU Country To Have A Full Ban On Abortion' (*The Economist*, 27 July 2019) www.economist.com/europe/2019/07/27/malta-is-the-last-eu-country-to-have-a-full-ban-on-abortion accessed 3 August 2025.

The issue of abortion *is barely divisive* in this homogenous microstate, and a survey reveals that 90 per cent of the Maltese citizens oppose unrestricted abortion in the first trimester.[186] Maltese law has a complete ban on abortion, and in Malta's 2003 accession agreement to the EU, it obtained Protocol No. 7, which leaves unaffected 'the application in the territory of Malta of national legislation relating to abortion'.[187]

Given this socio-cultural dynamic, it will be unwise and costly to social peace to disturb the small state and impose a top-down moral view, rather than leave their social actors to adhere to their Catholic heritage in the diverse EU landscape. And if social interaction with the borderless EU and with other EU legal systems instilled a seed for change, they may do so organically, gradually, and above all, without costly polarisation. I shall return to this discussion later.

c. EU Overview

The EU adhered to the convention of 'duty to respect' domestic moral choices and refrained from imposing top-down conformity,[188] while keeping the possibility of intervention to police market externalities and disproportionate or incohesive aspects within the national scheme. Abortion regulations in most states have changed considerably, gradually, and mainly peacefully.[189] Unmarred by extremities seen in America, most EU state legislatures and courts sought to reconcile the imperative of the right to life with decisional autonomy. Now, with some divergent details, 25 EU Member States allow abortion upon request, whether conditional or not on dissuasive counselling. Notably, there are no considerable attempts to reverse established constitutional principles as those common in American states, nor is the debate fraught with the fierce polarisation that defines the American tale of abortion.

IV. Why Conflict in America and Dialogue in Europe?

This section highlights three factors present in the EU and absent in the US, which explain how omitting the principle/interest distinction and its concomitant 'surface allure'[190] of impartiality contributed to the stark gulf between the two sides of the Atlantic.

[186] K Sansone, 'Malta Today Survey | No change in Malta's anti-abortion attitudes' (*Malta Today*, 15 July 2019) www.maltatoday.com.mt/news/data_and_surveys/96270/no_change_in_maltas_anti-abortion_attitudes#.YO4pjy1Q3ok accessed 3 August 2025.

[187] Protocol No 7 on Abortion in Malta (2003) OJ L236/947.

[188] L Azoulai, 'The European Court of Justice and the Duty to Respect Sensitive National Interests' in *Judicial Activism at the European Court of Justice* (Cheltenham, Edward Elgar Publishing, 2013).

[189] Erratic resistance occurred in Europe, but by no means comparable to the level of America, see the French Court of Cassation's holding on an abortion violence case: Bull crim. N 431 (27 November 1996) Cass Crim (France); discussed in Turenne (n 11) 1.

[190] ibid 647.

A. Federalism's Fourth Option as a Check on Normative Power[191]

The difference between the two types of factions warrants a shift from the triadic model of *judging* to the dyadic model of *mediation*. The increased diversification of interested factions allows resolution of conflict through a *triadic model* where parties resort to the relatively more impartial federal government as a third-party umpire. The lack of such impartiality in principle-based factions makes the triadic model unfeasible. An alternative, then, would be federalism's fourth option, which is akin to a dyadic model of mediation among non-neutral parties. Each party, as a co-mediator, gets a slice of leverage; the state has regulatory choice while the centre polices its arbitrariness, rationality, potential externalities, and other procedural checks needed for the mediation to continue.

The advantage of keeping the centre as a *co-mediator* rather than *an ultimate judge*[192] lies not only in fostering a multiplicity of 'norm entrepreneurs' but also in imbuing the contested issue with an element of 'indeterminacy' and 'open-endedness'.[193] Indeterminacy permits multi-level dialogue that, while open-ended, is safeguarded against extremes. The centre and states engage in deliberations on the rationality and 'procedural proportionality' of states' regulatory choices, as well as their potential externalities. The safeguard against the risk of either party adopting extreme measures resides in the fact that this dialogue occurs under the shadow of the mutual threat of potential centralisation by the centre or revolt by the state. This 'mutually asserted' threat creates an *implicit convention*, inducing each interlocutor to tread carefully and avoid radical solutions.[194] The fourth option is preferable to complete decentralisation because it better advances the goals of limited government. It ensures that, on this particular issue, the powers of both levels are not unconditional but are checked through mutually asserted constraints.

Differently put, this approach makes better use of federalism's capacity to expand the 'menu of policy options',[195] and by creating options that simply cannot be available in federalism's 'unitary cousin'.[196] For instance, monistic states usually opt for and, thus, impose a top-down ideological choice which is either liberal or conservative oriented, with their varying versions. Conversely, federalism allows

[191] Here, I use the term 'normative' to denote all methods of norm articulation, be it legislative or judicial.

[192] ibid: 'Decentralized governance … provid[es] an institutional framework for mediating social conflict and making stable and productive the diversity of views'.

[193] RM Cover, 'The Uses of Jurisdictional Redundancy: Interest, Ideology, and Innovation' (1980) 22 *William & Mary Law Review* 662, 682.

[194] Similar to Walker's famous analysis of EU pluralism, see discussion in K Jaklic, *Constitutional Pluralism in the EU* (Oxford, Oxford University Press, 2014).

[195] An expression taken from AS Sweet, *The Judicial Construction of Europe* (Oxford, Oxford University Press, 2004) 135.

[196] Term taken from J Bednar, *The Robust Federation: Principles of Design* (Cambridge, Cambridge University Press, 2008) 2.

the centre, in many issues, a third option, which is to choose neither, ie, not to inhibit nor establish a top-down imposed view, leaving each state free to diverge on the issue across the spectrum. Further, polycentricism offers 'mediated plurality' as an additional *fourth option*. Instead of federal do-nothingness and relegating the matter fully to states, it keeps the centre as a co-mediator to apply procedural checks, examining the states' regulatory choice without dictating a particular substantive outcome, as illustrated in the European dynamics.[197]

Further safeguards against extremity lie in the fact that the centre, given that it is equipped with a wider calibre and eagle view of the union, can oversee the transcendental aspects or procedural checks required to ensure the stability of the dialogue without deciding on the contested core of the issue. As discussed, the ECtHR monitors the clarity and proportionality of the MS regulatory scheme to its professed goals without imposing a certain goal. Although the ECtHR is an international Court whose judgments are not necessarily binding, the threat to MS lies in that the CJEU, as it invariably does, may incorporate ECHR jurisprudence and extend it to the very constitutional systems of Member States.

B. Tolerance and Change Through Cross-Pollination All the Way Down

When teasing out the impartial side of human nature is not possible, mediated plurality can cultivate the tolerant side – a disposition grounded in an 'agree-to-disagree' approach. Tolerance differs both from 'indifference ('who cares?') and relativism ('anything goes')'.[198] As social psychologists remind us, 'tolerance is not neutrality, or an unwillingness to judge'. Rather, it combines 'principled disapproval' of others' beliefs with a commitment to non-interference.[199] This approach can also simultaneously work on in-group belief towards self-moderation.

Placing the divisive issue in 'mediated plurality' can 'dampen the fever' of 'polarization' since it 'guarantee[s] that neither side can use its momentary political power' to enforce their 'brand of morality' or 'suppress disagreement'.[200] Each group is guaranteed a sphere where it can 'live in accordance with their conscience'.[201] This way it allows supporters of rival views, while remaining a party in their local dispute, to become *attentive spectators* to the experience of the several states. Social and legal actors benefit from the 'explorative potential'

[197] Rodriquez argues for cases where the federal government 'will play a robust role without dictating outcome and in other cases true national norms eventually will emerge as the result of what has happened within and among states and localities, supplemented by the assertion of federal power.' C Rodríguez, 'Federalism and National Consensus' 5 (unpublished manuscript).

[198] M Verkuyten, K Yogeeswaran and L Adelman, 'The Social Psychology of Intergroup Tolerance and Intolerance' (2023) 34 *European Review of Social Psychology* 5.

[199] ibid 4.

[200] NS Chapman and MW McConnell, *Agreeing to Disagree: How the Establishment Clause Protects Religious Diversity and Freedom of Conscience* (Oxford, Oxford University Press, 2023) 190.

[201] ibid.

of observing, testing and 'multiple perspective rather than suppress[ing] them'.[202] Through inter-jurisdictional interactions, private actors become, as Cover puts it, 'carriers that pollinate one system … with the information about another system's experience'.[203] Polycentric norm articulation acts as a 'knowledge-creating [and sharing] process'.[204] This helps allay some of the suspicions of other beliefs/ideologies and brings them slowly into people's 'latitudes of acceptance'.[205]

Let's recall some examples. Cross-pollination of legal ideas can be seen, for instance, in how the permissive Dutch abortion law and abortion tourism to the Netherlands were raised in abortion debates in Germany in the 1990s,[206] as well as in the recent reforms in Belgium.[207] More formally, the preamble of the 2010 Spanish law refers to 'the legislative trend prevailing among [European] state'.[208] Cross-fertilisation found its way to judicial reasoning. In addition to the influential German FCC decision, which has migrated to many MS, we have seen Croatian and Slovak constitutional court judgments quoting at length and passionately comparing abortion regulations of other MS.[209]

At the popular level, the borderless EU allows citizens to shop for the legal system which better suits their needs, and in doing so, they revisit their locally idiosyncratic moral reasons.[210] Literature on Ireland and beyond has referred to the influence of social media documentation of abortion tourism in sister jurisdictions and its difficulties and questioned the logic of domestic regulation.[211] As David Cole, among others, has contended, the interplay between EU and domestic laws on abortion makes 'isolationism impossible, even on an issue as strongly felt as abortion'.[212]

Reminiscent of McCormick's institutional theory of law,[213] Gerken remarks that it is only through aligning social values with constitutional change that norms

[202] M Minow, 'Putting up and Putting Down: Tolerance Reconsidered' (1990) 28 *Osgoode Hall Law Journal* 409.

[203] Cover (n 193) 678.

[204] V Vanberg and W Kerber, 'Institutional Competition among Jurisdictions: An Evolutionary Approach' (1994) 5 *Constitutional Political Economy* 193.

[205] Verkuyten, Yogeeswaran and Adelman (n 198) 27.

[206] M Levels, R Sluiter and A Need, 'A Review of Abortion Laws in Western-European Countries. A Cross-National Comparison of Legal Developments between 1960 and 2010' (2014) 118 *Health Policy* 95; M Marx Ferree and others, *Shaping Abortion Discourse: Democracy and the Public Sphere in Germany and the United States* (Cambridge, Cambridge University Press, 2002).

[207] De Meyer (n 158) 5.

[208] Organic Law 2-2010 on Sexual and Reproductive Health and Voluntary Termination of Pregrnancy (Spain), pmbl II; translated in Fabbrini (n 77).

[209] See II.B.

[210] R Fletcher, 'National Crisis, Supranational Opportunity: The Irish Construction of Abortion as a European Service' (2000) 8 *Reproductive Health Matters* 35; CM Rodríguez, 'Negotiating Conflict through Federalism: Institutional and Popular Perspectives' (2013 123 *Yale Law Journal* 2127.

[211] Fabbrini (n 97) 1–3; Kurzer (n 5) 168; Levels, Sluiter and Need (n 206) 103; see also R Sluiter, 'The Diffusion of Morality Policies among Western European Countries between 1960 and 2010: A comparison of the temporal and spatial diffusion patterns of six morality and eleven nonmorality policies' (2012) Nijmegen: ICS Dissertation Series.

[212] D Cole, 'Going to England: Irish Abortion Law and the European Community' (1993) 17 *Hastings International & Comparative Law Review* 113, 115.

[213] N McCormick, *Institutions of Law* (Oxford, Oxford University Press, 2007).

endure and thereby 'convert the rights guarantees that lawyers dismiss as "parchment barriers" into robust shields'.[214] A judicial or legislative fiat cannot achieve this, but gradual multi-level dialogue can. One particular virtue of multiplicity of norms is the mathematically proven 'confirmatory redundancy'.[215] This denotes the case when a contentious issue arises in several jurisdictions, and more jurisdictions independently arrive at a similar result. Under some conditions detailed in law and economics literature, the redundant articulation of the 'central core' of the norm *mathematically diminishes* the risk that the finding was a product of 'error' or 'local prejudice'.[216]

To take an analogy, when one suspects the diagnosis of a doctor who suggests an 'invasive surgery', suspicion diminishes when the diagnosis is confirmed upon consulting more doctors.[217] Likewise, as the converging norm 'iterates', spectators in sister jurisdictions may observe the redundantly articulated norm with less suspicion and distrust.[218] This decrease of suspicion helps counter inclinations to delegitimise the other views and, thus, contributes to increased toleration of difference and builds a slowly ingrained agreement to disagree.[219]

Recall the discussion on different types of biases. It was argued that the impartiality argument works only with controlling 'group bias', but not cognitive and ideological bias. While cross-pollination does not eliminate ideological predetermination, it can gradually mitigate some of its malaise. As Tushnet remarked, having plural ports of norm articulation and the ensuing inter-jurisdictional interactions can, effectively yet indirectly, help revise fundamental ideologies that otherwise would not be 'revisable'.[220] Additionally, the decrease of suspicion coupled with exposure to the redundantly articulated norm may alternatively stir the '*seeds for change*'[221] when the 'taken-for-grantedness' of their existing norms is called into question and individuals incrementally ponder on adjustment to their norms.[222] When this happens, it is not done by a sudden top-down official fiat, but normative change is inextricably bound up with the evolving popular views, which serve as what Post terms a 'supportive constitutional culture'.[223]

[214] H Gerken, 'Second-Order Diversity: An Exploration of Decentralization's Egalitarian Possibilities' (2016) Yale Law School, Public Law Research Paper 2.

[215] Bednar (n 196) 176.

[216] EA Posner and CR Sunstein, 'Response: On Learning from Others' (2007) 59 *Stanford Law Review* 1309, 1309–10 (2006).

[217] Bednar (n 196) 176; Cover (n 193) 672.

[218] Cover terms it the suspicion of 'local error' or 'prejudice', 'jurisdictional doubt': ibid.

[219] M Tushnet, 'Federalism and Liberalism' (1996) 4 *Cardozo Journal of International & Comparative Law* 343; Cover (n 193).

[220] Tushnet (n 219) 342.

[221] M Aoki, *Toward a Comparative Institutional Analysis* (Cambridge, MA, MIT Press, 2001) 240.

[222] ibid 241.

[223] RC Post, 'Fashioning the Legal Constitution: Culture, Courts, and Law' (2003) 117 *Harvard Law Review* 4.

'[R]edundancy', 'gradualism',[224] coupled with 'bottom-up' constitutionalism,[225] help substitute 'control by others' with 'self-control'; the 'compulsory' imposition of a norm is replaced by what Stein terms the 'voluntary process' of change.[226] This, under the right conditions, produces more enduring norms. An indicative example is the shift of Irish people from endorsing a referendum banning abortion to incrementally endorsing the opposite amendment with the same sweeping two-thirds vote. Likewise, states with strong Catholic traditions, such as Portugal and Spain,[227] or with Orthodox influence, such as Cyprus, have expanded the decriminalisation of abortion.[228] In these states, we seldom see continuous attempts to reverse the change. And in the few occasions where such attempts occur, as in 2014 Spain, they are popularly defeated.[229] Contrast this with American states, which, empowered by sizable popular support, continuously attempt to contravene and effectively restrain the federally established abortion right.

By contrast, centralisation in America's 'coerce or be coerced' fashion created unmistakable incentives for like-minded factions to consolidate across the union. Instead of cross-fertilisation, the resulting polarisation leads to 'compression of information space', viewing the world in an all-or-none fashion.[230] Anti-abortion became 'a bridge' between different religious groups, including 'Protestants and Catholics who had been on opposite sides of practically every church-state issue since Catholics began to immigrate to America'.[231] This is not to say that complete decentralisation, as exemplified by *Dobbs*, makes coercion magically disappear, as polarised state majorities may feel free to impose their moral views on their ideological rivals. The future of abortion regulation is briefly discussed later on.

Some object to the incremental nature of cross-fertilisation on the premise that for years, in the EU restricting jurisdictions, women were denied abortion except through free movement.[232] This objection rests on a utopian view of the world

[224] G de Búrca, 'EU Race Discrimination Law: A Hybrid Model?' in G de Búrca and J Scott (eds), *Law and New Governance in the EU and the US* (Oxford, Hart Publishing, 2006) 98.

[225] ibid.

[226] E Stein, 'Uniformity and Diversity in a Divided Power System: The United States' Experience' (1986) 61 *Washington Law Review* 1081, 1084–1086 (1986).

[227] 'The lingering influence of Catholicism in increasingly secular Spain' (*The Economist*, 1 May 2021) www.economist.com/europe/2021/05/01/the-lingering-influence-of-catholicism-in-increasingly-secular-spain accessed 3 August 2025.

[228] See below.

[229] 'Dropped anti-abortion bill must usher in better protection of women's rights in Spain' (Amnesty International, 24 September 2014) www.amnesty.org.uk/press-releases/dropped-anti-abortion-bill-must-usher-better-protection-women's-rights-spain accessed 3 August 2025.

[230] J Bednar, 'Polarization, Diversity, and Democratic Robustness' (2021) 118 *Proceedings of the National Academy of Sciences* 118 (50) e2113843118.

[231] Feldman (n 50) 214.

[232] F Fabbrini, 'The "European" future of American Abortion Law: Dobbs, Federalism and Constitutional Equality' (2023) 62 *Columbia Journal of Transnational Law* 113, 149–153.

where choice among evils is not needed.[233] Differently put, the objection could be accepted only if the securing agreement on a deeply divisive moral issue is immediately and peacefully attainable by a federal fiat. However, coming back to reality, American women seeking abortion even after *Roe* were often worse off than EU women using EU free movement to obtain abortion.

Differently put, even during *Roe*'s reign, the mismatch between its holding and the moral conviction of some socio-political groups led to the well-known scarcity of abortion providers, which forced American women to travel interstate distances equivalent to those across neighbouring EU states. For instance, if we compare the EU's most restrictive jurisdiction with Mississippi, whose population is six times larger than Malta, but before *Dobbs* had only one abortion clinic. This made travel for many in Mississippi the only option.[234] Still, an EU citizen travelled without having to face the 'nightmare of jeering demonstrators' and the 'horror' of media broadcasting that American women often undergo in anti-abortion states.[235] This is not to mention the erratic risk of clinic violence.

A further point to respond to this objection is that mediated plurality and other species of decentralisation encourage extending 'federalism all the way down'.[236] Federalism does not need to be confined to a two-dimensional centre-state model. Regulatory autonomy can – and in some areas should – be extended to cities, counties, and sub-local levels. This federalism in 4D, with its interconnected layers of central, state, local, and sub-local governance, fosters 'dialogue, dissent, and resistance' within an integrated multi-layered system.[237] By multiplying the centres of norm articulation on divisive issues, such an approach encourages further cross-pollination of ideas and mitigates the costs of exit, travel and relocation for those who disagree with local rules. This does not imply moral relativism or the absence of shared values.[238] Centralisation remains appropriate for other matters, as discussed in earlier chapters. The question of how far diversity can or should be tolerated is a vast philosophical field, which need not be fully explored here; a brief discussion will follow in the final chapter.

[233] ibid. He does, however, recognise that argument from equality can equally cut 'both ways'. If a foetus is seen as a person, the right to abortion would have 'to be banned everywhere'.

[234] S Fowler, 'Can Mississippi's Last Abortion Clinic Survive?' (*Politico*, 26 May 2021) www.politico.com/news/magazine/2021/05/26/mississippi-last-abortion-clinic-490797 accessed 3 August 2025.

[235] Tribe (n 12) 171–172.

[236] Gerken (n 214).

[237] ibid 28.

[238] Federalism as much as it is pluralistic, requires a measure of common values, or as the CJEU terms it 'constitutional traditions common to Member States' through which to judge 'good diversity', which can be distinguished from 'bad diversity', which runs afoul of these values. See, eg, DL Horowitz, 'The Many Uses of Federalism' (2006) 55 *Drake Law Review* 967. I do not think uniformity on abortion is necessary though.

C. Non-Antagonistic Mediation and Balanced Compromises

This is not a factor but rather an outcome of the earlier ones. In constitutional settings, akin to individual ones, calm-minded negotiation is unlikely in polarising environments where each side delegitimises and antagonises the other. Once tension diffuses, extremities are avoided and balancing competing considerations becomes conceivable. Nowhere in the EU does one see the extreme measures passed in America, such as punishing abortion by lifetime imprisonment or deputising citizens to catch out one another. Rather, when most EU states decriminalised voluntary abortion, they did not opt for an extreme solution favouring one of the clashing rights to the disregard of the other, and they still adhere to a 'culture of life'.[239]

As charted earlier, in most jurisdictions, serious efforts have been exerted to balance the rights of the unborn with the mother's right to autonomy.[240] Courts have often invoked ensuring social and financial protection to mothers and 'student-parents' as measures to encourage motherhood and reduce the risk of unintended pregnancies, while '*also* consistent with women's autonomy'.[241] Notably, in most European countries, there is a system of social support that includes prenatal and postnatal medical care, paid parental leave, and availability of infant care for working parents – which are largely absent in the US. As Tushnet remarks, there is some reason to think that western European-style abortion policies 'reduce the incidence of abortion'.[242]

With this, I conclude the reasons that contributed to the difference in abortion polarisation across the Atlantic. Next, it is important to dispel two of the often-mistaken causes of polarisation in the US.

D. The Unlikely Culprits: What may not Explain the Differences

The jurisdictional question of federalisation/decentralisation is sometimes overlooked in contrasting the US and European abortion journeys. For some, continued US polarisation is attributed to judicial activism or to the US's exceptional religiosity. Here, I discuss why both are misattributions.

[239] M Tushnet, 'Abortion Policy Aimed at Promoting Life As Much As Possible' (unpublished manuscript).

[240] Reminiscent of Sunstein's statement that 'a women should be allowed to choose abortion; but it would be far better if that choice were never necessary': C Sunstein, *The Partial Constitution* (Cambridge, MA, Harvard University Press, 1993).

[241] *FCC Abortion II case* (n 137).

[242] Tushnet (n 239).

First, 'the judicial restraint' argument goes as follows:[243] in the US, it was the court's 'raw exercise of judicial power'[244] that wreaked 'havoc' by superintending on the abortion debate,[245] unlike European courts, which defer to the legislature's superior democratic apparatus.[246] This view rests on an incomplete description of the changes in Europe. Courts in Europe did not stand passively; rather, several European courts took the initiative of inviting or invalidating democratically adopted abortion laws. It started in 1975 when the Italian Constitutional Court held that although the Constitution 'protects unborn life, the right to life and to health of the pregnant woman has priority over the claim to life of the unborn during the early stages of pregnancy'.[247] The Court then invited the legislature to draft new abortion provisions legalising abortion, which the legislature did in 1978.[248] Twice, the German Court invalidated democratically adopted abortion laws.

More importantly, the German hybrid abortion regime, influential in Europe, was 'not chosen by the legislature but imposed by the Federal Constitutional Court',[249] which Neuman describes as 'an extraordinary example of judicial activism'.[250] Less extreme, yet important, three eastern European constitutions (Hungarian, Czech, and Slovak) contain provisions relating to prenatal life protection. Nonetheless, the constitutional courts of these states have construed these provisions as not recognising 'a special right to life of the unborn, but a constitutional value that enjoys special protection of the state'.[251] As summarised earlier, none of these states disallowed abortion based on these constitutional provisions.

Moreover, comparison is made in the American Court's approach to abortion, not based on *Roe* alone but holistically on other judgments such as *Harris v McRae* and obviously *Casey*. In fact, some comparativists have already drawn

[243] Tribe (n 12) 79–81.

[244] *Doe v Bolton* 410 US 179, 222 (1973) (White J, dissenting).

[245] ibid. For an analysis and critique of this argument, see Post and Siegel (n 34); Rodríguez (n 197) 31.

[246] M Ann Glendon, *Abortion and Divorce in Western Law* (Cambridge, MA, Harvard University Press, 1987); Turenne (n 11) 316; Glendon's analysis, however, overlooks the dynamics and the role of the European Community and ECtHR and, thus, fails to explain the difference between states in quasi-federal structure and insulated nation-states. For a thorough critique of her argument, see Tushnet (n 239) 105–111.

[247] *Cone Costituiionale, decision* of 18 Feb. 1975, no. 27, 20, at 117 ff. Translation in Comp. Const. L., op. ctf. note 1, p. 612 ff.; discussed in M Nijsten, *Abortion and Constitutional Law: A Comparative European-American Study* (European University Institute, 1990) 100–102.

[248] Nijsten (n 247) 99–102.

[249] ibid 273.

[250] ibid 314.

[251] Ruling of the Constitutional Court of the Republic of Croatia No U-I-60/1991 and others of 21 February 2017 and the dissenting opinion (Rjelenje Ustavnog suda Republike Hrvatske, broj: U-I-60/1991. i dr. od2l. veljade 2017. i izdvojeno miljenje), Official Gazette, No. 25/17, par. 31, [sljeme. usud.hr/usud/praksaw.nsf/7114c25caa361e3acl257f340032flle/cl2570d30061ce54cl2580d100416faf/$-FILE/U-I-60-1991%20i%20dr.pdf], accessed 30. January 2021. Unofficial abridged translation into English: [www.law.utoronto.ca/utflfile/count/documents/reprohealth/croatia-2017 constitutional.pdf], accessed 30. January 2021.

parallels between *Casey* and the FCC's 1995 ruling.[252] The joint result of the foregoing is that polarisation cannot be simply attributed to judicial activism without accounting for the issue of centralisation versus decentralisation that prevents cross-fertilisation and encourages factions to consolidate and intensely polarise.

The second argument is that the US polarisation is due to popular religiosity in 'Christian America' compared to secular Europe.[253] While it is true that a large part of American society is generally more religious, such claims overlook key counter examples. Permissive legislation found its way to Ireland, one of the world's strongest holds of Catholicism. Indeed, immigrants from Ireland have had a strong influence on the abortion debate in America, as well as other constitutional issues on religion.[254] Abortion was peacefully legalised in Cyprus despite some disagreement from the Church, which enjoys an influential role, and religion remains a marker among citizens. Other countries which have a form of legal secularism, like America, but continue to have an influential Christian tradition include Spain, Portugal, and Greece, which all legalised abortion.[255] In none of these cases does one see strong polarisation, nor the unceasing efforts to reverse the permissive legislation.

Moreover, many of those EU states take a much more religious approach to church-state relationship compared to the US. This includes EU states making explicit reference to God in their constitution's preamble (Germany) or to 'the Holy Trinity' (Ireland).[256] Other Member States' constitutions provide an 'institutionalized state church', such as the Greek and Danish Constitutions, and others.[257] Conversely, on issues like non-heterosexual marriage and medical marijuana – both of which may conflict with traditional religious values – many US states have adopted more permissive policies than their EU counterparts.

V. Future Abortion Regulation across the Atlantic

The goal of this analysis is not the prediction of the post-*Dobbs* future of abortion. Crystal ball gazing is difficult.[258] As Chemernisky noted, 'Dobbs won't end

[252] Neuman (n 136); Siegel (n 137) 24–28.

[253] Eg, M Minkenberg, 'Religion and Public Policy: Institutional, Cultural, and Political Impact on the Shaping of Abortion Policies in Western Democracies' (2002) 35 *Comparative Political Studies* 221; G Layman, *The Great Divide: Religious and Cultural Conflict in American Party Politics* (New York, Columbia University Press, 2001).

[254] Feldman (n 50) 125.

[255] See earlier discussion on Spain.

[256] Irish Constitution, art 6(1).

[257] For a comparative survey, see R McCrea, *Religion and the Public Order of the European Union* (Oxford, Oxford University Press, 2010) 22.

[258] The past analysis was on how to avoid polarisation, more than how to remedy its effects after it takes hold. Cross-pollination also takes time, which makes the prediction premature. Much like the human body avoiding a disease is easier than curing it at later stage.

the litigation over abortion.' States will adopt a 'plethora' of abortion-related laws which 'are likely to be challenged before the supreme court'.[259] Rather than speculation, hindsight can help abstract the normative lessons and preferred approach out of the theoretical and comparative analysis offered thus far. As Fabbrini's piece on '*The European Future of American Abortion Law*' highlights, many of the questions facing contemporary America provoke an EU 'déjà vu'.[260]

The main takeaway from the analysis thus far is that opting for either extreme will continue to unjustifiably violate the *nemo judex* rule, discard federalism's calculus of values, and fuel polarisation. By the first extreme, I mean full federal retreat through decentralising the issue completely to states, and by the second, I mean full federal legislative codification or a federalised abortion right or a federal abortion ban. Both approaches fall under a form of triadic model where either the state (in the former) or the federal level (in the latter) continues to act as the ultimate umpire and superimposes its unchecked moral view. Contrary to Justice Kavanaugh's misplaced 'neutrality' optimism, the increasing inter-jurisdictional clashes between liberal and conservative states[261] as the new abortion 'battleground' doubt the possibility of the federal stay being completely uninvolved and 'scrupulously neutral'.[262]

A better approach, as the EU experience shows, is a dyadic, 'mediated plurality' model. Suffice it to say that it is not completely without precedent in the US Supreme Court's jurisprudence to have a model of 'sharing constitutional decision-making' where state actors are authorised to adopt divergent moral choices while the Supreme Court maintains a supervisory 'backup review' of procedural 'balancing'[263] and proportionality without 'dictat[ing]' a uniform substantive outcome across the country.[264] Yes, there are downsides to the slow incremental nature of cross-fertilisation, but we have addressed this in the previous section.

Although this chapter has contrasted the American approach unfavourably with the more constructive European model, a cautionary note is warranted regarding a recent development in the EU. Europe may be overlooking the value of its own approach. If federalism's fourth option means the centre does little, it is often unnoticed and under-theorised. A recent proposal has made it through the

[259] E Chemernisky, *Constitutional Law* (Boston, Aspen, 2019) 912.

[260] Fabbrini (n 232) 116.

[261] See ch 4.

[262] 'Texas judge fines New York doctor for prescribing abortion pills to a woman near Dallas' (*NPR*, 14 February 2025) www.npr.org/2025/02/14/g-s1-48889/texas-judge-fines-new-york-doctor-abortion-pills accessed 3 August 2025; DS Cohen, G Donley and R Rebouché, 'The New Abortion Battleground' (2023) 123 *Columbia Law Review* 1.

[263] ET Sullivan and RS Frase, *Proportionality Principles in American Law: Controlling Excessive Government Actions* (Oxford, Oxford University Press, 2008).

[264] See, eg, analysis of the Court's approach to capital punishment in JS Liebman, 'Slow Dancing with Death: The Supreme Court and Capital Punishment, 1963-2006' (2007) 107 *Columbia Law Review* 124. I am grateful to Mark Tushnet for noting that while *Dobbs* takes a deferential approach to substantive regulations of abortion, it probably may not foreclose a less deferential approach to procedures associated with such regulations (including, for example, the procedures used to determine whether an abortion might be medically necessary where such an exception is allowed under state law).

Parliament to explicitly include abortion among a bundle of reproductive rights as a right in the European Charter.[265] Whilst amendment seems unlikely, if it happens, such a centralisation-minded approach risks provoking resistance from member states and could run counter to the EU's subsidiarity-oriented method, as well as the ECtHR's margin of appreciation.

In other words, the proposed amendment may risk bringing Europe into its own version of the American 'déjà vu'.[266] That said, the scope for backlash might be more limited in Europe, given that only two Member States currently impose a full ban on abortion. However, the amendment's underlying message to shift the EU's approach to morally divisive matters could reframe the Charter from a mechanism for safeguarding unity in diversity into a tool for enforcing moral conformity. This, in turn, risks generating unnecessary polarisation within the Union.

With this, we conclude the contrast of abortion's past and future. Readers might be thinking that abortion could be an outlier example and that we may need to look beyond it to test the argument further. This is what the next section attempts very briefly to do.

VI. Examples Beyond Abortion and a Caveat

The comparative analysis covered in this chapter illustrated a pattern whereby recourse to power to impose a top-down uniformity on a divisive moral value not only betrays impartiality but also tends to result in enduring polarisation. By contrast, a gradual organic bottom-up approach can diffuse tension. In the latter case, jurisdictions either gradually and voluntarily converge on the matter or reach an agreement to disagree. This pattern extends beyond abortion and even beyond western systems. While space does not permit a full exploration of additional case studies, a brief review of the established literature on these issues should suffice.

One example is the American story over the 'advent of non-fault divorce',[267] which is often termed 'the silent revolution'.[268] For a country with a Christian heritage, no-fault divorce was a morally 'controversial' issue pitting the sanctity of marriage against the rising tide of individual autonomy.[269] Relaxing divorce laws

[265] European Parliament, 'Resolution on Inclusion of the Right to Abortion in the EU Charter of Fundamental Rights' (2024) P9_TA(2024)0286 www.europarl.europa.eu/doceo/document/TA-9-2024-0286_EN.html accessed 3 August 2025.

[266] Fabbrini (n 232).

[267] DL Shapiro, *Federalism: A Dialogue* (Evanston, Northwestern University Press, 1995) 96–97.

[268] H Jacob, *Silent Revolution: The Transformation of Divorce Law in the United States* (Chicago, University of Chicago Press, 1988).

[269] Being divisive depends on the society in question; divorce was not a divisive issue in Muslim majority countries, for example, compared to the West.

was viewed by some as 'evil', and they fiercely 'campaigned' for divorce law reform.[270] Yet slowly, states like Nevada started to allow *ex parte* divorces 'on easy terms', which ushered in an era of 'migratory divorce' whereby unhappy spouses temporarily migrate to a sister state with relaxed laws to secure divorce.[271] To counter this phenomenon, many attempted unsuccessfully to amend the Constitution and centralise the divorce question. In 1906, President Roosevelt famously 'implored Congress to amend the Constitution to provide federal control over the laws of marriage and divorce'.[272] Other proposed amendments were explicitly couched in the language of America being a 'Christian nation'.[273]

The Supreme Court took a different approach, steering away from full centralisation by refraining from establishing a fundamental right to divorce while also not leaving states' discretionary authority entirely unconditional. In a number of decisions, the Court mediated the plurality of regulations amongst states.[274] Essentially, the Court held that according to the constitutional clause of 'full faith and credit', it entails that a divorce granted in one state is entitled to be recognised in every other as long as the plaintiff spouse has established the 'jurisdictional prerequisites' for obtaining the divorce.[275] The availability of migratory divorce, along with its resulting 'jurisdictional redundancy' and the underlying contradictions it exposed, sparked widespread discussion. These debates permeated popular culture, appearing in numerous movies, books, plays, and even music.[276] This cultural and social engagement played a role in facilitating a gradual convergence among states on divorce regulations.

The story of non-fault divorce is 'complicated', and it is fully covered in 'family law federalism' literature.[277] The point is that scholars concur that after a slow start, no-fault divorce 'became virtually universal' across various states, even though the states 'still differ in a number of significant details'.[278] Strikingly, one of the 'most morally freighted' and 'controversial'[279] issues was turned into what Herbert Jacob described 'as an instance of routine policymaking', which was made possible by shifting social and economic conditions. Importantly, this transformation unfolded 'largely without controversy'.[280] Differently put, the transformative

[270] See, eg, *Boddie v Connecticut* 401 US 371 (1971) [37].
[271] Shapiro (n 267).
[272] MJ Higdon, 'If You Grant It, They Will Come: The History and Enduring Legal Legacy of Migratory Divorce' (2022) *Utah Law Review* 295.
[273] The proposed amendment reads 'The Congress, as the highest law-making power of a Christian nation, shall have exclusive power to regulate marriage and divorce in the several States, Territories, and the District of Columbia.' Cited in ibid.
[274] For a summary of the 12 cases, see ibid.
[275] Shapiro (n 267) 96–97.
[276] Higdon (n 272) 310.
[277] AL Estin, 'Family Law Federalism: Divorce and the Constitution' (2007) 16 *William & Mary Bill of Rights Journal* 381.
[278] ibid 431.
[279] ibid.
[280] Estin citing H Jacob, *Silent Revolution: The Transformation of Divorce Law in The United States* (Chicago, University of Chicago Press, 1988) 36.

convergence occurred without mass polarisation or recourse to top-down value imposition of either of the competing views. This does not imply universal agreement with the outcome – disagreement, as discussed earlier, is inherent to human nature. Nevertheless, polarisation on this issue is minimal, largely confined even to the fringes, without involving significant segments of the population.[281]

Another example is how the EU has allowed a diversity of state-church arrangements, rather than pursuing a rigid de-establishment agenda as the US did from the mid-twentieth century onwards. This has been another arena for ideological confrontation in the US. By contrast, the approach adopted under Article 17 of the EU, which leaves states free to choose their arrangements, exemplifies how federalism can offer a fourth option on issues that may otherwise be divisive. While highly unlikely, a counterfactual scenario may be helpful here. Imagine if the CJEU had followed the US path, interpreting the Charter rights on freedom of religion as requiring strict separation, thereby compelling states such as Ireland or Denmark to disestablish their national churches. Such an approach would undoubtedly provoke backlash and unnecessary polarisation. We shall revisit state-church comparisons in the next chapter and explore how they overlap with other forms of factionalism to further illustrate the dangers of overcentralisation of factions of principle.

A non-western example is the discovery of Arabian and Turkish coffee. This triggered intense legal disagreement as to whether their energising effect should be considered intoxicating and, thus, banned.[282] After the prohibition advocates failed to effectively centralise a ban throughout the empire, gradually the tense disagreement evaporated, and it is now impossible to imagine Ottomans without Turkish coffee.[283] This can be contrasted with the US Temperance Movement's constitutional amendment centralising Alcohol Ban. That centralisation led to widespread conflict, social unrest, and organised crime – the era of Al Capone and Prohibition-era violence popularly portrayed in American films.[284] Yet, when the ban was repealed via another constitutional amendment, the national tension quickly dissipated. Importantly, this shift did not require Americans to abandon their principled convictions: as late as 40 years after repealing the amendment,

[281] For contemporary discussion, see JA Smith, 'Why Are Americans Fighting Over No-Fault Divorce? Maybe They Can't Agree What Marriage Is For' (*The Conversation*, 11 March 2023) theconversation.com/why-are-americans-fighting-over-no-fault-divorce-maybe-they-cant-agree-what-marriage-is-for-223422 accessed 3 August 2025.

[282] S Topik, 'Coffee as a Social Drug' (2009) 71 *Cultural Critique* 81.

[283] Another illustrative oriental example is the centralisation of the theological view of the faction known as the Mutazilites. Overzealous centralised enforcement was accompanied with polarisation and coercion. By contrast, when such matters were no longer centrally imposed, polarisation and the accompanying coercion subsided. Of course, differing opinions persisted – as disagreement is inherent to human nature – but, as discussed earlier, disagreement need not degenerate into polarisation or conflict.

[284] Contrast this with the bottom-up, gradual approach adopted toward banning alcohol in the Muslim world, which led to maximum adherence with minimum execution cost and without heavy state apparatus to enforce it. It also does not apply to religious minorities and alcohol abstinence acquired social acceptance for centuries since then. Contrary to the justification offered by C de Secondat Montesquieu, *The Spirit of the Laws* (Kitchener, Batoche Books, 2001).

many US counties' local jurisdictions stayed dry and kept a ban, but the issue was less polarising or divisive.[285] Examples abound in moral diffusion literature.[286]

A caveat is in order. Mediated diversity for factions of principle can be overridden by central intervention in cases where moral conformity is a necessity for the preservation of the Union *narrowly construed*. While federalism is inherently pluralistic, federalism also presumes a degree of moral unity or, as the CJEU terms it, 'constitutional traditions common to Member States'[287] through which to judge 'good diversity', which could be maintained from 'bad diversity', which runs afoul of these values.[288] These concrete moral commitments could be either universal or regionally contingent. Universal or near-universal examples include rules against murder or judicial impartiality. One could also use the example put forth by Sandel: the EU or US will not allow experimenting with the sale of children born into poor families to wealthy persons who could better take care of them. This would be unacceptable despite all stakeholders being, economically speaking, better off.[289]

Regionally contingent moral commitments are dictated by the *cultural imprint and the historical contingency* of a given society. Given that a constitutional convention 'designs' a constitution, not 'a society',[290] these values are needed to ensure '[social] solidarity'[291] or, as Dworkin puts it, a 'society cannot survive unless some standards of moral conformity' are in place.[292] He refers to monogamy in western democracies as an example of such standards. As is commonly known, six times the American Congress did not allow Utah to enter the Union unless its Constitution banned polygamy.[293] For example, while the temperance movement was highly divisive in the US, alcohol bans are widely accepted in Middle Eastern societies and maintained without heavy state intervention or social polarisation. This illustrates two broader points: first, some of the core moral commitments vary from one polity to another. Second, that

[285] Specifically, 'as late as 1973, 545 United States counties banned liquor sales and 672 banned liquor sales for consumption on premises': L McGirr, *The War on Alcohol: Prohibition and the Rise of the American State* (New York, WW Norton & Co, 2015).

[286] LG Sager, 'Cool Federalism and the Lifecycle of Moral Progress' (2004) 46 *William & Mary Law Review* 1389; in the EU, see R Sluiter, 'The Diffusion of Morality Policies among Western European Countries between 1960 and 2010' (2012) Nijmegen: ICS Dissertation Series.

[287] Eg, Case C-4/73 *Nold v Commission* ECLI:EU:C:1974:51, [1974] ECR 491, para 13; see J Lawrence, 'Constitutional Pluralism's Unspoken Normative Core' (2019) 21 *Cambridge Yearbook of European Legal Studies* 24, 28.

[288] 'Diversity is much trickier, because what we have to do is distinguish between good diversity and bad diversity.' Horowitz (n 237) 967.

[289] M Sandel, *What Money Can't Buy: The Moral Limits of Markets* (London, Penguin, 2013) 64–75.

[290] RA Dahl, *A Preface to Democratic Theory* (Chicago, University of Chicago Press, 2006) 89.

[291] A Hartman, *A War for the Soul of America: A History of the Culture Wars*, 2nd edn (Chicago, The University of Chicago Press, 2019) 290; RC Post, 'Democratic Constitutionalism and Cultural Heterogeneity' (2000) 25(2) *Australian Journal of Legal Philosophy* 185, 188.

[292] R Dworkin, *Taking Rights Seriously* (Richmond, Duckworth, 1977) 271; the foundational core of each polity is the subject of vast philosophical and jurisprudential scholarship in both the EU and the US – far beyond the scope of this chapter, but certainly a topic for future exploration. See, eg, R Forst, *Toleration in Conflict: Past and Present* (Cambridge, Cambridge University Press, 2013).

[293] Horowitz (n 237) 967.

mediated plurality is a tool to avoid polarisation, but if a particular (concrete, not abstract) moral commitment is extremely central to a society's identity and breaching it – through decentralisation – would risk disintegration, then the argument for decentralisation loses its rationale.[294]

In short, mediated plurality is not advisable where the issue at stake forms a core foundation of societal cohesion – without which the union risks losing either its functional viability or its long-established moral identity.[295] However, such exceptions must be interpreted narrowly. Abstract appeals to shared values should not become instruments for enforcing moral conformity in areas that, as discussed in chapter four, involve genuine value clashes. Since pluralism lies at the heart of federalism's constitutional DNA, moral conformity should be reserved only for cases of absolute necessity – not where two foundational principles are in legitimate conflict.

The examples explored in this chapter – abortion, no-fault divorce, temperance, and even illustrative cases from non-western contexts – demonstrate that moral conformity was not necessary in these domains. Although arguments grounded in autonomy, dignity, or public morality can be invoked to justify moral homogeneity and centralisation, such claims frequently overlook the fact that these are value-laden conflicts, marked by competing moral commitments of foundational weight genuinely advanced by both parties. As developed in the test outlined in chapter four and applied here, these conflicts support the case for a federal hands-off approach. Comparative analysis of the EU, reflection on American history, and even intuitive 'situation sense' all suggest that unity on such matters is not required for the moral or functional preservation of either union.[296] Indeed, attempts to impose moral conformity have often deepened polarisation rather than alleviated it – and have, at times, undermined the very moral principles they intended to defend, as seen in the American abortion context. By contrast, mediated plurality offers a framework capable of gradually balancing tensions between conflicting moral commitments, as Tushnet observed in his analysis of social welfare and abortion in Europe.[297]

VII. Concluding Remarks

Federalism is a double-edged sword that can be wielded for good – such as diffusing polarisation – or for ill, by inflaming it. Imposing top-down conformity

[294] To contrast concrete versus abstract: consider rule against murder which is concrete compared to the abstract appeal to a right to life.

[295] See, eg, the Utah example discussed earlier or the recent UK case limiting Scotland's ideological experimentation: *For Women Scotland v Lord Advocate* [2022] CSIH 4, [209].

[296] K Llewellyn, *The Common Law Tradition: Deciding Appeals* (Boston, Little, Brown & Co, 1960) 402.

[297] Tushnet (n 239) 351.

on a morally divisive issue is far more polarising in an integrative federation than in a unitary state because the sheer number of coerced groups is significantly larger. Such an overcentralising approach could even transform an issue that might otherwise remain non-divisive into a source of profound conflict. However, mediated plurality can help turn this federal risk into an added value. By enabling multiple jurisdictions to act as centres of norm articulation, federalism can gradually moderate disagreement over contentious issues. This process is supported by the educative effects of cross-pollination, where the free circulation of social and legal norms facilitates dialogue and builds compromises over time.

This dovetails with the previous chapters' discussion of impartiality and its impossibility. In divisive ideological issues, both state and federal majorities are non-neutral in seeking to impose their own moral view on the other faction, leaving 'no neutral' umpire on the horizon.[298] The impossibility of neutrality has eluded the attention of many, and the 'faux' neutrality argument is not confined to Justice Kavanaugh but equally caught the dissent, which claimed to represent the neutral side, and writers such as Sunstein, who argued that the 'impartial' constitutions ought to protect abortion rights. Alternatively, as chapter two explained, when impartiality is impossible, the jurisdictional question should be decided based on a 'calculus' determining which jurisdictional arrangement attains more 'optimisation' of federalism's matrix of objectives. Here, balancing the values of 'redundancy', 'cross fertilisation', and 'subsidiarity', as well as the benefit of averting unnecessary consolidation of social polarisation together, tips the scale in favour of mediated plurality as federalism's fourth option.

Thus far, the comparative cases have largely centred on issues dominated by one type of faction. The next chapter turns to compounded cases, where principle- and interest-based factions overlap. How might federalism navigate such layered conflicts?

[298] O'Connor (n 1).

6

Multi-Faceted Factions and the Flexibility of Boundaries: The Case of Religion

I. Introduction: A Fable of Two Factions

The previous chapters have examined two types of cases: factions of group interest, such as minority rights (where federal impartiality can check group bias), and factions of conflicting moral principle, such as abortion (where federal impartiality cannot check ideological/moral bias). What remains is the case in which these two types overlap yet remain analytically separable – a situation referred to as *multi-faceted factions*. This refers to constitutional conflicts which *can* be broken into two issues: involving both majority bias (faction of interest) as well as ideological bias (faction of principle).[1]

Poignant examples emerge from cases involving religion. As a 'multifaceted'[2] phenomenon, religion can be 'both a matter of identity (akin to race) and a matter of belief (akin to political opinion)'.[3] Differently put, religion can act as a cause of interest-based faction when used as 'a marker of group membership (chosen or otherwise)' based on ethnic 'immutable characteristics' of its group members.[4] On the other hand, religion can take on a positively ideological dimension by aligning with and indirectly shaping culture wars that divide society, without being limited to the concerns of a specific religious minority. This is evident in many religiously influenced debates on issues such as abortion, assisted dying, and others.[5] As

[1] Occasionally, separating the two cannot be achieved as discussed later.

[2] T Khaitan and JC Norton, 'The Right to Freedom of Religion and the Right against Religious Discrimination: Theoretical Distinctions' (2019) 17 *International Journal of Constitutional Law* 1132, 1132–1134, 1144.

[3] R McCrea, 'I Faith at Work: The CJEU's Headscarf Rulings' (*EU Law Analysis*, 14 March 2017) eulawanalysis.blogspot.com/2017/03/faith-at-work-cjeus-headscarf-rulings.html accessed 3 August 2025.

[4] Khaitan and Nortin (n 2).

[5] Khaitan brilliantly captures the distinction between the ideological-driven groups and that of minorities. The former are 'politically optimistic and therefore seek expressive recognition of their agendas [unlike the latter who simply seek] political insurance through constitutionally guaranteed power-sharing'. T Khaitan, 'Directive Principles and the Expressive Accommodation of Ideological Dissenters' (2018) 16 *International Journal of Constitutional Law* 394.

McCrea noted, what is lacking in case law is a 'criteria to work out when it is right to treat religion as belief and when it is right to treat it as identity'.[6]

The debate on the proper classification of the underlying cause of disagreement is clear, for example, in the EU cases concerning religious clothing. AG Sharpston in *Bougnaoui* saw these symbols as an 'inseparable' marker of group identity[7] – so did AG Medina in *SCRL*[8] – compared to merely an ideological 'choice' incomparable to race, as AG Kockott argued.[9] This classification of the nature of the issue involved significantly affects the choice of comparator and the consequent federal allocation of authority. The case law will be explored later, but the following fable can capture the institutional aspect of the distinction.

Certain intercollegiate universities, such as Cambridge, operate as a kind of federal system, comprising several colleges, each with its own sphere of divergent regulatory rules. Unlike other universities, such as the LSE or Harvard, this two-tier membership entails belonging to two parallel polities: one's *college* and one's *faculty*. Colleges differ not only in age and architecture but also in their relationship to religion. Many maintain historic Protestant chapels such as the renowned King's Chapel, while one retains a Catholic chapel, and newer colleges often have no religious affiliation at all. Importantly, each college is left free to decide whether to have a religious building or not and to regulate the governance and funding of these religious buildings.

In constitutional terms, this freedom falls under the institutional dimension of *establishment* – the relationship between the state (here college) and religion – which can be distinct from *the religious freedom* question. Many religious minority students and academics at Cambridge may observe the grandeur of its chapels without feeling coerced or excluded. What matters is not the presence of these symbols of faith but the freedom to practise one's own beliefs. A student or an academic from a minority religion, for example, is not concerned about the college having a chapel. Instead, they are concerned about being allowed to access prayer space, observe dietary laws, or wear religious attire without interference.

Now, imagine if Cambridge were to adopt a model drawn from a blend of the American Establishment Clause jurisprudence and French *laïcité*. Call this *Alternative Cambridge*. In such a system, religion would be pushed entirely out of the public sphere, and colleges would be asked to disestablish their historical chapels and pursue an exclusive neutrality policy whereby all symbols of

[6] R McCrea, 'Religious Discrimination in the Workplace: Which Approach Should the CJEU Follow?' (*EU Law Analysis*, 14 July 2016) eulawanalysis.blogspot.com/2016/07/religious-discrimination-in-workplace.html accessed 3 August 2025.

[7] Case C-188/15 *Asma Bougnaoui and Association de défense des droits de l'homme (ADDH) v Micropole SA* ECLI:EU:C:2016:553, Opinion of AG Sharpston, para 118. See also, Shadow Opinion of former Advocate General Sharpston: Headscarves at Work (Cases C-804/18 and C-341/19) (EU Law Analysis, 23 March 2021), eulawanalysis.blogspot.com/2021/03/shadow-opinion-of-former-advocate.html.

[8] Case C-344/20 *LF v SCRL* EU:C:2022:328, Opinion of AG Medina, para 61.

[9] Case C-157/15 *Samira Achbita and Centrum voor gelijkheid van kansen en voor racismebestrijding v G4S Secure Solutions NV* EU:C:2016:382, Opinion of AG Kokott, paras 45–52, 116.

belief – such as the Muslim headscarf, the Sikh turban, or the Jewish yarmulke – are prohibited in classrooms or graduation ceremonies. For many minority students, such policies would likely be far more exclusionary than the presence of a chapel on college grounds. The point is this: moderate forms of religious establishment and secular non-establishment can be distinguished from coercion or denial of religious rights. The mere preference for or symbolic alignment with a religious or secular tradition does not necessarily violate religious freedom, provided that the exercise of dissenting beliefs is not unduly burdened.

The *Cambridge/Alternative Cambridge* fable aims to simplify two points. First, to remind the reader of federalism's third option. While unitary systems must choose either to allow establishment or not, federalism can give the option of both *allowing and disallowing establishment in the same breath*. It can disallow religious establishment at the federal level but leave states free to allow it or not at the local level. Second, and importantly, the analogy shows that the question of establishment can, in many cases, be distinct from the question of the free exercise of manifest beliefs, despite some obvious overlaps.

This has implications for the federal boundary. Much like the Cambridge fable, the locus of power can be broken down into two issues. States are free to choose different answers to the question of church-state and the role of religion in the public sphere, but the Centre's impartiality ensures protection of minorities for the question of exercise. These might seem like straightforward observations, but as we shall see from contrasting the EU and the US, they are in fact often overlooked in federal analysis or case law, which has made matters confusing and more socially divisive. As discussed below, the two questions appeal to two interrelated yet distinct types of factionalism (moral conviction and group interest), and federalism can allocate power differently to each when possible.

A preliminary point must be made about why the two aspects of religion – establishment and religious freedom/discrimination – can be animated by different, though sometimes interconnected, types of social disagreement (tribal/group-based inclinations compared to ideological impulses). The debate over religion's role in the public sphere (if we guarantee non-coercion to minorities) is not exclusive to majority faiths and is not group-based. Within almost all religions, adherents are divided between secularists who advocate a strict separation of religion and state and traditionalists who favour religious integration into public life.[10] Viewed this way, the establishment question becomes a matter of ideological commitment on religion's role in public life – not group identity. As Judge Power put it, 'secularism [is], in itself, one ideology among others. A preference for secularism over alternative world views – whether religious, philosophical or otherwise – is not a neutral option.'[11] Additionally, the content of the debate does not change with the enlargement of the political orbit. The debate is equally

[10] See generally N Feldman, *Divided by God: America's Church-State Problem-- and What We Should Do About It* (New York, Farrar, Straus and Giroux, 2006).

[11] *Lautsi v Italy* App no 30814/06 (ECtHR, 18 March 2011), [45] (Power L, concurring) (Lautsi) (emphasis added).

contentious in small states like San Marino as in larger federations like the US or the EU. This is a domain where no stance is truly neutral, in the federal sense of the word, and mediated decentralisation may be a more viable way to minimise ideological conflict.

If impartiality over the question of establishment is not possible and choosing a partial view becomes a necessity, the necessity must be understood narrowly. This 'necessarily unavoidable' preference of one ideological view – be it laic or religious – cannot license unnecessary avoidable coercion of other groups. A state's preference – such as religious public holidays or chapels – cannot extend to unnecessary oppression or discrimination.[12] This includes restrictions on dress, dietary practices, or public participation, which is seen in militant theological or militant secular systems like France. Unavoidable ideological preference must not become a licence for avoidable oppression.

This is where religious group diversity within a federation can serve as a constitutional safeguard. The larger the federation, the more religious groups it typically contains – making it harder for one group to dominate and strip others of rights. Maintaining the issue at the centre ensures more groups are involved, rather than leaving each minority at the mercy of the local majority. As the case law illustrates, the federal level can intervene more impartially to shield minorities from discriminatory practices. As the subsequent case law analysis will show, it includes bans on religious clothing (as in *Abercrombie*), denial of ritual practice (as in the legislative reversal of *Smith*), or discrimination in recruitment based on religious affiliation (as in *Egenberger*) or lack thereof (*Religious Testing cases*).[13]

This reflects the argument that stresses the Union's broader political orbit, which includes a wider array of groups and faith traditions with distinct yet overlapping interests. Restrictions imposed on one group often implicate others, generating wider opposition and making it harder to isolate any single group for oppression at the federal level compared to the state level. This usual correlation between federation size and overlapping religious diversity is illustrated by the extensive jurisprudence on religious accommodation. In the US, for example, one study identified over 2,000 federal and state accommodations for various religious practices, ranging from dietary laws to military dress and conscription.[14]

With this distinction and overlap in mind, the argument made here is that the boundary question should be addressed, when possible, in a *two-tracked approach*. First, considerable discretion can be granted to states regarding the role of religion in the public sphere within a framework of mediated plurality (ie, a hands-off

[12] Coercion understood in its core uncontested sense as 'compelling' a person to profess or practice religious orthodoxy and of 'financial support by force of law and threat of penalty'. This excludes the debated soft and indirect coercion, or psychological discomfort; see *Espinoza v Montana Department of Revenue* 591 US 464 (2020) (Thomas J, concurring); I Leigh and R Ahdar, 'Post-Secularism and the European Court of Human Rights: Or How God Never Really Went Away' (2012) 75 *The Modern Law Review* 1064, 1085–1091.

[13] Eg, *Torcaso v Watkins* 367 US 488 (1961).

[14] NS Chapman and MW McConnell, *Agreeing to Disagree: How the Establishment Clause Protects Religious Diversity and Freedom of Conscience* (Oxford, Oxford University Press, 2023) 99–100.

approach). Second, and at the same time, the establishment of a minimum floor for the protection of religious minorities/dissenters should be entrusted to the central government, which is better positioned to offer a more impartial perspective pursuant to Madison's federalist argument. It is worth reminding the reader that Madison's argument on impartiality was initially inspired by the clash of religious sects as discussed in chapter two. Of course, some cases defy easy categorisation, where the line between ideological and group-based claims becomes blurred and tension is unavoidable.

It is important to note that the chapter does not – and indeed cannot – undertake a comprehensive comparison of the constitutional treatment of religion in the EU and the US, which would require a dedicated study of its own. The objective of this brief comparison is to shed light on the boundary question – namely, to illustrate how the two questions of: (i) church-state arrangement; and (ii) religious freedom can be approached by a combination of a central hands-off/hands-on approach, respectively. Comparatively, the chapter shows that this two-layered jurisdictional approach aligns – at least in some cases – with Article 17, TFEU, which addresses the role of religious and philosophical organisations. It also briefly compares this approach to the historical interpretation of the First Amendment in the US Constitution, which appears to support a compounded approach to the boundary question. This stands in contrast to the mid-twentieth-century decisions of the US Supreme Court, which merged the two questions into an over-centralised approach to the Establishment Clause. As a result, this approach, as Feldman observes, led to unnecessary doctrinal complexity and social division.[15] However, both sides of the Atlantic exhibit a mixed-bag approach to religious freedom when it comes to minorities.

To this end, the chapter is structured as follows. Sections II and III respectively, provide a brief analysis of the key constitutional provisions and key case law on establishment and freedom of conscience in both the US and EU. Each section considers whether there is a difference in how establishment and free exercise are treated in terms of centralisation. Is one dimension more centralised than the other, and if so, why? Second, it explores the extent to which the allocation of power aligns with the federal impartiality argument, the implications of each system's approach on doctrinal consistency, social polarisation, and protection of rights.

II. US Religion Clauses and the Question of Boundaries

Unlike EU primary law, where the two aspects of religion are addressed in provisions located in separate places, the First Amendment of the US Constitution

[15] Feldman (n 10).

contains two religion clauses, 'yoked together in a single grammatical unit'.[16] The first is the *Establishment Clause*, which concerns the relationship between church and state and details that 'Congress shall make no law respecting an establishment of religion.' The second is the *Free Exercise Clause*, which guarantees religious freedom by stating that Congress shall make no law 'prohibiting the free exercise thereof'.

Despite the 'interconnected' nature of the religion clauses, the Supreme Court usually addresses matters related to the *Establishment Clause* within 'one doctrinal framework and *Free Exercise Clause* issues within another'.[17] This division is a useful starting point, as it reflects the core of this chapter's *multi-faceted faction* thesis – namely, that establishment and free exercise, sometimes, raise distinct, though overlapping, types of constitutional conflicts and can be addressed through different jurisdictional approaches. However, the Supreme Court often gets the wrong end of the stick. As we shall see, there has been an over-centralisation of the *Establishment Clause*, which runs counter to the argument for federal impartiality in matters of principle. Conversely, the treatment of free exercise and religious minority claims has often been marked by under-centralisation or inconsistency, failing to fully utilise federalism's capacity to deliver more impartial protections for vulnerable groups.

This brings us back to chapter one's discussion on the incorporation of the US Bill of Rights – that is, its centralisation, in European terms – and its application to the states. Until the twentieth century, it was widely understood that the Bill of Rights applied only to the federal government, not to the states. As a result, the Religion Clauses could not be invoked against state-level legislation. However, in the mid-twentieth century, the Supreme Court adopted the doctrine of *incorporation*, gradually applying the Bill of Rights to the states via the Due Process Clause of the Fourteenth Amendment. The Free Exercise Clause was the first of the two religion clauses to be incorporated, in *Cantwell v Connecticut* (1940).[18] The Establishment Clause followed in *Everson v Board of Education* (1947).[19] Both clauses are discussed in turn.

A. The Overcentralisation of the Establishment Clause

Unlike the incorporation of the Free Exercise Clause, which clearly safeguards individual and corporate religious liberty, the extension of the Establishment Clause to states has proven more 'controversial'.[20] This is because the Establishment

[16] Chapman and McConnell (n 14). The US First Amendment reads 'Congress shall make no law respecting an establishment of religion, or prohibiting the free exercise thereof.'

[17] RH Fallon Jr, *The Dynamic Constitution: An Introduction to American Constitutional Law and Practice*, 2nd edn (Cambridge, Cambridge University Press, 2013) 79.

[18] *Cantwell v Connecticut* 310 US 296 (1940).

[19] *Everson v Board of Education* 330 US 1 (1947).

[20] E Chemernisky *Constitutional Law*, 7th edn (Burlington, Aspen, 2020) 1300.

Clause arguably has a primarily institutional or federal dimension – concerning the structural relationship between not only church and state, but also the federal government and constituent states. Many scholars take the wording – 'Congress [not states] shall make no law respecting an establishment of religion' – to mean that Congress and the federal level more broadly 'simply lacked enumerated power to intrude into religious freedom in the several states'.[21] Put differently, the clause serves two functions: (i) it prohibits the establishment of religion at the federal level; and (ii) it bars federal interference with existing state establishments and churches.[22] In this view, the Establishment Clause is a 'pro-state' provision which maintains their regulatory autonomy, and it would be 'paradoxical' to incorporate it against them.[23]

There are plausible historical arguments both for and against the incorporation of the Establishment Clause, which are thoroughly discussed elsewhere.[24] What is most relevant here is Madison's view – and particularly his proposed draft of the Religion Clauses. Interestingly, similar to the current EU framework, Madison's original proposal separated the two religion clauses and placed them in distinct sections of the Constitution – each location is quite revealing. One clause, which closely resembles the language of today's First Amendment, was appended to Article I, Section 9, which *contains restrictions on federal power*. This version addressed the issue of establishment and was designed to limit the federal government from interfering with religious matters or compelling religious practice in general.

By contrast, Madison's second provision – concerned with protecting the *rights of conscience*, as well as jury rights, and freedom of the press – was directed at the states and appended *to Section 10, which restricts state power*. Madison considered this amendment 'the most valuable in the whole list', as it embodied his cherished logic of Federalist No. 10: that *states* were more *likely than the federal government to oppress religious minorities*.[25] The way Madison sought to 'interweave' the amendment in two different locations can be read to reflect a key theme of this chapter: the establishment of religion is a matter that ought to be decentralised and left to the states to determine, whereas the protection of freedom of religion and conscience warrants a more active role for the Union, to ensure impartiality and guard against the risks of religious factionalism.[26] Madison's proposal against the centralisation of the right to conscience against the state was rejected at the time, but 'arguably' the Fourteenth Amendment incorporation discussed in chapter one constitutes a revival of his view.

[21] AR Amar, *The Bill of Rights: Creation and Reconstruction* (New Haven, Yale University Press, 1998) 42.

[22] Chapman and McConnell (n 14) 80.

[23] Amar (n 21) 37.

[24] ibid.

[25] MW McConnell, 'The Fourteenth Amendment: A Second American Revolution or the Logical Culmination of the Tradition' (1991) 25 *Loyola of Los Angeles Law Review* 1159.

[26] Amar (n 21) 37.

The 'pro-state' nature of the Establishment issue is summed up by Amar's remark that the Clause constitutes a 'home rule-local option provision'[27] which is '*agnostic* on the substantive issue of establishment versus no establishment and simply calls for the issue *to be decided locally*'. To him, this has *deeper historical roots* and represents 'the American equivalent of the European Peace of Augsburg in 1555 and Treaty of Westphalia in 1648, which decreed that religious policy would *be set locally rather than imperially*'.[28] Therefore, he finds it 'paradoxical' to make such a 'local option clause be mechanically incorporated against localities'.[29]

While this view has wide support academically, it remains a minority position judicially, with Justice Thomas being its most prominent advocate on the current Supreme Court. Recently, in his concurring opinion in *Espinoza*, he argues that:

> [e]ven assuming that the [Establishment] Clause creates a right and that such a right could be incorporated, however, it would only protect against an 'establishment' of religion as understood at the founding, i.e., coercion of religious orthodoxy and of financial support by force of law and threat of penalty.[30]

As Amar and others have noted, such coercion can be adequately addressed through the Free Exercise Clause and general equality guarantees and does not justify wholesale centralisation of the establishment question, as the case law below illustrates.[31]

This over-centralisation and imposition of a rigid *separationist* view, symbolised by the 'metaphorical' wall of separation between church and state, has had significant consequences beyond legal doctrine.[32] As Feldman vividly illustrates, this judicial centralisation has helped deepen societal divisions.[33] A particularly poignant example is the controversy surrounding religious symbols in public spaces – such as crosses or displaying the Ten Commandments. The 'separationist Justices' have often relied on the widely critiqued *Lemon* test,[34] which bars any governmental action that has the purpose or primary effect of *advancing religion* or that results in 'excessive *entanglement*' between government and religion.[35] The resulting case law has been highly fact-dependent, creating precedents that are difficult to apply consistently, which often 'ultimately boil down to raw interest-balancing exercises'.[36]

[27] ibid 246 (he adds that the rule mandates 'imperial (ie, Union) neutrality').
[28] ibid (emphasis added).
[29] ibid.
[30] *Espinoza* (n 12) [I.A] (Thomas J, Concurring).
[31] Amar (n 21).
[32] RH Fallon, Jr, 'Tiers for the Establishment Clause' (2017) 166 *University of Pennsylvania Law Review* 59, 90.
[33] Feldman (n 10).
[34] Fallon (n 17) 90.
[35] *Lemon v Kurtzman* 403 US 602 (1971).
[36] Case Comment, 'Espinoza v. Montana Department of Revenue, 140 S. Ct. 2246 (2020)' (2020) *134 Harvard Law Review* 470, 476–77. See, eg, *Lynch v Donnelly* 465 US 668 (1984); *County of Allegheny v American Civil Liberties Union* 492 US 573 (1989).

Take *County of Allegheny v ACLU* (1989), in which the Court, lacking a clear majority opinion, struck down a nativity scene displayed in a courthouse – a depiction of the birth of Jesus featuring Mary, Joseph, and baby Jesus.[37] By contrast, the Court upheld a nearby display of a menorah placed alongside a large Christmas tree and a sign saluting liberty.[38] The key difference, at least for Justices Blackmun and O'Connor, who cast the decisive votes, was that the menorah had been placed next to recognisably secular symbols, making the overall display appear more inclusive.

Doctrinal inconsistency aside, the over-centralisation of the ideologically divisive Establishment-related matter has had profound socio-political consequences. Prior to centralisation, and for nearly two centuries after the ratification of the US Constitution, few considered public religious displays to violate the Establishment Clause, making litigation on this issue unthinkable. However, once the issue was judicially centralised, litigation 'proliferated'.[39] This shift has fuelled the polarisation of American society. As Feldman observes, the debate has divided the country into two dominant camps: 'value evangelicals', who defend the role of religion in the public sphere, and 'legal secularists', who advocate for a strict separation between church and state.[40]

The demographic makeup of these groups reflects what the present book terms *consolidated polarisation*, a condition that emerges when *factions of principle* are centralised – contrary to the vision of balanced diversity in Federalist No. 10 (see chapters four and five). Notably, *value evangelicals* are not confined to one religion; they can 'include Jews, Catholics, Muslims, and even people who do not focus on particular religious traditions, united by a shared commitment to traditional moral values'.[41] This kind of *cross-faith alignment* was something that Madison feared: religious diversity might 'cease' to serve as a constitutional check when 'different religious denominations … form alliances'.[42] Rather than fostering diversity through inter-group balance, this has created entrenched, bipartisan ideological blocs.

Another flashpoint in this battle was school prayer. In *Engel v Vitale*, the Supreme Court invalidated a state policy permitting non-denominational prayer in state schools.[43] Although students were not compelled to participate, and could remain silent or be excused, the Court found that the state violated the Establishment Clause.[44] No discretion was given to states or their

[37] *County of Allegheny v American Civil Liberties Union* 492 US 573 (1989).
[38] ibid.
[39] Chapman and McConnell (n 14) 80.
[40] Feldman (n 10) 8.
[41] ibid.
[42] ibid 55.
[43] LM Friedman, *A History of American Law*, 4th edn (Oxford, Oxford University Press, 2019) 699–701.
[44] *Engel v Vitale* 370 US 421 (1962).

constitutional identity, to use European terminology.[45] Even a state law authorising a moment of silence in the public schools 'for meditation or voluntary prayer' was found unconstitutional.[46] These rulings were met with strong public backlash and proved difficult to enforce.[47] The judgments clashed with social beliefs, leading to widespread non-compliance. *Engel* catalysed a powerful 'populist backlash forging a coalition of conservative forces under the banner of "traditionalism"'.[48] Overall, the Court's intervention did the opposite of what Madison envisioned: rather than diffusing factional intensity, it consolidated it.

That said, recent developments in the US establishment jurisprudence have shifted the legal landscape. Changes in the Court's composition have finally overruled the widely critiqued yet persistent *Lemon* test.[49] What replaces *Lemon* 'remains unclear'.[50] For symbols, a recent case adopted a '*passage of time* approach', holding that longstanding religious symbols need not be removed.[51] The unfolding of new jurisprudence has split commentators. For some, this signals the arrival of a more coherent, 'streamlined' approach,[52] while for others, it represents a step towards the 're-establishment of religion'[53] and an attack on regression in rights protections.[54]

What is striking, however, is that these new decisions continue to apply the same test uniformly to both federal and state governments – overlooking Amar's remark that the First Amendment was originally a 'home-rule' provision which is 'agnostic' as to the policy choice of state-level religious arrangements and the possibility of mediated plurality as a federalism third option.[55] Additionally, the confusion over federalism becomes more apparent in the context of *free exercise* jurisprudence, where justices who have explicitly praised Federalist No. 10 have, in practice, undermined its logic in cases affecting religious minorities.

[45] Treaty on European Union (Maastricht Treaty) art 4(2).
[46] *Wallace v Jaffree* 472 US 38, 40–41 (1985).
[47] K Orren and JW Compton, *The Cambridge Companion to the United States Constitution* (Cambridge, Cambridge University Press 2018) 93.
[48] BJ Dierenfield, *The Battle Over School Prayer: How Engel v. Vitale Changed America* (Manhattan, University Press of Kansas, 2007) x.
[49] *Lamb's Chapel v Center Moriches Union Free School District* 508 US 384, 398–99 (1993) (Scalia J, dissenting).
[50] Chemernisky (n 20) 1325.
[51] *American Legion v American Humanist Association* 588 US 29 (2019); Chapman and McConnell (n 14) 170–171.
[52] Case Comment, Espinoza (n 36) 476–77.
[53] RC Schragger, M Schwartzman and N Tebbe, 'Reestablishing Religion' (2025) 92 *University of Chicago Law Review* 199.
[54] G Sullivan, 'Symposium: What Play in the Joints Remains after Espinoza?' (*SCOTUSblog*, 1 July 2020) www.scotusblog.com/2020/07/symposium-what-play-in-the-joints-remains-after-espinoza/ accessed 3 August 2025.
[55] Amar (n 21) 37.

B. Free Exercise in Three Frames: Between Under-Centralisation, Balance, and Recent Shifts

The controversy over Free Exercise in America and its federal implications revolves around the cases of *Smith* and *Boerne*, which will form the main part of the (critical) analysis. This will be followed by an examination of the Court's occasionally more balanced approaches to religious minorities, along with a brief overview of recent developments seeking to revisit *Smith* and revitalise the Free Exercise Clause.[56]

i. Smith *and* Boerne's *Legislative Under-Centralisation*

As discussed earlier, Madison's proposal to extend the right to conscience against state violations was rejected, but almost a century later, its 'logic' was revived through Section 5 of the Fourteenth Amendment.[57] Bingham – the architect of the Fourteenth Amendment – saw the lack of application of the Bill of Rights, including the Free Exercise Clause against state violations, as the main 'defect' of the Constitution. The purpose of the Fourteenth Amendment – and, in particular, its Section 5 – was to remedy this defect by empowering Congress to address state violations of minority rights. As Rakove puts it, this is 'the most Madisonian element' of the US Constitution, as it reflects Madison's belief that the federal government is more impartial than the states in protecting religious minorities.[58]

However, in *Boerne*, the Court curtailed this Madisonian logic. In stark contrast to its over-centralised approach to the Establishment Clause – where it has imposed a near-uniform standard at both state and federal levels – the Court adopted a markedly decentralised posture toward Free Exercise claims. Three cases mark the shift: (i) *Sherbert* (which set a more religious freedom-friendly test); (ii) *Smith* (which replaced *Sherbert*); and (iii) *Boerne* (which relied on *Smith* to limit Congressional intervention to reinstate *Sherbert* and to protect religious minorities from state violations).

In *Sherbert v Verner* (1963), a Seventh-Day Adventist was denied unemployment benefits after refusing to work on her Sabbath, Saturdays. The Court held that she was entitled to an exemption from a 'facially neutral' rule disqualifying from benefits those who voluntarily left their jobs. For the next 27 years following *Sherbert*, the Court applied strict scrutiny to governmental actions that burdened religious freedom, even when the law was 'facially neutral' and 'generally applicable',

[56] CC Lund, 'Religious Minorities in the Free Exercise Revolution' (forthcoming) law.yale.edu/sites/default/files/area/clinic/document/lund_religious_minorities.pdf accessed 3 August 2025.

[57] McConnell (n 25).

[58] JN Rakove, *A Politician Thinking: The Creative Mind of James Madison* (Oklahoma, University of Oklahoma Press, 2017) 191.

and did not directly discriminate against religion.[59] Under this test, individuals were entitled to religious exemptions unless the government could demonstrate a compelling interest – the highest standard of constitutional justification, and one that is, as famously described, 'strict in theory, but fatal in fact'.[60]

Smith changed this approach.[61] At issue was a state law that criminalised possession of the mildly hallucinogenic drug peyote. The applicants in the case were denied employment benefits after ingesting peyote for sacramental purposes as members of the Native American Church. Justice Scalia, writing for the majority, held that no exemption was constitutionally required. According to *Smith*, 'neutral and generally applicable laws' do not raise any issue under the First Amendment, and their application against religious adherents does not trigger *strict scrutiny*, nor do they require a 'compelling state interest' justification.[62] States only need to meet the 'extremely deferential' rational basis review. This way, *Smith* leaves religious adherents with what Justice Stewart termed 'a cruel choice' of either breaching their religious duties or violating the law.[63]

In institutional terms, *Smith* entails that religious exemptions 'are not to be provided by Courts and religious groups should go to state legislature'.[64] This leaves minority rights at the mercy of 'vicissitude of state majorities'.[65] Taken to its logical conclusion, the decision entails that the US Constitution offers no protection if Jewish prisoners were denied kosher food, 'Muslim or Hindu girls were required to wear what their religion deems to be immodest dress during gym classes', or 'if priests or ministers were required to testify to what they have learned in the confessional'.[66] Or, along the same logic, to penalise Sikhs for not taking their turbans off while entering the airport departure lounge.[67] We shall later see how this institutional dimension contrasts with comparable developments in the EU.

The *Smith* decision sparked backlash. At the time, free exercise was 'a bipartisan' cause, and Congress responded with near-unanimous support by passing the Religious Freedom Restoration Act ('RFRA'), which passed the House unanimously and the Senate by a vote of 97–3.[68] The Act sought to overrule *Smith* and

[59] Chemernisky (n 20) 1372; 'strict in theory, but fatal in fact'. G Gunther, 'Foreword: In Search of Evolving Doctrine on a Changing Court' (1972) 86 *Harvard Law Review* 1, 8.

[60] See generally Fallon (n 17) 93.

[61] ibid 94.

[62] ibid 94.

[63] *Braunfeld v Brown* 366 US 599, 616 (1961) (Stewart J, dissenting).

[64] Lund (n 56).

[65] *Employment Division v Smith* 494 US 872, 902 (1990) (O'Connor J, concurring); see L Epstein and EA Posner, 'The Roberts Court and the Transformation of Constitutional Protections for Religion: A Statistical Portrait' (2022) 2021 *The Supreme Court Review* 315, 318.

[66] M McConnell, 'Institutions and Interpretation: A Critique of City of Boerne V. Flores' (1997) 111 *Harvard Law Review* 153, 159.

[67] ibid.

[68] Z Rothschild, 'Free Exercise Partisanship' (2021) 107 *Cornell Law Review* 1067, 1085.

reinstate the *strict scrutiny* standard for all Free Exercise Clause claims. The core provision of RFRA states:

> [g]overnment may substantially burden a person's exercise of religion only if it demonstrates that application of the burden to the person (1) is in furtherance of a compelling governmental interest; (2) is the least restrictive means of furthering that compelling government Interest.[69]

Seemingly unimpressed with the bipartisan support for reinstating strict scrutiny, the Court partially invalidated the RFRA as it applied to states. It held that Congress overstepped its power under Section 5 of the Fourteenth Amendment. The judgment rested on two dimensions: *horizontal* separation of powers and *vertical* allocation of powers (ie, federalism). First, the Court's definition of a particular right (such as religious freedom in *Smith*) constitutes a ceiling for Congress to adhere to, not a floor to go above. It unequivocally reasoned that 'Congress does not enforce a constitutional right by changing what the right is; it has been given the power *"to enforce,"* not the power to determine what constitutes a constitutional violation.'[70] This enforcing legislation must be 'congruent[t] and proportional' to an underlying pattern of identified constitutional violations. The Court surveyed the country and found that at the time, there were no sweeping patterns of targeting religion that warranted such a sweeping legislative intervention.

Second – and perhaps more surprisingly – the Court grounded its decision in *Boerne* on principles of federalism. According to the Court, RFRA unconstitutionally infringed upon state powers by compelling them to exempt individuals engaged in religiously motivated conduct from otherwise generally applicable laws. In terms of the boundary question, this reflects a *legislative decentralisation-leaning approach*. It drew the jurisdictional boundary widely in favour of the states, to the detriment of congressional authority. This move significantly curtailed the federal government's ability to ensure the protection of religious exercise across the Union.

The judgment triggered harsh criticism.[71] Let us pause to consider why *Boerne* stands in direct tension with the argument for federal impartiality, as originally articulated by Madison and arguably extended through the Reconstruction Amendments. This contradiction can be sharply illustrated by contrasting Justice Scalia's own characterisation of Federalist No. 10 with his interpretation in *Boerne*. In an earlier opinion, Justice Scalia enthusiastically reaffirmed Madison's argument, stating that '[a]n acute awareness of the heightened *danger of oppression from political factions in small, rather than large, political units dates to the very beginning of our national history*'. He further added, '[t]o the children of the Founding Fathers, this should come as no surprise'. He then went on to provide an extensive

[69] US Code, s 2000bb–1(b).

[70] *City of Boerne v Flores* 521 US 507 (1997); Fallon (n 17) 349.

[71] Eg, RC Post and RB Siegel, 'Protecting the Constitution from the People: Juricentric Restrictions on Section Five Power' (2003) 78 *Indiana Law Journal* 1.

survey evidencing the Madisonian 'prophecy' of the 'dangers of [factional] oppression' at the state level.[72]

Surprisingly, however, in his concurring opinion in *Boerne*, Justice Scalia reversed this logic. The crux of his opinion, as McConnell observed, was that 'the people of each individual state – each individual locality – should decide the outcome of … concrete cases involving the clash between religious freedom and generally applicable laws'. In other words, the scope of Free Exercise rights would vary by jurisdiction.[73] Recall that the Federalist No. 10 argument requires union-wide uniformity in safeguarding religious freedom through floor-level centralisation, based on the logic that states are more vulnerable to factional pressures. Yet, *Boerne* cuts in the opposite direction, *decentralising* those protections. This is simply 'misplaced' and 'misguided federalism'.[74] *Boerne* preventing the Congress from replacing *Smith* leaves religious minorities 'at the mercy of [facially] neutral acts of state and local governments'.[75]

ii. Balanced Minority Hands-On Cases: Lessons for Europe

Setting aside the debate over *Smith*, there are commendable *hands-on/centralisation* examples of US case law with regard to religious minorities that have successfully resolved issues that continue to trouble the Court of Justice of the European Union ('CJEU'). One such example is the US Supreme Court's decision in *EEOC v Abercrombie & Fitch Stores, Inc.*, which addressed the question of religious garb in the workplace. Here, the Court considered whether an employer violated Title VII of the Civil Rights Act by refusing to hire a Muslim applicant who wore a headscarf to her interview, citing a conflict with the company's 'look policy' that prohibited headwear.[76]

Writing for the majority, Justice Scalia made it clear that religious accommodation under Title VII requires not equal treatment but *favoured treatment*. He noted that the statute 'gives religious practices favored treatment, affirmatively obligating employers' to accommodate them – even when otherwise neutral workplace policies are at issue. As he explained:

> An employer is surely entitled to have, for example, a no-headwear policy as an ordinary matter. But when an applicant requires an accommodation as an 'aspect of religious … practice,' it is no response that the subsequent failure to hire was due to an otherwise neutral policy.

[72] *City of Richmond v JA Croson Co* 488 US 469 (1989) (Scalia J, concurring) citing examples of cases where Madison's argument has been proven: *Yick Wo v Hopkins* 118 US 356 (1886); *Hernandez v Texas* 347 US 475 (1954); *Cooper v Aaron* 358 US 1 (1958).

[73] McConnell (n 66) 193.

[74] Terminology inspired by PJ Henning, 'Misguided Federalism' (2003) 68 *Missouri Law Review* 389.

[75] McConnell (n 66) 162.

[76] *EEOC v Abercrombie & Fitch Stores, Inc.* 575 US 768, 775 (2015). See, eg, CA Sullivan, 'Accommodating Religion after Groff' (2024) 77 *SMU Law Review* 655, 664–665.

Justice Thomas dissented, adopting a European-style approach that stressed the neutrality of the policy notwithstanding the disparate impact on the applicant.[77] The majority rejected this reasoning. They clarified that Title VII does not merely ensure that religious practices are 'treated no worse than other practices'. Rather, it imposes an *affirmative duty* to reasonably accommodate religious observance – even if doing so requires exceptions to neutral rules.

Likewise, *Church of the Lukumi Babalu Aye v City of Hialeah* addressed the constitutionality of a Florida ordinance banning the ritual sacrifice of animals. Animal sacrifice is a core ritual of the Afro-Cuban Santería religion, with the animals slowly cooked and eaten afterward.[78] In response to public outcry over the establishment of a Santería church, the city of Hialeah convened an emergency session and enacted a series of ordinances prohibiting the ritual killing of animals. The Supreme Court *unanimously* ruled that the ordinances violated the Free Exercise Clause because they were neither *neutral* nor *generally applicable*. First, the laws failed the neutrality test, as they were clearly enacted with the specific objective to target and burden Santería religious practices. Second, the ordinances lacked general applicability because they carved out numerous secular exceptions. Hialeah permitted animal killings for food production, pest control, hunting, fishing, clothing manufacture, and pet euthanasia – but prohibited them when done for religious purposes. The Court concluded that the object of the ordinance was to 'suppress religion'.[79]

iii. Unfolding Shifts of Free Exercise

We began with a critique of *Smith* and *Boerne*, but the Court's change of membership has brought renewed pressure on *Smith*, though its status remains in flux. Justice Gorsuch observed, '[n]o fewer than ten Justices – including six sitting Justices – have questioned [*Smith's*] fidelity to the Constitution'. Since 2020, the Supreme Court has embarked on what might be called a 'revitalisation' of the Free Exercise Clause within *Smith*'s constraints – that is, without formally overruling *Smith*, the Court has stretched its doctrine to accommodate religious exemptions in several high-profile cases.[80]

An indicative example is *Fulton v City of Philadelphia* (2021). In this case, the Court unanimously held that Philadelphia violated the Free Exercise Clause by refusing to contract a Catholic foster care agency that declined to certify same-sex couples as foster parents. The legal issue centred on whether the city's anti-discrimination rule qualified as a generally applicable law under the *Smith*

[77] *EEOC v Abercrombie & Fitch Stores, Inc.* 575 US 768, 777–782 (2015) (Thomas J, concurring).
[78] *Church of the Lukumi Babalu Aye* v *City of Hialeah* 508 US 520 (1993).
[79] ibid 543.
[80] Lund (n 56) 22. Eg, *Roman Catholic Diocese of Brooklyn v Cuomo* 141 S Ct 63 (2020). (New York's lockdown order violated the Free Exercise Clause); *Tandon v Newsom* 141 S Ct 1294 (2021) (partially struck down Covid Restriction on Church Services in California).

framework. Here, the Court stretched the *Smith* test by focusing on how to define 'general applicability'.[81] It held that the city's policies lacked general applicability because they included a 'system of individual exemptions', giving city officials discretionary authority – even though no secular or religious exemptions had actually been granted. This discretion, the Court reasoned, triggered the application of strict scrutiny, which Philadelphia failed to meet.

While the Court did not overrule *Smith* – despite calls to do so from three justices – it significantly reshaped its scope. The *Fulton* decision reflects the rise of the so-called 'most favoured nation' ('MFN') interpretation of *Smith*.[82] Under this view, 'the denial of a religious exemption is presumptively unconstitutional' if the state treats some comparable secular activities more favourably.[83] In other words, if a law exempts secular activity that undermines the government's interests to a similar degree, then denying an exemption to religious activity renders the law not generally applicable and, therefore, requires the demanding justification of strict scrutiny.

Fulton was a unanimous judgment – denying the Catholic agency an exemption would have effectively ended its foster care services for thousands of children. But in other cases, the MFN approach has led to more contentious outcomes by forcing comparisons between religious and not immediately analogous secular activities. The jury is still out on the new development, where some see it as the beginning of the Court cleaning its 'multilayered mess',[84] while others perceive it as 'unworkable',[85] despite its radical reach that under-protects minorities.[86] However, given this book's jurisdictional focus and the still-evolving nature of this unfolding doctrine, a deeper engagement with the substantive content of MFN is beyond its scope – particularly as the Court may soon revisit *Smith*, potentially refining or overturning the current framework.

Another deeply divisive issue that marks a sharp divergence from the European practice is financial aid to religious schools. America's longstanding resistance to funding such schools has no real parallel in Europe, largely due to differing historical trajectories. The roots of this resistance lie in the nineteenth-century waves of Catholic immigration from famine-stricken Ireland and the subsequent backlash from a predominantly Protestant majority.[87] This culminated in the failed federal Blaine Amendment, which sought to bar public funding for 'sectarian' schools – a term widely understood to target Catholic institutions. For minority faiths, however, 'non-sectarian' public schools were simply Protestant schools in

[81] EU Scholars might recognise an analogy between *Smith*'s general applicability and *Keck's* universality requirement.
[82] NS Champan, 'The Case for the Current Free Exercise Regime' (2022) 108 *Iowa Law Review* 2115, 2148.
[83] *Tandon v Newsom* 141 S Ct 1294, 1297 (2021).
[84] Case Comment, Espinoza (n 36) 476–77.
[85] Z Rothschild, 'The Impossibility of Religious Equality' (2025) 125 *Columbia Law Review* 453, 529.
[86] See generally Lund (n 56).
[87] Feldman (n 10) 11–12; see also *Espinoza* (n 12) (Alito J, Concurring).

disguise – what Feldman aptly terms 'Protestant sectarianism' imposed through state power.[88] Far from fostering 'civic unity', this dynamic ignited deep and sometimes violent conflict over state funding.[89]

To further entrench Protestant dominance, the Blaine Amendment sought to ban public funds for 'sectarian' schools – a euphemism for Catholic ones – while continuing to support Protestant-oriented public education. Though the amendment ultimately failed at the federal level, it took root in over 35 state constitutions through the so-called 'mini-Blaine Amendments', many of which still shape educational funding debates today.[90] The Supreme Court's approach to these state constitutions and to funding religious schools generally has shifted significantly over the last two decades.

In *Locke v Davey* (2004), the Court upheld a Washington State ban on funding devotional theology degrees, invoking the 'play in the joints' between the Free Exercise and Establishment Clauses – a zone of state discretion between what is *not prohibited* by the Establishment Clause but *not required* by the Free Exercise Clause.[91] This approach partly mirrors the current European model, which allows states a 'wide' margin of discretion in church–state funding arrangements.[92]

However, in *Trinity Lutheran, Espinoza*, and *Carson*, the Court shifted course and partially narrowed the zone of state autonomy. According to these cases, states can choose whether or not to fund private schools, and if they do, they cannot exclude religious institutions simply because they are religious. In a nutshell, states retain the discretion to level down (ie, eliminate funding altogether for all schools), and if they choose to fund, they must extend all public benefits to religious institutions. The controversial trick here is choosing the comparators. The comparison is not between religions or denominations (eg, Protestants vs. Catholics), but between religious and secular institutions more broadly. *Trinity Lutheran* invalidated Missouri's denial of a church preschool's access to playground grants because of its availability to other non-faith preschools.[93] *Espinoza* went further, striking down Montana's exclusion of religious schools from a tax credit programme.[94] In *Carson*, the Court held that Maine could not exclude schools with a 'sectarian' curriculum from its tuition assistance scheme.[95]

Interestingly, this particular area is a clear example of an overlap between factions of group interest and moral principle. The historical refusal to fund religiously affiliated institutions originally stemmed from 'virulent' group-based

[88] Feldman (n 10) 12.
[89] ibid.
[90] Dierenfield (n 48) 33.
[91] *Locke v Davey* 540 US 712, 718–719 (2004).
[92] K Alexopoulou, 'The Margin of Appreciation in Freedom of Thought, Conscience, and Religion under Article 9 of Echr' (2022) 11 *Oxford Journal of Law and Religion* 220, 220.
[93] *Trinity Lutheran Church of Columbia, Inc. v Comer* 582 US 449 (2017).
[94] *Espinoza* (n 12).
[95] *Carson v Makin* 596 US 767 (2022).

bias,[96] particularly anti-Catholic sentiment, as seen in the Blaine Amendments. Over time, however, this issue has evolved into an ideological clash between 'modern separationists' and religious traditionalists across faiths.[97] Given this dual character, it may be preferable to leave the question to states – unless state policy is clearly used to target a particular sect,[98] as Wisconsin recently did, in which case federal intervention becomes justified.[99]

A final question on the new case law from a federalism perspective is what this MFN redefinition of 'general applicability' and the expansion of Free Exercise means for *City of Boerne*'s under-centralisation. Recall that the fate of *City of Boerne* is partly tied to the fate – and reinterpretation – of *Smith*. The new interpretation of *Smith* has prompted an argument that if a new version of the Religious Freedom Restoration Act were enacted today, it would not be 'doomed' by *Boerne*.[100] Two reasons are offered in support of this claim. First, the definition of the Free Exercise Clause has effectively widened through the Court's evolving jurisprudence – particularly in cases like *Fulton* – meaning Congress would no longer be 'redefining' the right, as the Court held it had done in *Boerne*.

Second, the *Boerne* decision emphasised that any federal intervention under Section 5 must be *congruent and proportional* to a demonstrated pattern of constitutional violations. In 1997, the Court found no such widespread pattern of religious discrimination at the state level. By contrast, the recent wave of litigation and government responses to religious practices – especially during the pandemic – has arguably shown an increased tendency to 'single out' religious 'people and practices'.[101] This claim regarding the constitutionality of a hypothetical future RFRA remains untested – both politically and judicially.

[96] *Espinoza* (n 12) [3] (Alito J, Concurring).

[97] Feldman notes this 'ugly bias' was predated by institutional separation philosophy: Feldman (n 11) 246.

[98] *Catholic Charities Bureau, Inc. v Wisconsin Labor & Industry Review Commission* 605 US ____ (2025) (No. 24-154), decided 5 June 2025; see commentary in A Howe, 'Supreme Court sides with Catholic social ministry over tax exemption' (*SCOTUSblog*, 5 June 2025) www.scotusblog.com/2025/06/supreme-court-sides-with-catholic-social-ministry-over-tax-exemption/ accessed 3 August 2025.

[99] Unlike the core discrimination cases involving assessment of equality between *different religions*, the comparability of religious and secular institutions is epistemically, metaphysically complex, and parties often disagree on what counts as a valid analogue, especially in disputes over public benefits or legal exemptions. In my view, this places the issue beyond the scope of Federalist No. 10. As discussed in chs 1 and 4, Madison's model assumes a shared moral or conceptual baseline among factions. When that common foundation is lacking, centralisation cannot generate impartiality, and the Madisonian logic does not hold. On the philosophical debate of whether religion and secularism are always analogues as subset of a belief, see C Laborde, 'Dworkin's Freedom of Religion without God' (2014) 94 *Boston Universty Law Review* 1255.

[100] Case comment, *Harvard Law Review* [Vol. 137:1050]; *MA v Rockland County Department of Health* 53 F.4th 29 (2d Cir 2022) 1057. Additionally, case law in the EU, ECHR, as well as the US, deals extensively with group-based claims (such as ministerial exception) for religious groups, but we do not have corresponding development of similar claims to secular/humanist groups. (See, eg, Case C-414/16 *Egenberger v Diakonie* ECLI:EU:C:2017:851, Opinion of AG Tanchev, para 106, and case cited; *Center for Inquiry v Marion Circuit Court Clerk* 758 F.3d 869 (7th Cir 2014).)

[101] ibid.

iv. Concluding Remarks on the US Religious Clauses

Until recent developments, the US had followed a mostly consistent pattern: hands-on centralisation for Establishment Clause issues (as seen in school prayer and religious symbol cases) and hands-off decentralisation when it came to religious minorities under the Free Exercise Clause (*Smith*/*Boerne*). This dynamic runs counter to the combined logic of Federalist No. 10 and the interpretation of the Establishment Clause advanced by scholars such as Amar, who argue that Congress should keep its 'hands off' questions of establishment – leaving them to state-level discretion – while actively protecting free exercise rights across the Union.[102] This pattern is qualified by some minority-friendly case law (eg, religious clothing in the workplace and ritual slaughter) and with the current court's unfolding shift since 2020.

Strikingly, free exercise was once a 'bipartisan', relatively non-divisive issue – as evidenced by the near-unanimous passage of RFRA.[103] Yet, recent empirical evidence suggests that it has become deeply polarised – socially, politically, and judicially.[104] One explanation is that the centralisation of culture wars on establishment and marriage equality – examples of *factions of principle* – has increasingly intersected with religious liberty. Religious adherents have invoked free exercise to shield their practices, while their rival separations have sought to overcentralise many aspects of the culture war.

An alternative route – partly visible in the EU – is a *two-track* or *compounded approach*: hands-off for establishment as well as other ideologically divisive culture war matters through mediated plurality, and hands-on for religious minorities via a centralised floor of protection. For example, whether to allow school prayer should be decided locally. But if no opt-out is available or if prayer spaces exclude minority faiths, federal intervention is warranted to protect equal rights. The strengths and limits of the EU's approach to this boundary question are discussed in the following section.

III. Religion, the EU, and Member States

Resembling, in part, Madison's original dual structure, the EU's legal framework for religion is similarly divided across different locations. The institutional dimension is governed by Article 17, TFEU, which provides that '[t]he Union respects and does not prejudice the status under national law of churches and religious associations or communities in the Member States'. This provision grants no corresponding EU competence to legislate in this area. By contrast, the rights-oriented dimension is governed by Articles 10 and 21, CFR, covering freedom of religion

[102] Amar (n 21) 246.
[103] Rothschild (n 68) 1084–1093.
[104] ibid.

and non-discrimination, respectively. The legislative competence underpinning these rights falls primarily under Article 19, TFEU (anti-discrimination), which requires unanimity for legislative action (as discussed earlier in chapter three). While the text of Article 10, CFR, mirrors that of Article 9, ECHR, for space constraints, ECtHR's case law will not be explored in detail here. Additionally, the CJEU has already referenced and incorporated many of the ECtHR decisions in the judgment, which will be discussed below.[105]

What is of relevance is that the interaction between the institutional aspect (Article 17, TFEU) and religious freedom (Articles 10 and 21, CFR) has generated cases of overlap that contrast sharply with the US experience. The next sections examine, first, cases involving Article 17 that intersect with discrimination issues and, second, cases focused more directly on minority rights, where Article 17 plays a lesser role, if any.

A. Article 17, TFEU, Case Law: *Egenberger* and *IR*

The inclusion of this article emerged from an 'explicit' debate 'on the role of God and Religion' during the drafting of the ill-fated EU Constitutional Treaty (later reproduced into the Lisbon Treaty).[106] Religious organisations (including the Catholic Church) 'vigorous[ly]' lobbied for explicit references to Europe's religious – and specifically Christian – heritage, while secular groups pushed back with equal intensity.[107] The eventual compromise was Article 17, TFEU, whose institutional implications can provide opponents of incorporating the Establishment Clause a vivid modern concretisation of their theory. Akin to Amar's argument of the Establishment Clause being 'agnostic' to state arrangement, AG Bobek in *Cresco* notes that Article 17, TFEU, suggests that 'indeed' the EU is '*agnostic* – towards how the Member States have organised their relationship to religion'.[108]

An overview of Member States' constitutions bears testimony to the divergence of church-state arrangements within the EU.[109] This ranges from the French *laïcité* embodied in Article 1 of the Constitution to states making explicit reference to God in their constitution preamble (Germany) or to 'the Holy Trinity' (Ireland).[110] Even further, other Member States' constitutions provide an 'institutionalized state church', such as the Greek and Danish Constitutions, and others.[111] The variety of

[105] The ECHR, which in many EU states is only binding under international, not constitutional law, does and does not have a direct third-party effect, and binds 'states as such': A Tischbirek, 'A Double Conflict of Laws: The Emergence of an EU "Staatskirchenrecht"?' (2019) 20 *German Law Journal* 1066.

[106] R McCrea, 'Religion in the Constitutional Order of the European Union' in *Constitutions and Religion* (Cheltenham, Edward Elgar Publishing, 2020) 308.

[107] *Egenberger*, Opinion of AG Tanchev (n 100) para 97.

[108] C-193/17 *Cresco Investigation* EU:C:2018:614, Opinion of AG Bobek, para 26 (emphasis added).

[109] For a survey of church-state relationship across EU members, see R Mccrea, *Religion and the public order of the European Union* (Oxford, Oxford University Press, 2010) 22–48.

[110] Irish Constitution, art 6(1).

[111] K Jaklic, *Constitutional Pluralism in the EU* (Oxford, Oxford University Press, 2014) 83–94.

European models is 'an inconvenient truth' for those who claim that separatism is the European norm for religion-state relations.[112]

It is true that, as McCrea notes, the EU is not 'ideologically neutral' on the religion/secularism question and expresses explicit policy preference towards what the Commission called 'democratic secularism'.[113] Yet, Article 17, TFEU, safeguards 'federalism's fourth option' against the US equivalent of 'invocation of EU law to overturn arrangements such as recognition of state churches in the member states'.[114] This is given some qualified 'protection' to read EU law in line with Article 4(2), which protects 'national constitutional identities and structures of the Member States'.[115] Arguably, church-state arrangements are linked to specific 'constitutional moments', such as the French Revolution or German Religious Wars.[116]

Notably, Article 17, TFEU, does not create a 'block exemption' or reserve religion as 'an exclusive' state domain in the dual federalism sense.[117] Some overlap and the EU intervention remain inevitable, as will be seen shortly. However, it has allowed Europe to avoid the kind of centralised ideological factional struggle that has plagued the US, particularly over financial aid to religion and public symbols. Even in France, 'there is certain tax reductions for the benefit of religious associations as well as a governmental system of prison and military chaplaincy'.[118]

The only case in the Court's docket to date examined whether a Spanish Catholic school's tax exemption violated EU state aid law.[119] The CJEU did not address Article 17, TFEU, or frame the issue as one of religious freedom but applied a purely economic analysis. It instructed the national court to determine whether the school's activities were 'strictly religious' as a public 'social' function or economic in nature.[120] If economic, the exemption would constitute state aid, as it could confer 'a considerable economic advantage over other European companies' creating market distortions the EU seeks to prevent.[121]

Another culture war battle the EU avoids concerns religious symbols in public spaces. Given the allocation of powers in EU law, the religious symbols over public space are 'unlikely to be placed in EU institutions and the CJEU is, therefore,

[112] Leigh and Ahdar (n 12) 1093; As the ECtHR observed in *Otto-Preminger-Institut v Austria* (1995) 19 EHRR 34, paras 57–58: 'it is not possible to discern throughout Europe a uniform conception of the significance of religion in society; even within a single country such conceptions may vary'.

[113] McCrea (n 106) 313, 319.

[114] ibid 309.

[115] Eg, *Egenberger*, Opinion of AG Tanchev (n 100) paras 94–95; *Achbita*, Opinion of AG Kokott (n 9) para 32: 'National identity does not therefore limit the scope of the Directive as such, but must be duly taken into account in the interpretation of the principle of equal treatment which it contains and of the grounds of justification for any differences of treatment.'

[116] Tischbirek (n 105) 1068.

[117] *Cresco Investigation*, Opinion of AG Bobek (n 108).

[118] Tischbirek (n 105) 1067.

[119] Case C-74/16 *Congregación de Escuelas Pías Provincia Betania v Ayuntamiento de Getafe* ECLI:EU:C:2017:496.

[120] ibid paras 50–52.

[121] Tischbirek (n 105) 1072.

unlikely to have to rule on this kind of challenge'.[122] Even when the Crucifix issue in public schools reached the ECtHR in the well-known case of *Latusi*, the Grand Chamber reversed the Second Chamber's decision and deferred to Member States' discretion.[123] Notably, eight of the ten third-party intervening states criticised the Second Chamber's ruling as an 'Americanisation' of Europe, accusing it of attempting to impose 'a single European laïc model'.[124] The Grand Chamber avoided the American trap and adopted a hands-off approach.

That said, as previously noted, overlap between the institutional/ideological aspects of establishment and the individual/group rights of religious freedom is often unavoidable. Two cases, in my view, offer a particularly reasonable balance between these dimensions. *Egenberger* is a key case on multifaceted, 'interlocked' conflicts.[125] A charitable organisation connected to the German Protestant Church advertised a fixed-term employment position tasked with producing a report on the UN Convention on Racial Discrimination for discrimination on grounds of belief. Ms Egenberger's application was denied for being non-denominational.[126]

The dispute centred on interpreting Article 4(2), FED, which allows religious organisations to require faith-based qualifications where religion is a 'genuine, legitimate and justified occupational requirement'.[127] German law afforded religious organisations wide autonomy, which can (subject to light-touch plausibility review) 'decide for themselves' whether their 'own ethos' requires a particular role be reserved for persons of their own faith.[128] The referring court asked whether EU law requires stricter scrutiny.

The CJEU reiterated that while Germany is free to structure its church-state relationship in line with Article 17, TFEU, to grant the defendant institutional autonomy, this freedom cannot be unlimited and must comply with the Charter.[129] The CJEU's hands-off approach to questions of religious establishment is balanced by a hands-on, strict scrutiny standard for any discrimination not necessary or not objectively dictated by religious autonomy. In *Egenberger*, the Court required the referring German court to rigorously assess whether Ms Egenberger's rejection was 'objectively dictated' by a 'genuine, legitimate and justified occupational requirement' in accordance with the principle of proportionality.[130] It added that

[122] R McCrea, 'Singing from the Same Hymn Sheet? What the Differences Between the Strasbourg and Luxembourg Courts Tell Us About Religious Freedom, Non-Discrimination, and the Secular State' (2016) 5 *Oxford Journal of Law and Religion* 183, 194.

[123] *Lautsi* (n 11).

[124] Leigh and Ahdar (n 12) 1093.

[125] Case C-414/16 *Egenberger v Diakonie* ECLI:EU:C:2018:257, paras 60–69.

[126] L Lourenço, 'Religion, Discrimination and the EU General Principles' Gospel: Egenberger' (2019) 56 *Common Market Law Review* 193.

[127] Council Directive (EC) 2000/78/EC establishing a general framework for equal treatment in employment and occupation [2000] OJ L303/16, art 4(2) ('FED').

[128] *Egenberger*, Opinion of AG Tanchev (n 100) para 64.

[129] *Egenberger* (n 125) paras 56–58.

[130] ibid paras 60–69, 83.

protection of the right to an effective (and impartial) remedy required that acts of discrimination in employment be capable of being challenged in the courts.[131]

The Court's careful balancing in this case was subsequently affirmed in *IR*. There, a Catholic hospital dismissed its director of internal medicine following his divorce and remarriage.[132] As a Catholic, the hospital argued, he had a special 'duty of loyalty' to safeguard 'the image of the Catholic Church' – a duty not required of his non-Catholic medical colleagues.[133] The CJEU reiterated its deference to respect church-state autonomy while ensuring it does not go into unnecessary discrimination.[134] The Court emphasised the internal inconsistency in the hospital's treatment of its employees: while the latter were allowed to divorce and remarry without a 'fear of negative consequences', Catholics could not.[135] Therefore, the Court 'primarily sanctioned this inconsistency'.[136] The Court 'strongly suggested' to the referring national court (which remains responsible for applying the ruling to facts) that requiring a duty of loyalty to a medical position was likely disproportionate.[137]

Read together, *Egenberger* and *IR* reflect the CJEU's broader effort to balance two competing dimensions: a *qualified hands-off* approach that preserves mediated diversity in institutional church–state arrangements (largely avoiding the establishment clause conflicts seen in US jurisprudence) and a *hands-on*, strict proportionality review to prevent unnecessary or excessive discrimination. Particularly, two key elements emerge: first, the Court applies a consistency requirement (as in *IR*); and second, it subjects employer justifications based on religious *ethos* or institutional *image* to strict scrutiny (as in *Egenberger* and *IR*). Strikingly, however, both elements are almost entirely absent in the Court's later case law involving non-Christian faiths or secular neutrality claims discussed below, where the Court goes even further by limiting state legislative efforts to protect religious minorities.

B. The CJEU's Misguided Federalism on Religious Minorities

Nothing better captures the Court's approach to religious minorities than the religious clothing (Muslim headscarves) case law. To properly grasp the issue, a few words must be said on the CJEU's distinction between direct and indirect discrimination and their federal implications. Direct discrimination occurs when 'one person is treated less favourably than another is, has been or would be treated in a

[131] ibid para 59. The CJEU reflects the spirit of *the nemo judex rule which underpins article 47 CFR*. It held that *the employer cannot be their own judge*.

[132] Case C-68/17 *IR v JQ* ECLI:EU:C:2018:696.

[133] ibid para 57; see McCrea (n 106) 315.

[134] *IR* (n 132) paras 40, 55.

[135] Tischbirek (n 105); McCrea (n 106) 315.

[136] McCrea (n 106).

[137] ibid 315.

comparable situation',[138] whereas indirect discrimination occurs when 'an apparently neutral provision, criterion or practice would put persons having a particular [characteristic] at a particular disadvantage compared with other persons'.

The way each discrimination is justified varies considerably. Direct discrimination is subject to, as AG Medina noted, 'a *closed-justification regime*, including, for instance, public security and the prevention of criminal offences, occupational requirements and positive action'. By contrast, 'indirect discrimination responds to a more *consequentialist approach*, because it allows for justification on the basis of the balancing of opposing rights and freedoms, namely the right to conduct a business and the freedom of religion, conscience and thought'. There will be cases then where the right to conduct a business will prevail over the freedom of religion, conscience, and thought.[139] In doing so, the defendant must establish this multifactorial test: there must be: (i) a legitimate aim; the means to achieve it must be; (ii) appropriate; and (iii) necessary.[140] If less discriminatory practices are available to achieve the same goal, the defence is 'defeated'.[141]

The choice between direct and indirect discrimination has institutional and federal implications, too. The Union – particularly the CJEU – plays a stronger role in policing direct discrimination, whereas indirect discrimination gives more room to national discretion. However, justifications for indirect discrimination also fall across a spectrum.[142] The Court's review can range from strict scrutiny to near-total deference. For victims of religious discrimination, the ideal scenario is to have their case classified as direct discrimination; failing that, they would at least hope for meaningful scrutiny of indirect discrimination claims. Yet, as we shall see, Muslim women are often denied both options.

Circling back to the headscarf cases, they all share a common pattern: Muslim women were either dismissed[143] or denied employment[144] due to conflict with dress codes that prohibit all 'visible signs of religious, philosophical, or political belief'. In a minority of cases, employers were less subtle; instead of a 'comprehensive ban', they explicitly prohibited only 'large-sized' religious signs. These large-sized

[138] N Dube, 'A Typology of Comparators and Comparisons in EU Equality Law' (2025) 62 *Common Market Law Review* 49, 51–52.

[139] *SCRL*, Opinion of AG Medina (n 8) para 55.

[140] Others argue that a further limb of strict proportionality should apply, which extends to contrasting the benefits of the measure which must be proportionate to the damage caused to the rights and liberties of individuals (proportionality *stricto sensu*). However, Van Den Brink notes that the language of Art 2(2) of FED excludes this limb: M van den Brink, 'The Protected Grounds of Religion and Belief: Lessons for EU Non-Discrimination Law' (2023) 24 *German Law Journal* 855, 876.

[141] D Chalmers, G Davies and G Monti, *European Union Law* (Cambridge, Cambridge University Press, 2019) 562.

[142] See, eg, the contrast offered by: *Wabe*, Shadow Opinion of AG Sharpston (n 7).

[143] Case C-157/15 *Samira Achbita and Centrum voor gelijkheid van kansen en voor racismebestrijding v G4S Secure Solutions NV* EU:C:2017:203; Case C-188/15 *Asma Bougnaoui and Association de défense des droits de l'homme (ADDH) v Micropole SA* ECLI:EU:C:2017:204; Cases C-804/18 *IX v Wabe eV* and C-341/19 *MH Müller Handels GmbH v MJ* ECLI: EU:C:2021:594 (Wabe).

[144] Case C-344/20 *LF v SCRL* ECLI: EU:C:2022:774 (the applicant was denied internship).

bans were found as directly discriminatory,[145] but for all other cases, the judgments have been consistently minority unfriendly. Take *Achbita* as an illustrative example. There, a long-serving receptionist at a Belgian branch of a global security company was dismissed after she began wearing a hijab, which covers the hair and chest but leaves the face visible. Her decision conflicted with the company's internal policy of 'neutrality', which barred displaying any visible signs of political, philosophical, or religious beliefs. When she declined to remove the hijab as instructed by her supervisor, the company terminated her employment.[146]

The Court excluded direct discrimination because the ban is comprehensive to all sorts of beliefs (religious, philosophical, and others), and since 'everyone may have … a belief', Muslim women are not explicitly targeted.[147] The Court then classified the ban as a prima facie indirect discrimination. The Court took a *hands-off* deferential approach to justification. It first classified this exclusive neutrality policy as a legitimate aim 'to project an image of neutrality towards customers', which the Court grounded in the freedom to conduct a business that is recognised in Article 16 of the Charter.[148] The only concession the Court requested from the employer was the so-called 'back office' compromise.[149] The CJEU asked the national court to inquire whether, instead of 'dismissing' Achbita, it would have been possible to demote her to a post not involving 'visual contact with customers'.[150] This case is distinguished from the facts of *Bougnaoui*, where a design engineer was dismissed following a complaint by a customer, who, after meeting, requested 'no veil next time'.[151] This 'subjective consideration' in the absence of any internal rule banning such symbols was insufficient to justify the discriminatory dismissal.[152]

The *Achbita* approach (and leaving aside *Bougnaoui's* particular factual context) was largely upheld in *Wabe* and subsequently *SCRL*. The facts in the joint cases of *WABE* and *Muller Handel* resemble those of *Achbita*. Once again, the employer sought to enforce a so-called 'neutrality policy' which either prohibited the wearing of all signs of a political, philosophical or religious nature (*WABE*), or the wearing of those which were conspicuous or large-sized (*Muller Handel*).[153] The *Achbita* criticism led to one improvement in *Wabe*, where the Court developed 'the genuine need' test.[154] It held that the employer has to prove that 'there was a genuine need' for the apparel ban, which included showing that without it, the business

[145] For a critique of the large size distinction, see van den Brink (n 140).
[146] *Achbita* (n 143).
[147] This line of reasoning is more explicit in *Wabe* (n 143) para 52; see also *SCRL* (n 146) para 34.
[148] *Achbita* (n 143) paras 30–32.
[149] R Xenidis, 'From Religious Neutrality to Religious Discrimination in the Public and the Private Sector: Commune D'ans and Scrl' (2025) 62 *Common Market Law Review* 513, 529.
[150] *Achbita* (n 143) para 43.
[151] *Bougnaoui* (n 143) para 14.
[152] ibid para 40.
[153] M Hunter-Henin, 'Religious Neutrality at Europe's Highest Courts: Shifting Strategies' (2022) 11 *Oxford Journal of Law and Religion* 23, 33.
[154] *Wabe* (n 143) para 64.

would suffer real harm.[155] Namely, if one's consumers have a traceable strong anti-religion (or practically anti-religious minority) zeal that could genuinely harm one's business, then the indirect discrimination is justifiable. While this makes the employer's case more difficult, the test has 'antithetical rationale' to non-discrimination law by legally 'pandering' to discriminatory prejudice.[156] The same approach was further confirmed in *SCRL*.

These judgments have been widely criticised[157] for invoking a 'false' concept of neutrality[158] as a 'loincloth for prejudice',[159] particularly against 'minority faiths',[160] for conflating state neutrality with that of a private corporation';[161] avoidance of 'multiple discrimination';[162] legally 'pandering' to social hatred,[163] discarding the legal text;[164] 'and for formulating a 'tautological' test'[165] which easily 'license discriminatory attitudes'.[166] I will not explore these critiques here. Instead, this section highlights four main points which are relevant to the book's institutional focus. First, the rulings reflect a misguided understanding of federalism. From this perspective, the CJEU's approach is arguably worse than the much-criticised *Smith* decision in the US, as it undermines the diversity logic underpinning the Federalist No. 10 argument and unduly restrains EU states from offering a more favourable treatment of minorities. It is also less minority-friendly than the US's *Abercrombie* approach.

Second, it stresses the relevance of the faction typology offered in chapter two to these cases. Recognising that the conflict over religious clothing involves a faction of group interest, since these symbols are an 'inseparable' marker of group identity – as argued by AG Sharpston in *Bougnaoui*[167] and AG Medina in *SCRL*[168] – rather than merely an ideological choice, as AG Kokott argued, is crucial. This proper classification of the faction involved and its concomitant source of potential bias significantly affects the choice of comparator and the consequent allocation of authority. Third, while I disagree with much of the Court's reasoning,

[155] E Howard, 'LF v SCRL and the CJEU's Failure to Engage with the Reality of Muslim Women in the Labour Market' (2023) *Industrial Law Journal* 52, 997.

[156] van den Brink (n 140) 878.

[157] '[A]lmost everyone seems to agree that the CJEU erred': ibid.

[158] *Wabe*, Shadow Opinion of AG Sharpston (n 7) para 265.

[159] E Bribosia and I Rorive, 'ECJ Headscarf Series (4): The Dark Side of Neutrality' (*Strasbourg Observers*, 14 September 2016) strasbourgobservers.com/2016/09/14/ecj-headscarf-series-4-the-dark-side-of-neutrality/ accessed 3 August 2025.

[160] McCrea (n 107) chs 6 and 7.

[161] Howard (n 155); M Bell, 'Leaving Religion at the Door? The European Court of Justice and Religious Symbols in the Workplace' (2017) 17 *Human Rights Law Review* 787, 795.

[162] Dube (n 138).

[163] E Howard, 'Headscarves and the Cjeu: Protecting Fundamental Rights and Pandering to Prejudice, the Cjeu Does Both' (2022) 29 *Maastricht Journal of European and Comparative Law* 245.

[164] Xenidis (n 149) 531.

[165] ibid; Howard (n 155).

[166] *Wabe*, Shadow Opinion of AG Sharpston (n 7).

[167] *SCRL*, Opinion of AG Medina (n 8).

[168] *Achbita*, Opinion of AG Kokott (n 9).

I seek to contextualise why the veto requirement, among other factors, may help explain – though not fully justify – the current jurisprudence. Fourth, I will explore the implications of this case law on harder cases involving hijab bans in public employment and ritual slaughter.

i. Why is it Federally Wrong?

The judgments reflect two key federal missteps. First, they represent a failure of central hands-on intervention to protect minorities – undermining the logic of federal impartiality, which calls for a stronger Union role in safeguarding minority rights. Second, they go further by restricting Member States from adopting more protective measures toward religious minorities. I will address each of them in turn. The first institutional failure is illustrated by the Court's excessive deference to Member States' assessments in these cases. Whenever a conflict occurs between religious minorities and so-called workplace neutrality, it effectively triggers a 'duty of non-intervention' and a full retreat from Union-level scrutiny. This runs contrary to the *nemo judex* rule underpinning federalism, as the Court is essentially leaving the state majority as *judges of their* own controversy with the minority. Chapters two to four thoroughly explain why the Union is more impartial in this regard and why minority rights require stronger central intervention. This has also been illustrated through a wide range of case law in both the EU and the US. For the Court to overlook its own key case law would constitute *federal amnesia*.

Additionally, this approach negatively affects 'the level of diversity' within the society, which, in turn, undermines the logic of federalism.[169] AG Medina illustrated how uniformity and diversity represent 'two opposing views as to how to address prejudice against differences arising from religion or religious beliefs in society'.[170] To take the point further, a survey of constitutional theory and history indicates that there are two overarching ways to manage religious factionalism.[171] One is the pursuit of *uniformity*, attempting to mould citizens into a shared identity by erasing or 'diluting religious and cultural differences', after which the chance of conflict is trimmed – an aspiration often contradicted by reality.[172]

The other is *balanced diversity* (or unity in diversity), affirming unity around certain core values while recognising group diversity as constitutionally valuable

[169] *SCRL*, Opinion of AG Medina (n 8) para 56.

[170] ibid.

[171] See generally DJ Elazar, *Exploring Federalism* (Tuscaloosa, University of Alabama Press, 1987); J Tully, *Strange Multiplicity: Constitutionalism in an Age of Diversity* (Cambridge, Cambridge University Press, 1995).

[172] R Pierik and W Van der Burg, 'What Is Neutrality?' (2014) 27 *Ratio Juris* 496, 498 (critiquing the unrealistic assumption of exclusive neutrality).

and necessary. This latter approach underpins the logic of *integrative federalism* (thoroughly unpacked in chapter two). Europe, as the historical cradle of nationalism, has witnessed the failures of the uniformity approach, which helped catalyse the Union model. As Monnet, among others, understood, 'the abuse' and cost of national homogeneity were too high.[173] Likewise, the genesis of modern federalism, as explained in Federalist No. 10, itself drew inspiration from America's religious diversity to resolve problems. The basics of the federal approach are to '[e]ncourage – not compression, reduction, homogeneity – but a broad extent of territory … and a wide diversity of [group] interest'.[174]

Consistently targeting a weaker faith group erodes federalism's very requisite diversity, weakening its function as a constitutional check. Alas, while the Court pays 'lip service to diversity', its decisions reflect a 'preoccupation with maintaining uniformity and homogeneity'.[175] If the functional role of natural group diversity – as one of federalism's key added values – were properly understood, rather than treated as a rhetorical device, the Court's invocation of 'impartiality' and 'neutrality' would have been accompanied by assessing the functional role of diversity in attaining impartiality through checking majoritarian bias via federalism.[176] It is, therefore, myopic to apply the nation-state's fully-fledged uniformity logic to a Union whose constitutional DNA and impartiality are premised on diversity. This is akin to installing *a lawnmower engine in a spaceship*.[177] Further, if history offers any guide, pursuing uniformity is unlikely to resolve the underlying social conflict or deliver justice to minorities.

ii. Why is it Federally Worse than the US's Smith *Approach?*

The severity of the critique levelled against *Achibita* and its progeny is analogous to that received by *Smith* in the US. Both represent *a decentralising abandonment of religious minorities*. Yet, the *Achbita* approach is still federally worse. Recall that *Smith* was deferential to the state legislatures, which are free to decide whether to grant more favourable treatment to religion or not. AG Medina and the referring Belgian Court in *SCRL* proposed a similar *Smith* approach as a 'way out' by allowing state legislative reform to create more favourable and 'autonomous protection

[173] JHH Weiler, *The Constitution of Europe: Do the New Clothes Have an Emperor?and Other Essays on European Integration* (Cambridge, Cambridge University Press, 1999) 340, analysed in Jaklic (n 111) 82–84; see also 'Monnet's conception of Europe was rooted in his desire to remove forever the causes of war – what he regarded as a civil war – that periodically served to tear Europe apart.' M Burgess, *Comparative Federalism: Theory and Practice* (Abingdon, Routledge, 2006) 228.

[174] FW Matson, 'Party and Faction: The Principles of Politics vs. The Politics of Principle' (1958) 18 *The Antioch Review* 341.

[175] Xenidis (n 149) 535.

[176] Eg, Case C-148/22 *OP v Commune D'Ans* ECLI:EU:C:2023:924, para 32.

[177] Xenidis (n 149) 533.

for religious belief'.[178] The CJEU unequivocally refused and 'authoritatively' asserted that such legislative effort 'would be contrary to EU law'.[179]

The institutional implication of *SCRL* is that EU states cannot 'a *priori*' – *ie, through legislation* – provide stronger protection of religious minorities. Rather, the margin of discretion afforded to states can only be exercised 'a *posteriori*' in judicial interpretation, not through 'legislative action'.[180] The Court suggests that national judges can exercise this discretion while carrying the balancing of proportionality by giving more weight to religious over economic freedoms. As Xenidis notes, this 'displaces a controversial political choice' from the prerogative of the national legislature to that of 'the [EU state] judiciary'.[181] This is puzzling. If the Union's legislature is constrained by the veto requirement in Article 19, TFEU, why does the Court restrain the hands of national legislators through its own judicial veto? The approach is also perplexing on textual grounds. As highlighted by AG Medina and AG Sharpton's shadow opinion, the Framework Equality Directive contains two textual provisions that explicitly allow Member States greater discretion to provide more favourable protection.[182]

Beyond *Smith*, the EU approach diverges sharply from the more minority-friendly strand of US jurisprudence. AG Kokott's opinion cites the US Supreme Court's judgment in *Abercrombie & Fitch*, where an 8–1 majority held that employers have a duty to accommodate religious workers and rejected the employer's argument of a neutral dress code policy.[183] But 'the AG wanted none of this for Europe',[184] warning that such an approach may constitute a 'significant organisational burden' for employers,[185] who would then be required to accommodate religious needs regardless of cost or inconvenience.[186]

iii. *Why does the Typology of Faction/Bias Matter Here?*

Religion, as many noted, is a 'multi-faceted' phenomenon.[187] At least four of these facets can be mentioned here. It can fuel ideological conflicts, such as culture war debates on abortion or assisted dying, or church/state institutional choice. It can serve as a marker of group identity, 'akin to race'.[188] In its negative aspect, it can

[178] ibid 556.
[179] ibid 556.
[180] ibid.
[181] ibid 531.
[182] *Bougnaoui*, Opinion of AG Sharpston (n 7) paras 274–276.
[183] *Achbita*, Opinion of AG Kokott (n 9) para 110.
[184] J Witte Jr, 'Meet the New Boss of Religious Freedom: The New Cases of the Court of Justice of the European Union' in J Witte Jr (ed), *The Blessings of Liberty: Human Rights and Religious Freedom in the Western Legal Tradition* (Law and Christianity, Cambridge, Cambridge University Press, 2021) 267.
[185] *Achbita*, Opinion of AG Kokott (n 9) para 110.
[186] Witte Jr (n 184) 267.
[187] Khaitan and Norton (n 2).
[188] McCrea (n 3).

signal the rights of individuals to be independent of the group (freedom not to believe, or to join or exit a faith group). And finally, this is not to mention the non-legal, ascetic dimension of religion as a truth claim, along with its theological corollaries. For the purposes of this chapter, the first two are particularly relevant – namely, the contrast between group interest and ideology – as they were at the heart of the disagreement between AG Kokott in *Achbita* and AG Sharpston in *Bougnaoui*. Therefore, the distinction is crucial for both jurisprudential and federal implications.

AG Kokott saw religious clothing as a 'subjective decision or conviction'[189] comparable to an ideological/philosophical choice.[190] AG Sharpston countered that to describe it as a 'choice' of 'ideologically determined clothing' is 'fundamentally to misunderstand … the two non-Christian religions in question (Islam, Judaism)'.[191] She added that 'it would be entirely wrong to suppose that, whereas one's sex and skin colour accompany one everywhere, somehow one's religion does not'.[192] McCrea captures the contrast in simple terms. If religion is viewed as a 'group identity marker', then refusing to allow someone to wear a headscarf or kippah when interacting with the public is 'akin to' preventing 'a worker with brown skin from serving customers'.[193] Conversely, if it is viewed as a 'form of ideology', then this ban 'is no less justifiable' than banning a worker from wearing a Labour Party/Les Republicans/British National Party/Jobbik badge while at work.[194]

From a federal lens, if we subscribe to AG Kokott's view that religious apparel is comparable to ideological choice, then – following federal theory and the Hume/Madison analysis outlined in chapters two to four – the decision should lean more towards decentralisation, and the CJEU was right to retreat from this area. By contrast, if the ban reflects a majoritarian bias and affects the group interests of minorities, then it is an archetypal case of factional group interest – the very type of dynamic that inspired Madison to argue for federalism and centralisation. Chapter four has already illustrated why the religious apparel ban (in a private workplace setting) predominantly involves a factional group interest.[195] In fact, the CJEU already treats this as a form of indirect discrimination against members of religious groups, though it has found such discrimination to be justifiable in certain cases. The Court also balances discrimination against an unmistakably interest-based issue: the right to

[189] *Achbita*, Opinion of AG Kokott (n 9) para 45.
[190] ibid para 52.
[191] *Bougnaoui*, Opinion of AG Sharpston (n 7) para 129.
[192] ibid.
[193] ibid para 129.
[194] McCrea (n 106) 318.
[195] This faction, as defined earlier, combines principles (militant secularism, certain view on integration, nativity, or anti-immigration) with interests emanating from different economic and moral interests of different racial groups.

conduct business.[196] The same classification would follow from the proposed four-factorial test proposed in chapter four.

First, it meets the linchpin of Madison's argument that diversification increases with the number of groups involved. The larger the federation, the more religious groups it typically contains, making it harder for one group to dominate and strip others of rights without affecting other groups involved and the economic interests tied to them. Religious apparel – such as Sikh turbans, Muslim headscarves, or Jewish yarmulkes – is most often worn by individuals from minority ethnic backgrounds.[197] As critics of *Smith* have noted, accepting the doctrine of restricting religious freedom under the so-called 'neutral' rules can have far-reaching implications beyond headscarves, affecting a broad spectrum of insulated minorities.[198] Further, the bans have economic implications. They generate tangible economic harm and 'exclusion from the labour market',[199] particularly for Muslim women, as confirmed by the European Network Against Racism's CV-testing data.[200] These are precisely the kinds of 'group-based disadvantages' that non-discrimination law aims to address.[201] As resources remain scarce, protecting minority rights can be seen as coming at a cost to majority interests – intensifying group-based and tribal instinct biases.

Second, as per the demographic make-up of dissenters to the right to wear religious clothing, it is implausible to find an economically active woman wearing a headscarf or a turbaned Sikh arguing for the ban. The dissenters are the *hijab/kippa/dastar-free population*. Third, consider the financial incentives. If, in the spirit of American 'contract compliance', the EU offered a tax holiday or conditioned funding to those employers hiring people with diverse backgrounds, including those with religious symbols, judging from the sex equality experience, this would, as it did with equal pay, alter the calculus of employers. Possibly, even many of the defendants in the headscarf cases would have approached their hiring policy quite differently.[202]

Fourth, unlike the epistemic divergence in culture war issues like abortion, parties here generally do not contest the departure point: non-discrimination. The dispute lies in how it is interpreted as direct or justifiable indirect discrimination. Madison's theory is useful here: it calls for structural safeguards to check bias in applying shared principles. The conflict between economic freedom and religious freedom here is a matter of relative weight, not mutual exclusivity. Contrast this with the context of abortion, where the rights asserted are often seen as irreconcilable. The German Constitutional Court has described the conflict as

[196] Eg, *Wabe* (n 143) paras 63–67 (referring to art 16 of the Charter); *Achbita* (n 143).
[197] See *Wabe, Shadow* Opinion of AG Sharpston (n 7).
[198] See, eg, US 522, 593–600 (2021) (Alito J, concurring).
[199] *SCRL*, Opinion of AG Medina (n 8) paras 60, 68–75.
[200] D Sena, *Forgotten Women: The Impact of Islamophobia on Muslim Women* (European Network Against Racism 2016) 19; Howard (n 155) 1010.
[201] van den Brink (n 140) 859.
[202] On how religion is a multifaceted phenomenon, see Khaitan and Norton (n 2).

'impossible'[203] to resolve fully, while Justice Blackmun warned that recognising foetal personhood would 'collapse' the constitutional right to abortion.[204] Taken together, these four factors make the private workplace ban on religious clothing a textbook example of a faction grounded in group identity and economic interest – precisely the kind of pressure that, under the logic of federal impartiality, warrants oversight by central institutions.

There is another utility of the classification of which facet of religion is involved. It is one of the ways to help address the 'inappropriate comparator objection', which determines whether discrimination is direct and, consequently, affects the level of discretion states enjoy.[205] By treating religious dress as a manifestation of ideological belief rather than as a marker of group identity, the Court included in the definition of belief secular or philosophical beliefs – thereby excluding the possibility of direct discrimination. Because the rule applies to all theistic and atheistic beliefs, it is deemed not to explicitly target a particular group and, thus, facially neutral. But if the category of belief is expanded to include everything from political to secular convictions, then – as the Court itself has observed – 'everyone has a belief',[206] making the concept practically ineffective.[207]

Succinctly put, narrowing the circle of the disadvantaged group enhances the protection of equality law.[208] When the comparison is between those whose religion mandates specific clothing (a narrowly defined underprivileged group) and those without such obligations (a broader privileged group), direct discrimination becomes clearer. However, the Court's current approach reverses this logic: it broadens the group which theoretically may be targeted by the rule and narrows the group used as a comparator. By expanding the concept of belief to include atheistic or philosophical ideologies, the category becomes so wide that the comparator group effectively includes almost everyone – while the privileged group shrinks to a near non-existent set of people with no moral conviction or ideological beliefs. This renders direct discrimination almost impossible to establish because technically *it compares almost everyone to no-one*.[209] As some have shown, this expansion of the legal meaning of belief is comparatively exceptional.[210]

[203] A 'compromise which guarantees the protection of the life of the one to be born and permits the pregnant woman the freedom of abortion is not possible'. Quoted in M Nijsten, *Abortion and Constitutional Law: A Comparative European-American Study* (European University Institute, 1990) 100–102.

[204] If foetal 'personhood is established, the foetus's right to life would then be guaranteed', and any right to abortion would 'collapse'.

[205] van den Brink (n 140) 868.

[206] *Wabe* (n 143) para 52; see also, *SCRL* (n 146) para 34.

[207] Reformulating the Belgian Court's referral in *SCRL*, it would be like saying a rule targeting 'Black individuals is not discriminatory because everyone has a [race].'

[208] While simultaneously widening the circle of the comparator to a reasonable extent.

[209] Even according to settled case law and literature, 'not every personal belief is protected for the purpose of non-discrimination law': van den Brink (n 140) 870. The ECtHR noted that only 'views that attain a certain level of cogency, seriousness, cohesion and importance' are covered by the Convention: see *Eweida and Others v United Kingdom* App nos 48420/10, 59842/10 and 36516/10 (ECtHR, 15 January 2013) para 81.

[210] For a comparative survey, see van den Brink (n 140) 870.

For that reason, AG Sharpston's shadow opinion, as well as AG Medina and the Belgian Court in *SCRL*, invited the Court to change its '*modus comparationis*'[211] by narrowing the disadvantaged group circle – but the Court ultimately 'demurred'.[212] It reasoned that splitting the notion of 'religion or belief' into 'several grounds' instead of being 'two facets of the same ground' would have 'the result of *creating* more *sub-groups* of workers' in assessing EU equality law.[213] What is missed in this reasoning is that these sub-groups are *not legally created*; they '*already exist*' *out there*, and the proper constitutional framework is the one that harnesses the sub-group diversity rather than seeing it as a problem.[214] Recall that what inspired the reincarnation of modern federalism was Madison's realisation of how the diversity of *predominantly Christian sub-groups* checks one another. Seeing sub-groups as a constitutional blessing, he went on to write his influential Federalist No. 10. The CJEU, with prominent federal scholars on its bench, would be expected to be aware of this and to jurisprudentially embrace sub-group diversity rather than suppressing it.

This is not to say that religion and ideology are never comparable. As McCrea observed, what is lacking in current CJEU jurisprudence are 'criteria to work out when it is right to treat religion as belief and when it is right to treat it as identity'.[215] Some facets of religion have a clear ideological edge, such as culture war issues – where religious and secular worldviews are comparable in both acting as a 'sword' to impose a policy choice rather than a shield to secure 'conscientious exemption'.[216] This is evident in debates over abortion, assisted dying, or the non-coercive elements of church–state arrangements where theistic and atheistic ideologies clash. In hybrid cases that straddle both identity and ideology, a *rigorous* proportionality scrutiny – as seen in *Egenberger* – can help mediate the tension, at least to some degree.

iv. Why is Legislative Intervention Needed, and does its Absence Partly Explain the Court's Approach?

While I disagree with the Court's judgments, certain institutional dynamics help explain its approach. The first of which is the Council veto. As discussed in chapter three, Article 19, TFEU, requires unanimity for anti-discrimination legislation, effectively restraining Union-level intervention. This can allow militantly secular

[211] Xenidis (n 149) 117.

[212] Chalmers, Davies and Monti (n 141) 562.

[213] *SCRL* (n 146) para 55 (emphasis added).

[214] '[O]ne key difference between Madison's and Calhoun's diagnosis is that for Madison the interest that generate factions (creditors, debtors … different opinion concern ion religion) already exist in society prior to any action of government': J Read, *Majority Rule versus Consensus* (Lawrence, Kansas University Press, 2009) 50.

[215] McCrea (n 6).

[216] T Khaitan, 'Directive Principles and the Expressive Accommodation of Ideological Dissenters' (2018) 16 *International Journal of Constitutional Law* 389, 392.

states like France and Belgium to act as judges in their own cause, vetoing any legislative effort to protect religious minorities – even where the European Parliament's intersectional discrimination report has advocated for 'more capacious interpretation' and stronger protection under the EU law.[217]

Xenidis adds an economic angle. Pursuing diversity means that employers 'internalise' the cost of societal prejudice – such as client discomfort with a diverse workforce.[218] By contrast, enforcing uniformity shifts this burden to workers. Correcting this skewed incentive market structure typically requires comprehensive legislative intervention, which can, to use Madison's words, 'gradually induce' resisting groups to uphold rights.[219] As chapter three showed, the US system's use of contract compliance and the 'carrot-and-stick' federal approach helped erode segregation by reshaping economic incentives.[220] As Sunstein notes, it was the 'dramatic shift' away from 'compensatory' adjudication to 'administration' that helped positively alter race relations in America.[221] Additionally, judicial remedies, as Fredman remarks, 'are limited by their focus on the individual' rather than 'engaging' in 'forward-looking reform'.[222] In the absence of federal legislation and faced with a strong current of anti-minorities social hatred, the CJEU has 'limited latitude' deciding on 'controversial' matters against the resistant Member States.[223]

Finally, federalism is not a mechanistic or self-correcting system. It does not operate like a 'Newtonian' machine that automatically produces rights.[224] Unlike the US civil rights or equal pay movements, minority religious groups in the EU have not mobilised in ways that trigger intra-EU clashes of interest capable of activating the federal checks. Strengthening the rights of veiled Muslim women may upset powerful Member States like France and Belgium,[225]

[217] European Parliament, Report on Intersectional Discrimination in the European Union: the Socio-economic Situation of Women of African, Middle-Eastern, Latin-American and Asian Descent (Committee on Women's Rights and Gender Equality, Rapporteur: Alice Kuhnke, A9-0190/2022, 22 June 2022) www.europarl.europa.eu/doceo/document/A-9-2022-0190_EN.html accessed 8 September 2025.

[218] Xenidis (n 149) 535.

[219] Madison, Federalist No. 51.

[220] *Marshall II* did this corrective incentive through removing the damage cap as Alter noted, but the intervention here was relatively possible judicially compared to the possible Trible discrimination at play in these cases intertwining racial, religious, and gender elements.

[221] CR Sunstein, *The Partial Constitution* (Cambridge, MA, Harvard University Press, 1993) 322.

[222] S Fredman, *Discrimination Law* (Oxford, Oxford University Press, 2011) 289.

[223] L Kaiser, A Knecht and LD Spieker, 'European Society Strikes Back: The Member States Embrace Article 2 TEU in Commission v Hungary' (*VerfBlog*, 26 November 2024) verfassungsblog.de/european-society-strikes-back/ accessed 3 August 2025; citing D Tsarapatsanis, 'A Political Approach to Lautsi and Others v Italy' in D Gonzalez-Salzberg and L Hodson (eds), *Research Methods for International Human Rights Law Beyond the Traditional Paradigm* (Abingdon, Routledge, 2019) 219.

[224] Reformulating B Ackerman, *We the People* (Cambridge, MA, Harvard University Press, 2014) vol 3, 61.

[225] R McCrea, 'Faith at Work: The European Court's Headscarf Ruling' (*UCL European Institute*, 28 March 2017) www.ucl.ac.uk/european-institute/news/2017/mar/faith-work-cjeus-headscarf-ruling accessed 3 August 2025.

but offers little political or economic gain to others – thus, weakening the role of the clash of interest condition logic of federal correction. This may explain the Court's reluctance in many cases. Yet, the puzzle remains why, in *SCRL*, the Court declined even to defer the matter to national legislatures, when it easily could have done so.[226]

v. Harder Overlapping Cases: Hijab Ban in Public Employment

While the classification of headscarf bans in private employment clearly involves a faction of economic interest, the situation is more complex in the public sector. In the latter, if a state's policy on religious symbols reflects an ideological choice – such as a militant secularism or the so-called 'exclusive neutrality' – there may be a possible claim to discretion under the previous analysis of the establishment's hand-off approach. But this creates tension with the Union's duty to protect religious minorities.[227]

The *Commune d'Ans* case was the closest to this. The Belgian municipality introduced a so-called 'exclusive neutrality' ban across all symbols immediately after the employee (a legal officer) requested to wear a headscarf. Although the timing raises suspicion about the ban's motives – and it was not applied uniformly across similar bodies – the Court's approach was an even looser test than *Achbita*'s backdoor compromise and *Wabe*'s genuine need test. The Court invoked the state's 'margin of discretion' concept '*ex ante* … well ahead of the balancing stage of the objective justification test'.[228] This way, it managed to 'pre-empt' any assessment on the legitimacy of 'exclusive' neutrality policies.[229] Looking ahead, more difficult cases may soon emerge. France's intervention in *Commune d'Ans* – invoking constitutional identity under Article 4(2), TEU – signals that future challenges may concern more legally sophisticated bans on the hijab in public employment, framed under the French Constitutional doctrine of *laïcité*.[230]

Federal theory can offer two alternative routes. First, and ideally, one can think of secular/establishment as a spectrum and not a binary, and a federal union can attempt to moderate the extremes of each ideology.[231] Just as the Union would

[226] Possible explanations could either be federal misunderstanding or in a realist sense some judges might have a mix of 'overtly secular' bias combined with some negative stenotypes of 'non-Christian faith'. We cannot tell with confidence though.

[227] The ideological and non-pecuniary nature of the dispute can be also gleaned from the idea that strong economic incentives (eg, tax relief) are unlikely to shift entrenched attitudes in strong laïcité administrations.

[228] Xenidis (n 149) 530.

[229] ibid commenting on paras 32–34 from *Commune d'Ans* (n 176) where it held 'Each Member States including infra-state bodies' must be afforded 'margin of discretion' in designing 'workplace neutrality': paras 32–33.

[230] The referring Belgium Court noted that secularism is not a constitutional principle see Xenidis' translation of the point in Xenidis (n 149) fn 67.

[231] M Tushnet, 'Federalism and Liberalism' (1996) 4 *Cardozo Journal of International & Comparative Law* 343.

intervene against a conservative state requiring a declaration of faith for public employment, it can also challenge a secular state that excludes individuals who manifest religious belief.[232] From this perspective, such a ban on headscarves can be likened to a modern analogue of religious tests once struck down by the US Supreme Court.[233] It effectively conditions access to public office on showing allegiance to a particular worldview here: a secular one. This raises concerns about structural exclusion and group-based disadvantage of manifestly religious Muslim women and Sikh and Jewish males. Protecting minorities from religious persecution, after all, was the *eureka* moment in Federalist constitutional thought.

Alternatively, federal theory may yield to practical realities. In France, *laïcité* is a deeply rooted ideology, shaped by its historical animus toward religion (not necessarily against religious minorities despite its implications for them).[234] Therefore, the EU faces a hard case: how to balance the need to protect religious minorities (a central function of Union federalism) with the Member State's discretion over religion in the public sphere. In other words, how to reconcile the two factions: the ideological commitment to *laïcité* and the group-based claims of religious minorities. This answer is already there in *Egenberger* and should have been 'transposed' to *Commune d'Ans* and similar future cases.[235]

Instead of the automatic acceptance of public employers' invocation of neutrality, one can extend AG Sharpton's call to apply the *Egenberger/IR* approach to religious clothing cases. In both strands of cases (*Egenberger* and *Achbita*), employers relied on their institutional 'ethos', 'self-perception',[236] and the need to safeguard their 'image' (whether religious or neutral image), to justify limiting employees' rights.[237] Yet, as AG Sharpston suggested, these two types of ethos/philosophies have not been treated equally: the justification premised on the secular version of the employer's *image* is given hands-off/deferential review, while the religious image invoked in *IR* is given hands-on 'strict scrutiny'.[238]

The CJEU had previously required national courts to conduct 'detailed and rigorous scrutiny' of the justifications advanced by religious employers – whether

[232] After all, a comparison between two theological and modern states is not novel see, eg, 'All significant concepts of the modern theory of the state are secularized theological concepts.' C Schmitt, *Political Theology: Four Chapters on the Concept of Sovereignty* (George Schwab tr, Chicago, University of Chicago Press, 2005) 36; 'These two conceptions of [Parliament] omnipotence have their parallel in two conceptions of an omnipotent God': HLA Hart, *The Concept of Law*, 2nd edn (Oxford, Clarendon Press, 1994) 149.

[233] 367 US 488 (1961)).

[234] See generally M Verkuyten, K Yogeeswaran and L Adelman, 'The Social Psychology of Intergroup Tolerance and Intolerance' (2023) 34 *European Review of Social Psychology* 1, 12–13.

[235] *Wabe*, Shadow Opinion of AG Sharpston (n 7) para 260.

[236] On 'self-perception' of the Church, see *IR* (n 132) paras 34–35; on 'ethos', see paras 44–47.

[237] For invocation of religious image, see *IR* (n 132) para 57; and for secular image, see *Achbita* (n 143) para 38.

[238] *Wabe*, Shadow Opinion of AG Sharpston (n 7) para 285; eg *IR* (n 132) paras 58–60 (adherence to that notion of marriage does not appear to be necessary for the promotion of *IR*'s ethos). This disparity seems to betray Art 17, TFEU's professed neutrality towards religious and secular views. Consistently, the Court is favouring the secular view.

in not hiring a candidate (*Egenberger*) or in dismissing an employee (*IR*).[239] In both cases, the Court 'unequivocally' rejected a priori 'broad latitude' to employers applying their 'philosophy to recruitment'.[240] It insisted that the 'inevitable' connections between the employee's role and the employer's religious stipulations be carefully examined.[241] As AG Sharpston rightly asked: 'why a religious employer should be scrutinised carefully, but an employer who claims that he wishes to 'project a neutral image' … should (essentially) be taken at his word'.[242]

While the recommendation to follow *Egenberger/IR* was made in the context of *Wabe*'s private employment, it can be extended to public employment. While state neutrality may be invoked under Article 4(2), TEU, as an element of national constitutional identity, this – as AG Connells argued – must be balanced against the Union's strong commitment to Article 2, TEU, values, which play a central role in the CJEU's evolving jurisprudence.[243] Article 2 explicitly affirms the values of *non-discrimination* and *respect for minority rights*. These values require not *ex ante* judicial retreat but serious scrutiny of competing claims. Howard adds further provisions to the mix.[244] She refers to Article 3, TEU, whereby the Union 'shall combat social exclusion and discrimination', in addition to Articles 22 and 31(1) of the Charter, which, respectively, provide that 'the Union shall respect cultural, religious, and linguistic diversity' and that 'every worker has the right to working conditions which respect his or her … dignity'.[245] One can also add the requirement of impartiality (in a federal sense), which flows from the principle of *nemo judex* underpinning Article 47, CFR.

To harmoniously read these articles and Article 2, TEU, alongside Article 4(2), TEU, entails,[246] at minimum, that any state invocation of neutrality to exclude religious individuals from public employment must be '*put under the microscope*'.[247] The burden lies on the state to demonstrate such exclusion as strictly necessary. As AG Collins noted, neutrality might be required if the state can demonstrate 'strong community tensions or serious social problems', 'proselytising activities or a specific risk of conflicts between employees linked to such beliefs'.[248] Those factual justifications cannot be presumed – they should be demonstrated. After all, Article 4(2) was invoked in *IR* and *Egenberger* and did not prove conclusive.[249] There seems to be no reason to apply deferential review for one type of employer

[239] *Wabe*, Shadow Opinion of AG Sharpston (n 7) para 259.
[240] ibid.
[241] ibid.
[242] ibid 260.
[243] Case C-148/22 *OP v Commune D'Ans* ECLI:EU:C:2023:378, Opinion of AG Collins, paras 45–47.
[244] Howard (n 155) 1010–1011.
[245] ibid 1010–1011.
[246] 'A joined reading of Articles 2 and 4(2) TEU, however, reveals that the former cannot override the latter … Respect for constitutional identity is therefore a requirement under, not an exception to, the EU's founding values': TL Boekestein, 'Making Do With What We Have: On the Interpretation and Enforcement of the EU's Founding Values' (2022) 23 *German Law Journal* 431, 446.
[247] Reformulating *Wabe*, Shadow Opinion of AG Sharpston (n 7) para 259.
[248] *Commune D'Ans*, Opinion of AG Collins (n 243) para 73.
[249] *Egenberger*, Opinion of AG Tanchev (n 100) para 95.

and strict scrutiny for the other. As Chalmers and others note, the 'constitutional commitment to secularism is tempered by the EU equality policy'.[250]

vi. Harder Case II: Ritual Slaughter

Ritual slaughtering provides another example of a 'delicate case' that contrasts with the US.[251] The *Centraal* case involved a Flemish regulation (adopted in one of Belgium's cantons) requiring Jewish and Muslim butchers to perform a form of reversible stunning before slaughter. Flemish legislators cited some empirical evidence that reversible stunning would reduce the animal's suffering while still allowing the animal to regain consciousness, thus preserving the bleeding process required by religious law.[252] A 'consortium' of Jewish and Muslim groups challenged the law, arguing that it violated their religious freedom under EU law.[253]

Once again, the factional nature of the dispute overlaps multiple dimensions, and European history complicates the issue compared to the US. While bans on ritual slaughter in Europe have well-documented 'antisemitic' roots (as seen in Nazi Germany and early Swedish legislative bans), today the issue is increasingly tied to modern animal welfare activism.[254] These motives often converge, as can be seen in the parliamentary debates of similar bans across Europe, where sometimes far-right parties and liberal animal activists align for this cause.[255] Yet, at its core, this remains a moral division that directly implicates group rights for insular religious minorities against a legitimate aim of reducing animal suffering. While both Jewish and Muslim groups maintain that their faith traditions are also concerned with animal welfare, they challenge the empirical findings advanced by Belgium that reversible stunning is less painful.[256]

AG Hogan's opinion offers a balanced approach. He opined that the language of the relevant EU regulation contained an express derogation from the stunning requirement for religious minorities. Adding that while Member States enjoyed a 'certain level of subsidiarity' to provide more extensive protection of animal welfare,[257] they cannot 'effectively nullify' the EU legislature's policy choice to accommodate religious freedom.[258] The Court disagreed and upheld the Flemish law as a proportionate limitation of religious freedom to pursue the 'value' of

[250] Chalmers, Davies and Monti (n 141) 567.
[251] Case C-336/19 *Centraal Israëlitisch Consistorie* EU:C:2020:695, Opinion of AG Hogan, para 14.
[252] ibid.
[253] Witte Jr (n 184) 267.
[254] EZ Granet, '"As I Have Commanded Thee": Flemish Decrees and Cjeu Jurisprudence Put Religious Slaughter under the Knife' (2021) 46 *European Law Review* 380, 388.
[255] ibid citing M Valenta, 'Pluralist Democracy or Scientistic Monocracy: Debating Ritual Slaughter' (2012) 5 *Erasmus Law Review* 27, 34.
[256] ibid.
[257] Council Regulation (EC) 1099/2009 on the protection of animals at the time of killing OJ L303/1, recital 18.
[258] *Centraal*, Opinion of AG Hogan (n 251) para 70.

animal welfare.[259] Notably, the Court's reliance on state discretion permitted national legislatures to *restrict* religious freedom, while, contrastingly, in *SCRL*, it effectively denied Member States' legislatures the opportunity to *expand* religious freedoms.

The judgment diverges sharply from the previously discussed US Supreme Court ruling in *Hialeah*. Whereas the Flemish ban is narrower – it does not (in theory) prohibit ritual slaughter outright but adds a procedural modification – it nevertheless entangles the Court in theological questions. The CJEU ventured into religious doctrine by asserting that reversible stunning is limited to 'one aspect of the specific ritual act of slaughter, and that act of slaughter is not, by contrast, prohibited as such'.[260] To second-guess the theological view on whether this new component alters the ritual practice conflicts with a basic institutional tenet of church/state separation, often known as the 'ecclesiastical abstention doctrine'.[261] According to this doctrine, the separation cuts both ways, and state courts should avoid 'rul[ing] on the orthodoxy or heterodoxy of a given religious teaching'.[262] It is true that many mainstream Muslim institutions accept reversible stunning as permissible,[263] but the issue remains more problematic for large segments of Orthodox Judaism, for whom this modification renders the meat impermissible, and the Court should not entangle itself with theological debates for which it is not trained.[264]

An ideal approach, consistent with the logic of 'federalism all the way down'[265] and the organisational autonomy doctrine,[266] would treat religious communities as a non-territorial federal layer with a normative 'sphere' of autonomy over their religious affairs, subject only to strictly justified interventions.[267] This subsidiarity-based approach can offer some leeway in reconciling the competing issues at stake. As AG Hogan explained, Article 26 of the Regulation grants Member States some discretion but does not permit the 'quasi-elimination' of the religious practice.[268] He provided examples of permissible regulation, such as 'requiring qualified veterinarians to be present during ritual slaughter and ensuring slaughterers are appropriately trained'.

[259] Case C-336/19 *Centraal Israëlitisch Consistorie* EU:C:2020:1031.

[260] ibid para 61.

[261] Granet (n 254) fn 79.

[262] Case C-426/16 *Liga van Moskeeën* EU:C:2018:926, Opinion of AG Wahl, para 57.

[263] Al-Azhar Al-Sharif, 'A Communiqué from Al-Azhar Al-Sharif: Impermissibility of Animals Killed with Electrical Stunning' (*Al-Azhar Observatory for Combating Extremism*, 14 August 2015) www.azhar.eg/observer-en/details/ArtMID/1153/ArticleID/2005/A-Communiqu233-from-Al-Azhar-Al-Sharif-Impermissibility-of-animals-killed-with-electrical-stunning accessed 3 August 2025.

[264] See generally Granet (n 254).

[265] HK Gerken, 'Federalism All the Way Down' (2010) 124 *Harvard Law Review* 4.

[266] See EP report on religious tolerance citing *Schüth v Germany* App no 1620/03 (ECtHR, 23 September 2010); *Obst v Germany* App no 425/03 (ECtHR, 23 September 2010); *Fernández Martínez v Spain* App no 56030/07 (ECtHR, 15 May 2012).

[267] On the notion of religious societies as having spheres of sovereignty, see Leigh and Ahdar (n 12) citing GS Smith (ed), *God and Politics: Four Views on the Reformation of Civil Government* (Phillipsburg, Presbyterian & Reformed, 1989) 75–77.

[268] *Centraal*, Opinion of AG Hogan (n 251) para 67.

Such measures would avoid theological entanglement while still applying some soft pressure on these groups to further advance animal welfare.[269]

Additionally, as argued in chapter five, this subsidiarity/agreeing-to-disagree approach can enable gradual yet more enduring moral change.[270] A bottom-up approach to morally divisive matters substitutes 'control by others' with 'self-control'; the 'compulsory' imposition of a norm is replaced by what Stein terms the 'voluntary process' of change.[271] Many Muslim institutions, including Al-Azhar (Islam's oldest religious scholarly body), have found reversible stunning permissible, and some communities have voluntarily adopted it. Imposing top-down moral value, however, may delay or harden resistance to such internal evolutions. AG Sharpston made a similar point in her shadow opinion. However, this admittedly raises a tricky issue of which value society cannot allow divergence on. But the Court did not have to go there and could have minimised its theological/moral entanglement had it taken heed of the US approach.[272]

Alternatively, the Court could have employed its previously used consistency argument, which was also the crux of *Hialeah*, where the US Supreme Court scrutinised the selectivity of prohibiting ritual slaughter while permitting hunting, fishing, and other forms of animal killing. Conversely, the CJEU briefly dismissed the consistency argument, arguing that requiring prior stunning would render hunting and fishing 'meaningless'.[273] One can think of 'catch-and-release fishing' as a less restive measure.[274] By the same token, for many religious Jews and some Muslims, reversible stunning similarly renders their ritual *meaningless*, and it seems arbitrary to target 'the small communities of Jews and Muslims while leaving hunters and other sportsmen to kill animals without stunning'.[275]

Had the Court taken the inconsistency/arbitrary discrimination argument seriously, it would have been in line with its earlier case law, such as *IR*.[276] It would have also provided an 'exit route' that shifts the political cost of the ban to the national level, forcing local majorities to confront their own cultural contradictions with regard to un-stunned animal killing (eg, defending elite hunting traditions while restricting minority ritual slaughter). The advocates of the ban would have to overcome the cultural elite's resistance to secure its enactment. Such political dynamics could serve to indirectly insulate minority practices without requiring the Court to pronounce directly on the theological or proportionality merits of ritual slaughter itself.

[269] ibid para 69.
[270] ibid.
[271] E Stein, 'Uniformity and Diversity in a Divided Power System: The United States' Experience' (1986) 61 *Washington Law Review* 1081, 1084–1086.
[272] The Court could follow Hialeah which are grounded in the consistency requirement in *IR* without embracing the recent American MFN theory.
[273] Case C-336/19 *Centraal* (n 257) para 91 (emphasis added).
[274] Granet (n 254) 393.
[275] White Jr (n 186) 279.
[276] *Commune d'Ans* (n 176) para 38; *Wabe* (n 143) para 77; see the comment on consistency in *IR* case highlighted in Tischbirek (n 105) 1077.

Instead, by avoiding this path, the Court may have inadvertently opened the door for 'firmer' bans, several of which are pending across Europe and may eventually return to the CJEU's docket.[277] The Court may, thus, find itself even more entangled in this divisive debate. Either way, these are complex cases, given the shadow of the racist roots of these bans in Europe, the increasing challenges of multiculturalism, and the growing expansion of moral complicity claims underlying animal rights activism.[278] Striking a balance in this terrain is difficult and can lead to the critique that 'constitutional provisions are like the *animals* in George Orwell's barnyard: some are considerably more equal than others'.[279] Effectively, the Court has placed the welfare of animals – pun intended – above freedom to conduct business, which itself had previously been ranked above religious freedom.[280] The approach adopted by the US Supreme Court (and other European constitutional courts) may offer a more nuanced framework for navigating these tensions.[281]

IV. Concluding Remarks

This chapter addressed a multi-faceted form of faction, one that overlaps issues of religious freedom and church–state arrangements. The argument is that, when possible, the Union should have a hands-off (mediated plurality) approach to the institutional question of Establishment with hands-on oversight in questions of religious freedom/discrimination. Getting this balance wrong betrays Federalist No. 10, read in conjunction with Hume's faction typology. It was argued that impartiality, in the federal Madisonian sense, is unattainable for the question of Establishment. The question cuts across different groups, and its underpinning causes are not different at the federal compared to the state level. However, the impossibility of impartiality in this area must be understood narrowly. It should not license oppression of minorities or dissenting individuals. For example, in a secular state, religious groups should not be excluded from meaningful participation in the labour market. Likewise, in a state informed by religious values, there should be no coercive imposition on those who do not share those beliefs. In sum,

[277] White Jr (n 186) 279.

[278] The underlying moral harm or complicity motives of the ban are understandable. But moral complicity must have jurisdictional limits, otherwise it risks absurd results. Imagine a Muslim or otherwise alcohol-averse majority adopts a version of the US Volstead Act (banning alcohol consumption but with no religious exemption) effectively prohibiting Catholic Mass from using wine on public health grounds, arguing that banning alcohol in the sacrament is just introducing one modification to the rite which is proportionate because non-alcoholic substitutes exist.

[279] S Levinson and EA Young, 'Who's Afraid of the Twelfth Amendment' (2001) 29 *Florida State University Law Review* 925, 944.

[280] *Wabe*, Opinion of AG Sharpston (n 7) para 141.

[281] Granet (n 254) 293 (discussing that the German Constitution Court offers a more balanced analysis considering both economic and religion freedom involved) citing Schächten 1 BvR 1783/99, para 44.

it was argued that getting this federal balance wrong can lead to unnecessary politicisation and under-protects minorities.

The theoretical claim was tested comparatively through thorough case law. Until recent unfolding developments, the US had followed a mostly consistent pattern: *hands-on* centralisation for Establishment Clause issues (as seen in school prayer and religious symbol cases), and *hands-off decentralisation* when it came to religious minorities under the Free Exercise Clause (*Smith/Boerne*). The pattern is qualified by an occasionally more protective approach to minorities (in *Abercrombie*) and to their rituals (in *Hialeah*) as well as the unfolding shifts in free exercise jurisprudence.

This is contrasted with the EU's largely hands-off approach with regard to the establishment/church-state arrangement. The EU provides the US opponents of the incorporation of the Establishment Clause with a contemporary real-life instantiation of how their view would look if the Establishment Clause were read as a 'pro-state' decentralised provision, which is 'agnostic to the substance of the state choice'.[282] Conversely, the EU's approach to minorities is rather mixed. It almost commanded unanimous critique for its approach to religious clothing, which effectively weakens the economic opportunities available to manifestly religious Muslim women and potentially for Jews and Sikhs in the labour market. Perhaps, an ideal world would be to *Europeanise* the current US approach to the Establishment and to *Americanise* the EU case law on religious clothing.

When the two questions overlap, the CJEU *Egenberger* and *IR* offer a balanced *two-track* or *compounded approach*:[283] a qualified hands-off for establishment as well as other ideologically divisive matters through mediated plurality, and hands-on for religious minorities via a centralised floor of protection. Yet they are not followed with regard to religious apparel or ritual ban cases. This two-tracked approach – particularly the hands-off stance towards establishment – remains absent even in the US Supreme Court's recent revisionist cases.[284] Such an approach would require applying different tests at the state and federal levels – something that is yet to emerge in Establishment Clause jurisprudence.

The chapter further warns that conflating the hands-on/hands-off balance is not only federally erroneous but also socially divisive. The US offers a cautionary tale on the dangers of overcentralising the Establishment. Prior to centralisation, there were no cases on symbols, for example. Once centralised, litigation

[282] Amar (n 21) 37.

[283] This layered application of EU provisions is not unfamiliar to EU Law. Eg, Bogdandy suggested that the intensity of review should vary between acts of the Union and those of Member States: A von Bogdandy, 'The European Union as a Human Rights Organization?' (2000) 37 *Common Market Law Review* 1307; see also LD Spieker, *EU Values Before the Court of Justice: Foundations, Potential, Risks* (Oxford, Oxford University Press, 2023) ch 3.

[284] Whereas the CJEU widened the circle of belief, the new jurisprudence seemed to widen the corresponding circle of comparators to include things which are not immediately comparable to religion or things that are not necessarily areligious. Grocery or medication depending on objective or intention can be both religious and secular. The comparator in the MFN and the EU might require separate work to assess.

and its concomitant controversy 'proliferated'.[285] This has contributed to widespread social division and growing 'partisanship' over religion.[286] By contrast, the EU steered away from the entangled web of US jurisprudence. This is not 'idle scaremongering'.[287] In *Latusi*, when the Second Chamber followed a comparably American style of school crucifix, political rage ensued across Europe. The Italian Prime Minister denounced the decision publicly, and 10 states intervened. The Grand Chamber's hands-off approach diffused the tension.[288]

In the context of free exercise, Madison's prophecy has largely materialised. When the centre is restrained from acting – whether by *Boerne*'s judicial veto, the EU's Article 19, TFEU, veto, or the CJEU's deferential jurisprudence – religious minorities have often struggled and borne the cost. By contrast, when the centre adopts a more active role, it tends to reduce social exclusion. Case law demonstrates that federal intervention can offer more impartial protection to shield minorities from discrimination. Examples include headscarf bans (*Abercrombie*), denial of ritual sacraments (as in RFRA's reversal of *Smith*), discriminatory recruitment based on religious affiliation (*Egenberger*), or discrimination against non-believers (the *Religious Testing* cases). Abandoning this crucial federal function will not make the underlying controversies disappear, nor will it lead to assimilation of minorities or the smoothing out of social conflict. If the experience with racial and sex equality discussed in chapter three is any indication, an active federal role is far more likely to reduce social conflict rather than prolong it.

While there are cases which defy easy categorisation or where combining both centralisation with a hands-off approach might prove functionally difficult, the table below offers a typology of cases covered.

Table 6.1 Multi-faceted faction cases

Faction cause (Centre of Gravity)	**Group Interest / Majoritarian Bias**	**Cross-group ideological conflict**	**Compounded**
Federal Impartiality	Attainable	Unattainable	Mixed
Allocation of boundaries	Central Floor (hands-on)	Mediated Plurality (hand-off)	Combination of the two (when possible) + proportionality
Examples	*Smith* *Abercrombie* *Achbita*	Nativity Scene cases Article 17, TFEU *Latusi*	*Egenberger* Aid to religious schools in the US

285 Chapman and McConnell (n 14) 80.
286 Section II above.
287 Leigh and Ahdar (n 12) 1097.
288 See generally Feldman (n 10); Rothchild (n 68) 105.

7

Conclusion

The book has come full circle. It started with the centuries-old metaphor depicting constitutional systems as a human body. Building on this, it shared Madison's view of the human psyche as mixed – the better side appeals to fairness, the worse to 'despotism'.[1] Federalism holds the potential – under some conditions – to appeal to the *better side of our psyche*. However, just as our psyche is variable, so too are federal boundaries. Federal impartiality varies depending on its object. Madisonian impartiality theory, read alongside Hume's typology of faction and the common law distinction between causes of bias, suggests different approaches depending on the faction type.

In matters involving conflict of group interests, where tribal bias colours our judgment and lawmaking decisions, centralisation at the floor level can infuse an element of impartiality that checks (though does not eliminate) the effect of this *groupishness* bias and, thus, helps achieve more equitable outcomes. Madison even argued that this will 'gradually induce' groups to accept the egalitarian outcomes.[2] This argument was verified in examining the cases on American Civil Rights and EU equal pay, along with other cursory examples cited judicially and academically. We saw how centralisation did change a group's calculus of interest, which produced a clear, traceable pattern in softening (though not eliminating) prejudice and building gradual social change.

Conversely, in matters entangled with deeply divisive ideological or philosophical beliefs which cut cross group identities, federal impartiality is not attainable. Instead, federalism's mediated plurality approach can slowly evoke a *tolerant side* of our psyche. It enables citizenry not to abandon their convictions but to agree to disagree, thus sparing polarisation and fostering coexistence amid diversity when uniformity is unnecessary. This can revise ideologies that otherwise do not seem 'revisable'.[3] The divergent trajectories of abortion regulation in the EU and the US – and the accompanying levels of polarisation – illustrate this well. Instead of chasing an impartiality mirage, keeping factions of principle at the mezzanine level

[1] JF Kobylka and BK Carter, 'Madison, "the Federalist" & the Constitutional Order: Human Nature & Institutional Structure' (1987) 20 *Polity* 190, 195.

[2] Madison, *Federalist No. 51* 255.

[3] M Tushnet, 'Federalism and Liberalism' (1996) 4 *Cardozo Journal of International & Comparative Law* 329, 342.

of 'mediated plurality' leverages federalism's 'cross-pollination' of legal and social norms and helps gradually build an agreement to disagree.[4]

Beyond abortion, the book demonstrates how this argument holds for other examples of morally divisive matters falling under the category of 'faction of moral principle'. This included the stark polarisation on the Temperance movement, which receded following decentralisation, without people necessarily denouncing their conviction; matters of overcentralisation of the question of (dis)establishment of religion or even non-western moral conflict that was flared by centralisation, then cooled down by subsequent decentralisation.

But the two types of factions are *not mutually exclusive* and can be combined. Public decision-making can be coloured by both group and ideological bias, as we saw in the cases surrounding religion's multi-faceted nature in the final chapter. This included a wide array of cases, including bans on religious apparel in public employment or ritual slaughter, which reflects both the ideological disposition of separatism and some anti-minority impulses. Here, federalism's flexibility can, in many cases, allow a more nuanced approach to the overlapping issues. We have seen, for example, how judgments like *Egenberger* and *IR*, as well as AG Sharpton's Shadow opinion, provide some illustrative guidance on careful balancing in this regard. Of course, some hard cases defy neat categorisation, and functional considerations may override the decentralisation logic altogether, as discussed in the last two chapters.

In this way, the book makes both a theoretical and empirical contribution to the Madisonian tradition. Theoretically, it clarified the attributes of federal impartiality, the subsidiary mechanism of uncertainty, and the behavioural dynamics behind coalition stability when based on shared (though thin) conceptions of fairness. It also discussed the problem of institutional inertia that lies dormant in the Madisonian syllogism. Crucially, it offered a missing link in the literature by tracing Hume's influence on Madison – especially through the former's typology of faction – and connecting it with the British common law's distinction between types of bias.

Chapter four drew these threads together – Federalist No. 10, Hume's tripartite factional typology, and the common law doctrine on bias. The Madisonian theory becomes clearer when the distinction between factions of interest and factions of principle is restored and analogised to the established doctrines of pecuniary and non-pecuniary bias. This distinction has far-reaching implications for much of the substance of rights and intensity of conflict in many of the contemporary controversies, where the 'boundary question' is often the first site of constitutional contestation. Comparatively and empirically, the argument was illustrated by contrasting jurisprudence on racial minorities and equal pay with more ideologically contentious issues like abortion, no-fault divorce, the Temperance movement, and bans on religious symbols in public spaces, among many others.

[4] RM Cover, 'The Uses of Jurisdictional Redundancy: Interest, Ideology, and Innovation' (1980) *William & Mary Law Review* 639, 678.

That said, while factions of principle and interest are major sources of socio-political conflict, they are not exhaustive. Other significant factors can distort public decision-making, but these lie beyond the scope of this book. As such, some related questions remain open. For instance, this book has focused on the vertical dimension of federalism – rather than the horizontal balance between institutions, such as the judiciary and the legislature. Another important question concerns whether the *duration* of polarisation affects the effectiveness of the federal remedy. To reformulate Machiavelli's observation: after a time, the illness of a republic becomes 'easy to diagnose but difficult to cure'.[5] The book has also focused on the concept of impartiality, which underpins the EU's rule of law value expressed in Article 2, TEU. While space did not allow for a detailed exploration of how this insight connects to current debates surrounding the interpretation and enforcement of Article 2, this remains an area for future inquiry. After all, there is only so much that can be achieved in a single book.

In conclusion, one message must be emphasised: integrative federalism holds great potential but also significant risks if misunderstood. Revisiting Madison's insights shows that 'structure' not only shapes 'substance'[6] but also affects social acrimony. When the federal boundary is grounded in its first principles, it can help advance the rights of underprivileged groups – as demonstrated in chapter three – and even influence broader social attitudes. When misunderstood through the veto of Art 19 TFEU – a modern analogue of Calhoun's concurring majority theory – it negatively affected the EU's racial minority rights. Likewise, *Smith/Boerne*'s decentralising veto in the US and their European equivalent of *Achbita/SCRL* undermined religious minority rights. By contrast, for factions of moral principles, when federalism's potential has been properly harnessed – particularly through mediated plurality as its distinctive 'fourth option' – the EU has avoided the kind of polarisation that has plagued the United States in relation to abortion, the establishment of religion, and other morally divisive issues explored in the final two chapters.

Stated differently, Madison was right to liken integrative federalism to a medical 'remedy'.[7] But like any medicine, it must be 'applied wisely and appropriately' – or it can backfire.[8] Federalism, when properly understood, can enhance the protection of rights and help alleviate social tensions; when misapplied, it can undermine rights and inflame division. Understanding the object of federal impartiality is, therefore, crucial. In some matters, a stronger federal dose – through centralisation – can promote impartiality; in others, a lighter dose – a federal hands-off approach – may better foster cross-depolarisation and de-escalation of social tension. Conflate the two, and you risk achieving neither de-escalation nor impartiality.

[5] N Machiavelli, *The Prince* (Salt Lake City, Gutenberg 2002) ch 3, 303.

[6] M Tushnet, 'Constitutional and Statutory Analyses in the Law of Federal Jurisdiction' (1977) 25 *UCLA Law Review* 1301, 1336.

[7] Madison, Federalist No. 10, 48.

[8] M Nettesheim, 'European "Frankenstein Constitutionalism": TEU Article 2 as a Federal Homogeneity Clause' (2024) 118 *AJIL Unbound* 167, 171.

SELECTIVE BIBLIOGRAPHY

Ackerman, B, *We the People, Volume 1: Foundations* (Cambridge, MA, Harvard University Press, 1993)

——, *We the People, Volume 3: The Civil Rights Revolution* (Cambridge, MA, Harvard University Press, 2014)

Adair, D, '"That Politics May Be Reduced to a Science": David Hume, James Madison, and the Tenth Federalist' (1957) 20 *Huntington Library Quarterly* 343

Alexopoulou, K, 'The Margin of Appreciation in Freedom of Thought, Conscience, and Religion under Article 9 of ECHR' (2022) 11 *Oxford Journal of Law and Religion* 220

Albert, R, 'America's Amoral Constitution' (2021) 70 *American University Law Review* 773

Alexy, R, *A Theory of Constitutional Rights* (Oxford, Oxford University Press, 2010)

Alter, K, *The European Court's Political Power: Selected Essays* (Oxford, Oxford University Press, 2010)

Amar, AR, *The Bill of Rights: Creation and Reconstruction* (New Haven, Yale University Press, 1998)

Aoki, M, *Toward a Comparative Institutional Analysis* (Cambridge, MA, MIT Press, 2001)

Azoulai, L, 'The European Court of Justice and the Duty to Respect Sensitive National Interests' in Mark Dawson, Bruno de Witte and Elise Muir (eds), *Judicial Activism at the European Court of Justice* (Cheltenham, Edward Elgar, 2013)

Barnard, C, 'Restricting Restrictions: Lessons for the EU from the US?' (2009) 68 *Cambridge Law Journal* 575

Baumeister, RF and Vohs, KD (eds), *Encyclopedia of Social Psychology* (Thousand Oaks, SAGE Publications, 2007)

Bednar, J, *The Robust Federation: Principles of Design* (Cambridge, Cambridge University Press, 2008)

——, 'Polarization, Diversity, and Democratic Robustness' (2021) 118 *Proceedings of the National Academy of Sciences* e2113843118

Belavusau, U and Henrard, K, 'A Bird's Eye View on EU Anti-Discrimination Law: The Impact of the 2000 Equality Directives' (2019) 20 *German Law Journal* 614

Bell, M, *Racism and Equality in the European Union* (Oxford, Oxford University Press, 2008)

Bittker, BI, Idleman, SC and Ravitch, FS, *Religion and the State in American Law* (Cambridge, Cambridge University Press, 2015)

Blanchard, DA and Prewitt, TJ, *Religious Violence and Abortion: The Gideon Project* (Gainesville, University Press of Florida, 1993)

——, *The Anti-Abortion Movement and the Rise of the Religious Right: From Polite to Fiery Protest* (New York, Twayne Publishers, 1994)

Brennan, G and Buchanan, JM, *The Reason of Rules: Constitutional Political Economy* (Cambridge, Cambridge University Press, 1985)

Burgess, M, *In Search of the Federal Spirit* (Oxford, Oxford University Press, 2012)

Bulman-Pozen, J, 'Federalism as a Safeguard of the Separation of Powers' (2012) 112 *Columbia Law Review* 459

—— and Gerken, HK, 'Uncooperative Federalism' (2009) 118 *Yale Law Journal* 1256

Calabresi, G, *Ideals, Beliefs, Attitudes, and the Law: Private Law Perspectives on a Public Law Problem* (New York, Syracuse University Press, 1985)

Carolan, E, 'Constitutional Change Outside the Courts: Citizen Deliberation and Constitutional Narrative(s) in Ireland's Abortion Referendum' (2020) 48 *Federal Law Review* 497

Chalmers, D, Davies, G and Monti, G, *European Union Law* (Cambridge, Cambridge University Press, 2019)

Chapman, NS and McConnell, MW, *Agreeing to Disagree: How the Establishment Clause Protects Religious Diversity and Freedom of Conscience* (Oxford, Oxford University Press, 2023)

Chemerinsky, E, *Constitutional Law* (Burlington, Aspen Publishers, 2023)
——, 'Dunwody Distinguished Lecture in Law: The Values of Federalism' (1995) 47 *Florida Law Review* 499
Choudhry, S, *Constitutional Design for Divided Societies: Integration or Accommodation?* (Oxford, Oxford University Press, 2008)
Claus, L, 'Montesquieu's Mistakes and the True Meaning of Separation' (2005) 25 *Oxford Journal of Legal Studies* 419
Cover RM, 'The Uses of Jurisdictional Redundancy: Interest, Ideology, and Innovation' (1981) 22 *William & Mary Law Review* 639
Craig, P and de Búrca, G, *EU Law: Text, Cases, and Materials* (Oxford, Oxford University Press, 2015)
Czerwinski, A, 'Sex, Politics, and Religion: The Clash between Poland and the European Union over Abortion' (2004) 32 *Denver Journal of International Law and Policy* 653
Dahl, RA, *A Preface to Democratic Theory* (Chicago, University of Chicago Press, 2006)
Dawson, M and Muir, E, 'Individual, Institutional and Collective Vigilance in Protecting Fundamental Rights in the EU: Lessons from the Roma' (2011) 48 *Common Market Law Review* 751
de Búrca, G and Scott, J (eds), *Law and New Governance in the EU and the US* (Oxford, Hart Publishing, 2006)
——, 'The Evolution of EU Human Rights Law' in P Craig and G de Búrca (eds), *The Evolution of EU Law*, 2nd edn (Oxford, Oxford University Press, 2011)
——, 'EU Race Discrimination Law: A Hybrid Model?' in G de Búrca and J Scott (eds), *Law and New Governance in the EU and the US* (Oxford, Hart Publishing, 2006)
De Meyer, F, 'Abortion Law Reform in Europe: The 2018 Belgian and Irish Acts on Termination of Pregnancy' (2020) 20 *Medical Law International* 3
De Witte, F, 'Sex, Drugs & EU Law: The Recognition of Moral and Ethical Diversity in EU Law' (2013) 50 *Common Market Law Review* 1545
Di Salvo, D, *Engines of Change: Party Factions in American Politics, 1868–2010* (Oxford, Oxford University Press, 2012)
Doan, AE, *Opposition and Intimidation: The Abortion Wars and Strategies of Political Harassment* (Ann Arbor, University of Michigan Press, 2007)
Dube, N, 'A Typology of Comparators and Comparisons in EU Equality Law' (2025) 62 *Common Market Law Review* 49
Dworkin, R, *Taking Rights Seriously* (Richmond, Duckworth, 1977)
Earner-Byrne, L and Urquhart, D, *The Irish Abortion Journey, 1920–2018* (Basingstoke, Palgrave Macmillan, 2019)
Eklund, H, 'The Margin of Discretion and the Boundary Question in EU Fundamental Rights Law' (2022) 59 *Common Market Law Review* 1407
Elazar, DJ, *Exploring Federalism* (Tuscaloosa, University of Alabama Press, 1987)
——, *American Federalism: A View from the States*, 3rd edn (New York, Harper & Row, 1984)
Elkins, Z, Ginsburg, T and Melton, J, *The Endurance of National Constitutions* (Cambridge, Cambridge University Press, 2009)
Eliason, A, 'With No Deliberate Speed: The Segregation of Roma Children in Europe' (2017) 27 *Duke Journal of Comparative & International Law* 191
Elliott, M and Varuhas, J, *Administrative Law: Text and Materials* (Oxford, Oxford University Press, 2017)
Ellis, E and Watson, P, *EU Anti-Discrimination Law* (Oxford, Oxford University Press, 2012)
Epstein, L and Posner, EA, 'The Roberts Court and the Transformation of Constitutional Protections for Religion: A Statistical Portrait' (2022) *2021 Supreme Court Review* 315
Erbsen, A, 'Horizontal Federalism' (2008) 93 *Minnesota Law Review* 493
Estin, AL, 'Family Law Federalism: Divorce and the Constitution' (2007) 16 *William & Mary Bill of Rights Journal* 381
Fabbrini, F, 'The European Court of Human Rights, the EU Charter of Fundamental Rights, and the Right to Abortion: Roe v. Wade on the Other Side of the Atlantic' (2011) 18 *Columbia Journal of European Law* 1

——, 'The Last Holdout: Ireland, the Right to Abortion and the European Federal Human Rights System' (2019) 42 *Dublin University Law Journal* 21

——, 'The "European" Future of American Abortion Law: Dobbs, Federalism and Constitutional Equality' (2023) 62 *Columbia Journal of Transnational Law* 113

Fallon, RH Jr, *The Dynamic Constitution: An Introduction to American Constitutional Law and Practice*, 2nd edn (Cambridge, Cambridge University Press, 2013)

Farkas, L, 'Limited Enforcement Possibilities under European Anti-Discrimination Legislation – A Case Study of Procedural Novelties: Actio Popularis Action in Hungary' (2010) 3 *Erasmus Law Review* 181

Feldman, N, *Divided by God: America's Church-State Problem – and What We Should Do About It* (New York, Farrar, Straus and Giroux, 2006)

——, *After Jihad: America and the Struggle for Islamic Democracy* (New York, Farrar, Straus and Giroux, 2007)

Filippov, M, Ordeshook, PC and Shvetsova, O, *Designing Federalism: A Theory of Self-Sustainable Federal Institutions* (Cambridge, Cambridge University Press, 2004)

Forst, R, *Toleration in Conflict: Past and Present* (Cambridge, Cambridge University Press, 2013)

Fox, D, 'Neuro-Voir Dire and the Architecture of Bias' (2014) 65 *Hastings Law Journal* 999

Fredman, S, *Discrimination Law* (Oxford, Oxford University Press, 2011)

Friedman, LM, *A History of American Law*, 4th edn (Oxford, Oxford University Press, 2019)

Galligan, DJ, *Due Process and Fair Procedures: A Study of Administrative Procedures* (Oxford, Clarendon Press, 1996)

Galle, B and Leahy, J, 'Laboratories of Democracy: Policy Innovation in Decentralized Governments' (2009) 58 *Emory Law Journal* 1333

Geiger, R, Kotzur, M and Khan, D-E, *European Union Treaties* (Munich, Beck, 2015)

Gerken, HK, 'Federalism All the Way Down' (2010) 124 *Harvard Law Review* 4

—— and Holtzblatt, A, 'The Political Safeguards of Horizontal Federalism' (2014) 113 *Michigan Law Review* 57

Gibson, A, 'Madison's Republican Remedy: The Tenth Federalist and the Creation of an Impartial Republic' in JN Rakove and CA Sheehan (eds), *The Cambridge Companion to The Federalist* (Cambridge, Cambridge University Press, 2020)

Givens, TE and Case, RE, *Legislating Equality: The Politics of Antidiscrimination Policy in Europe* (Oxford, Oxford University Press, 2014)

Glendon, MA, *Abortion and Divorce in Western Law* (Cambridge, MA, Harvard University Press 1987)

Goodwin, M, 'Romani Marginalisation after the Race Equality Directive' in U Belavusau and K Henrard (eds), *EU Anti-Discrimination Law Beyond Gender* (Oxford, Hart Publishing, 2019)

Granat, M and Granat, K, *The Constitution of Poland: A Contextual Analysis* (Oxford, Hart Publishing, 2019)

Granet, EZ, '"As I Have Commanded Thee": Flemish Decrees and CJEU Jurisprudence Put Religious Slaughter Under the Knife' (2021) 46 *European Law Review* 380

Greenhouse, L and Siegel, RB (eds), *Before Roe v. Wade: Voices That Shaped the Abortion Debate Before the Supreme Court's Ruling* (Wokingham, Kaplan Publishing, 2010)

Griffiths, AP, Montefiore, A and others, *Neutrality and Impartiality: The University and Political Commitment* (Cambridge, Cambridge University Press, 1975)

Haidt, J, *The Righteous Mind: Why Good People Are Divided by Politics and Religion* (London, Vintage, 2012)

Halberstam, D, 'Federalism: Theory, Policy, Law' in M Rosenfeld and A Sajó (eds), *The Oxford Handbook of Comparative Constitutional Law* (Oxford, Oxford University Press, 2012) 576

Hall, DE and Feldmeier, JP, *Constitutional Law: Governmental Powers and Individual Freedoms* (London, Pearson, 2012)

Hamilton, A, Madison, J and Jay, J, *The Federalist Papers* (Ian Shapiro ed, New Haven, Yale University Press, 2009)

Harlow, C and Rawlings, R, *Pressure Through Law* (Abingdon, Routledge, 2013)

Hartman, A, *A War for the Soul of America: A History of the Culture Wars*, 2nd edn (Chicago, University of Chicago Press, 2019)
Henning, PJ, 'Misguided Federalism' (2003) 68 *Missouri Law Review* 389
Higdon, MJ, 'If You Grant It, They Will Come: The History and Enduring Legal Legacy of Migratory Divorce' (2011) *Utah Law Review* 295
Hills, RM Jr, 'Federalism and the Culture Wars' (2006) 31 *Oklahoma City University Law Review* 507
Hobson, CF, 'The Negative on State Laws: James Madison, the Constitution, and the Crisis of Republican Government' (1987) 44 *William and Mary Quarterly* 215
Horowitz, DL, 'The Many Uses of Federalism' (2007) 55 *Drake Law Review* 953
Howard, E, 'Headscarves and the CJEU: Protecting Fundamental Rights and Pandering to Prejudice – The CJEU Does Both' (2022) 29 *Maastricht Journal of European and Comparative Law* 245
——, 'LF v SCRL and the CJEU's Failure to Engage with the Reality of Muslim Women in the Labour Market' (2023) 52 *Industrial Law Journal* 997
Howe, DW, 'The Political Psychology of *The Federalist*' (1987) 44 *William and Mary Quarterly* 485
Hunter-Henin, M, 'Religious Neutrality at Europe's Highest Courts: Shifting Strategies' (2022) 11 *Oxford Journal of Law and Religion* 23
Huq, AZ, 'Tiers of Scrutiny in Enumerated Powers Jurisprudence' (2013) 80 *University of Chicago Law Review* 575
Jaklic, K, *Constitutional Pluralism in the EU* (Oxford, Oxford University Press, 2014)
Kahneman, D, Knetsch, JL and Thaler, RH, 'Fairness as a Constraint on Profit Seeking: Entitlements in the Market' (1986) 76 *American Economic Review* 728
Kelemen, RD, 'The European Union's Authoritarian Equilibrium' (2020) 27 *Journal of European Public Policy* 481
Kelly, AH, Harbison, WA and Belz, H, *The American Constitution: Its Origins and Development*, 7th edn (New York, WW Norton, 1991) vols 1& 2.
Kerr, KA, 'Organizing for Reform: The Anti-Saloon League and Innovation in Politics' (1980) 32 *American Quarterly* 37
Khaitan, T, 'Directive Principles and the Expressive Accommodation of Ideological Dissenters' (2018) 16 *International Journal of Constitutional Law* 389
Khaldun, I, *The Muqaddimah: An Introduction to History* (abridged edn) (Princeton, Princeton University Press, 1967)
Klamert, M, Kellerbauer, M and Tomkin, J (eds), *Commentary on the EU Treaties and the Charter of Fundamental Rights* (Oxford, Oxford University Press, 2019)
Klarman, MJ, *Brown v. Board of Education and the Civil Rights Movement* (Oxford, Oxford University Press, 2007)
——, *From Jim Crow to Civil Rights: The Supreme Court and the Struggle for Racial Equality* (Oxford, Oxford University Press, 2006)
——, *The Framers' Coup: The Making of the United States Constitution* (Oxford, Oxford University Press, 2016)
Kobylka, JF and Carter, BK, 'Madison, "The Federalist", & the Constitutional Order: Human Nature & Institutional Structure' (1987) 20 *Polity* 190
Kramer, L, 'Understanding Federalism: Federalism's Future' (1994) 47 *Vanderbilt Law Review* 1485
——, 'Putting the Politics Back into the Political Safeguards of Federalism' (2000) 100 *Columbia Law Review* 215
Kramer, M, *Objectivity and the Rule of Law* (Cambridge, Cambridge University Press, 2007)
Kurzer, P, *Markets and Moral Regulation: Cultural Change in the European Union* (Cambridge, Cambridge University Press, 2001)
Laborde, C, 'Dworkin's Freedom of Religion Without God' (2014) 94 *Boston University Law Review* 1255
Layman, G, *The Great Divide: Religious and Cultural Conflict in American Party Politics* (New York, Columbia University Press, 2001)
Leconte, C, 'The EU Fundamental Rights Policy as a Source of Euroscepticism' (2014) 15 *Human Rights Review* 83

Leigh, I and Ahdar, R, 'Post-Secularism and the European Court of Human Rights: Or How God Never Really Went Away' (2012) 75 *Modern Law Review* 1064
Lenaerts, K, 'Federalism and Rights in the European Community' in E Katz and GA Tarr (eds), *Federalism and Rights* (Lanham, Rowman & Littlefield, 1996) 139
—— 'Constitutionalism and the Many Faces of Federalism' (1990) 38 *American Journal of Comparative Law* 205
Levels, M, Sluiter, R and Need, A, 'A Review of Abortion Laws in Western European Countries: A Cross-National Comparison of Legal Developments between 1960 and 2010' (2014) 118 *Health Policy* 95
Levinson, DJ and Pildes, RH, 'Separation of Parties, Not Powers' (2006) 119 *Harvard Law Review* 2312
Levinson, S and Young, EA, 'Who's Afraid of the Twelfth Amendment?' (2002) 29 *Florida State University Law Review* 925
Lourenço, L, 'Religion, Discrimination and the EU General Principles "Gospel": *Egenberger*' (2019) 56 *Common Market Law Review* 585
Locke, J, *Second Treatise of Government and A Letter Concerning Toleration* (Oxford, Oxford University Press, 2016)
Lucy, W, 'The Possibility of Impartiality' (2005) 25 *Oxford Journal of Legal Studies* 3
MacCormick, N, *Questioning Sovereignty: Law, State, and Nation in the European Commonwealth* (Oxford, Oxford University Press, 1999)
Machiavelli, N, *Discourses on Livy* (Chicago, University of Chicago Press, 2009)
Mann, R, *When Freedom Would Triumph: The Civil Rights Struggle in Congress, 1954–1968* (Baton Rouge, LSU Press, 2007)
Mazey, S and Richardson, J, 'Institutionalizing Promiscuity: Commission–Interest Group Relations in the European Union' in AS Sweet, W Sandholtz and N Fligstein (eds), *The Institutionalization of Europe* (Oxford, Oxford University Press, 2001) 71
McCarty, N, *Polarization: What Everyone Needs to Know* (Oxford, Oxford University Press, 2019)
McConnell, MW, 'Institutions and Interpretation: A Critique of City of Boerne v. Flores' (1997) 111 *Harvard Law Review* 153
——, 'The Fourteenth Amendment: A Second American Revolution or the Logical Culmination of the Tradition?' (1992) 25 *Loyola of Los Angeles Law Review* 1159
McCrea, R, 'Religion in the Constitutional Order of the European Union' in Susanna Mancini (ed), *Constitutions and Religion* (Cheltenham, Edward Elgar, 2020)
——, 'Singing from the Same Hymn Sheet? What the Differences Between the Strasbourg and Luxembourg Courts Tell Us About Religious Freedom, Non-Discrimination, and the Secular State' (2016) 5 *Oxford Journal of Law and Religion* 183
McKevitt, T, 'The Rule of Necessity: Is Judicial Non-Disqualification Really Necessary?' (1996) 24 *Hofstra Law Review* 817
McGirr, L, *The War on Alcohol: Prohibition and the Rise of the American State* (New York, W.W. Norton, 2015)
Meltzer, DJ, 'Member State Liability in Europe and the United States' (2006) 4 *International Journal of Constitutional Law* 39
Minkenberg, M, 'Religion and Public Policy: Institutional, Cultural, and Political Impact on the Shaping of Abortion Policies in Western Democracies' (2003) 35 *Comparative Politics* 221
Minow, M, 'Putting Up and Putting Down: Tolerance Reconsidered' (1990) 28 *Osgoode Hall Law Journal* 409
Morgan, ES, 'Safety in Numbers: Madison, Hume, and the Tenth "Federalist"' (1986) 49 *Huntington Library Quarterly* 95
Moussa, M, 'Expanding the Nemo Judex Rule: Reflections on Non-Pecuniary Bias' (forthcoming, *Judicial Review*)
——, 'The Shackles of Veto: The American Parallel of Art 19 TFEU and Its Tension with Procedural Justice' (2023) 25 *Cambridge Yearbook of European Legal Studies* 122
Muir, E, 'Fundamental Rights: An Unsettling EU Competence' (2014) 15 *Human Rights Review* 25

Mullally, S, 'Debating Reproductive Rights in Ireland' (2005) 27 *Human Rights Quarterly* 78
Neuman, GL, 'Casey in the Mirror: Abortion, Abuse and the Right to Protection in the United States and Germany' (1995) 43 *American Journal of Comparative Law* 273
Nijsten, M, *Abortion and Constitutional Law: A Comparative European-American Study* (European University Institute, 1990)
Nettesheim, M, 'European "Frankenstein Constitutionalism": TEU Article 2 as a Federal Homogeneity Clause' (2024) 118 *AJIL Unbound* 167
O'Connor, K, *No Neutral Ground? Abortion Politics in an Age of Absolutes* (Abingdon, Routledge, 2020)
Olowofoyeku, AA, 'The "Nemo Judex" Rule: The Case Against Automatic Disqualification' (2000) *Public Law* 456
Ostrom, V and Allen, B, *The Political Theory of a Compound Republic: Designing the American Experiment*, 2nd edn (New York, Lexington Books, 2008)
Pech, L and Scheppele, KL, 'Illiberalism Within: Rule of Law Backsliding in the EU' (2017) 19 *Cambridge Yearbook of European Legal Studies* 3
Pérez, A, 'Rights and Powers in the European Union: Towards a Charter That Is Fully Applicable to the Member States?' (2020) 22 *Cambridge Yearbook of European Legal Studies* 279
Pillinger, J, *Feminising the Market: Women's Pay and Employment in the European Community* (Cham, Springer, 2016)
Post, R and Siegel, R, 'Popular Constitutionalism, Departmentalism, and Judicial Supremacy' (2004) 92 *California Law Review* 1027
Post, RC, 'Democratic Constitutionalism and Cultural Heterogeneity' (2000) 25 *Australian Journal of Legal Philosophy* 185
Rakove, JN, *A Politician Thinking: The Creative Mind of James Madison* (Oklahoma, University of Oklahoma Press, 2017)
Rapaczynski, A, 'From Sovereignty to Process: The Jurisprudence of Federalism After *Garcia*' (1985) *Supreme Court Review* 341
Resnik, J, 'Accommodations, Discounts, and Displacement: The Variability of Rights as a Norm of Federalism(s)' (2014) *Jus Politicum* (online) 1
Risen, C, *The Bill of the Century: The Epic Battle for the Civil Rights Act* (London, Bloomsbury, 2014)
Rodríguez, CM, 'Negotiating Conflict Through Federalism: Institutional and Popular Perspectives' (2014) 123 *Yale Law Journal* 2094
Rothschild, Z, 'Free Exercise Partisanship' (2022) 107 *Cornell Law Review* 1067
——, 'The Impossibility of Religious Equality' (2025) 125 *Columbia Law Review* 453
Ryan, E, *Federalism and the Tug of War Within* (Oxford, Oxford University Press 2011)
Sandel, M, *What Money Can't Buy: The Moral Limits of Markets* (London, Penguin, 2013)
Saurette, P and Gordon, K, *The Changing Voice of the Anti-Abortion Movement* (Toronto, University of Toronto Press, 2018)
Schabas, WA, *The European Convention on Human Rights: A Commentary* (Oxford, Oxford University Press, 2015)
Schapiro, RA, *Polyphonic Federalism: Toward the Protection of Fundamental Rights* (Chicago, University of Chicago Press, 2009)
Schütze, R, *From Dual to Cooperative Federalism: The Changing Structure of European Law* (Oxford University Press 2009)
——, *European Constitutional Law*, 2nd edn (Cambridge, Cambridge University Press, 2016)
Schuck, PH, 'Against (and for) Madison: An Essay in Praise of Factions' (1997) 15 *Yale Law & Policy Review* 553
Sears, DO and Funk, CL, 'The Role of Self-Interest in Social and Political Attitudes' (1991) 24 *Advances in Experimental Social Psychology* 1
Shapiro, DL, *Federalism: A Dialogue* (Evanston, Northwestern University Press, 1995)
Shepsle, KA and Weingast, BR, 'The Institutional Foundations of Committee Power' (1987) 81 *American Political Science Review* 85

Siegel, RB, 'Dignity and the Politics of Protection: Abortion Restrictions Under *Casey/Carhart*' (2008) 117 *Yale Law Journal* 1694

——, 'The Constitutionalization of Abortion' in RJ Cook, JN Erdman and BM Dickens (eds), *Abortion Law in Transnational Perspective: Cases and Controversies* (Philadelphia, University of Pennsylvania Press, 2014)

Sluiter, R, *The Diffusion of Morality Policies Among Western European Countries Between 1960 and 2010* (PhD thesis, Radboud University Nijmegen, 2012)

Spencer, MG (ed), *David Hume and Eighteenth-Century America* (New York, Boydell & Brewer, 2005)

Stepan, AC, *Arguing Comparative Politics* (Oxford, Oxford University Press, 2001)

Stone, SA, *The Judicial Construction of Europe* (Oxford, Oxford University Press, 2004)

Sunstein, CR, *The Partial Constitution* (Cambridge, MA, Harvard University Press, 1993)

——, 'Interest Groups in American Public Law' (1985) 38 *Stanford Law Review* 29

——, 'Moral Heuristics' (2005) 28 *Behavioral and Brain Sciences* 531

Thaler, RH and Sunstein, CR, *Nudge: Improving Decisions About Health, Wealth, and Happiness* (London, Penguin, 2009)

Tischbirek, A, 'A Double Conflict of Laws: The Emergence of an EU "Staatskirchenrecht"?' (2019) 20 *German Law Journal* 1066

Touchie, JC, 'On the Possibility of Impartiality in Decision-Making' (2001) 1 *Macquarie Law Journal* 21

Tridimas, T, 'Constitutional Review of Member State Action: The Virtues and Vices of an Incomplete Jurisdiction' (2011) 9 *International Journal of Constitutional Law* 737

Tucak, I and Blagojević, A, 'Abortion in Europe' (2020) 4 *EU and Comparative Law Issues and Challenges Series* 1135

Tully, J, *Strange Multiplicity: Constitutionalism in an Age of Diversity* (Cambridge, Cambridge University Press, 1995)

Turenne, S, *Le juge face à la désobéissance civile en droits américain et français comparés* (LGDJ, 2007)

Tushnet, M, *Taking the Constitution Away from the Courts* (Princeton, Princeton University Press, 2000)

——, *Taking Back the Constitution: Activist Judges and the Next Age of American Law* (New Haven, Yale University Press, 2020)

——, 'Constitutional and Statutory Analyses in the Law of Federal Jurisdiction' (1978) 25 *UCLA Law Review* 1301

——, 'Federalism and Liberalism' (1996) 4 *Cardozo Journal of International & Comparative Law* 329

van Beest, I, van Dijk, E, De Dreu, CKW and Wilke, HAM, 'Do-No-Harm in Coalition Formation: Why Losses Inhibit Exclusion and Promote Fairness Cognitions' (2005) 41 *Journal of Experimental Social Psychology* 609

van den Brink, M, 'The Protected Grounds of Religion and Belief: Lessons for EU Non-Discrimination Law' (2023) 24 *German Law Journal* 855

van der Vleuten, A, *The Price of Gender Equality: Member States and Governance in the European Union* (Abingdon, Routledge, 2016)

Vanberg, V and Buchanan, JM, 'Interests and Theories in Constitutional Choice' in *Perspectives on Positive Political Economy* (Cambridge, Cambridge University Press, 1990) 246

Vanberg, V and Kerber, W, 'Institutional Competition Among Jurisdictions: An Evolutionary Approach' (1994) 5 *Constitutional Political Economy* 193

Vermeule, A, 'Veil of Ignorance Rules in Constitutional Law' (2001) 111 *Yale Law Journal* 399

——, 'Contra Nemo Iudex in Sua Causa: The Limits of Impartiality' (2012) 122 *Yale Law Journal* 384

Voigt, S, *Institutional Economics: An Introduction* (Cambridge, Cambridge University Press, 2019)

——, 'Veilonomics: On the Use and Utility of Veils in Constitutional Political Economy' in M Albertone and A Stella (eds), *The Banker's and the Smith's Tales* (Farnham, Ashgate, 2009) 9

Vile, MJC, *Constitutionalism and the Separation of Powers* (Carmel, Liberty Fund, 2012)

Weiler, J, 'Je Suis Achbita' (2017) 28 *European Journal of International Law* 989

Whalen, CW and Whalen, B, *The Longest Debate: A Legislative History of the 1964 Civil Rights Act* (Santa Ana, Seven Locks Press, 1989)

Wharton, GF, *Legal Maxims, with Observations and Cases: In Two Parts, with Translations* (Chicago, Alpha Editions, 1865)

White, M, *Philosophy, The Federalist, and the Constitution* (Oxford, Oxford University Press, 1989)

Williams, RF, 'In the Supreme Court's Shadow: Legitimacy of State Rejection of Supreme Court Reasoning and Result' (1984) 35 *South Carolina Law Review* 353

Xenidis, R, 'From Religious Neutrality to Religious Discrimination in the Public and the Private Sector: *Commune d'Ans*' (2025) 62 *Common Market Law Review* 513

Young, AL, *Turpin and Tomkins' British Government and the Constitution: Text and Materials*, 8th edn (Cambridge, Cambridge University Press, 2021)

Young, EA, 'What Can Europe Tell Us About the Future of American Federalism?' (2017) 49 *Arizona State Law Journal* 1109

Ziegler, M, *Abortion and the Law in America: Roe v. Wade to the Present* (Cambridge, Cambridge University Press, 2020)

INDEX

NB – page locators in **bold** indicate information to be found in tables and/or figures

www.ingramcontent.com/pod-product-compliance
Ingram Content Group UK Ltd.
Pitfield, Milton Keynes, MK11 3LW, UK
UKHW020811290926
15470UKWH00003B/1080

9 781509 98728